9

ASSASSINATION
CLASSROOM

TIME FOR THE GRIM REAPER

YUSEI MATSUI

SHONEN JUMP ADVANCED

Koro Tribune

October Issue 2

Published by: Class 3-E Newspaper Staff

Although we have a lot of data on his weaknesses, we are still far from successfully assassinating Koro Sensei...

Story Thus Far

Kunugigaoka Junior High, Class 3-E is led by a monster who has disintegrated the moon and is planning to do the same to the Earth next March.

I EXPECT TO SEE YOU EXECUTE THE BEST ASSAS-SINATION ATTEMPT YOU ARE CAPABLE OF.
MAKE THE MOST OF YOUR KNOWLEDGE, INGENUITY AND HARD WORK.
THIS IS MY IDEA OF THE MOST FUN EVER.

Even the armies of the world with the latest technology can't kill the super creature Koro Sensei (and collect the 30 billion yen (300 million dollar) bounty for a group assassination)! So it comes down to his Kunugigaoka Junior High students in 3-E, the so-called "End Class," whom he has promised not to harm. Thanks to Koro Sensei's dedication, his charges are turning into fine students. Likewise, the 3-E students' athleticism and mental concentration are rapidly improving as the Ministry of Defense's Mr. Karasuma molds them into a professional team of assassins. Will the misfit students of 3-E manage to assassinate their target before graduation...?!

Koro Sensei

A mysterious, man-made, octopus-like creature whose name is a play on the words "koro senai," which means "can't kill." He is capable of flying at Mach 20 and his versatile tentacles protect him from attacks and aid him in everyday activities. Nobody knows who created him or why he wants to teach Class 3-E, but he has proven to be an exceptional instructor.

And what's with the smug face?!
TING

Nagisa Shiota

Class E student. Skilled at information gathering, he has been taking notes on Koro Sensei's weaknesses. He has a hidden talent for assassinations and even the Assassin Broker Lovro sees his potential.

Thanks to their new gear, the students are one step closer to assassinating Koro Sensei!
AFTER

Uh-huh.

Kaede Kayano

Class E student. She's the one who named Koro Sensei. She sits at the desk next to Nagisa, and they seem to get along well.

Sumire Hara pick up!

Not physically adept, but the explosive power she shows at certain moments can put her male friends to shame. A protective homebody,she excels in housewife-style ambush assassinations.

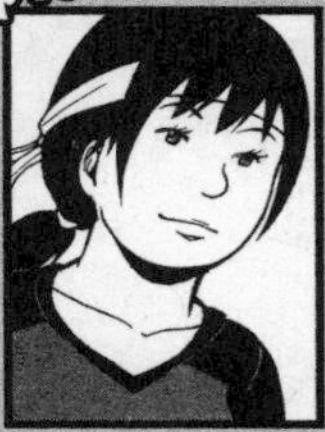

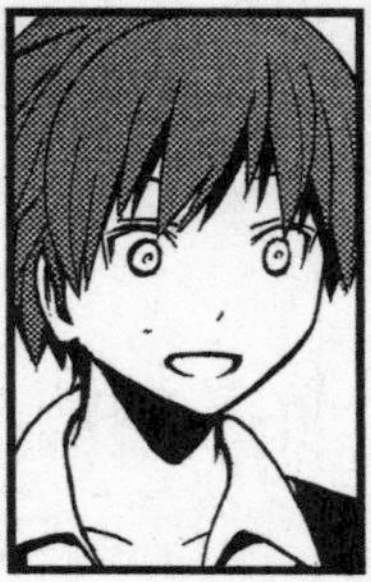

Karma Akabane

Class E student. A natural genius who earns top grades. His failure in the final exam of the first semester has forced him to grow up and take things a bit more seriously.

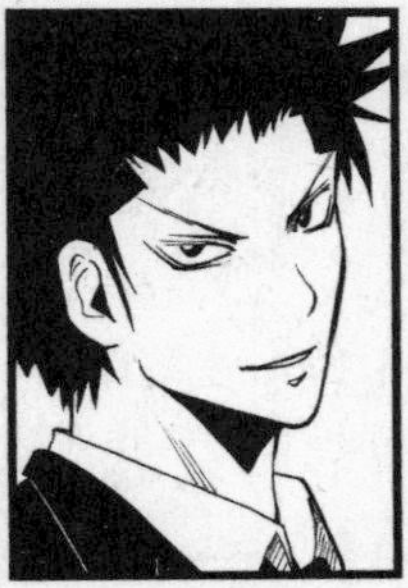

Tadaomi Karasuma

Member of the Ministry of Defense and the Class E students' P.E. teacher. Though serious about his duties, he is successfully building good relationships with his students.

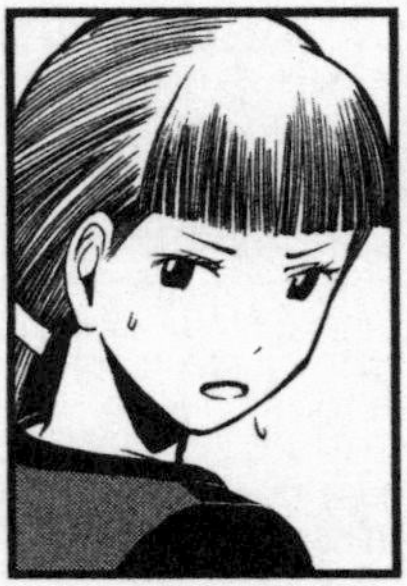

Meg Kataoka

A class representative with a strong sense of responsibility and leadership. Whenever the class is split into several groups for an assassination, she takes on the role of team leader.

THE YOSHIDA TRIKE!

Since the Ministry of Defense will financially assist the students with any assassination project, Yoshida has been building super modified power-assisted bicycles. Will the day come when his mechanical knowledge is put to use?!

Or is he just blowing the government's budget?!

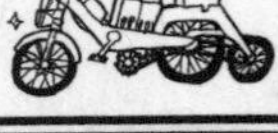

Irina Jelavich

A sexy assassin hired as an English teacher. She's known for using her "womanly charms" to get close to a target. She often flirts with Karasuma, but hasn't made any progress with him yet.

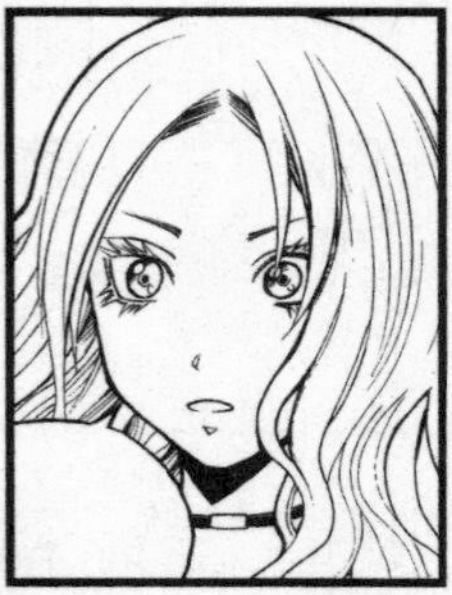

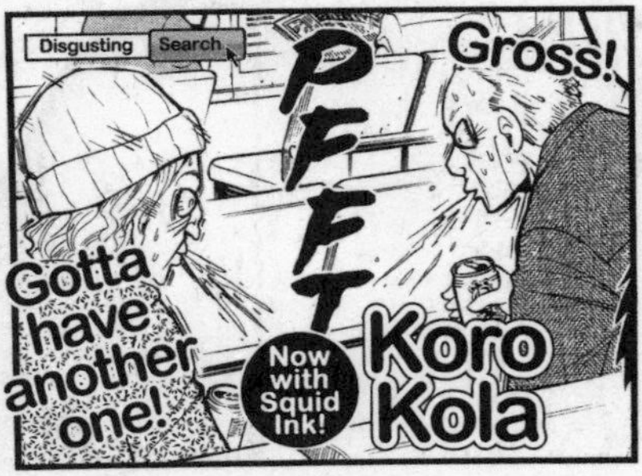

Disgusting
Search
Gross!
PFFT
Gotta have another one!
Now with Squid Ink!
Koro Kola

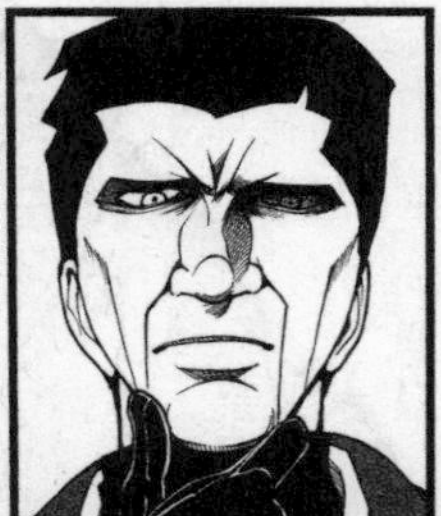

Lovro

An Assassin Broker in charge of introducing assassins to Karasuma. He has been out of touch ever since he was attacked by the Grim Reaper.

Assassination Class Roster

Always assassinate your target using a method that brings a smile to your face.

I'm available for assassinations anytime. But don't let them get in the way of your studies.

I won't harm students who try to assassinate me. But if your skills are rusty, expect a good scrubbing!

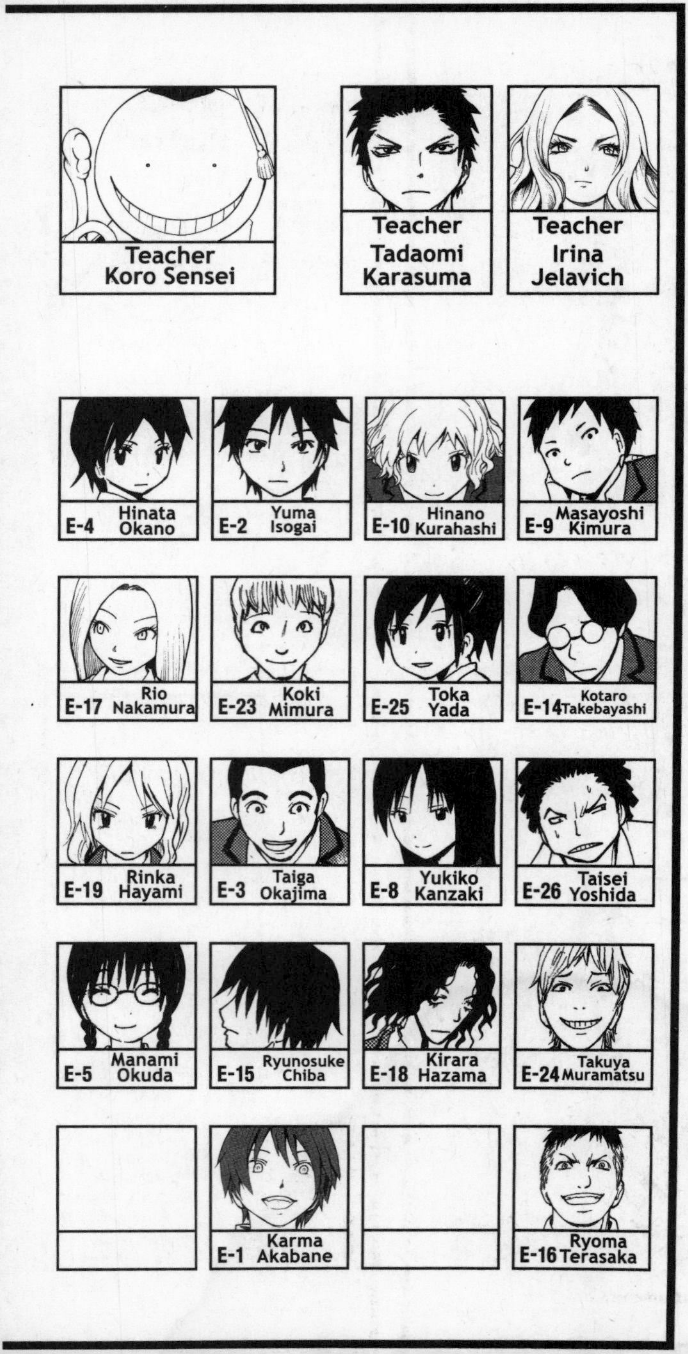

Teacher Irina Jelavich
Teacher Tadaomi Karasuma
Teacher Koro Sensei
E-9 Masayoshi Kimura
E-10 Hinano Kurahashi
E-2 Yuma Isogai
E-4 Hinata Okano
E-14 Kotaro Takebayashi
E-25 Toka Yada
E-23 Koki Mimura
E-17 Rio Nakamura
E-26 Taisei Yoshida
E-8 Yukiko Kanzaki
E-3 Taiga Okajima
E-19 Rinka Hayami
E-24 Takuya Muramatsu
E-18 Kirara Hazama
E-15 Ryunosuke Chiba
E-5 Manami Okuda
E-16 Ryoma Terasaka
E-1 Karma Akabane

Kunugigaoka Junior High

3-E

Koro Sensei Class

Seating Arrangement

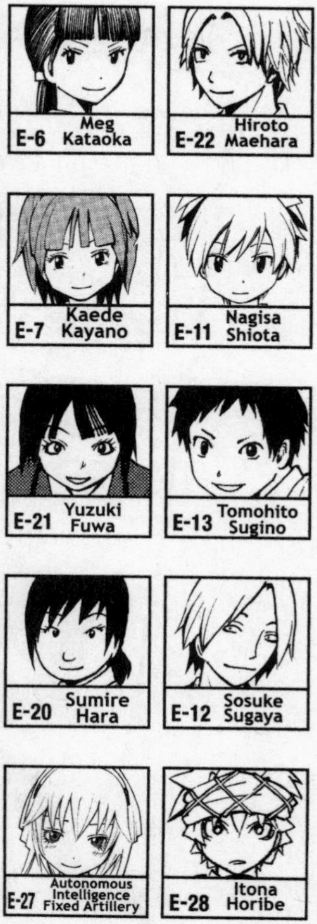
E-22 Hiroto Maehara
E-6 Meg Kataoka
E-11 Nagisa Shiota
E-7 Kaede Kayano
E-13 Tomohito Sugino
E-21 Yuzuki Fuwa
E-12 Sosuke Sugaya
E-20 Sumire Hara
E-28 Itona Horibe
E-27 Autonomous Intelligence Fixed Artillery

Individual Statistics

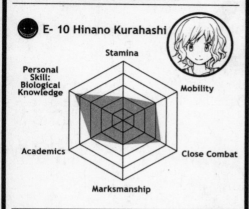

E- 10 Hinano Kurahashi

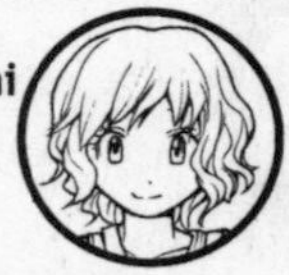

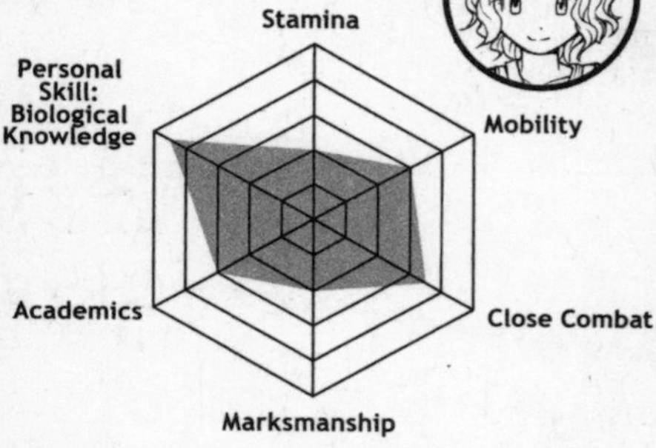
Stamina
Mobility
Close Combat
Marksmanship
Academics
Personal Skill: Biological Knowledge

E-11 Nagisa Shiota

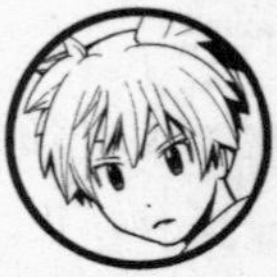

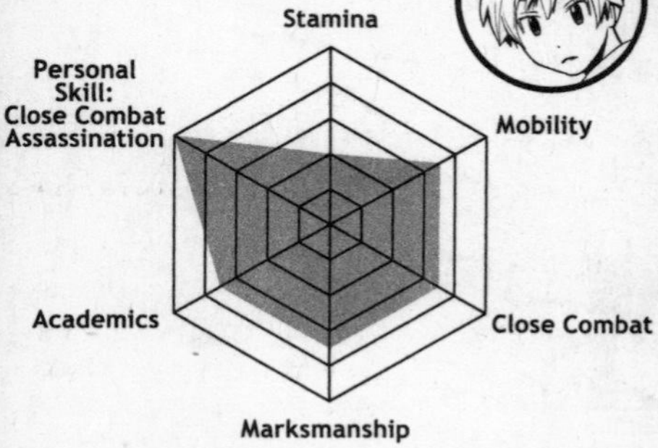
Stamina
Mobility
Close Combat
Marksmanship
Academics
Personal Skill: Close Combat Assassination

E-12 Sosuke Sugaya

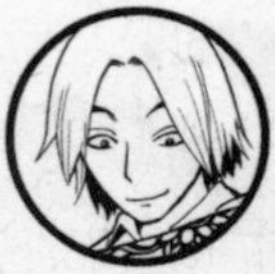

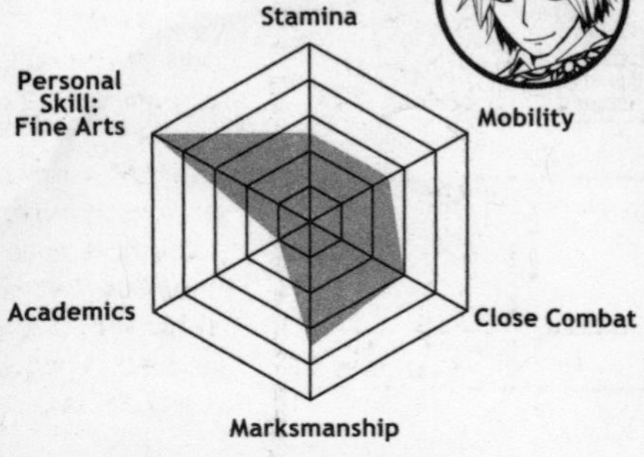
Stamina
Mobility
Close Combat
Marksmanship
Academics
Personal Skill: Fine Arts

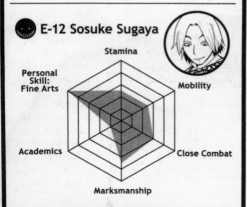

ASSASSINATION CLASSROOM ⑫ CONTENTS

English Test

(Question 1): Choose the best word to fill in the blank ( ) out of the four choices.

(1) Nagisa broke his right ( )
  1 ankle 2 wrist

(2) O
  Al
  1 pr

(3) Kata
  Kaya

  1 fall

(Question 2):
The dialogue
Choose the bes

No.1 1 To the K
     2 To a base
     3 To Isogai's
     4 To his aunt

No.2 1 Looking for a
     2 Taking an assa
     3 Borrowing som
     4 Making a bomb

| Grade | 3 | Class | E | Name | CONTENTS | Score |

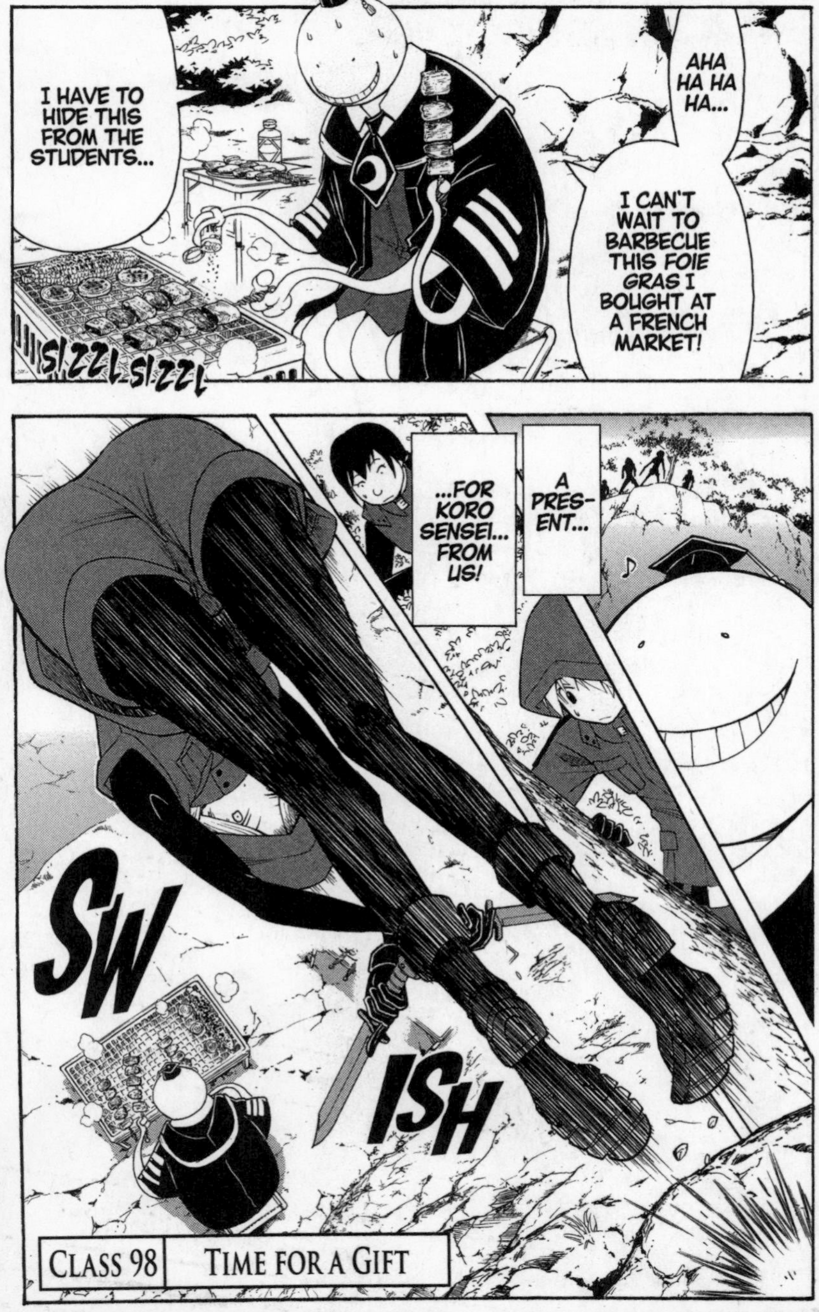
AHA HA HA HA...
I CAN'T WAIT TO BARBECUE THIS FOIE GRAS I BOUGHT AT A FRENCH MARKET!
I HAVE TO HIDE THIS FROM THE STUDENTS...
SIZZL SIZZL
A PRES-ENT...
...FOR KORO SENSEI... FROM US!
SWISH

Class 98 Time for a Gift

Class 98 Time for a Gift

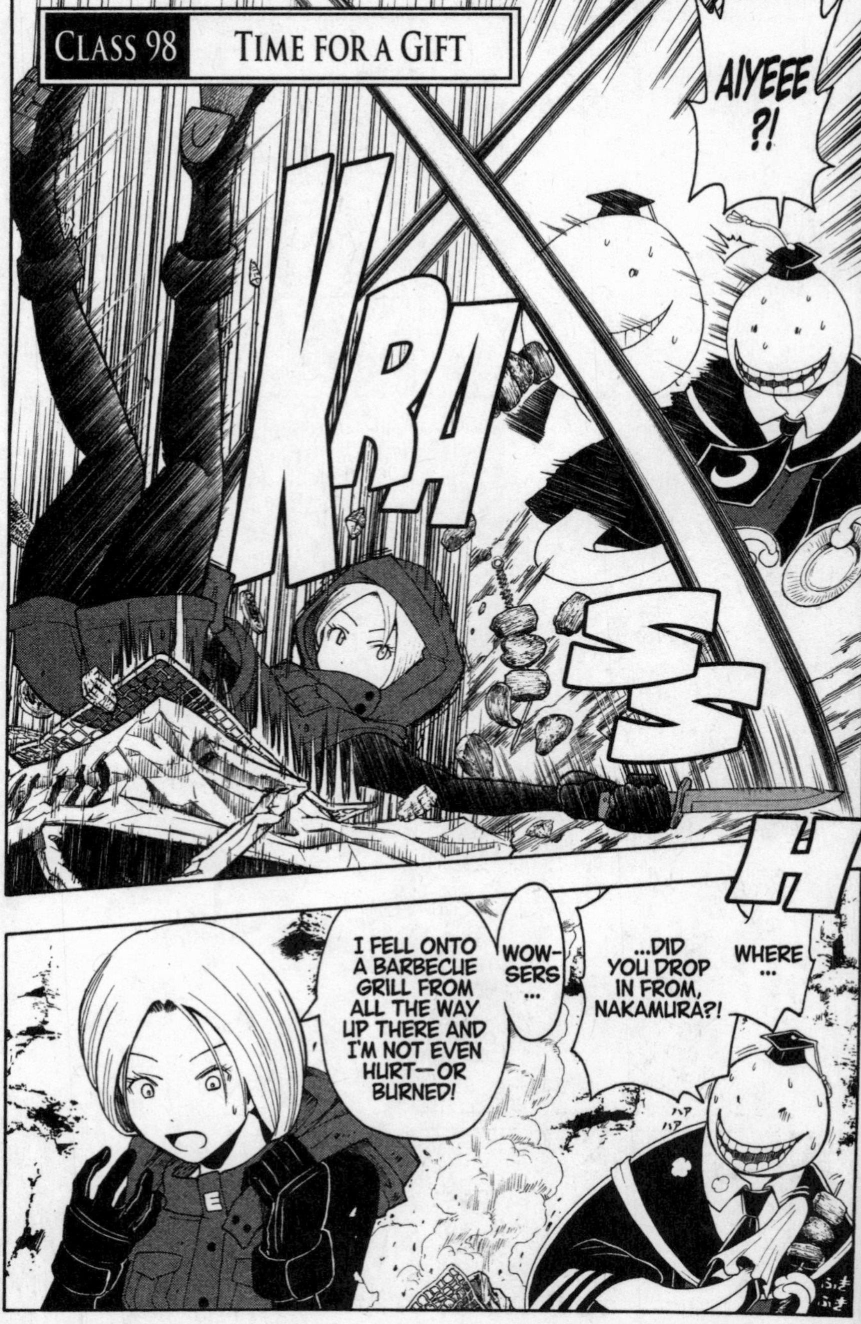

AIYEEE ?!
WHASSH
WHERE ...
...DID YOU DROP IN FROM, NAKAMURA?!
ハァ ハァ
WOW-SERS ...
I FELL ONTO A BARBECUE GRILL FROM ALL THE WAY UP THERE AND I'M NOT EVEN HURT—OR BURNED!
ふき ふき

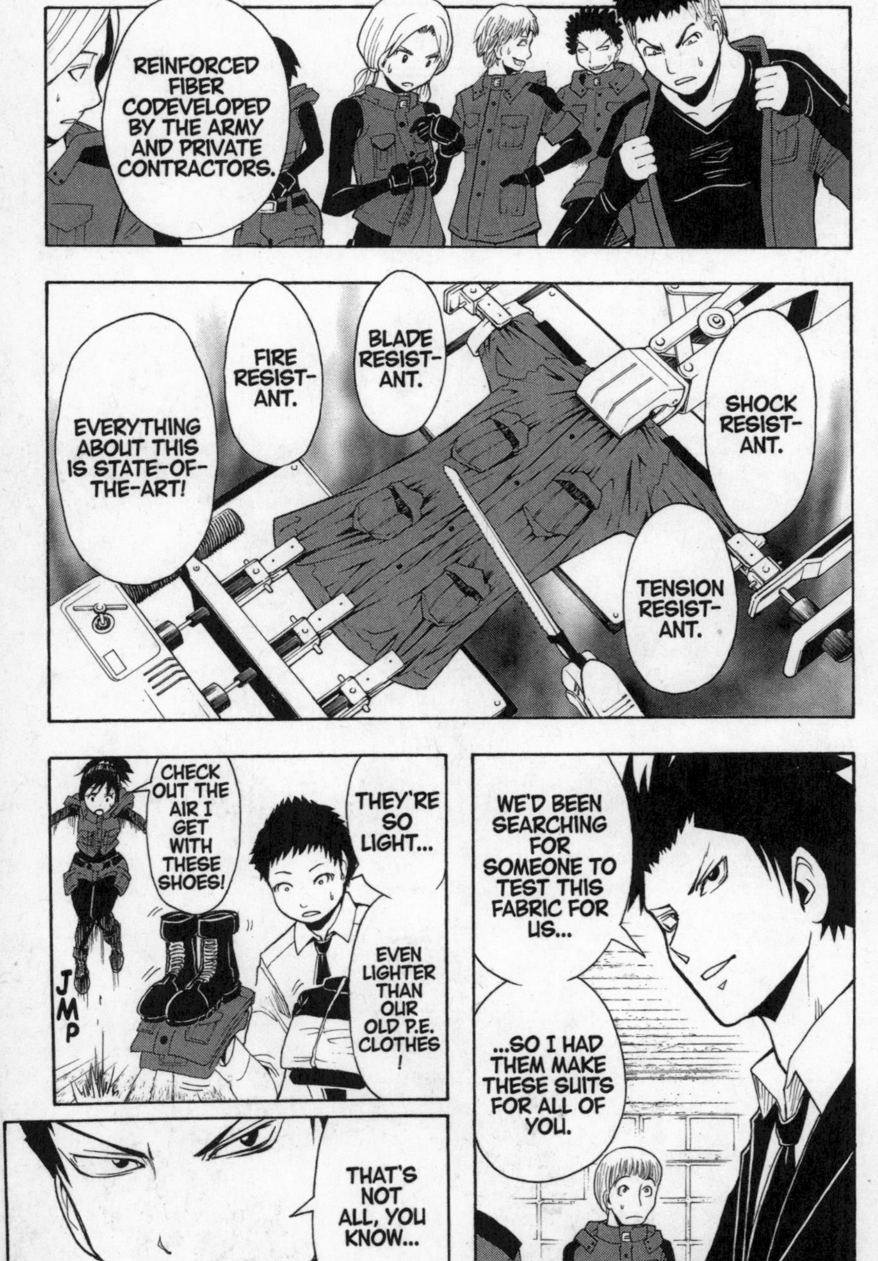
REINFORCED FIBER CODEVELOPED BY THE ARMY AND PRIVATE CONTRACTORS.
SHOCK RESIST-ANT.
TENSION RESIST-ANT.
BLADE RESIST-ANT.
FIRE RESIST-ANT.
EVERYTHING ABOUT THIS IS STATE-OF-THE-ART!
WE'D BEEN SEARCHING FOR SOMEONE TO TEST THIS FABRIC FOR US...
...SO I HAD THEM MAKE THESE SUITS FOR ALL OF YOU.
THEY'RE SO LIGHT...
EVEN LIGHTER THAN OUR OLD P.E. CLOTHES!
CHECK OUT THE AIR I GET WITH THESE SHOES!
JMP
THAT'S NOT ALL, YOU KNOW...

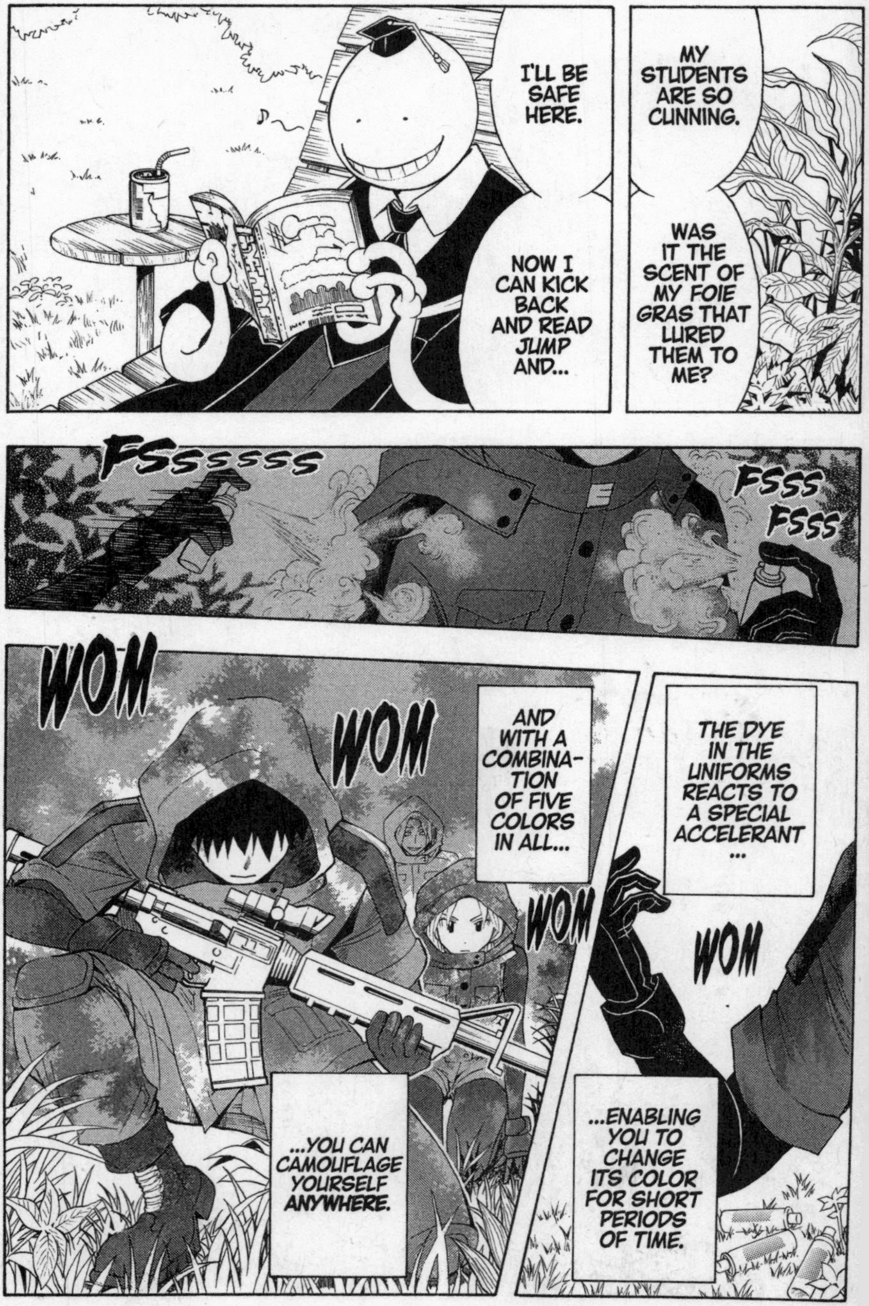

MY STUDENTS ARE SO CUNNING.
WAS IT THE SCENT OF MY FOIE GRAS THAT LURED THEM TO ME?
I'LL BE SAFE HERE.
NOW I CAN KICK BACK AND READ JUMP AND...
FSSS FSSS
FSSSSSS
THE DYE IN THE UNIFORMS REACTS TO A SPECIAL ACCELERANT ...
WOM
...ENABLING YOU TO CHANGE ITS COLOR FOR SHORT PERIODS OF TIME.
WOM
AND WITH A COMBINATION OF FIVE COLORS IN ALL...
WOM
WOM
...YOU CAN CAMOUFLAGE YOURSELF ANYWHERE.

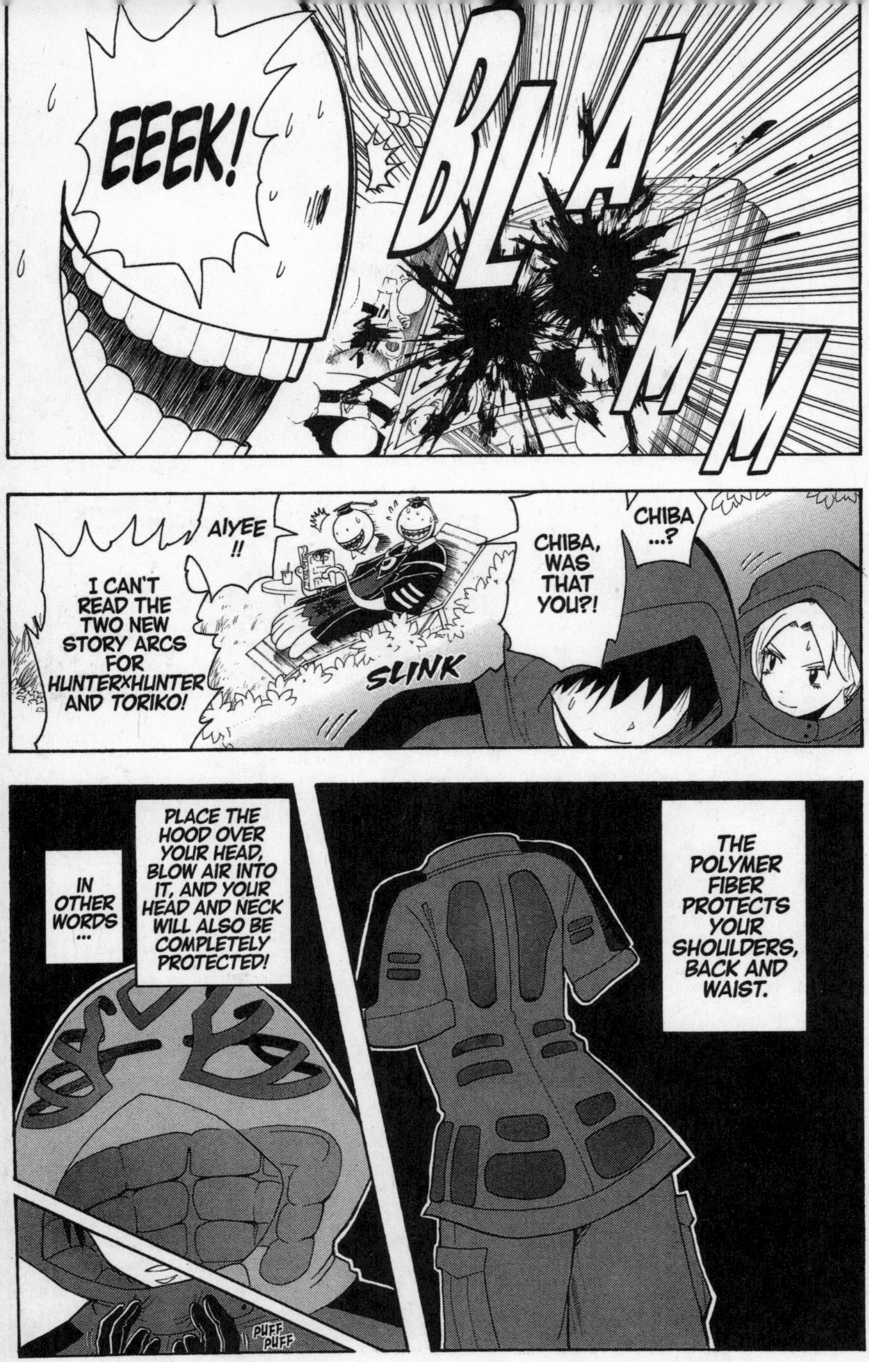
BLAMM
EEEK!
CHIBA ...?
CHIBA, WAS THAT YOU?!
AIYEE !!
SLINK
I CAN'T READ THE TWO NEW STORY ARCS FOR HUNTERxHUNTER AND TORIKO!
THE POLYMER FIBER PROTECTS YOUR SHOULDERS, BACK AND WAIST.
PLACE THE HOOD OVER YOUR HEAD, BLOW AIR INTO IT, AND YOUR HEAD AND NECK WILL ALSO BE COMPLETELY PROTECTED!
IN OTHER WORDS ...
PUFF PUFF

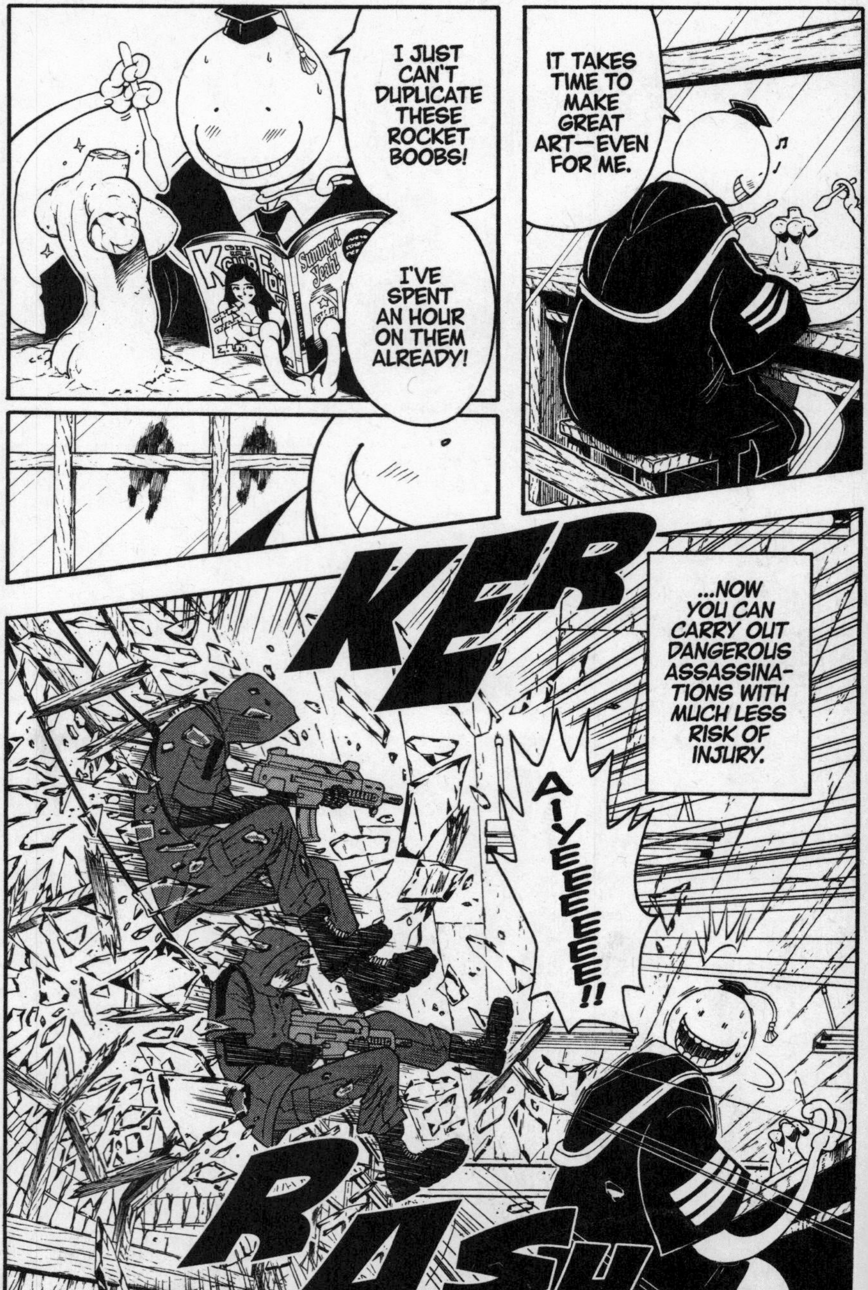
IT TAKES TIME TO MAKE GREAT ART—EVEN FOR ME.
I JUST CAN'T DUPLICATE THESE ROCKET BOOBS!
I'VE SPENT AN HOUR ON THEM ALREADY!
...NOW YOU CAN CARRY OUT DANGEROUS ASSASSINATIONS WITH MUCH LESS RISK OF INJURY.
KER
AIYEEEEEEEE!!
RASH

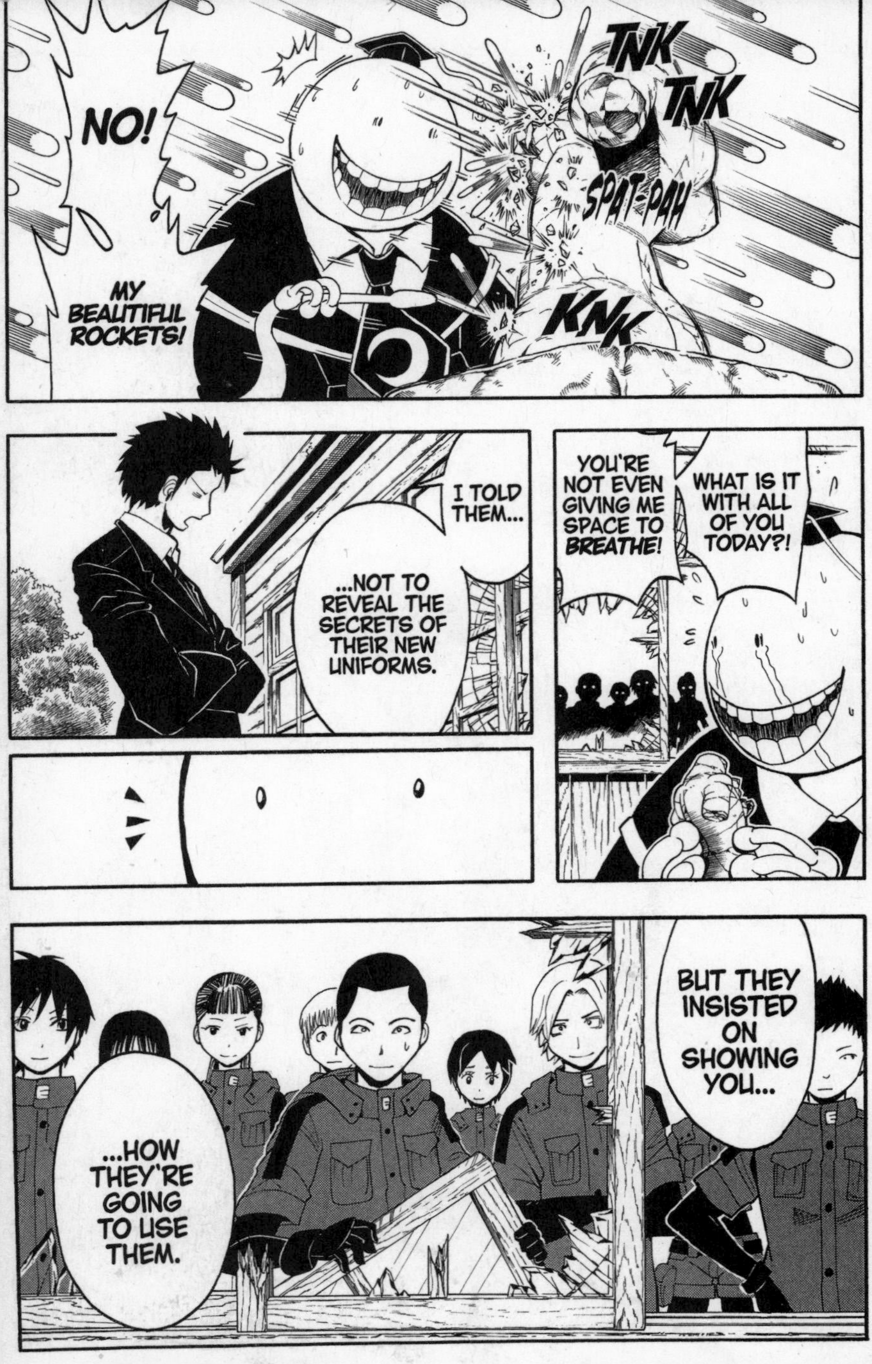
TNK
TNK
NO!
SPAT-PAH
MY BEAUTIFUL ROCKETS!
KNK
WHAT IS IT WITH ALL OF YOU TODAY?!
YOU'RE NOT EVEN GIVING ME SPACE TO BREATHE!
I TOLD THEM...
...NOT TO REVEAL THE SECRETS OF THEIR NEW UNIFORMS.
BUT THEY INSISTED ON SHOWING YOU...
...HOW THEY'RE GOING TO USE THEM.

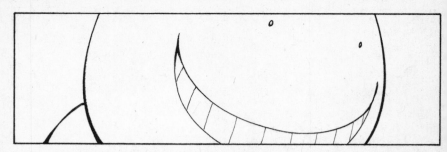

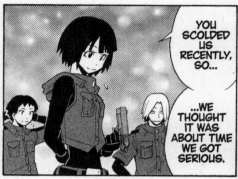

WE WANT TO EXPRESS OUR GRATITUDE FOR TEACHING US HOW TO DO ASSASSINA-TIONS.
THAT'S HOW WE DO THINGS HERE IN CLASS E.
YOU SCOLDED US RECENTLY, SO...
...WE THOUGHT IT WAS ABOUT TIME WE GOT SERIOUS.
YOU HAVE OUR WORD, KORO SENSEI!
WE WILL NEVER USE OUR POWERS...
...FOR ANYTHING OTHER THAN TO PROTECT OTHERS!

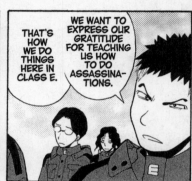

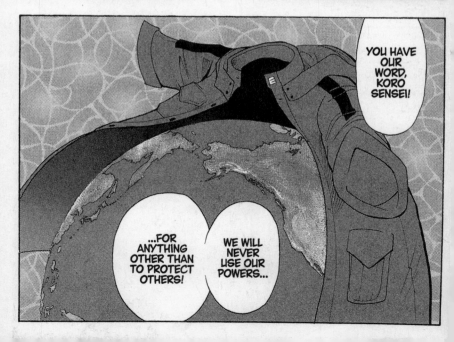

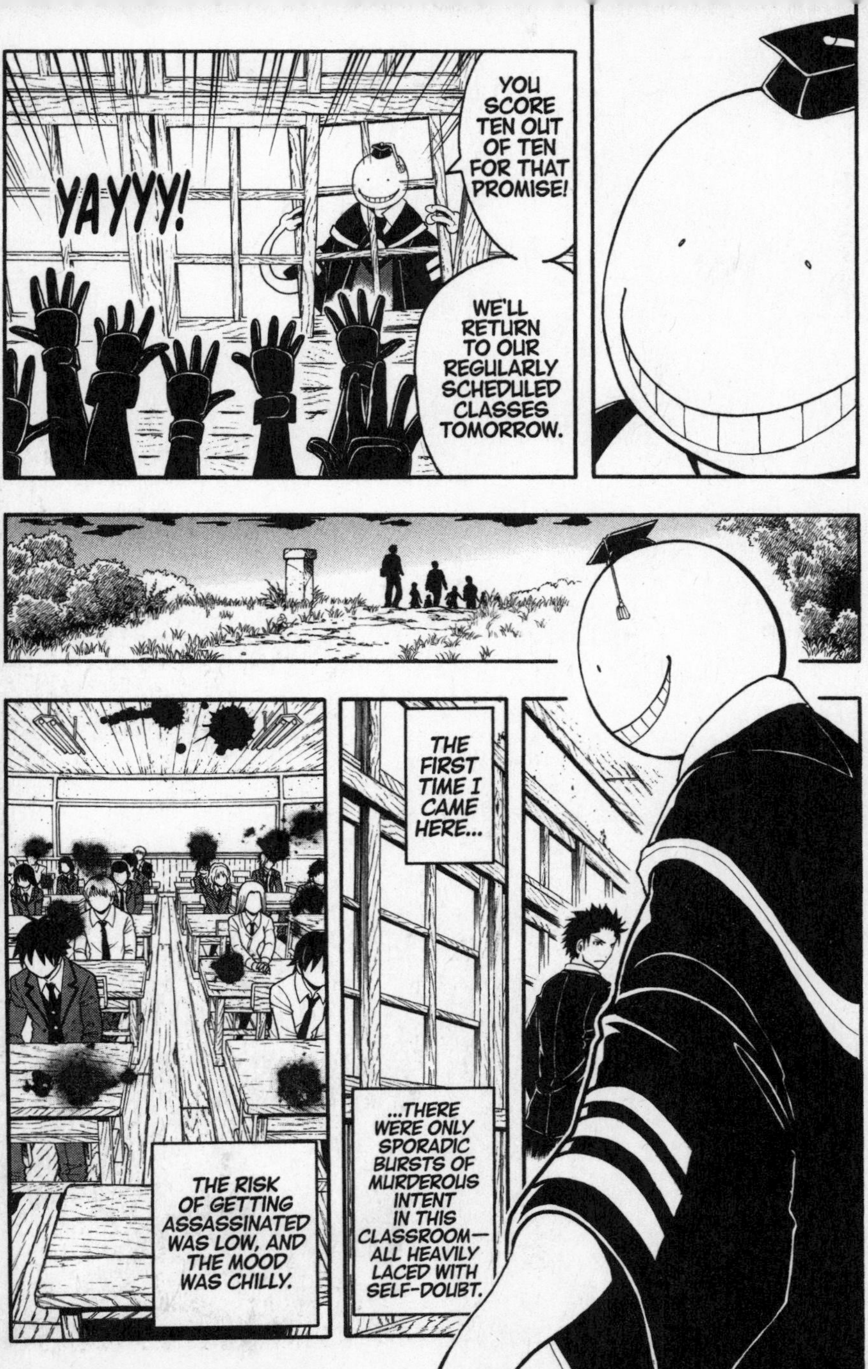
YOU SCORE TEN OUT OF TEN FOR THAT PROMISE!
YAYYY!
WE'LL RETURN TO OUR REGULARLY SCHEDULED CLASSES TOMORROW.
THE FIRST TIME I CAME HERE...
...THERE WERE ONLY SPORADIC BURSTS OF MURDEROUS INTENT IN THIS CLASSROOM—ALL HEAVILY LACED WITH SELF-DOUBT.
THE RISK OF GETTING ASSASSINATED WAS LOW, AND THE MOOD WAS CHILLY.

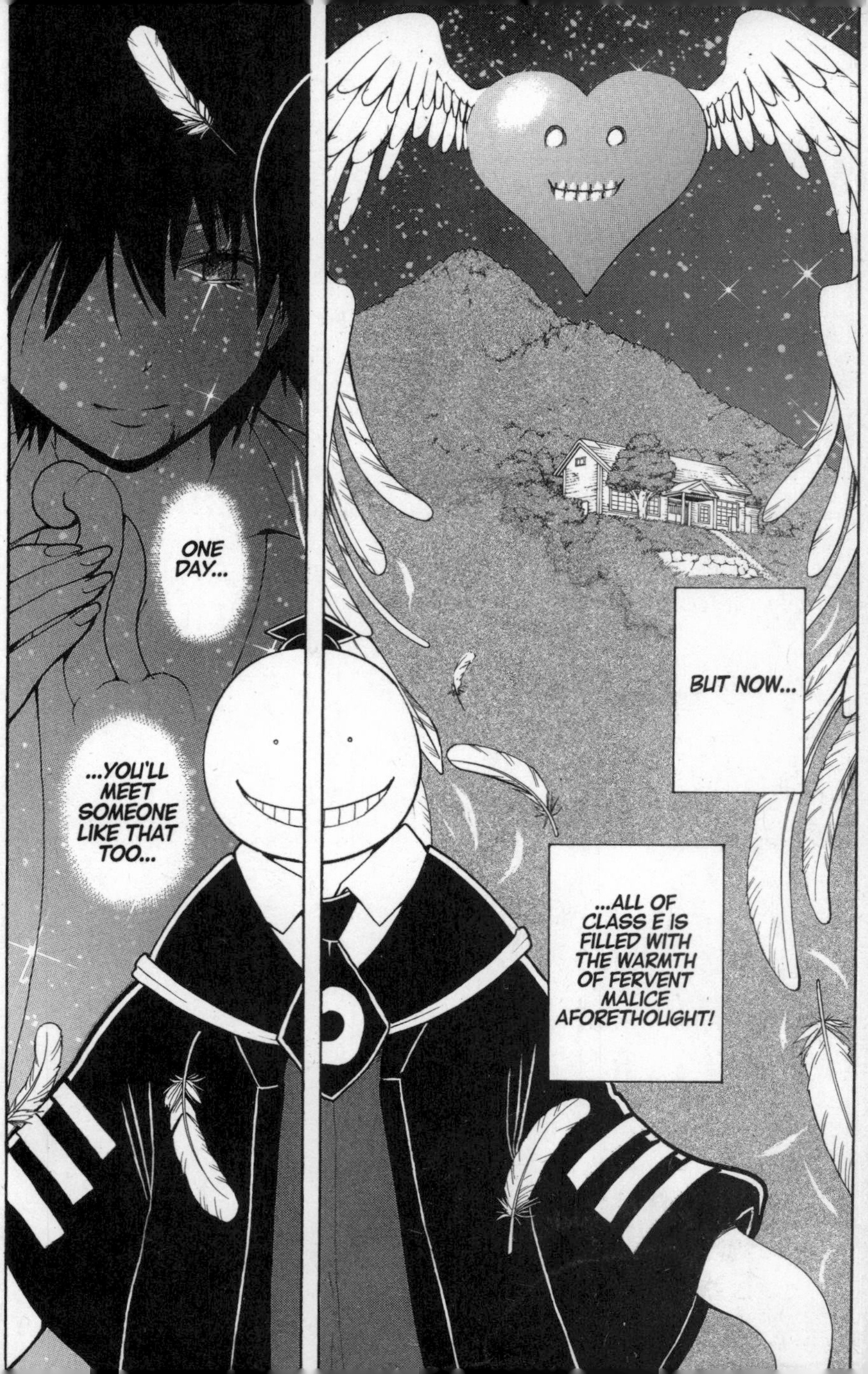
ONE DAY...
...YOU'LL MEET SOMEONE LIKE THAT TOO...
BUT NOW...
...ALL OF CLASS E IS FILLED WITH THE WARMTH OF FERVENT MALICE AFORETHOUGHT!

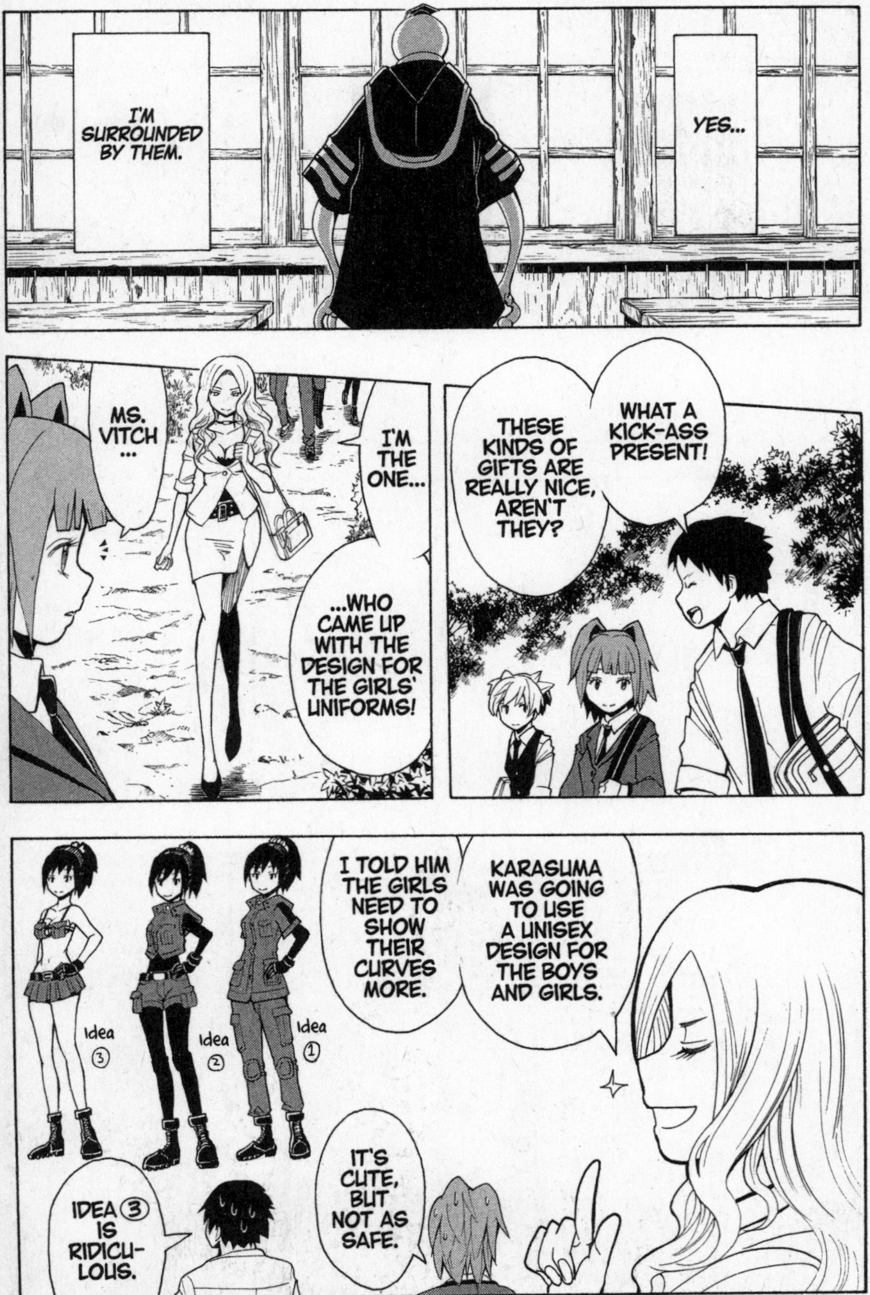
YES...
I'M SURROUNDED BY THEM.
WHAT A KICK-ASS PRESENT!
THESE KINDS OF GIFTS ARE REALLY NICE, AREN'T THEY?
I'M THE ONE...
MS. VITCH ...
...WHO CAME UP WITH THE DESIGN FOR THE GIRLS' UNIFORMS!
KARASUMA WAS GOING TO USE A UNISEX DESIGN FOR THE BOYS AND GIRLS.
I TOLD HIM THE GIRLS NEED TO SHOW THEIR CURVES MORE.
Idea ①
Idea ②
Idea ③
IT'S CUTE, BUT NOT AS SAFE.
IDEA ③ IS RIDICU-LOUS.

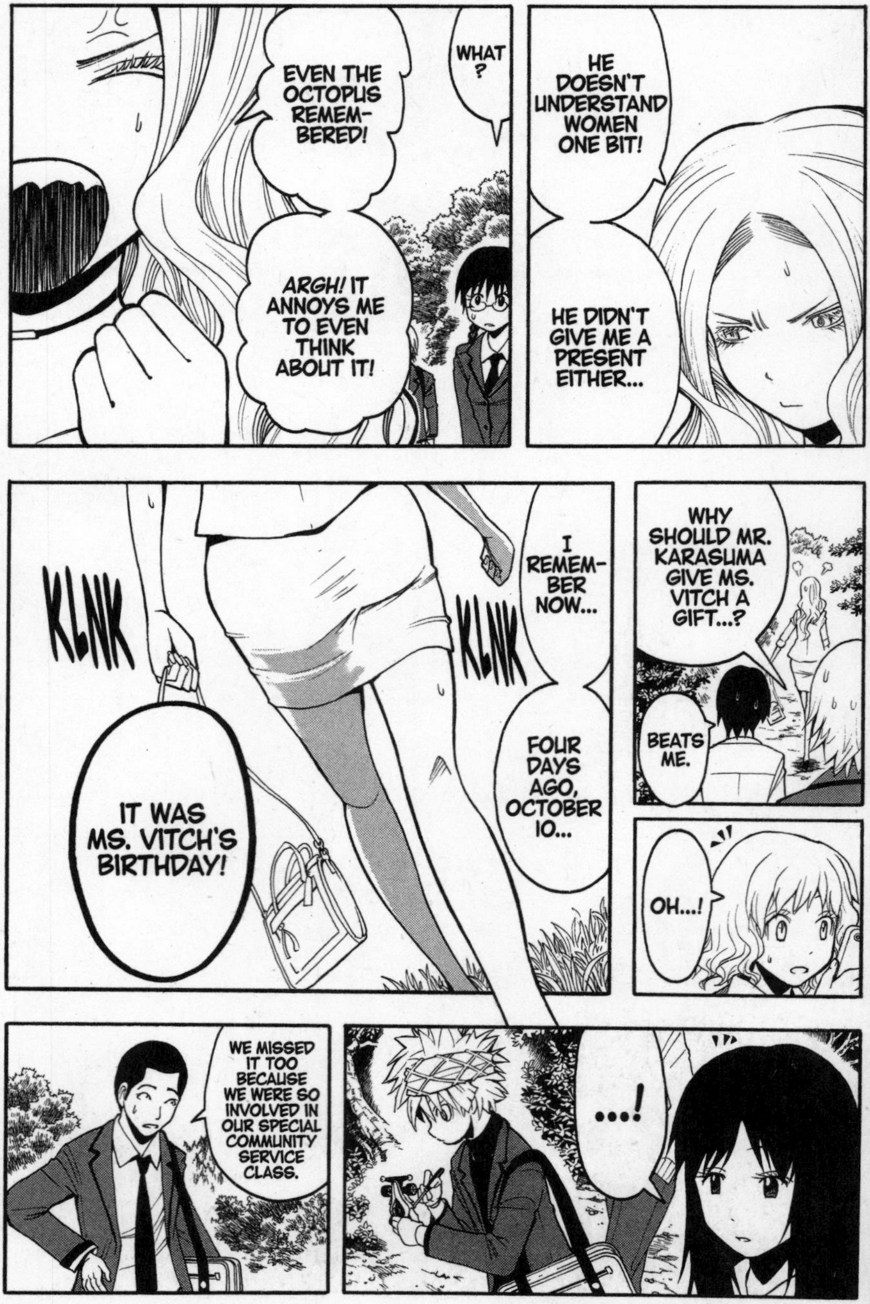
HE DOESN'T UNDERSTAND WOMEN ONE BIT!
HE DIDN'T GIVE ME A PRESENT EITHER...
WHAT?
EVEN THE OCTOPUS REMEMBERED!
ARGH! IT ANNOYS ME TO EVEN THINK ABOUT IT!
WHY SHOULD MR. KARASUMA GIVE MS. VITCH A GIFT...?
BEATS ME.
OH...!
I REMEMBER NOW...
FOUR DAYS AGO, OCTOBER 10...
KLNK
KLNK
IT WAS MS. VITCH'S BIRTHDAY!
...!
WE MISSED IT TOO BECAUSE WE WERE SO INVOLVED IN OUR SPECIAL COMMUNITY SERVICE CLASS.

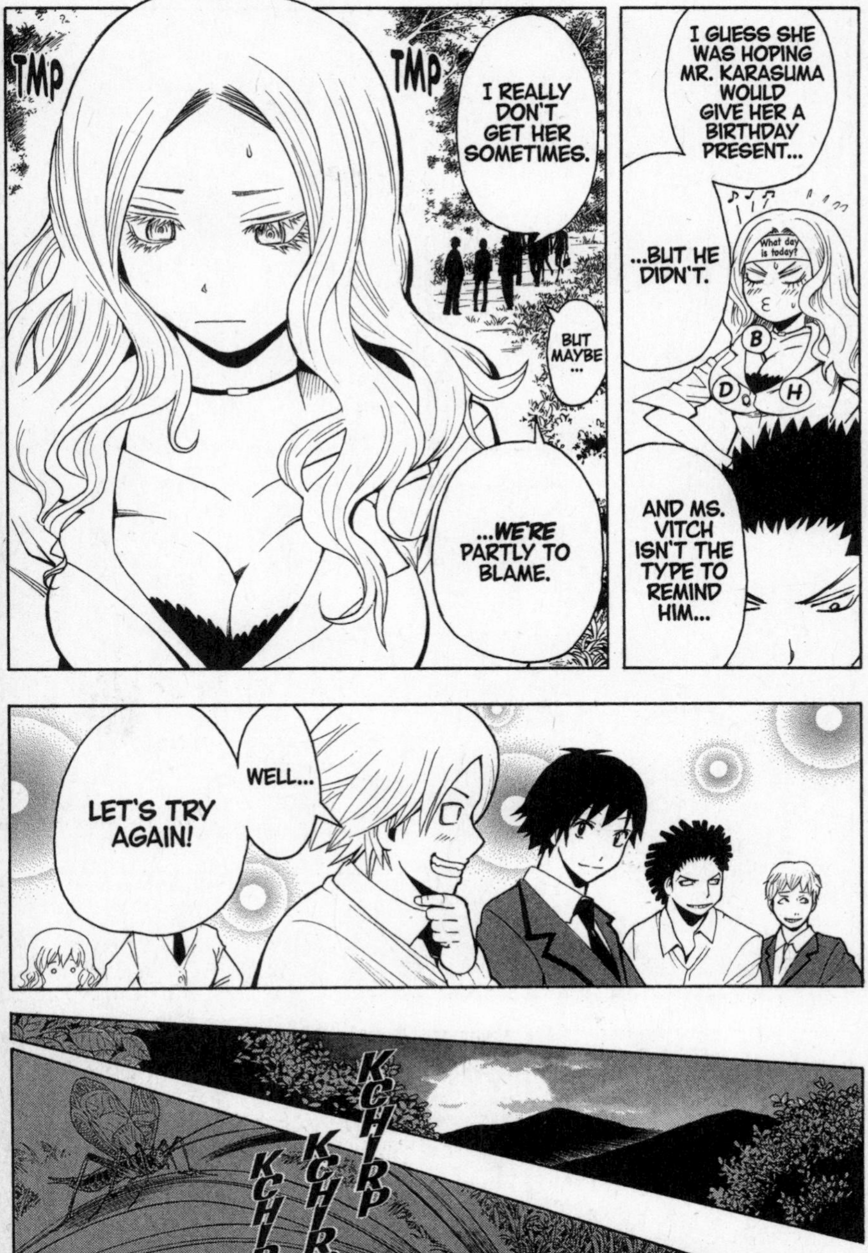
I GUESS SHE WAS HOPING MR. KARASUMA WOULD GIVE HER A BIRTHDAY PRESENT...
...BUT HE DIDN'T.
What day is today?
B
D
H
AND MS. VITCH ISN'T THE TYPE TO REMIND HIM...
TMP
TMP
I REALLY DON'T GET HER SOMETIMES.
BUT MAYBE...
...WE'RE PARTLY TO BLAME.
WELL...
LET'S TRY AGAIN!
KCHIRP
KCHIRP
KCHIRP

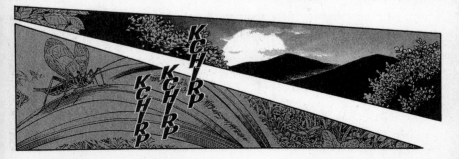

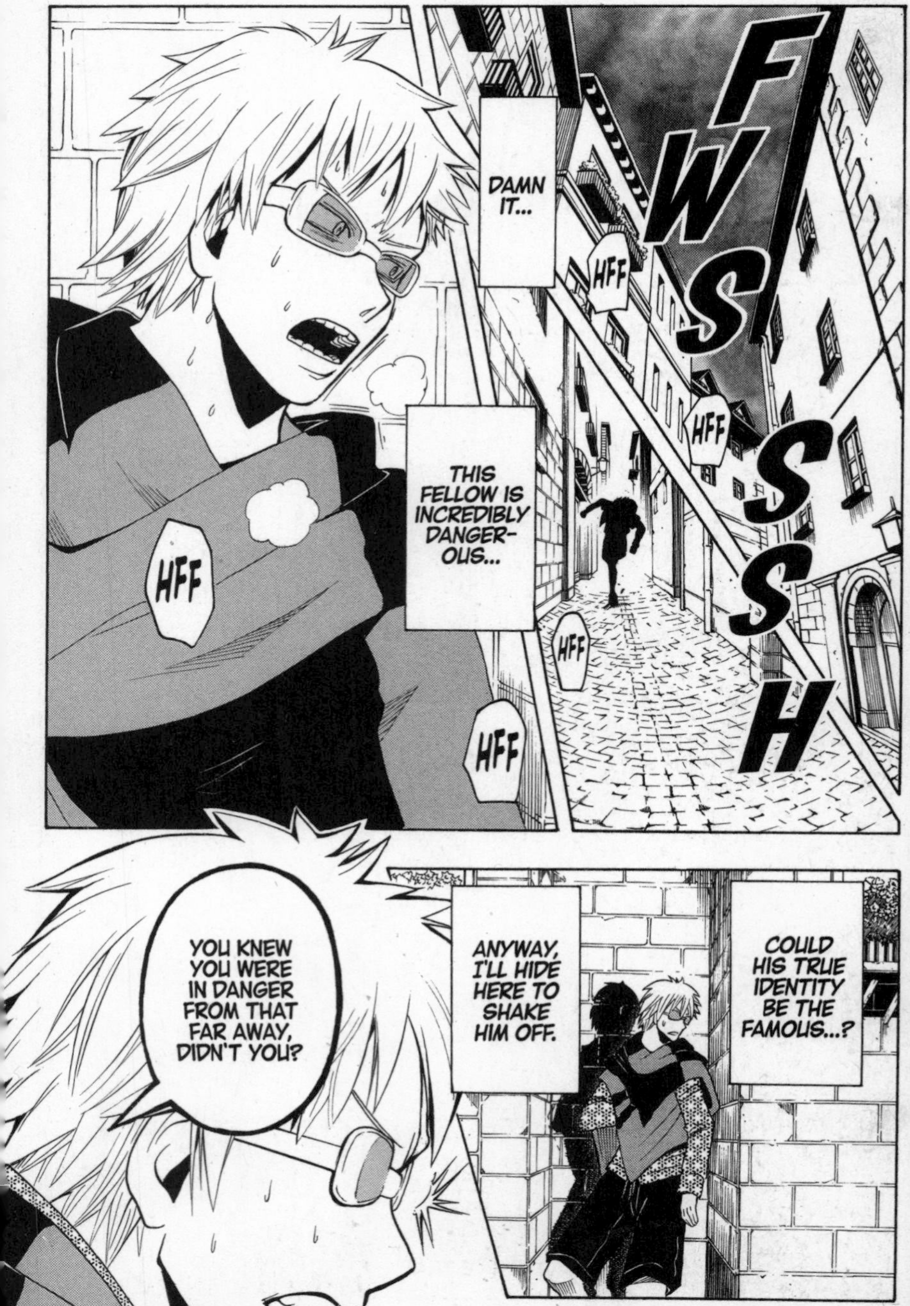
FWSSSH
DAMN IT...
HFF
HFF
THIS FELLOW IS INCREDIBLY DANGER-OUS...
HFF
HFF
HFF
COULD HIS TRUE IDENTITY BE THE FAMOUS...?
ANYWAY, I'LL HIDE HERE TO SHAKE HIM OFF.
YOU KNEW YOU WERE IN DANGER FROM THAT FAR AWAY, DIDN'T YOU?

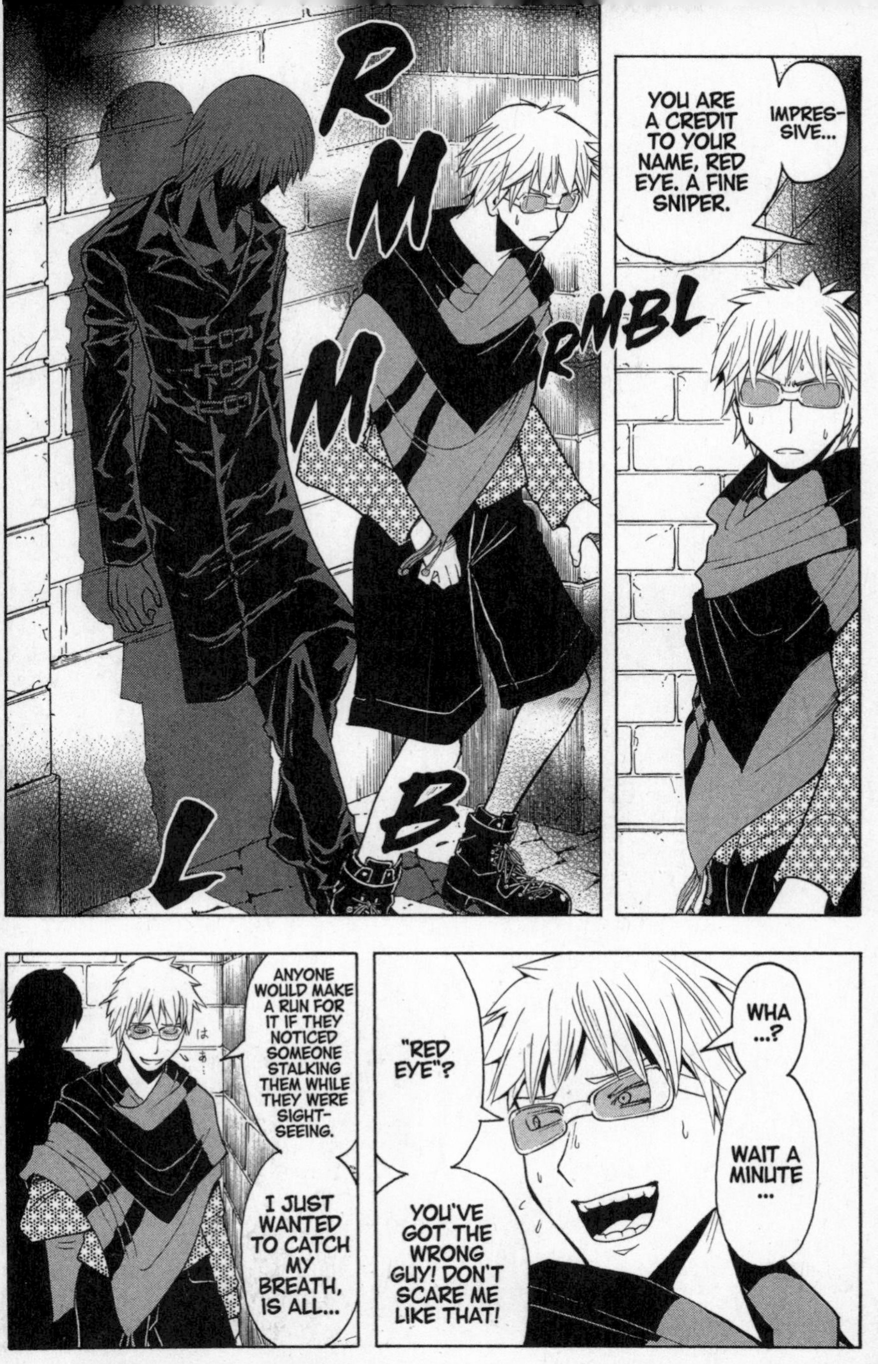
IMPRESSIVE...
YOU ARE A CREDIT TO YOUR NAME, RED EYE. A FINE SNIPER.
RMM
RMBL
BL
WHA ...?
WAIT A MINUTE ...
"RED EYE"?
YOU'VE GOT THE WRONG GUY! DON'T SCARE ME LIKE THAT!
ANYONE WOULD MAKE A RUN FOR IT IF THEY NOTICED SOMEONE STALKING THEM WHILE THEY WERE SIGHT-SEEING.
はあ…
I JUST WANTED TO CATCH MY BREATH, IS ALL...

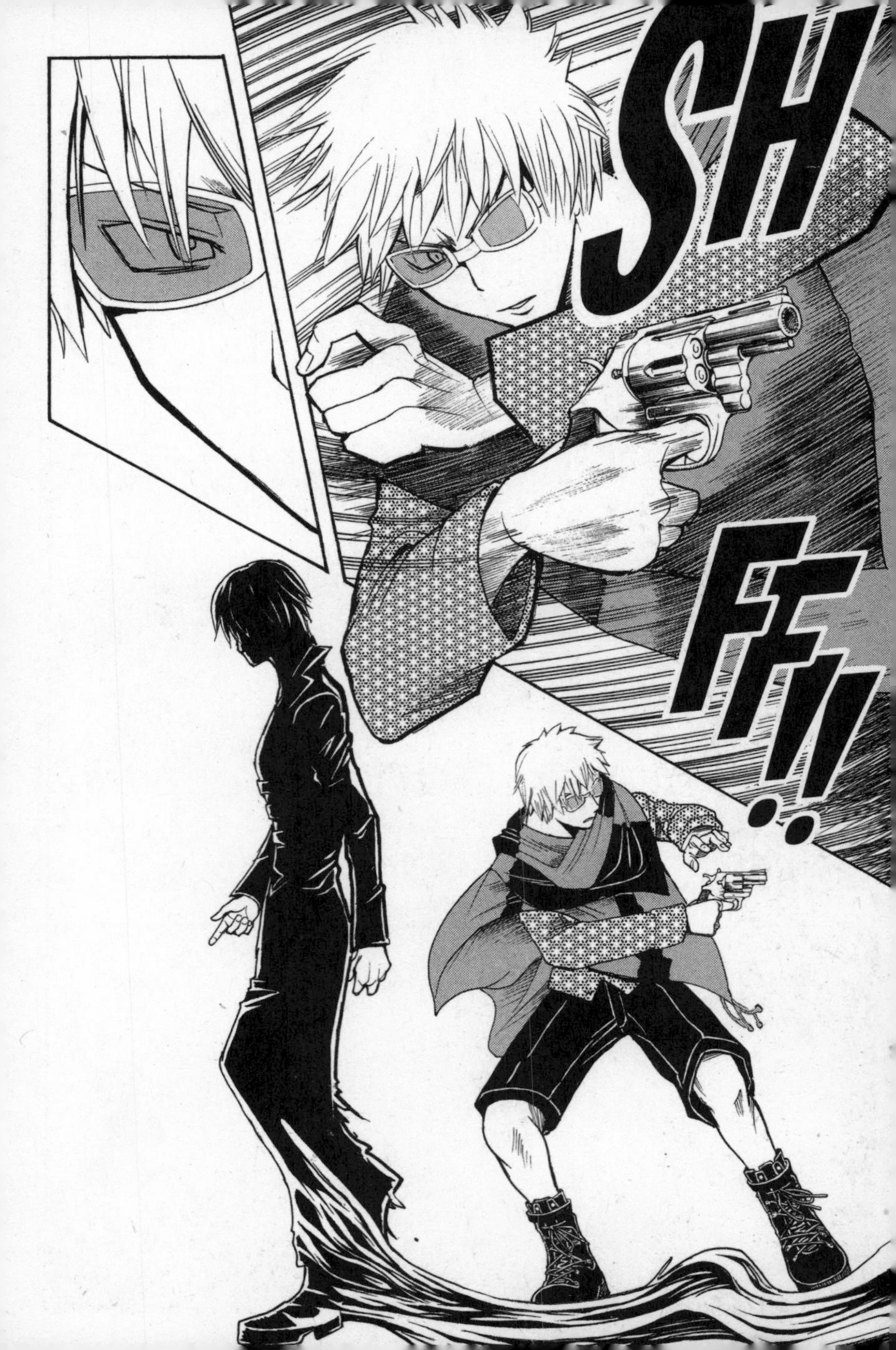
SHFT!!

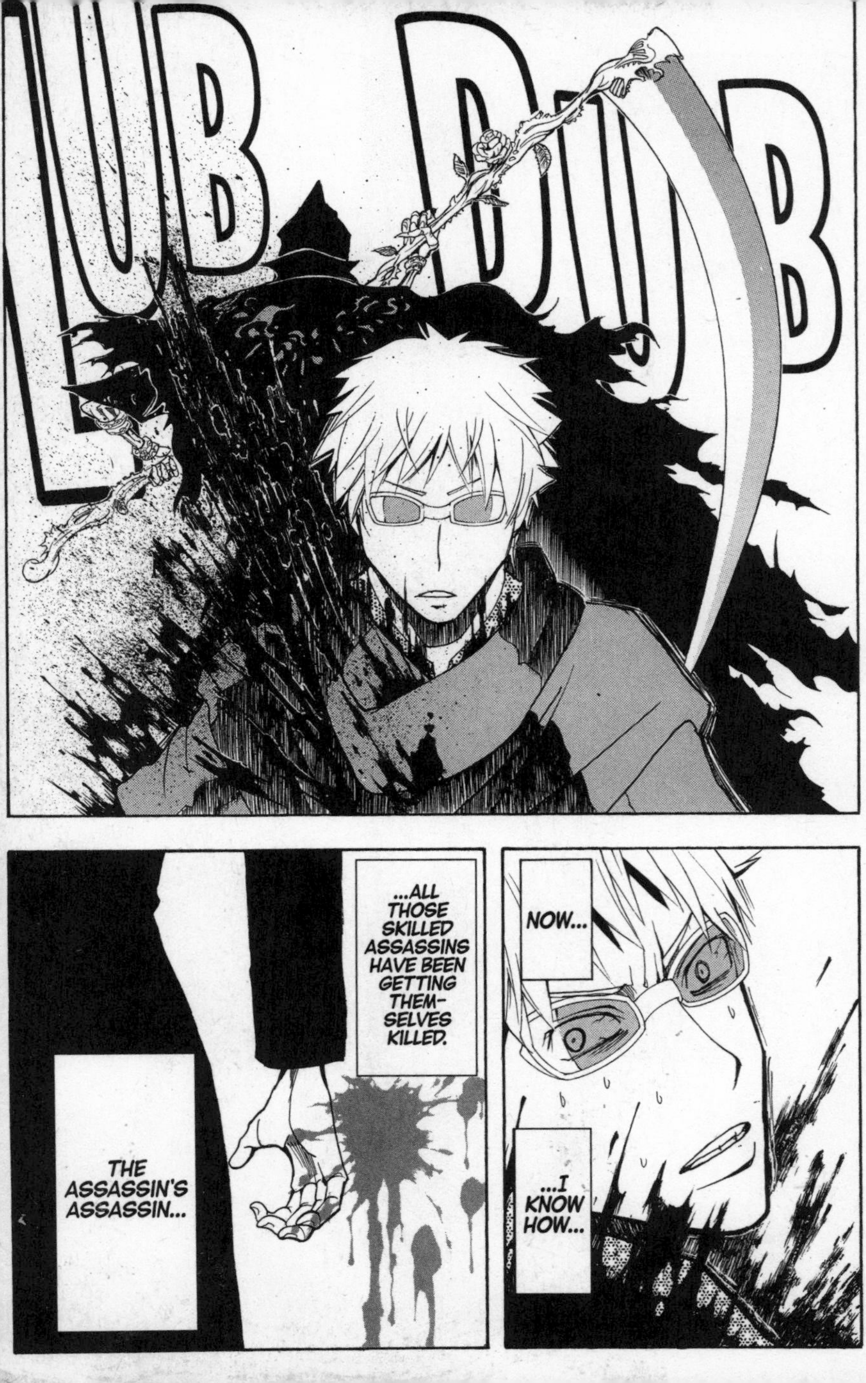

LUB DUB
NOW...
...I KNOW HOW...
...ALL THOSE SKILLED ASSASSINS HAVE BEEN GETTING THEM-SELVES KILLED.
THE ASSASSIN'S ASSASSIN...

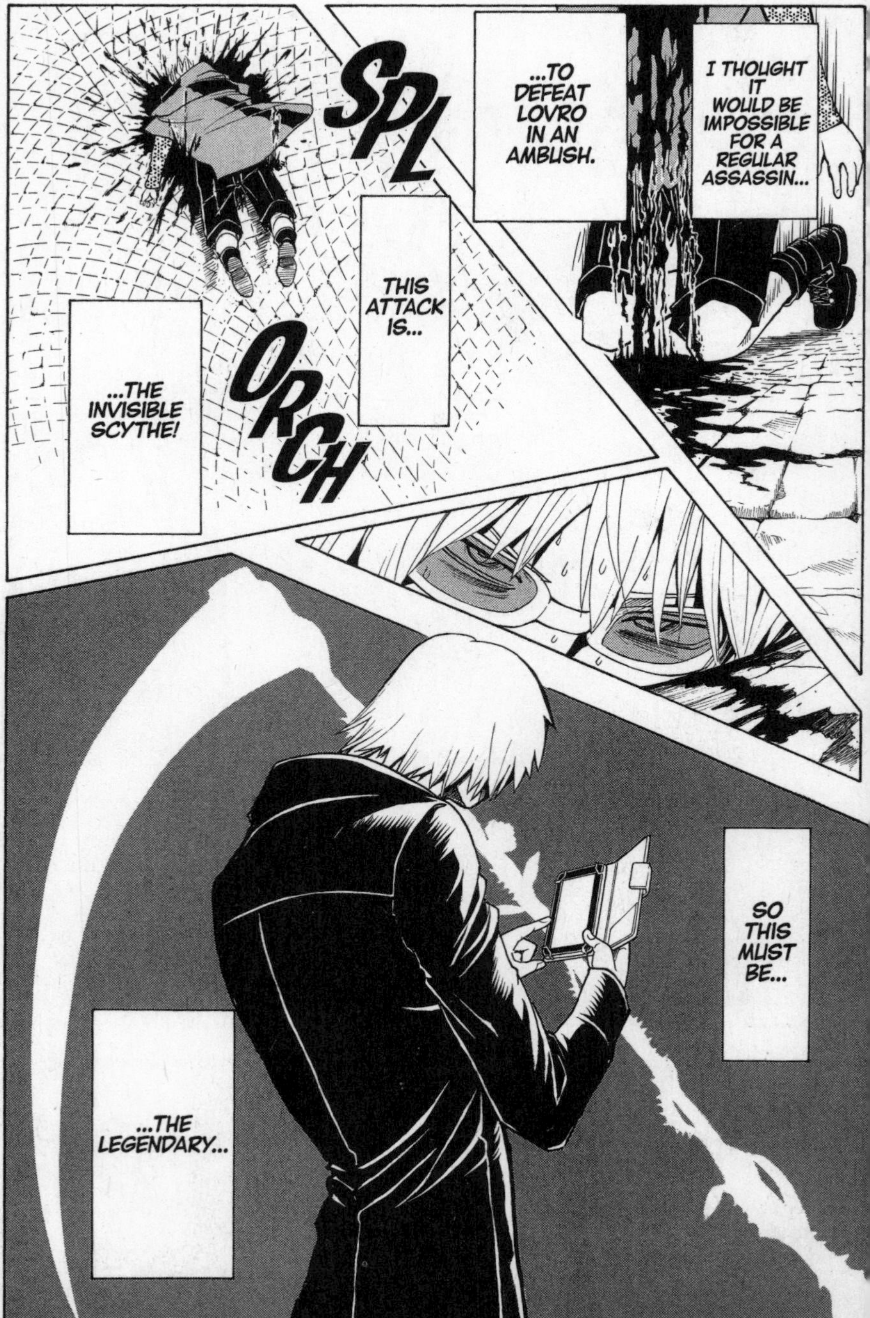
I THOUGHT IT WOULD BE IMPOSSIBLE FOR A REGULAR ASSASSIN...
...TO DEFEAT LOVRO IN AN AMBUSH.
SPLORCH
THIS ATTACK IS...
...THE INVISIBLE SCYTHE!
SO THIS MUST BE...
...THE LEGENDARY...

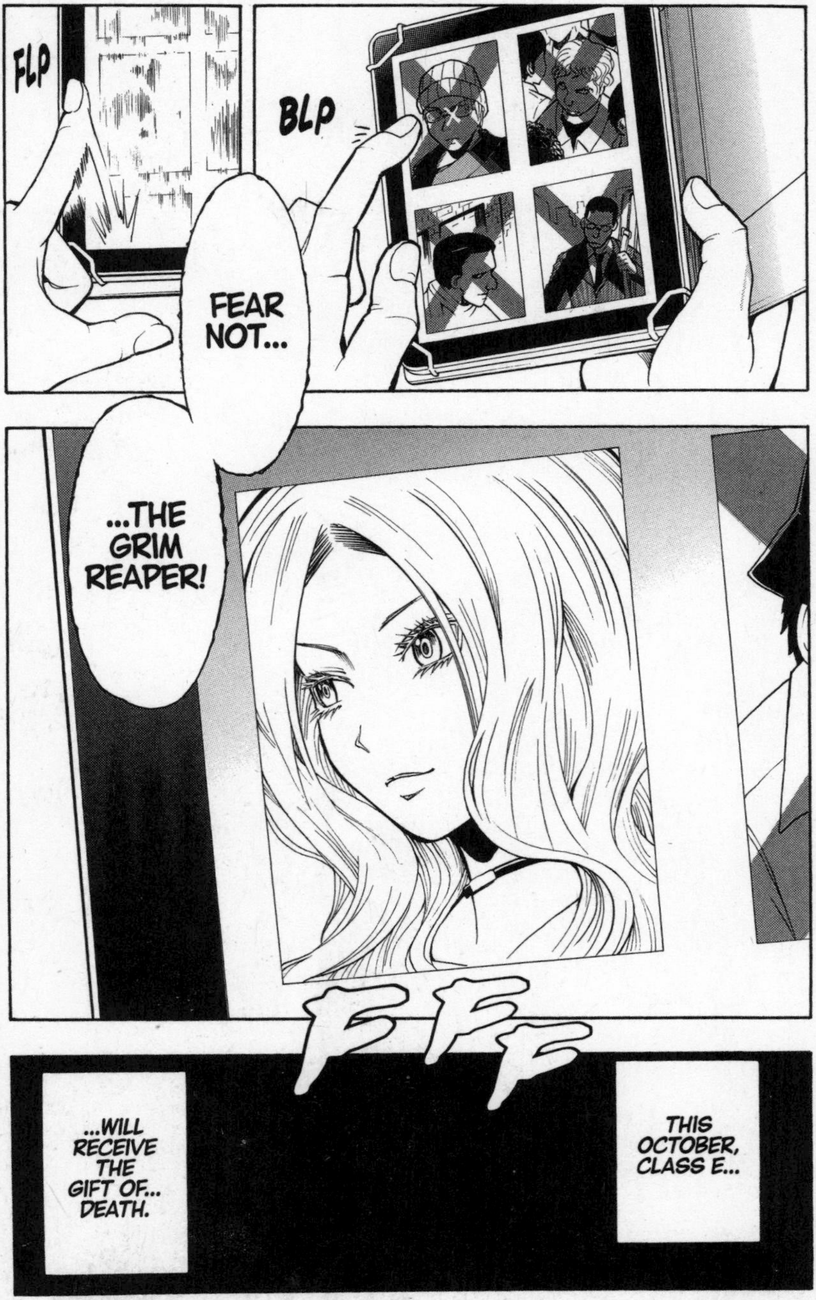
BLP
FEAR NOT...
FLP
...THE GRIM REAPER!
FFF
THIS OCTOBER, CLASS E...
...WILL RECEIVE THE GIFT OF... DEATH.

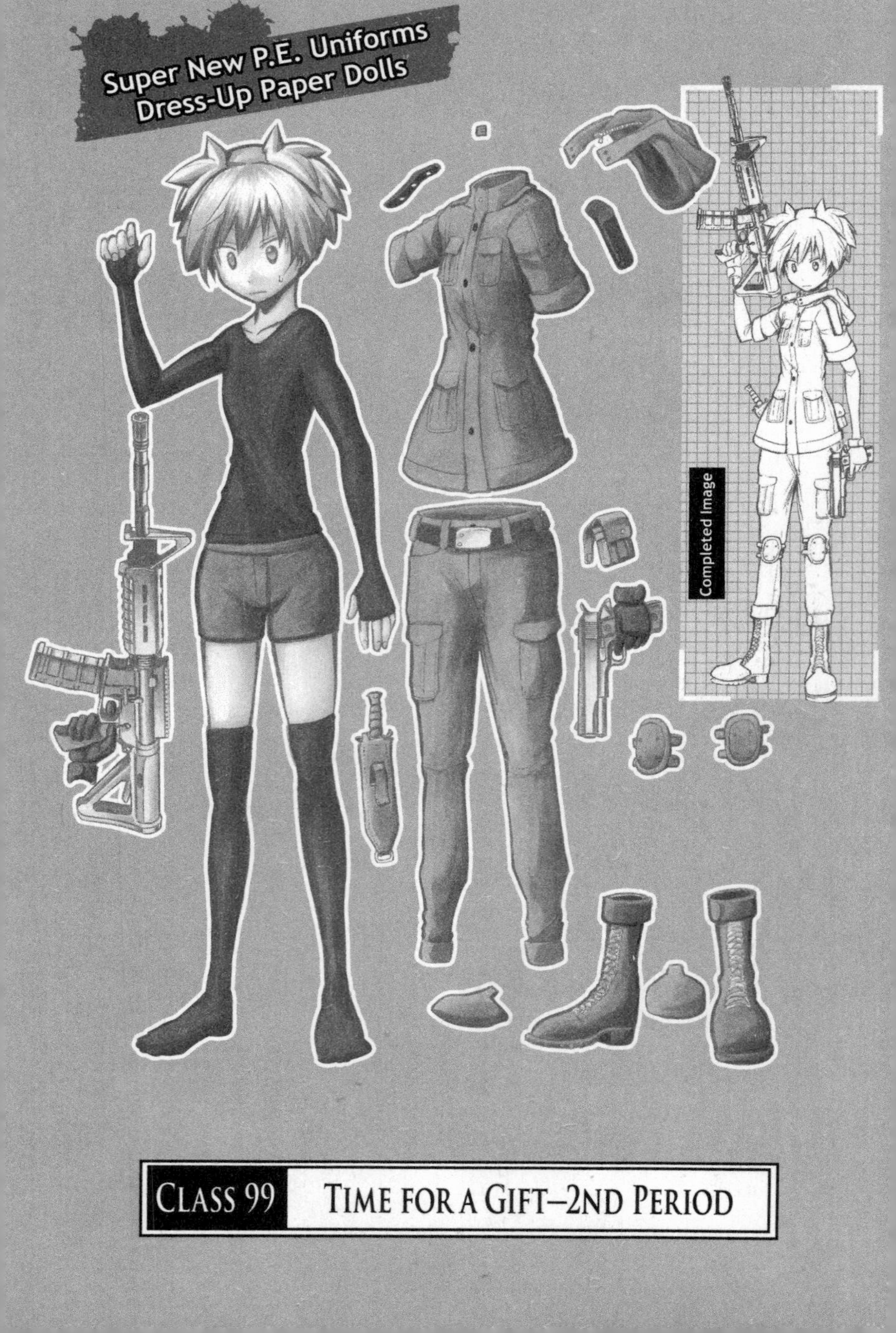
Super New P.E. Uniforms
Dress-Up Paper Dolls
Completed Image

CLASS 99 TIME FOR A GIFT—2ND PERIOD

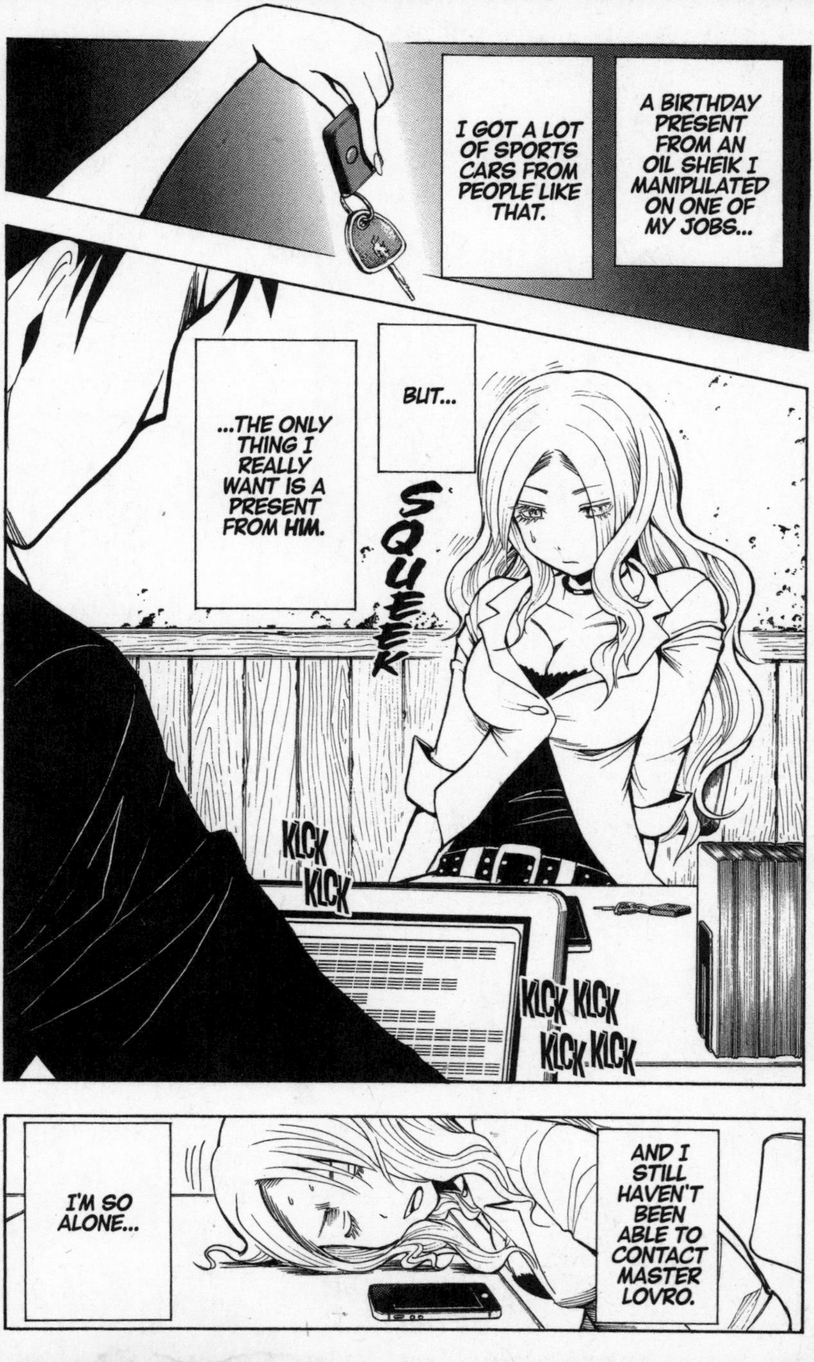
A BIRTHDAY PRESENT FROM AN OIL SHEIK I MANIPULATED ON ONE OF MY JOBS...
I GOT A LOT OF SPORTS CARS FROM PEOPLE LIKE THAT.
BUT...
...THE ONLY THING I REALLY WANT IS A PRESENT FROM HIM.
SQUEEK
KLCK KLCK
KLCK KLCK KLCK KLCK
AND I STILL HAVEN'T BEEN ABLE TO CONTACT MASTER LOVRO.
I'M SO ALONE...

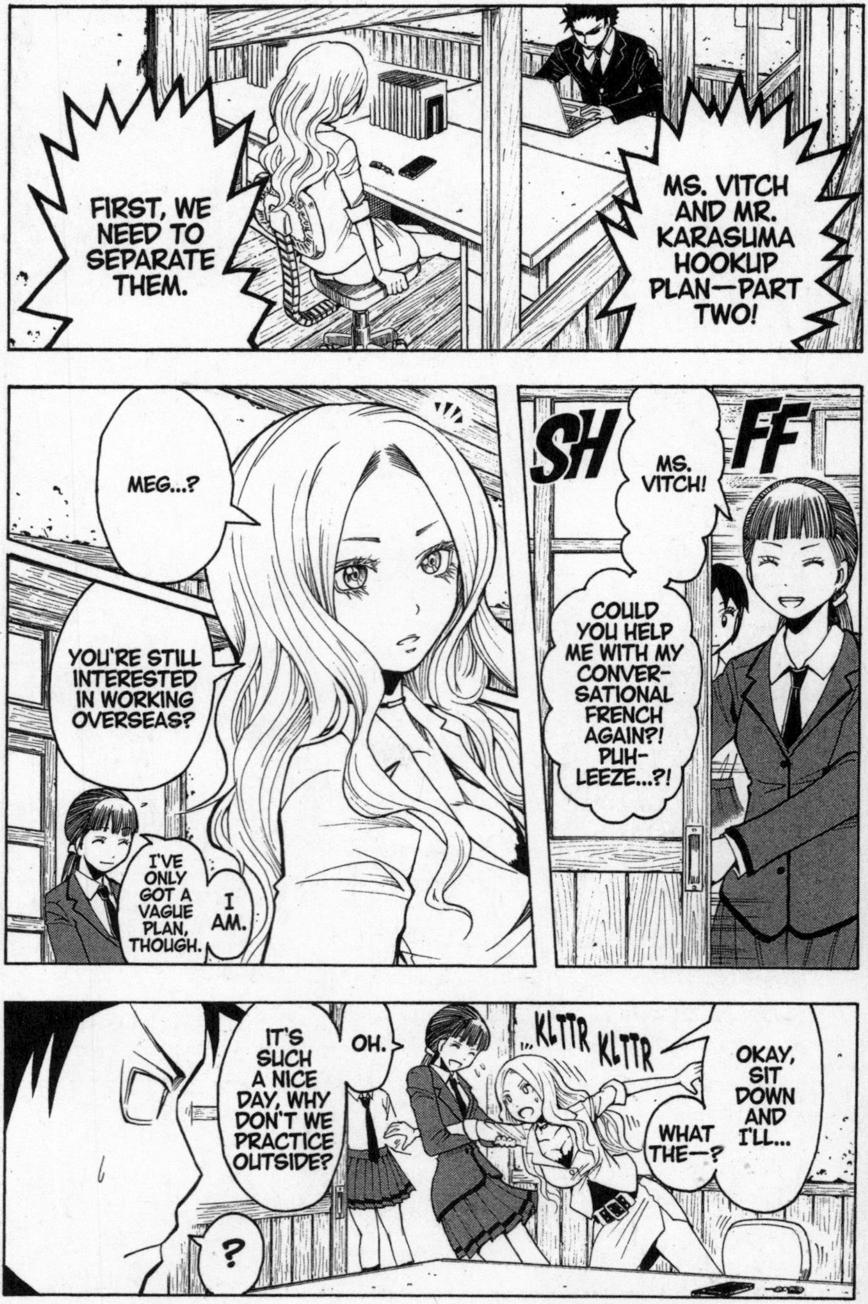
MS. VITCH AND MR. KARASUMA HOOKUP PLAN—PART TWO!
FIRST, WE NEED TO SEPARATE THEM.
SHFF
MS. VITCH!
COULD YOU HELP ME WITH MY CONVERSATIONAL FRENCH AGAIN?! PUH-LEEZE...?!
MEG...?
YOU'RE STILL INTERESTED IN WORKING OVERSEAS?
I AM.
I'VE ONLY GOT A VAGUE PLAN, THOUGH.
OKAY, SIT DOWN AND I'LL...
KLTTR KLTTR
WHAT THE—?
OH.
IT'S SUCH A NICE DAY, WHY DON'T WE PRACTICE OUTSIDE?
?

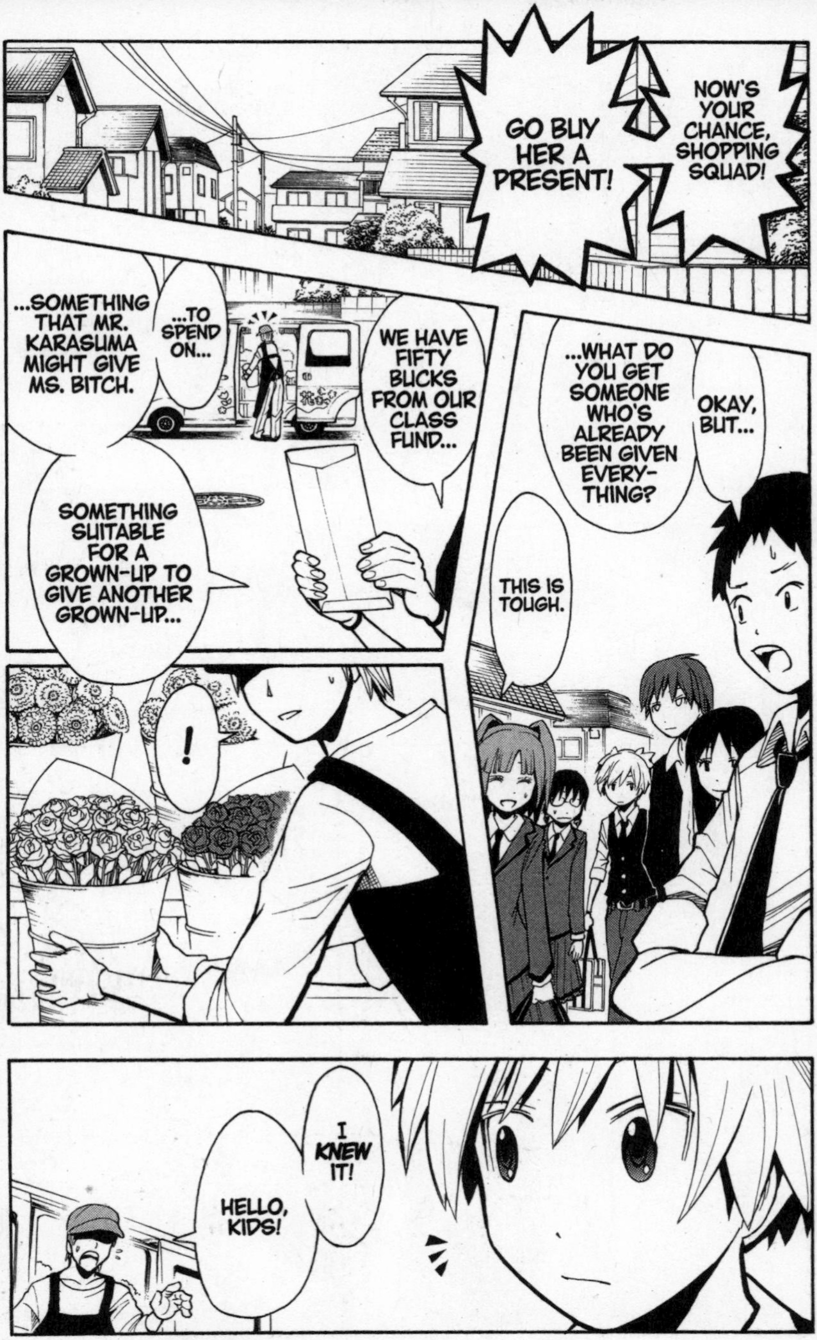

NOW'S YOUR CHANCE, SHOPPING SQUAD!
GO BUY HER A PRESENT!
OKAY, BUT...
...WHAT DO YOU GET SOMEONE WHO'S ALREADY BEEN GIVEN EVERY-THING?
THIS IS TOUGH.
WE HAVE FIFTY BUCKS FROM OUR CLASS FUND...
...TO SPEND ON...
...SOMETHING THAT MR. KARASUMA MIGHT GIVE MS. BITCH.
SOMETHING SUITABLE FOR A GROWN-UP TO GIVE ANOTHER GROWN-UP...
!
I KNEW IT!
HELLO, KIDS!

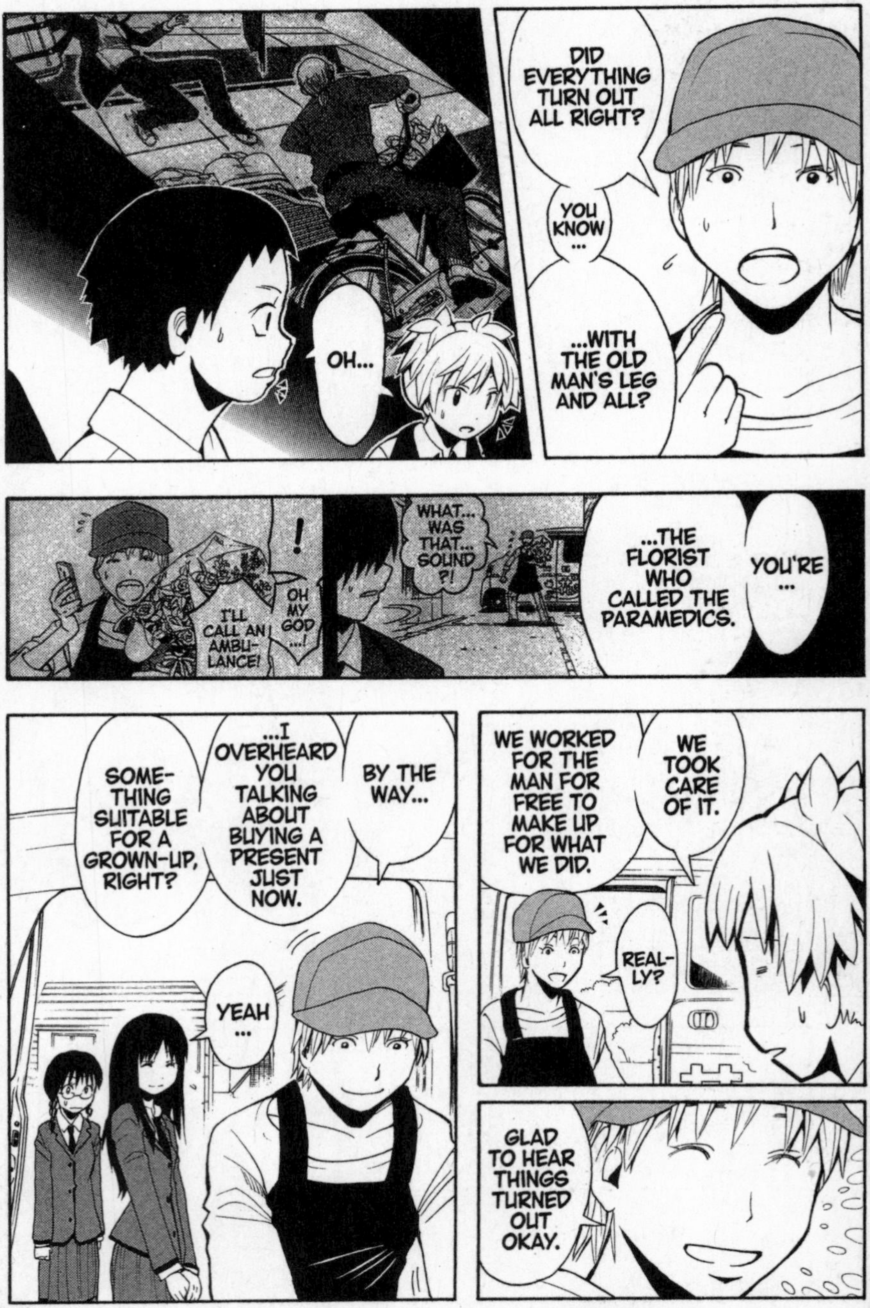
DID EVERYTHING TURN OUT ALL RIGHT?
YOU KNOW ...
...WITH THE OLD MAN'S LEG AND ALL?
OH...
YOU'RE ...
...THE FLORIST WHO CALLED THE PARAMEDICS.
WHAT... WAS THAT... SOUND ?!
!
OH MY GOD ...!
I'LL CALL AN AMBU-LANCE!
WE TOOK CARE OF IT.
WE WORKED FOR THE MAN FOR FREE TO MAKE UP FOR WHAT WE DID.
REAL-LY?
GLAD TO HEAR THINGS TURNED OUT OKAY.
BY THE WAY...
...I OVERHEARD YOU TALKING ABOUT BUYING A PRESENT JUST NOW.
SOME-THING SUITABLE FOR A GROWN-UP, RIGHT?
YEAH ...

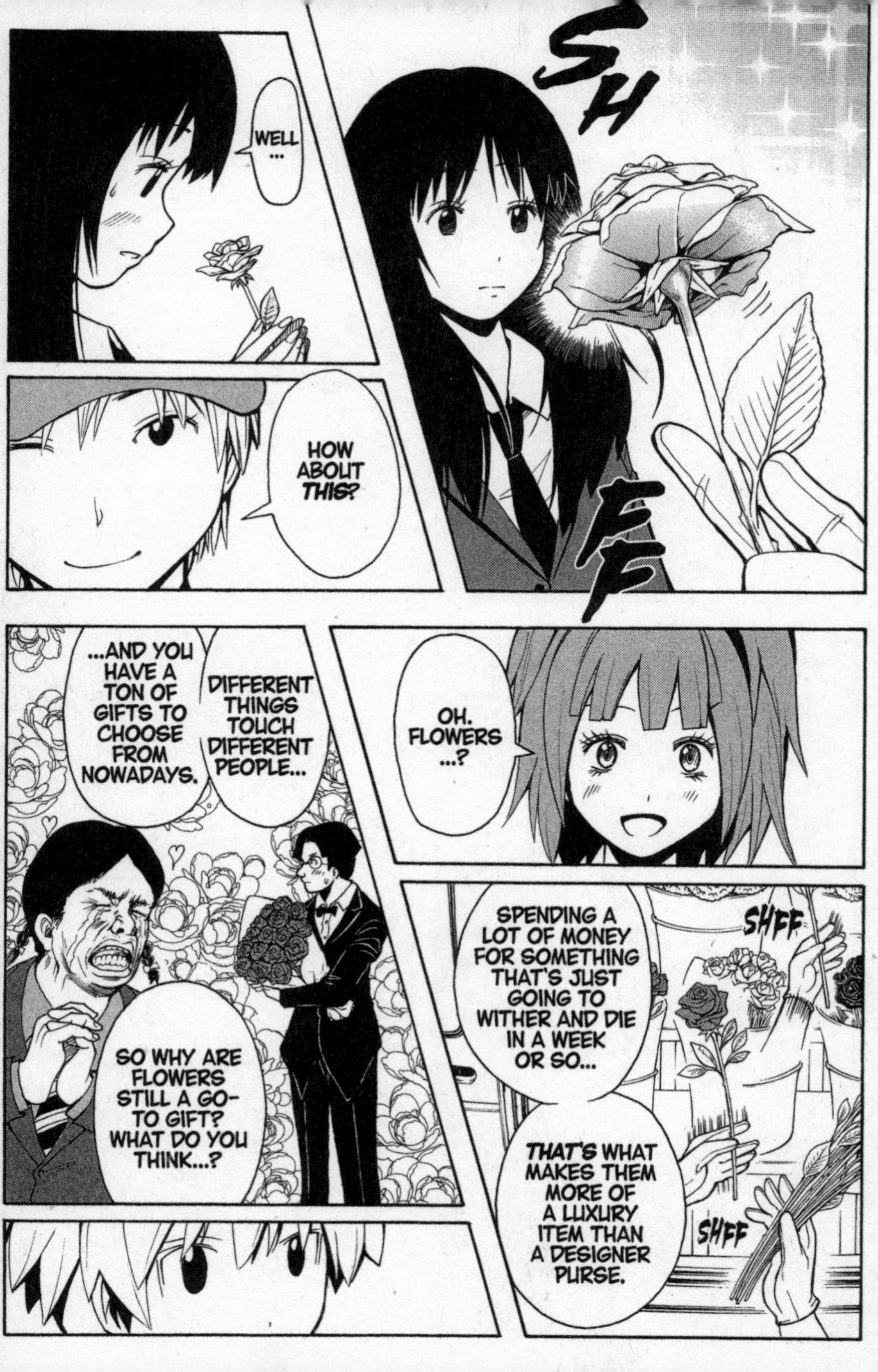
SH
FF
WELL...
HOW ABOUT THIS?
OH. FLOWERS...?
SPENDING A LOT OF MONEY FOR SOMETHING THAT'S JUST GOING TO WITHER AND DIE IN A WEEK OR SO...
SHFF
THAT'S WHAT MAKES THEM MORE OF A LUXURY ITEM THAN A DESIGNER PURSE.
SHFF
DIFFERENT THINGS TOUCH DIFFERENT PEOPLE...
...AND YOU HAVE A TON OF GIFTS TO CHOOSE FROM NOWADAYS.
SO WHY ARE FLOWERS STILL A GO-TO GIFT? WHAT DO YOU THINK...?

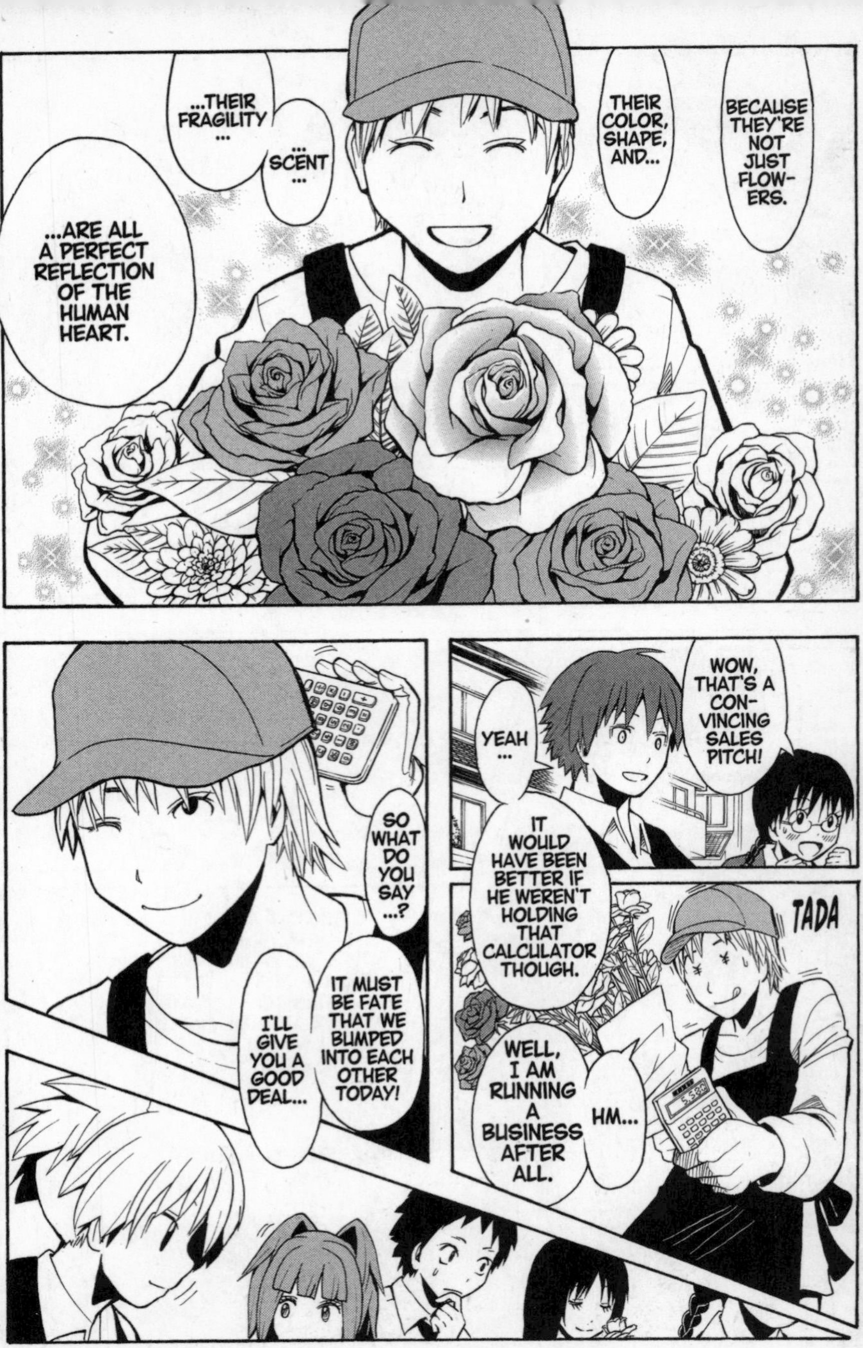
BECAUSE THEY'RE NOT JUST FLOWERS.
THEIR COLOR, SHAPE, AND...
...SCENT...
...THEIR FRAGILITY...
...ARE ALL A PERFECT REFLECTION OF THE HUMAN HEART.
WOW, THAT'S A CONVINCING SALES PITCH!
YEAH...
IT WOULD HAVE BEEN BETTER IF HE WEREN'T HOLDING THAT CALCULATOR THOUGH.
TADA
HM...
WELL, I AM RUNNING A BUSINESS AFTER ALL.
SO WHAT DO YOU SAY...?
IT MUST BE FATE THAT WE BUMPED INTO EACH OTHER TODAY!
I'LL GIVE YOU A GOOD DEAL...

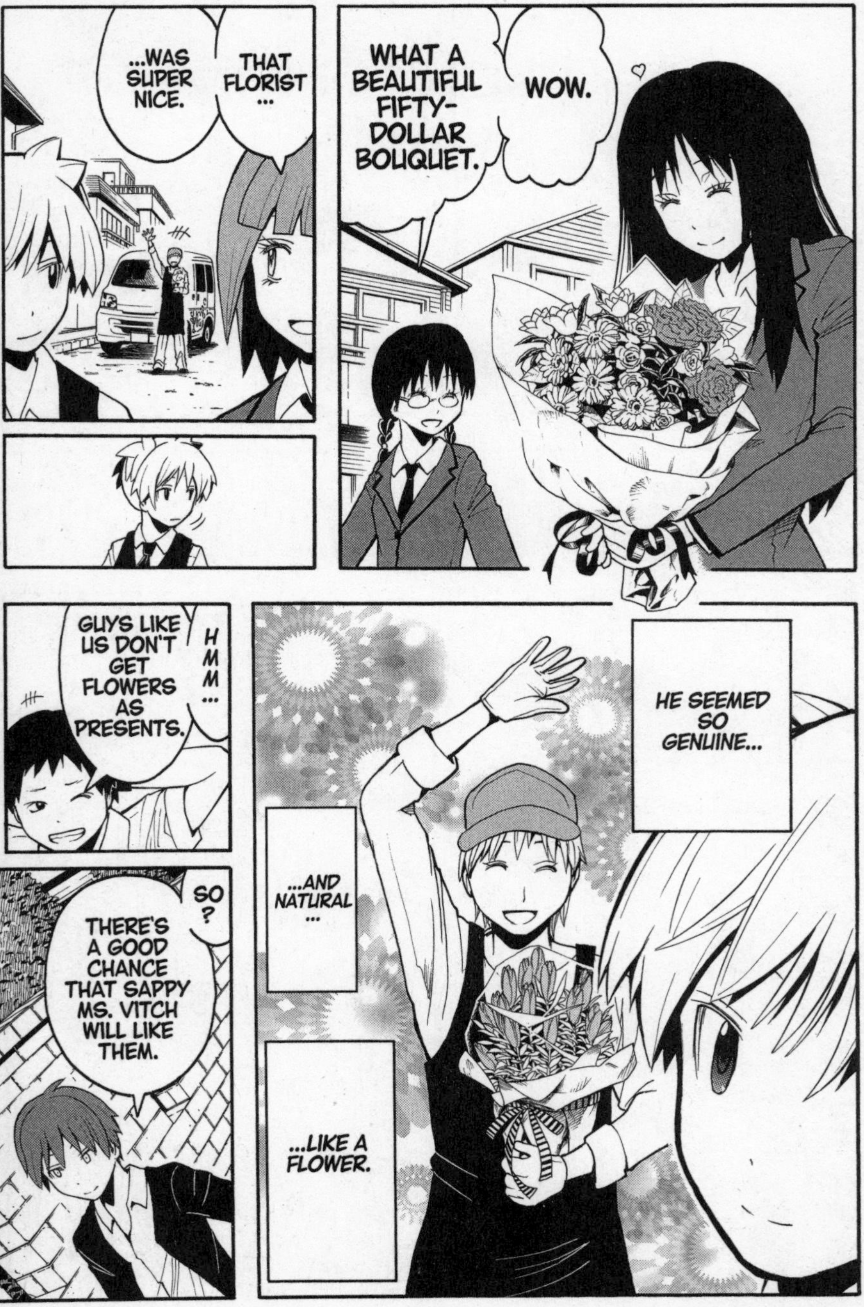
WOW.
WHAT A BEAUTIFUL FIFTY-DOLLAR BOUQUET.
THAT FLORIST...
...WAS SUPER NICE.
HE SEEMED SO GENUINE...
...AND NATURAL...
...LIKE A FLOWER.
HMM...
GUYS LIKE US DON'T GET FLOWERS AS PRESENTS.
SO?
THERE'S A GOOD CHANCE THAT SAPPY MS. VITCH WILL LIKE THEM.

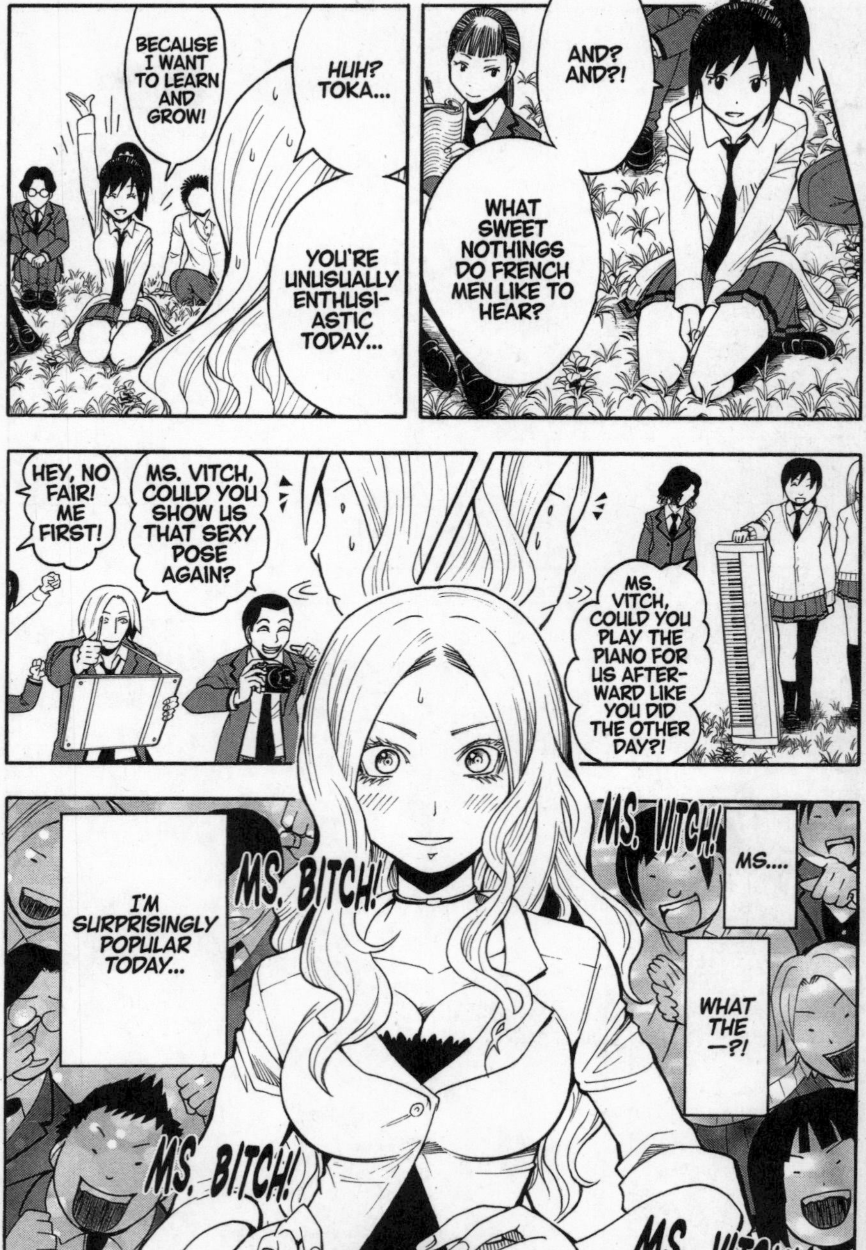
AND? AND?!
WHAT SWEET NOTHINGS DO FRENCH MEN LIKE TO HEAR?
BECAUSE I WANT TO LEARN AND GROW!
HUH? TOKA...
YOU'RE UNUSUALLY ENTHUSI-ASTIC TODAY...
MS. VITCH, COULD YOU PLAY THE PIANO FOR US AFTER-WARD LIKE YOU DID THE OTHER DAY?!
MS. VITCH, COULD YOU SHOW US THAT SEXY POSE AGAIN?
HEY, NO FAIR! ME FIRST!
MS....
WHAT THE —?!
MS. VITCH!
MS. BITCH!
I'M SURPRISINGLY POPULAR TODAY...
MS. BITCH!
MS. VITCH!

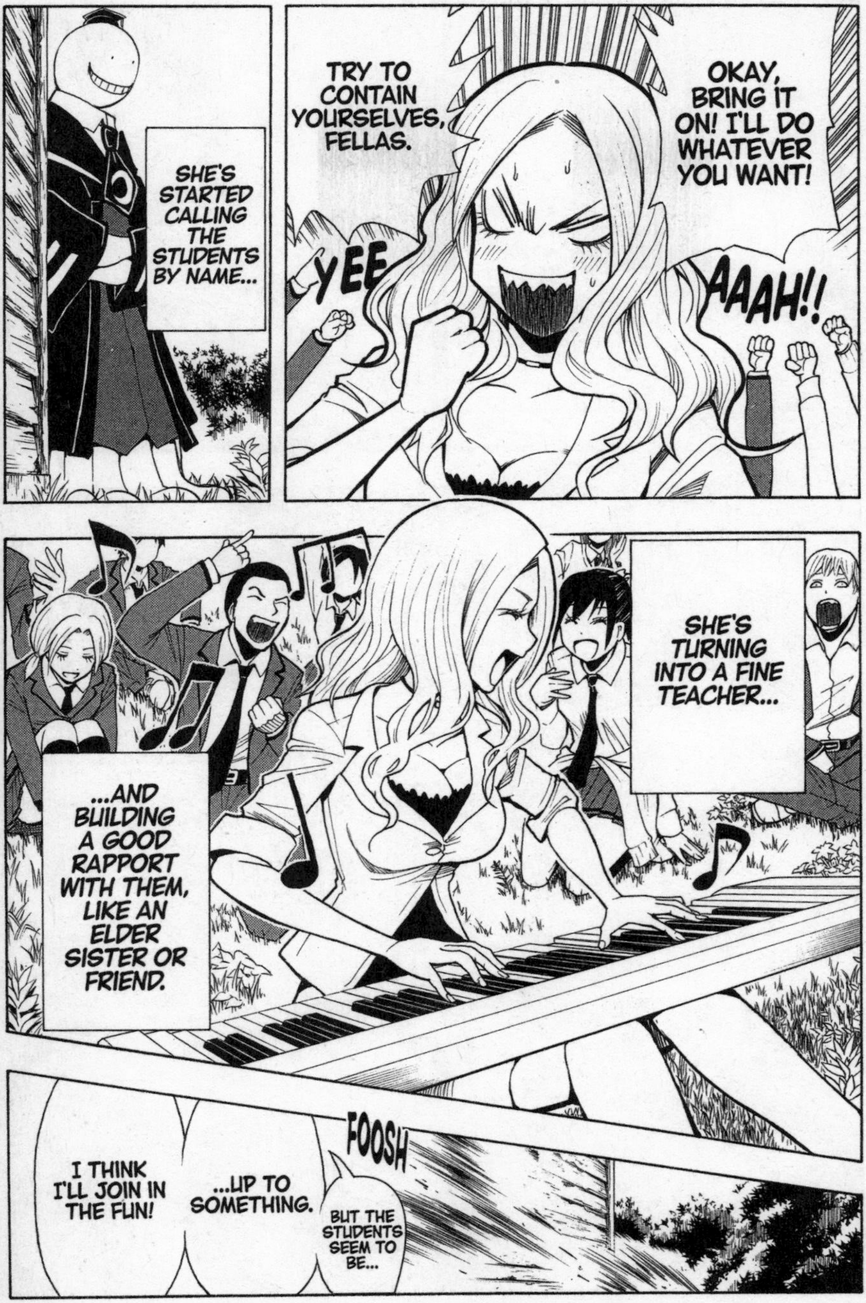
OKAY, BRING IT ON! I'LL DO WHATEVER YOU WANT!
TRY TO CONTAIN YOURSELVES, FELLAS.
YEE AAAH!!
SHE'S STARTED CALLING THE STUDENTS BY NAME...
SHE'S TURNING INTO A FINE TEACHER...
...AND BUILDING A GOOD RAPPORT WITH THEM, LIKE AN ELDER SISTER OR FRIEND.
BUT THE STUDENTS SEEM TO BE...
FOOSH
...UP TO SOMETHING.
I THINK I'LL JOIN IN THE FUN!

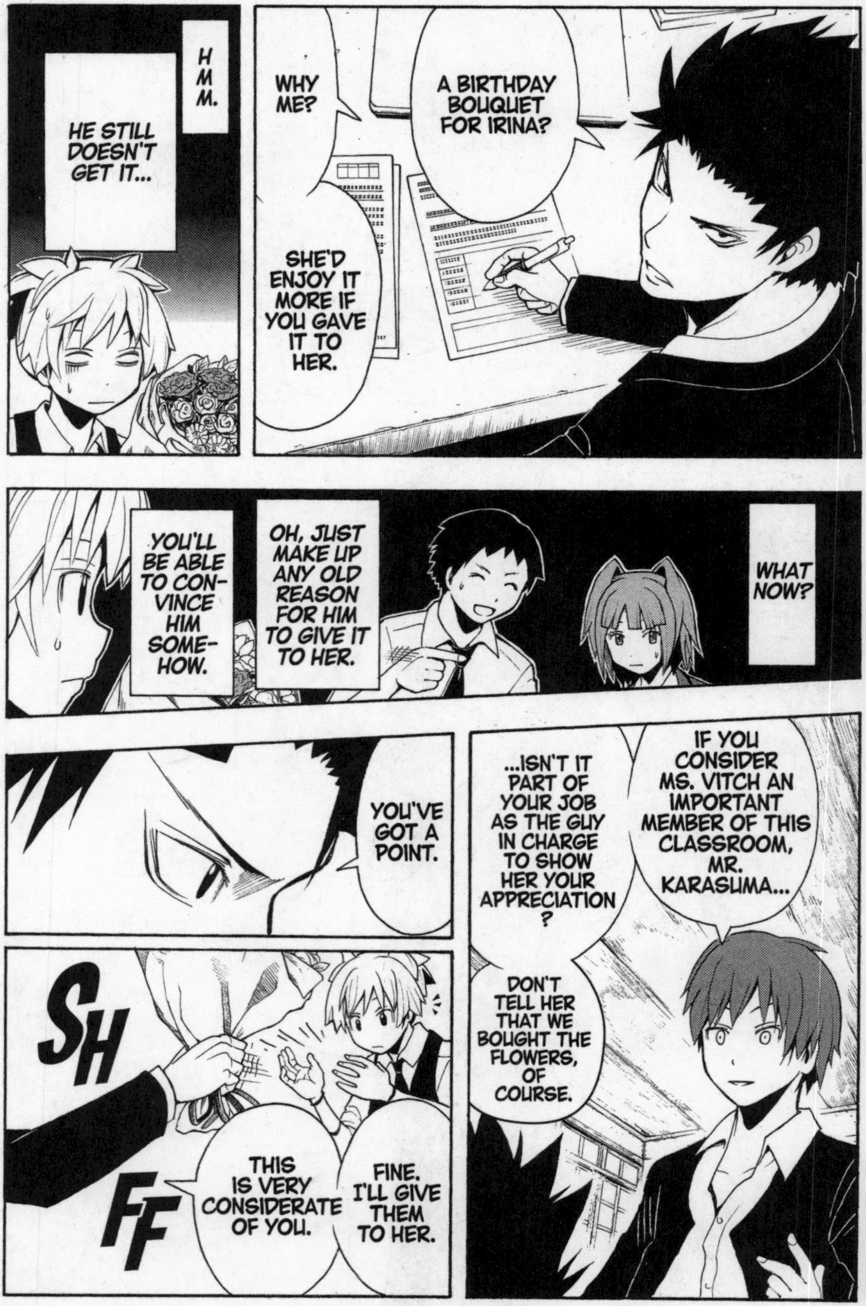
A BIRTHDAY BOUQUET FOR IRINA?
WHY ME?
SHE'D ENJOY IT MORE IF YOU GAVE IT TO HER.
HMM.
HE STILL DOESN'T GET IT...
WHAT NOW?
OH, JUST MAKE UP ANY OLD REASON FOR HIM TO GIVE IT TO HER.
YOU'LL BE ABLE TO CONVINCE HIM SOMEHOW.
IF YOU CONSIDER MS. VITCH AN IMPORTANT MEMBER OF THIS CLASSROOM, MR. KARASUMA...
...ISN'T IT PART OF YOUR JOB AS THE GUY IN CHARGE TO SHOW HER YOUR APPRECIATION?
DON'T TELL HER THAT WE BOUGHT THE FLOWERS, OF COURSE.
YOU'VE GOT A POINT.
FINE. I'LL GIVE THEM TO HER.
THIS IS VERY CONSIDERATE OF YOU.
SHFF

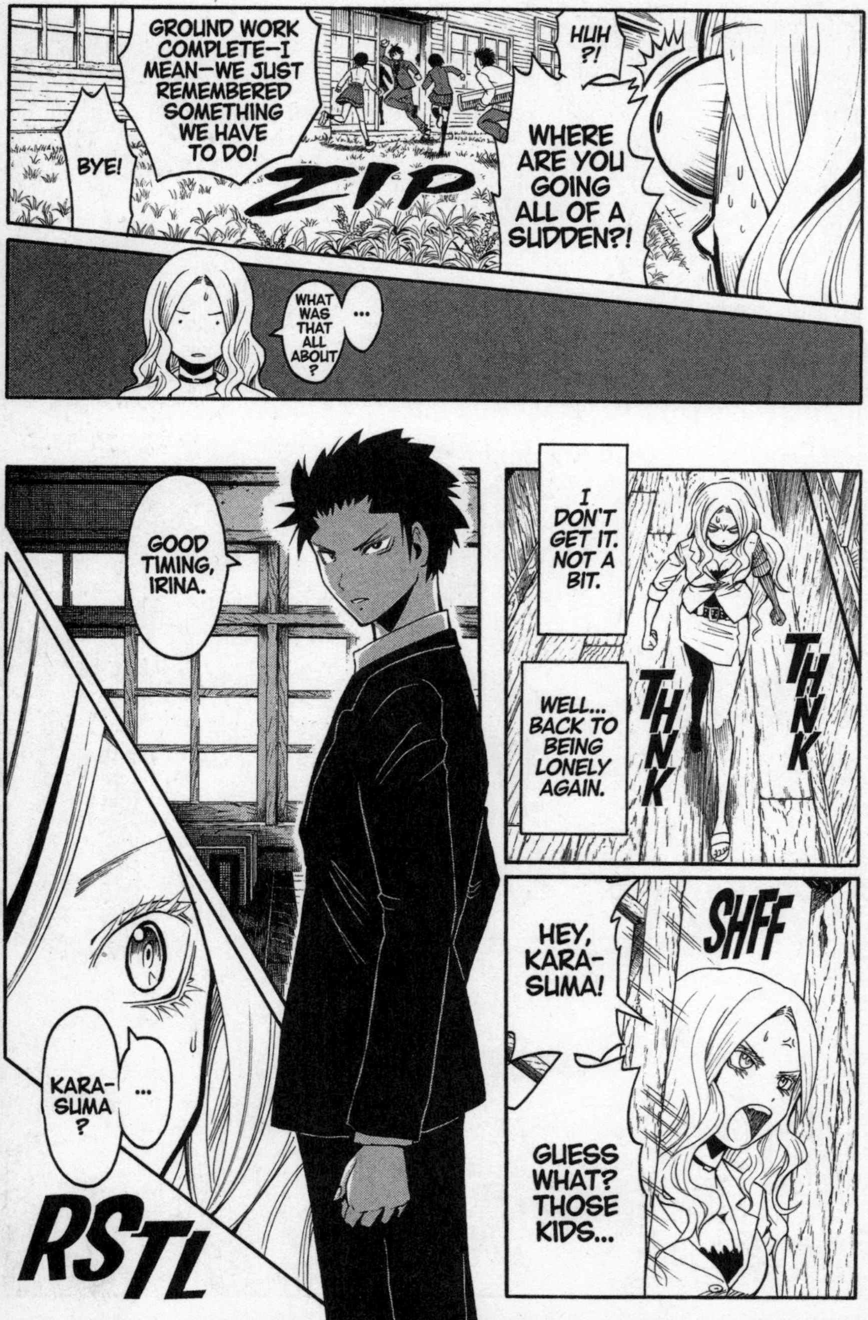
HUH?!
GROUND WORK COMPLETE—I MEAN—WE JUST REMEMBERED SOMETHING WE HAVE TO DO!
WHERE ARE YOU GOING ALL OF A SUDDEN?!
ZIP
BYE!
...
WHAT WAS THAT ALL ABOUT?
I DON'T GET IT. NOT A BIT.
WELL... BACK TO BEING LONELY AGAIN.
THNK
THNK
SHFF
HEY, KARA-SUMA!
GUESS WHAT? THOSE KIDS...
GOOD TIMING, IRINA.
...
KARA-SUMA?
RSTL

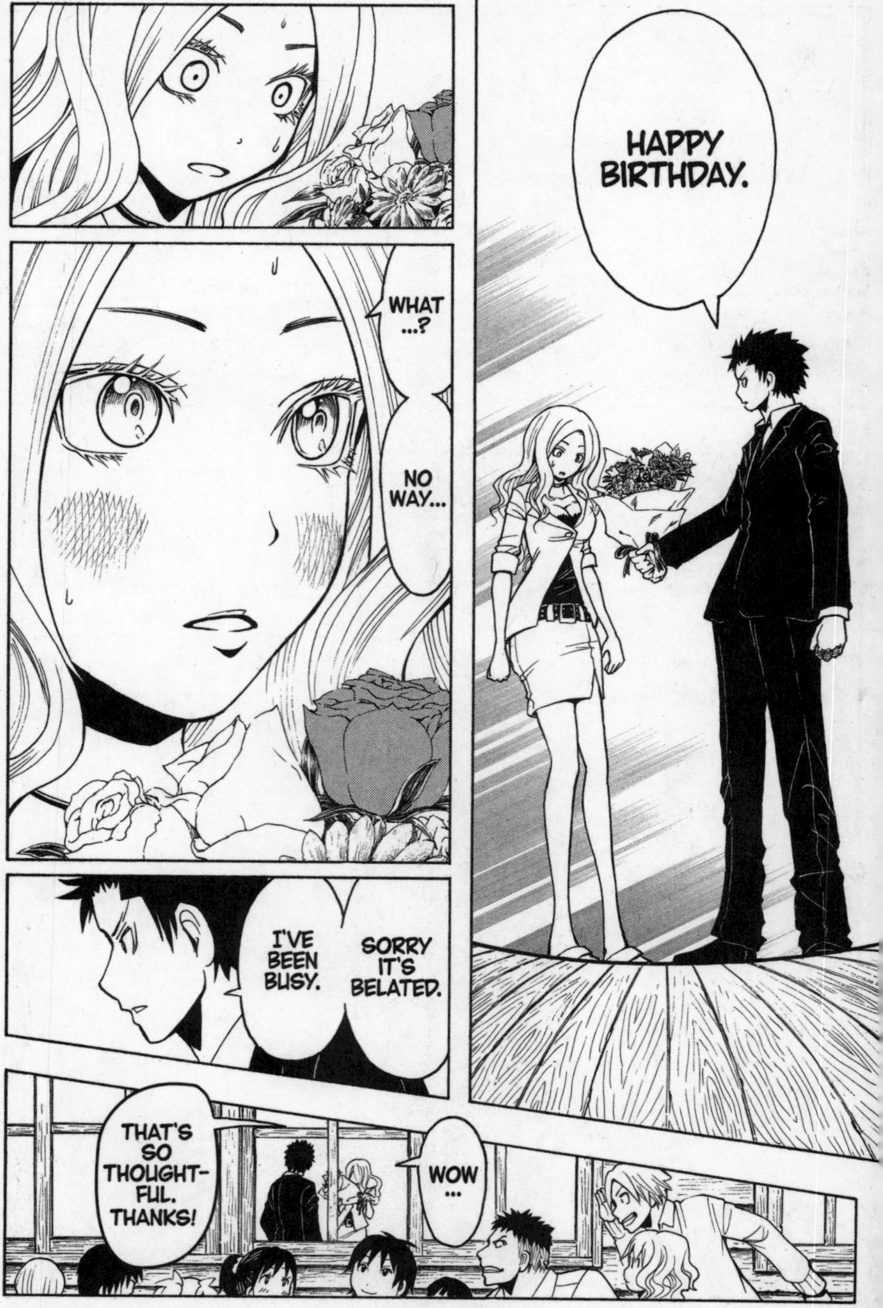
HAPPY BIRTHDAY.
WHAT ...?
NO WAY...
SORRY IT'S BELATED.
I'VE BEEN BUSY.
WOW ...
THAT'S SO THOUGHT-FUL. THANKS!

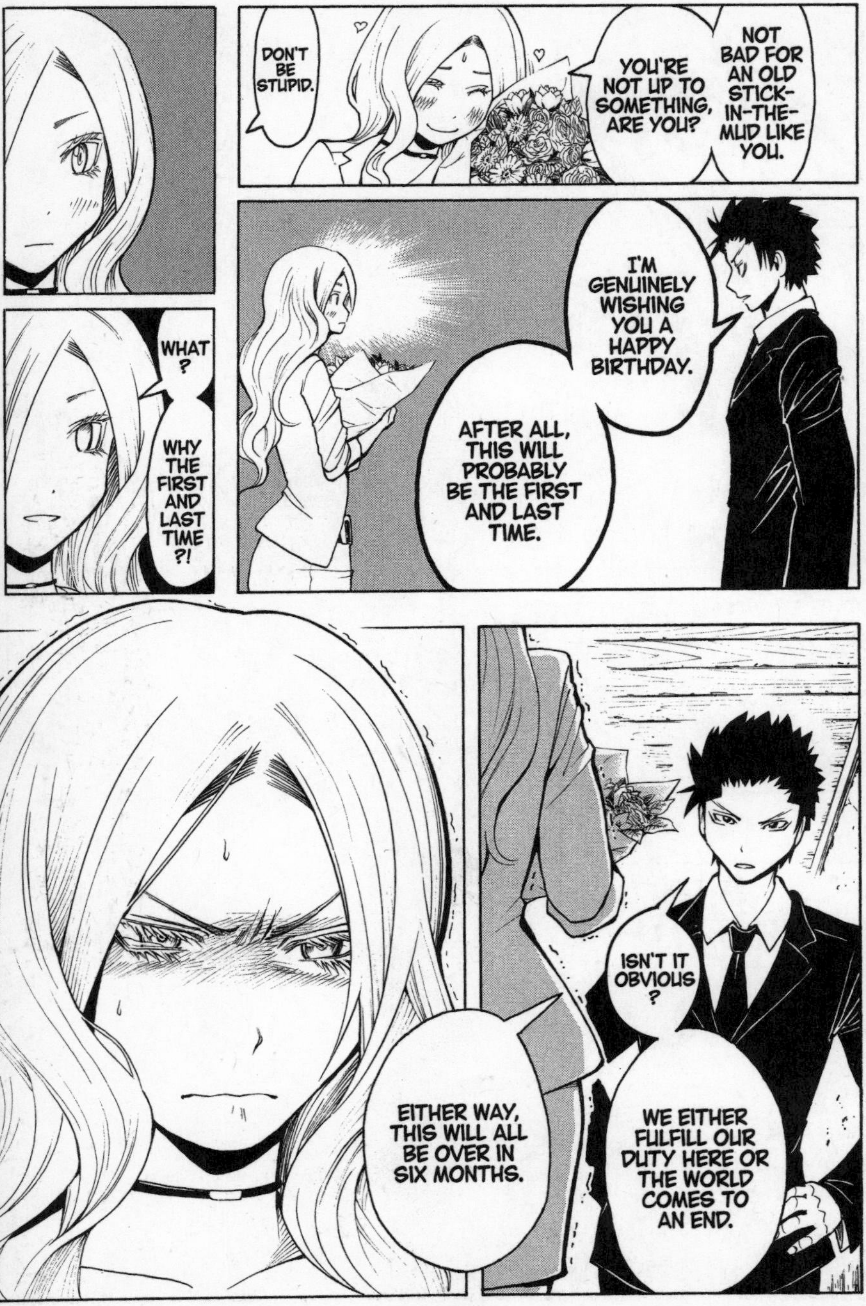
NOT BAD FOR AN OLD STICK-IN-THE-MUD LIKE YOU.
YOU'RE NOT UP TO SOMETHING, ARE YOU?
DON'T BE STUPID.
I'M GENUINELY WISHING YOU A HAPPY BIRTHDAY.
AFTER ALL, THIS WILL PROBABLY BE THE FIRST AND LAST TIME.
WHAT?
WHY THE FIRST AND LAST TIME?!
ISN'T IT OBVIOUS?
WE EITHER FULFILL OUR DUTY HERE OR THE WORLD COMES TO AN END.
EITHER WAY, THIS WILL ALL BE OVER IN SIX MONTHS.

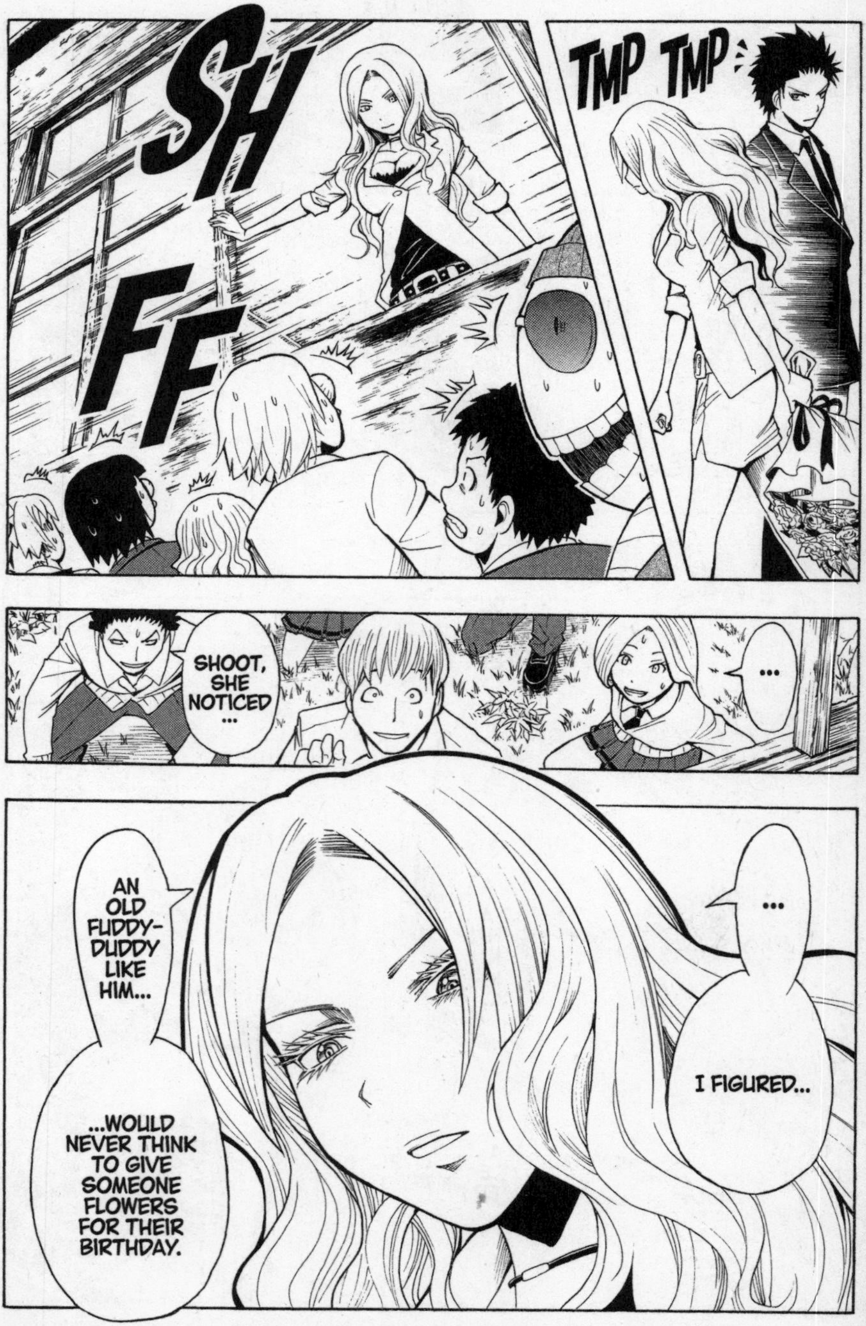
TMP TMP
SHFF
...
SHOOT, SHE NOTICED ...
...
I FIGURED...
AN OLD FUDDY-DUDDY LIKE HIM...
...WOULD NEVER THINK TO GIVE SOMEONE FLOWERS FOR THEIR BIRTHDAY.

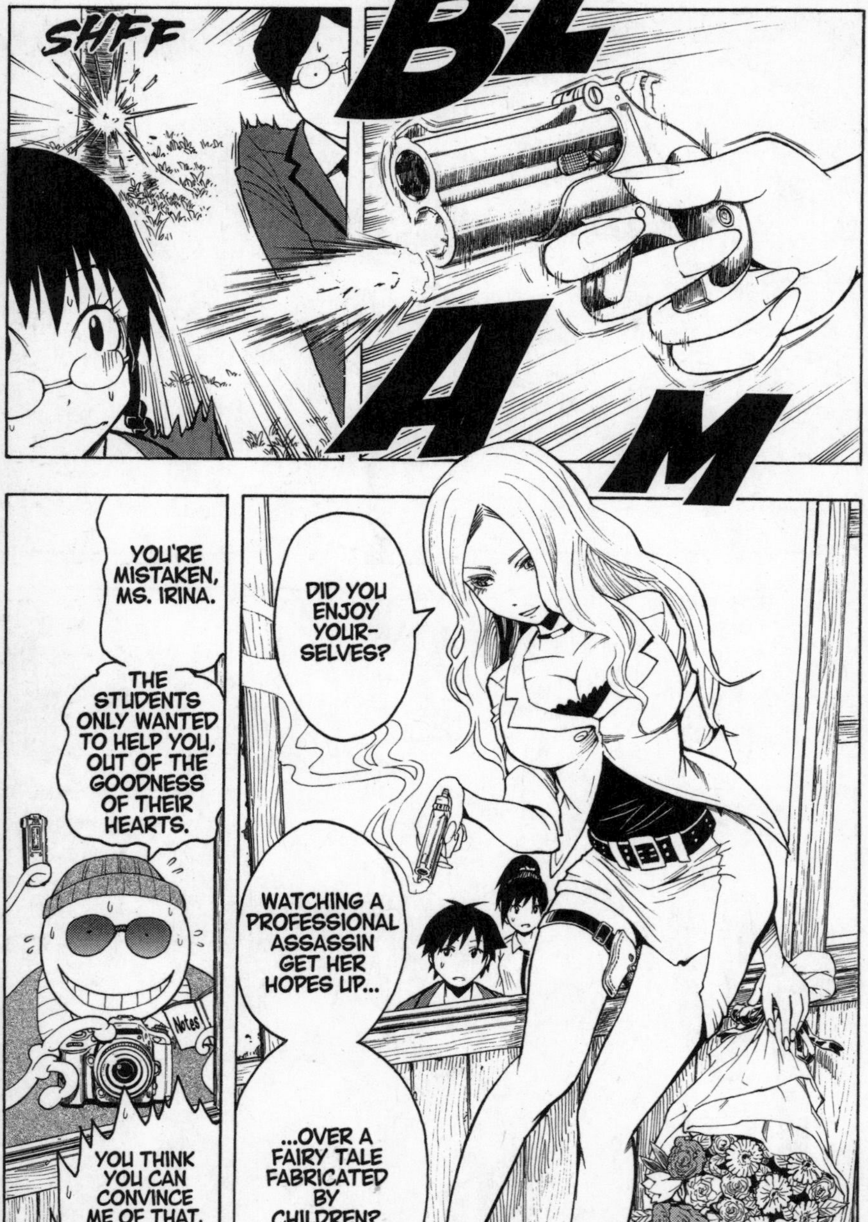
BLAM
SHFF
DID YOU ENJOY YOURSELVES?
WATCHING A PROFESSIONAL ASSASSIN GET HER HOPES UP...
...OVER A FAIRY TALE FABRICATED BY CHILDREN?
YOU'RE MISTAKEN, MS. IRINA.
THE STUDENTS ONLY WANTED TO HELP YOU, OUT OF THE GOODNESS OF THEIR HEARTS.
Notes
YOU THINK YOU CAN CONVINCE ME OF THAT, YOU, YOU... PAPARAZZI OCTOPUS?!

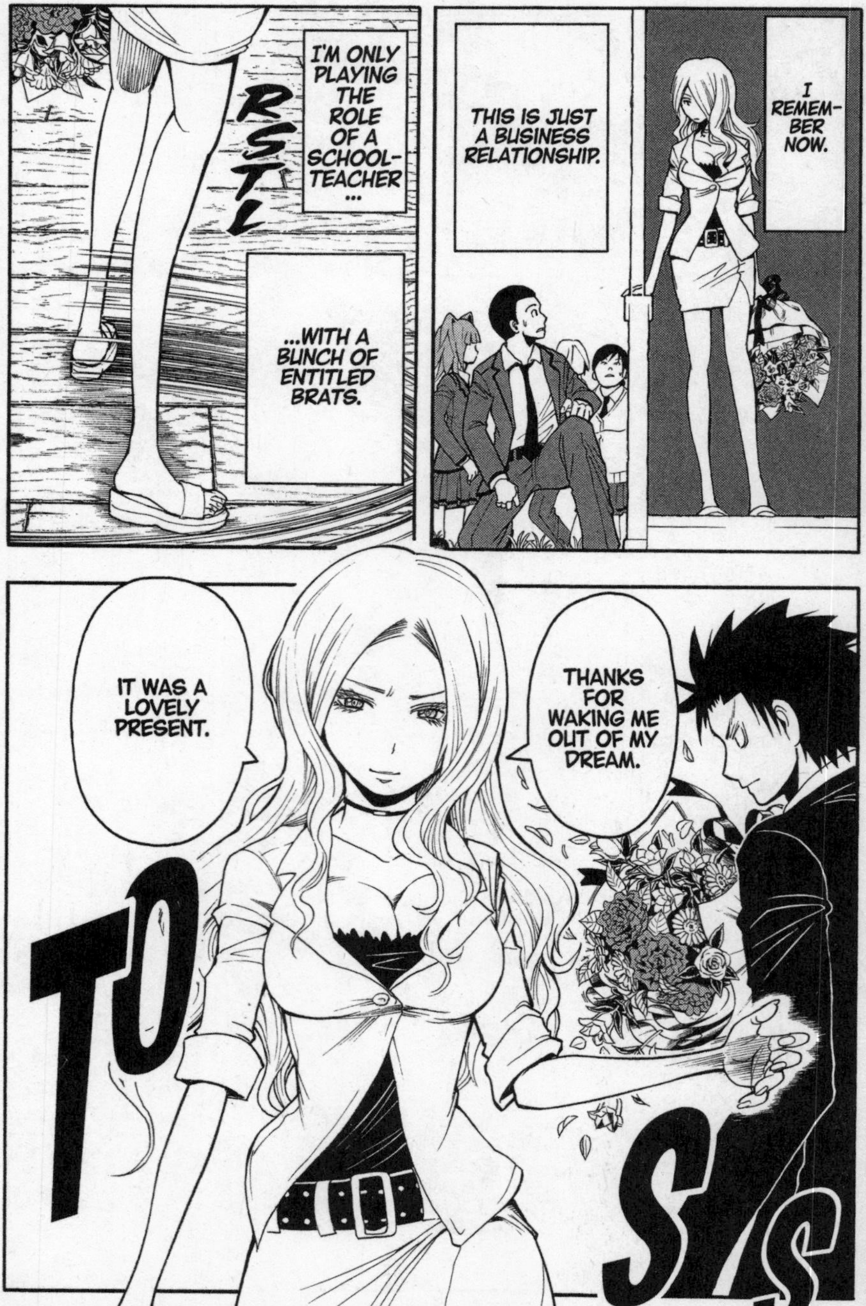
I REMEMBER NOW.
THIS IS JUST A BUSINESS RELATIONSHIP.
I'M ONLY PLAYING THE ROLE OF A SCHOOLTEACHER...
RSTL
...WITH A BUNCH OF ENTITLED BRATS.
THANKS FOR WAKING ME OUT OF MY DREAM.
IT WAS A LOVELY PRESENT.
TO
SS

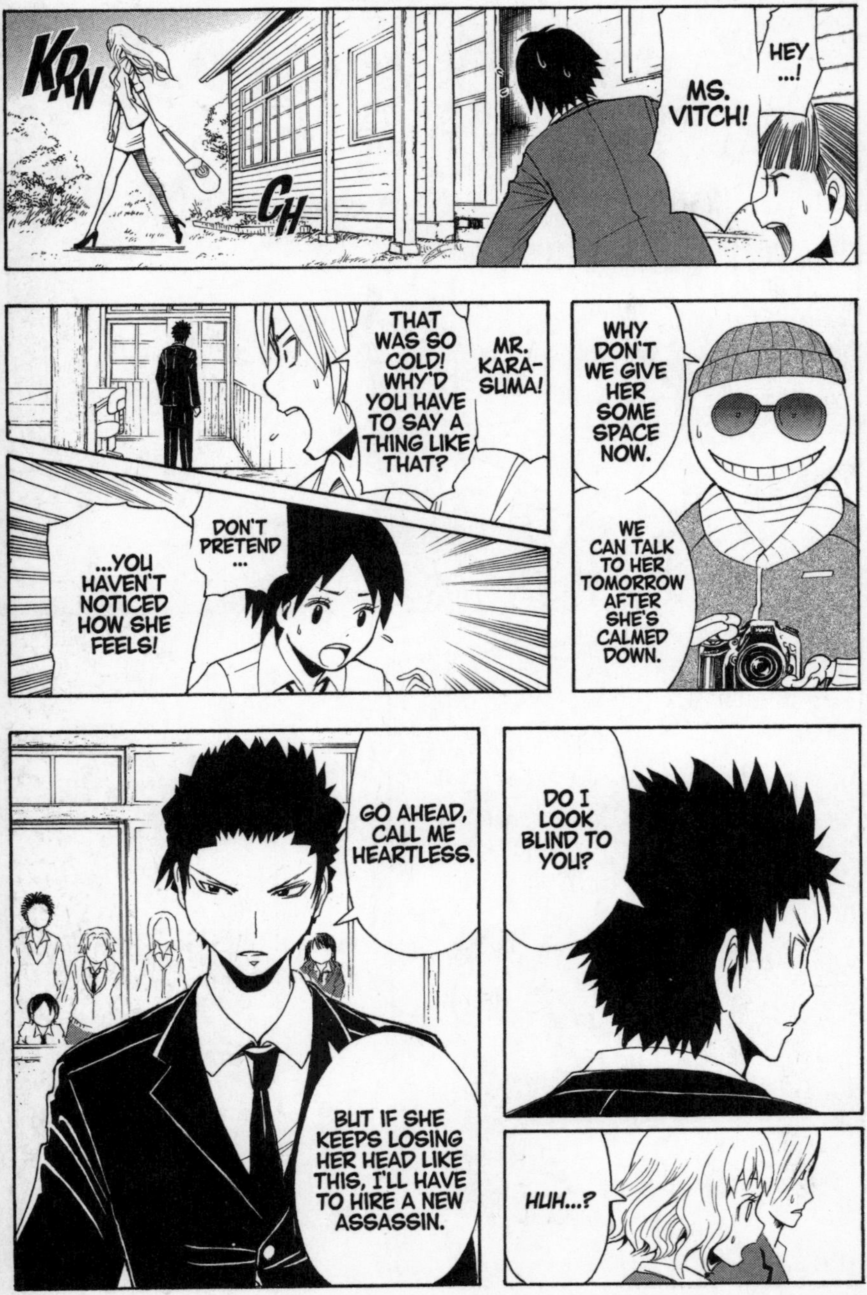
HEY ...!
MS. VITCH!
KRN
CH
WHY DON'T WE GIVE HER SOME SPACE NOW.
WE CAN TALK TO HER TOMORROW AFTER SHE'S CALMED DOWN.
MR. KARASUMA!
THAT WAS SO COLD! WHY'D YOU HAVE TO SAY A THING LIKE THAT?
DON'T PRETEND ...
...YOU HAVEN'T NOTICED HOW SHE FEELS!
DO I LOOK BLIND TO YOU?
HUH...?
GO AHEAD, CALL ME HEARTLESS.
BUT IF SHE KEEPS LOSING HER HEAD LIKE THIS, I'LL HAVE TO HIRE A NEW ASSASSIN.

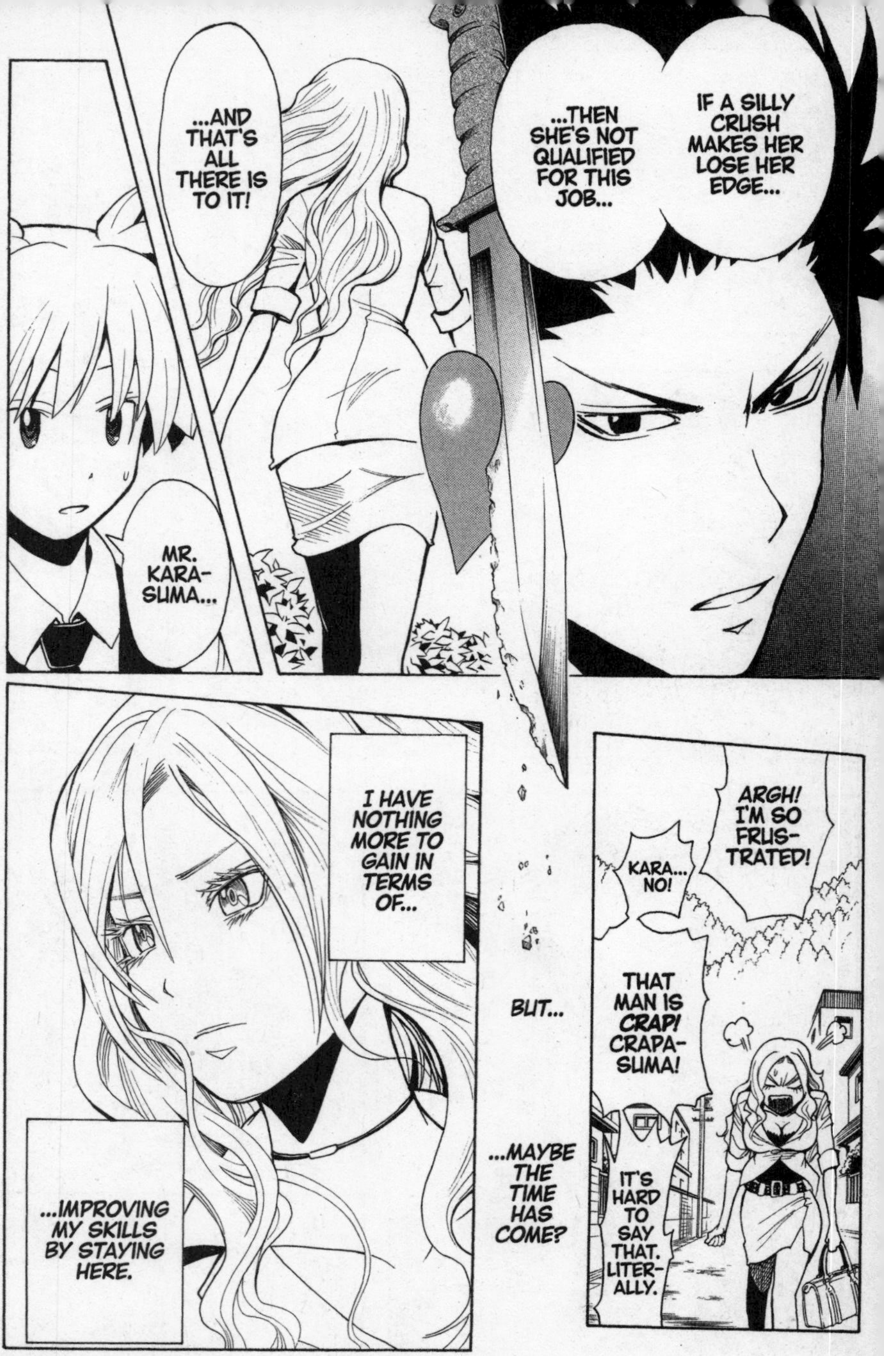
IF A SILLY CRUSH MAKES HER LOSE HER EDGE...
...THEN SHE'S NOT QUALIFIED FOR THIS JOB...
...AND THAT'S ALL THERE IS TO IT!
MR. KARA-SUMA...
ARGH! I'M SO FRUS-TRATED!
KARA... NO!
THAT MAN IS CRAP! CRAPA-SUMA!
IT'S HARD TO SAY THAT. LITER-ALLY.
I HAVE NOTHING MORE TO GAIN IN TERMS OF...
...IMPROVING MY SKILLS BY STAYING HERE.
BUT...
...MAYBE THE TIME HAS COME?

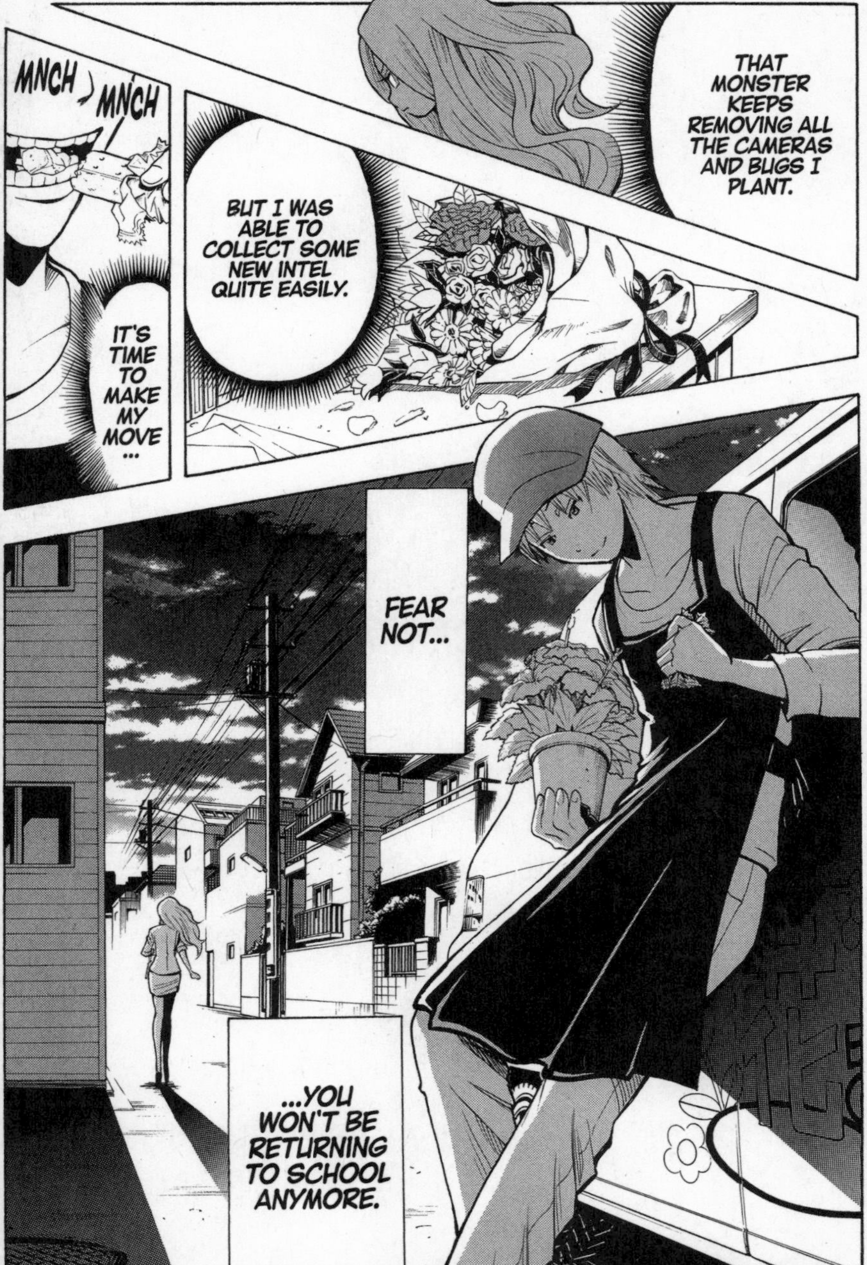
THAT MONSTER KEEPS REMOVING ALL THE CAMERAS AND BUGS I PLANT.
BUT I WAS ABLE TO COLLECT SOME NEW INTEL QUITE EASILY.
MNCH MNCH
IT'S TIME TO MAKE MY MOVE...
FEAR NOT...
...YOU WON'T BE RETURNING TO SCHOOL ANYMORE.

E-25 TOKA YADA

 BIRTHDAY: AUGUST 1

 HEIGHT: 5' 3"

 WEIGHT: 112 LBS.

 FAVORITE SUBJECT: JAPANESE

 LEAST FAVORITE SUBJECT: MATHEMATICS

 HOBBY/SKILL: MS. VITCH-STYLE "SKILLS"

 FUTURE GOAL: SALES REPRESENTATIVE

 WHAT SHE ENJOYS ABOUT "E": BEING IN SCHOOL SINCE SHE JOINED CLASS E.

 WHAT DEPRESSES HER ABOUT "E": FINDING A BRA TO FIT HER SIZE E BOOBS.

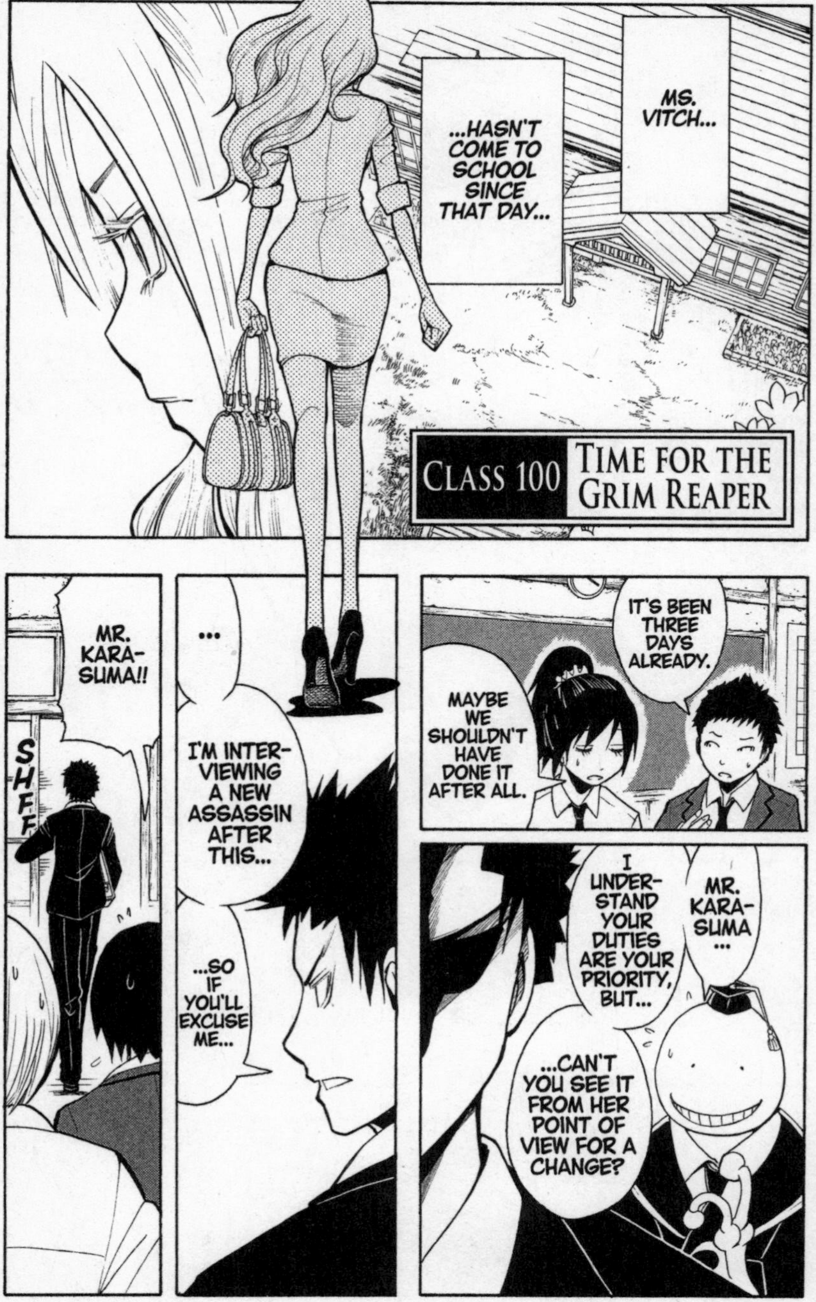
MS. VITCH...
...HASN'T COME TO SCHOOL SINCE THAT DAY...
CLASS 100 TIME FOR THE GRIM REAPER
IT'S BEEN THREE DAYS ALREADY.
MAYBE WE SHOULDN'T HAVE DONE IT AFTER ALL.
MR. KARA-SUMA...
I UNDER-STAND YOUR DUTIES ARE YOUR PRIORITY, BUT...
...CAN'T YOU SEE IT FROM HER POINT OF VIEW FOR A CHANGE?
...
I'M INTER-VIEWING A NEW ASSASSIN AFTER THIS...
...SO IF YOU'LL EXCUSE ME...
MR. KARA-SUMA!!
SHFF

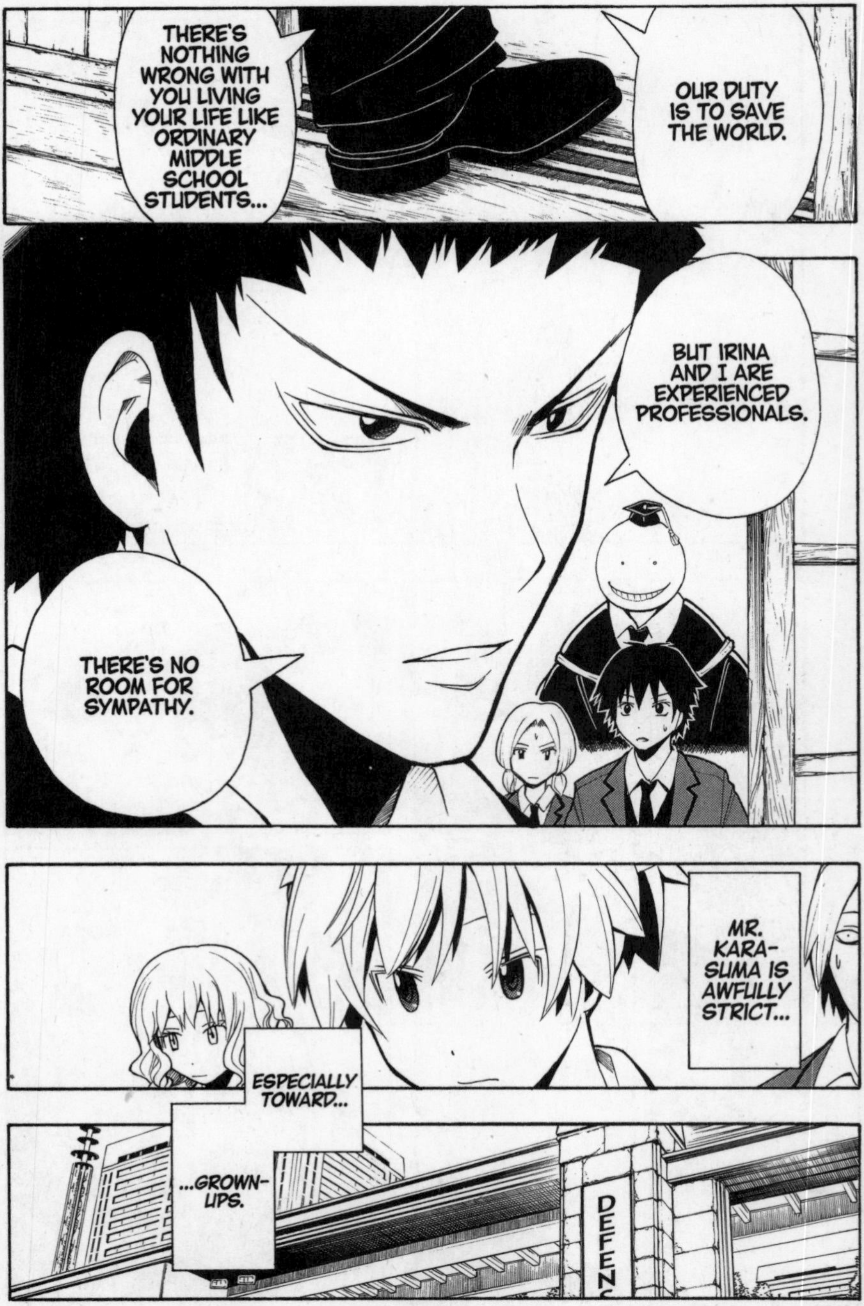
OUR DUTY IS TO SAVE THE WORLD.
THERE'S NOTHING WRONG WITH YOU LIVING YOUR LIFE LIKE ORDINARY MIDDLE SCHOOL STUDENTS...
BUT IRINA AND I ARE EXPERIENCED PROFESSIONALS.
THERE'S NO ROOM FOR SYMPATHY.
MR. KARA-SUMA IS AWFULLY STRICT...
ESPECIALLY TOWARD...
...GROWN-UPS.
DEFEN

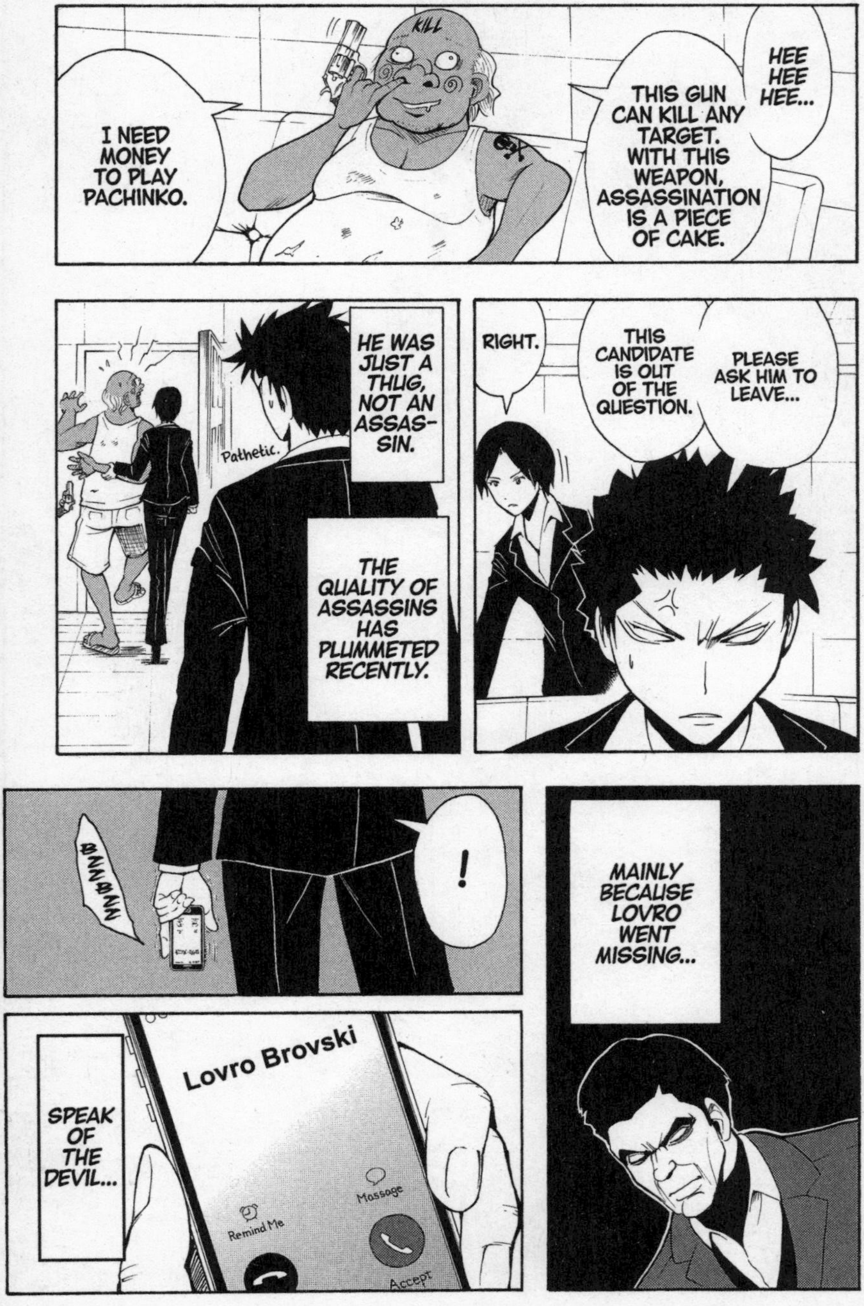
HEE HEE HEE...
KILL
THIS GUN CAN KILL ANY TARGET. WITH THIS WEAPON, ASSASSINATION IS A PIECE OF CAKE.
I NEED MONEY TO PLAY PACHINKO.
PLEASE ASK HIM TO LEAVE...
THIS CANDIDATE IS OUT OF THE QUESTION.
RIGHT.
HE WAS JUST A THUG, NOT AN ASSAS-SIN.
Pathetic.
THE QUALITY OF ASSASSINS HAS PLUMMETED RECENTLY.
MAINLY BECAUSE LOVRO WENT MISSING...
!
BZZ BZZ
Lovro Brovski
SPEAK OF THE DEVIL...
Massage
Remind Me
Accept

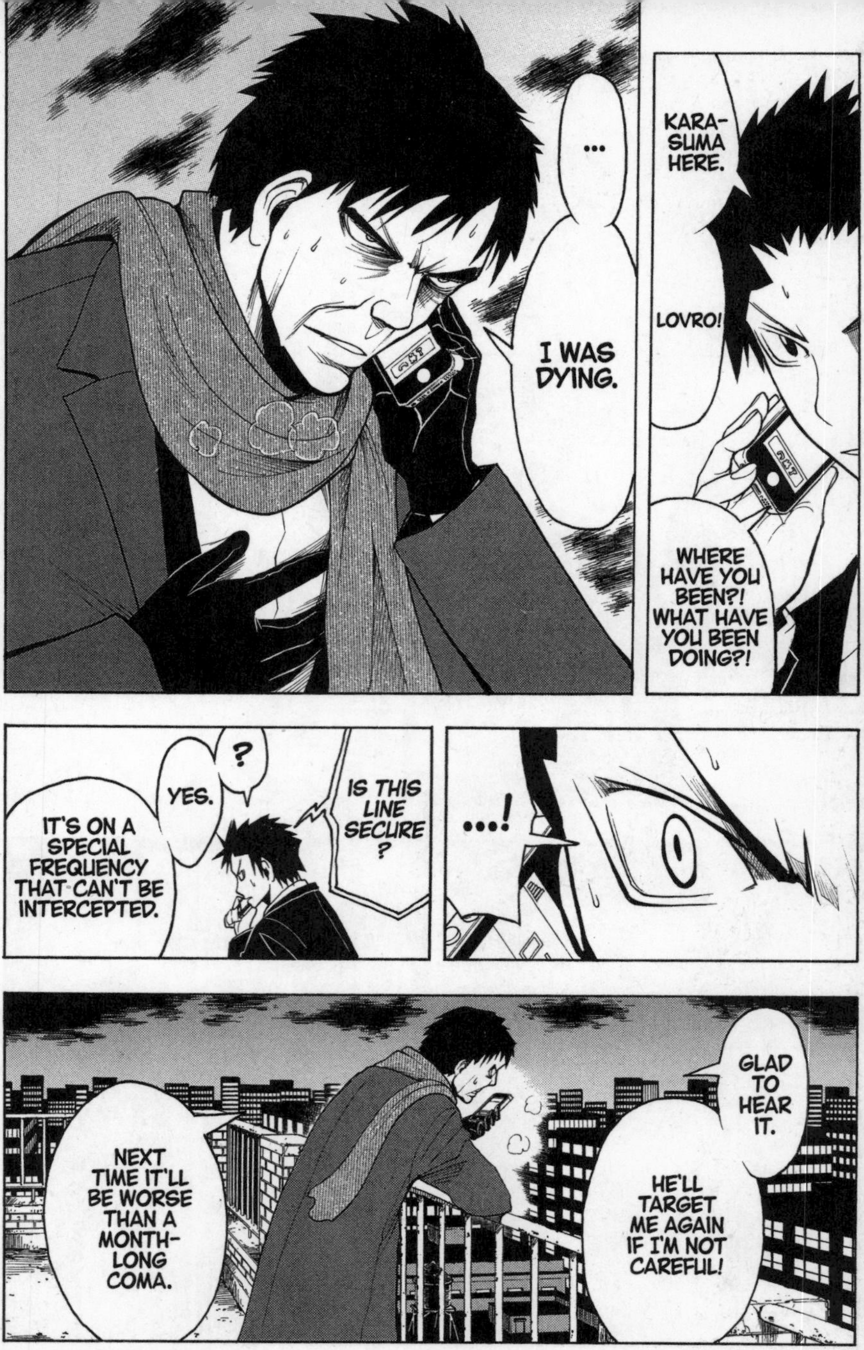
KARA-SUMA HERE.
LOVRO!
WHERE HAVE YOU BEEN?! WHAT HAVE YOU BEEN DOING?!
...
I WAS DYING.
...!
IS THIS LINE SECURE?
?
YES.
IT'S ON A SPECIAL FREQUENCY THAT CAN'T BE INTERCEPTED.
GLAD TO HEAR IT.
HE'LL TARGET ME AGAIN IF I'M NOT CAREFUL!
NEXT TIME IT'LL BE WORSE THAN A MONTH-LONG COMA.

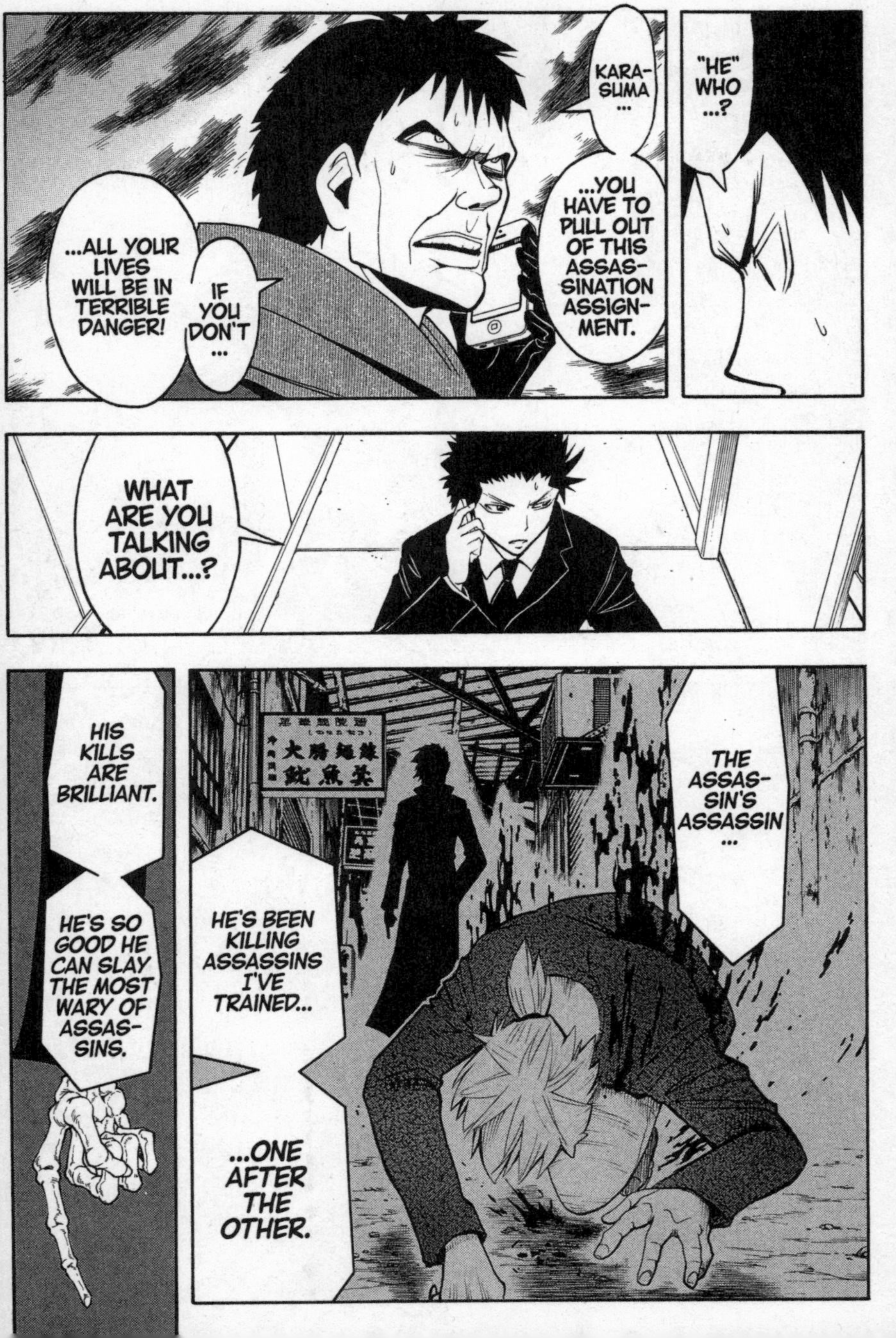
"HE" WHO ...?
KARASUMA...
...YOU HAVE TO PULL OUT OF THIS ASSASSINATION ASSIGNMENT.
IF YOU DON'T...
...ALL YOUR LIVES WILL BE IN TERRIBLE DANGER!
WHAT ARE YOU TALKING ABOUT...?
THE ASSASSIN'S ASSASSIN...
HE'S BEEN KILLING ASSASSINS I'VE TRAINED...
...ONE AFTER THE OTHER.
HIS KILLS ARE BRILLIANT.
HE'S SO GOOD HE CAN SLAY THE MOST WARY OF ASSASSINS.

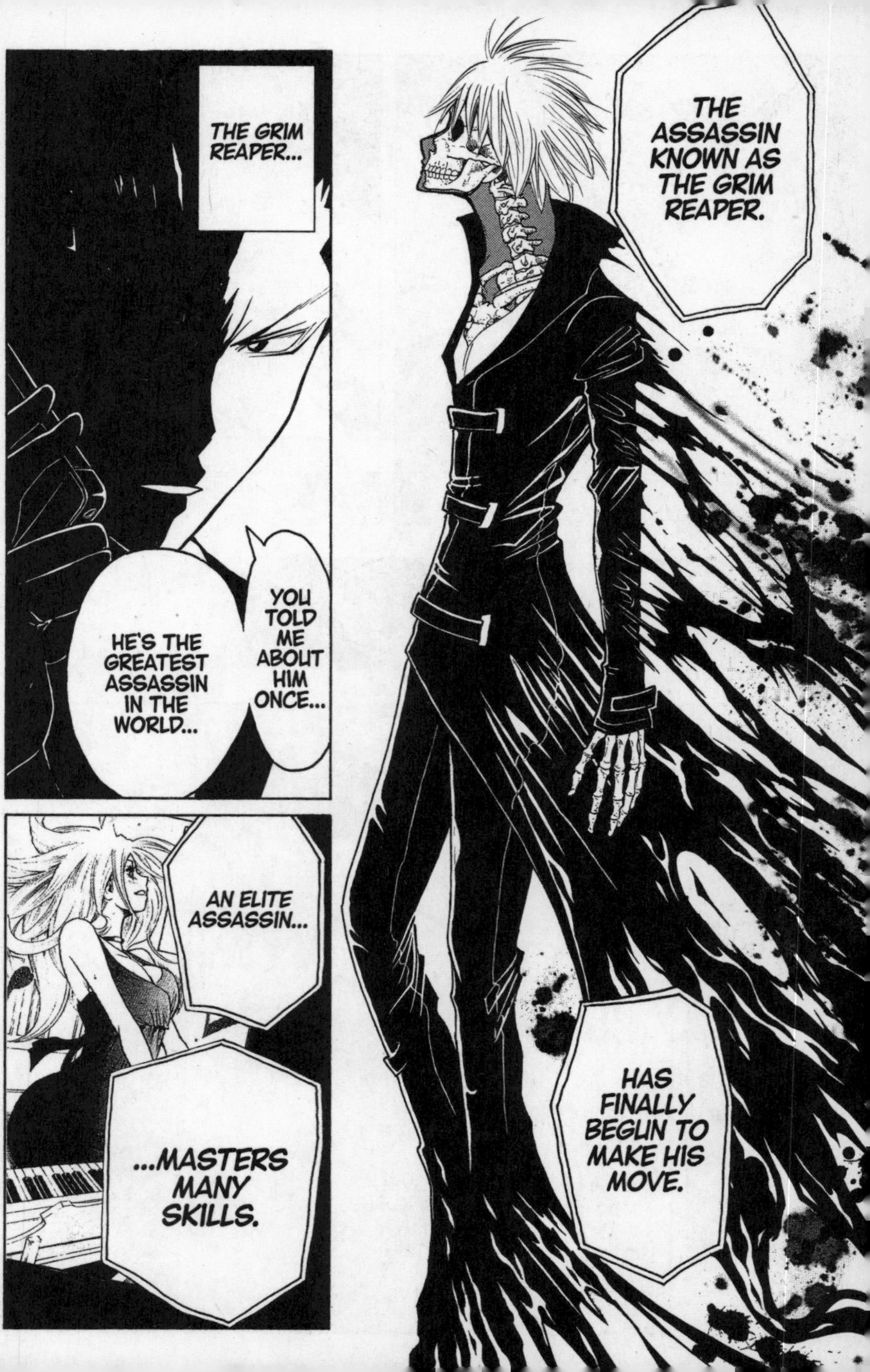
THE ASSASSIN KNOWN AS THE GRIM REAPER.
HAS FINALLY BEGUN TO MAKE HIS MOVE.
THE GRIM REAPER...
YOU TOLD ME ABOUT HIM ONCE...
HE'S THE GREATEST ASSASSIN IN THE WORLD...
AN ELITE ASSASSIN...
...MASTERS MANY SKILLS.

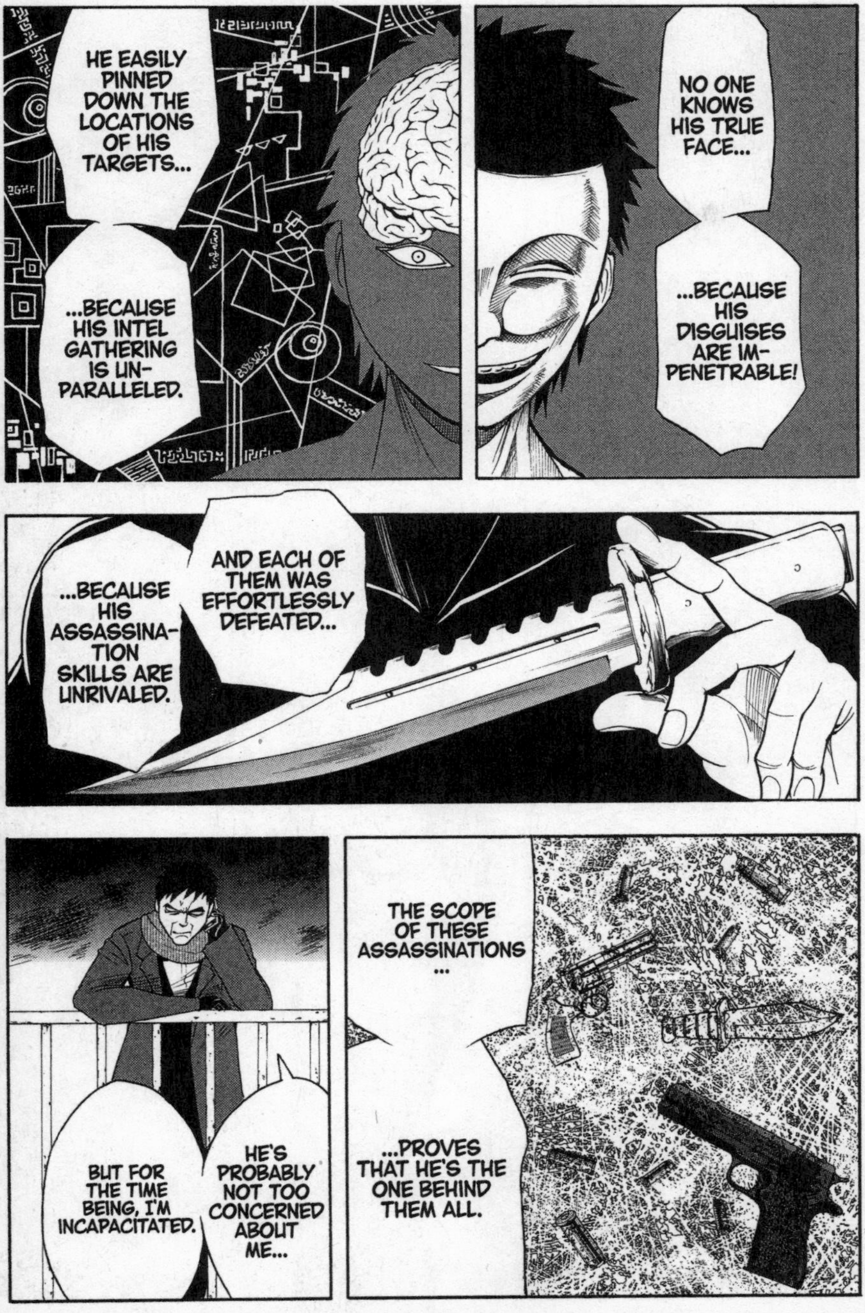
NO ONE KNOWS HIS TRUE FACE...
...BECAUSE HIS DISGUISES ARE IM-PENETRABLE!
HE EASILY PINNED DOWN THE LOCATIONS OF HIS TARGETS...
...BECAUSE HIS INTEL GATHERING IS UN-PARALLELED.
AND EACH OF THEM WAS EFFORTLESSLY DEFEATED...
...BECAUSE HIS ASSASSINA-TION SKILLS ARE UNRIVALED.
THE SCOPE OF THESE ASSASSINATIONS ...
...PROVES THAT HE'S THE ONE BEHIND THEM ALL.
HE'S PROBABLY NOT TOO CONCERNED ABOUT ME...
BUT FOR THE TIME BEING, I'M INCAPACITATED.

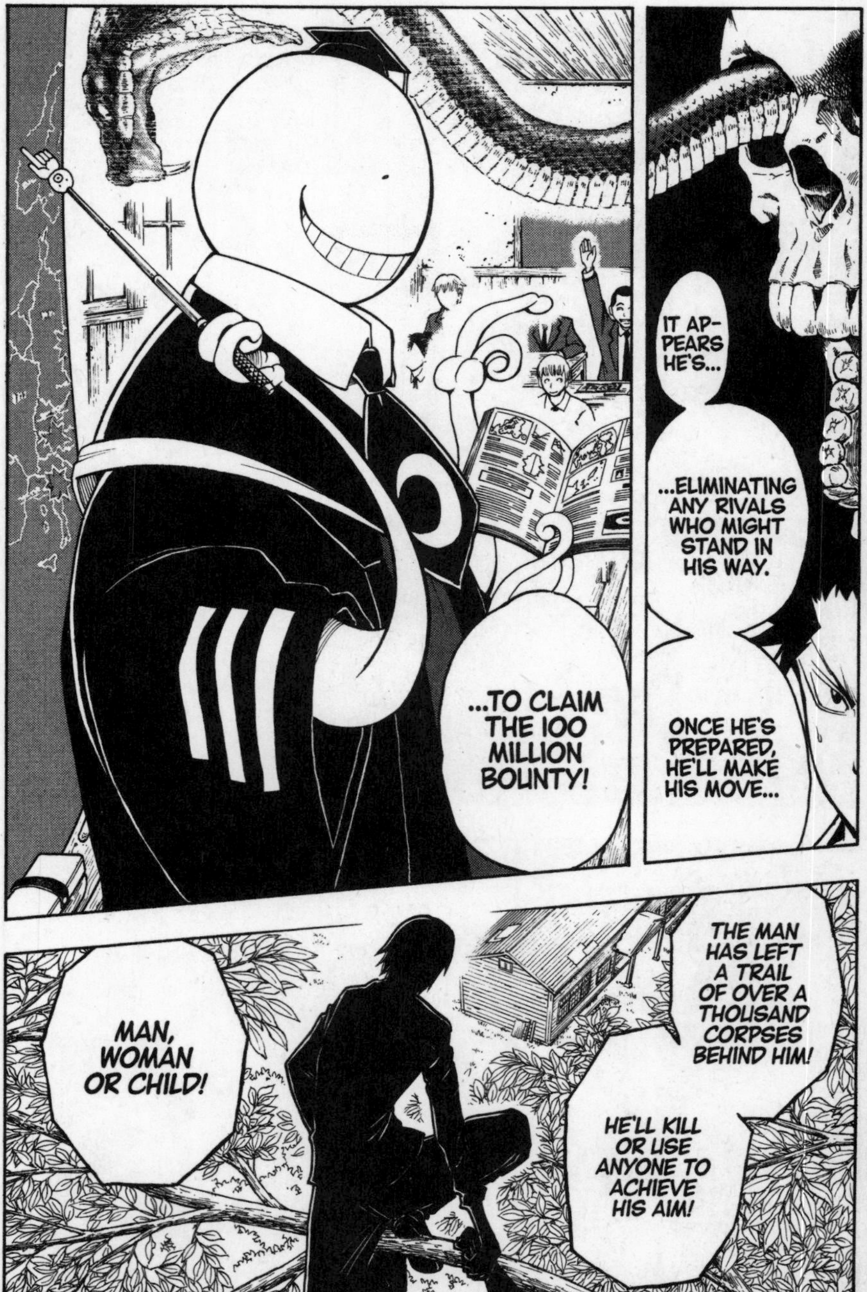
IT AP-PEARS HE'S...
...ELIMINATING ANY RIVALS WHO MIGHT STAND IN HIS WAY.
ONCE HE'S PREPARED, HE'LL MAKE HIS MOVE...
...TO CLAIM THE 100 MILLION BOUNTY!
THE MAN HAS LEFT A TRAIL OF OVER A THOUSAND CORPSES BEHIND HIM!
HE'LL KILL OR USE ANYONE TO ACHIEVE HIS AIM!
MAN, WOMAN OR CHILD!

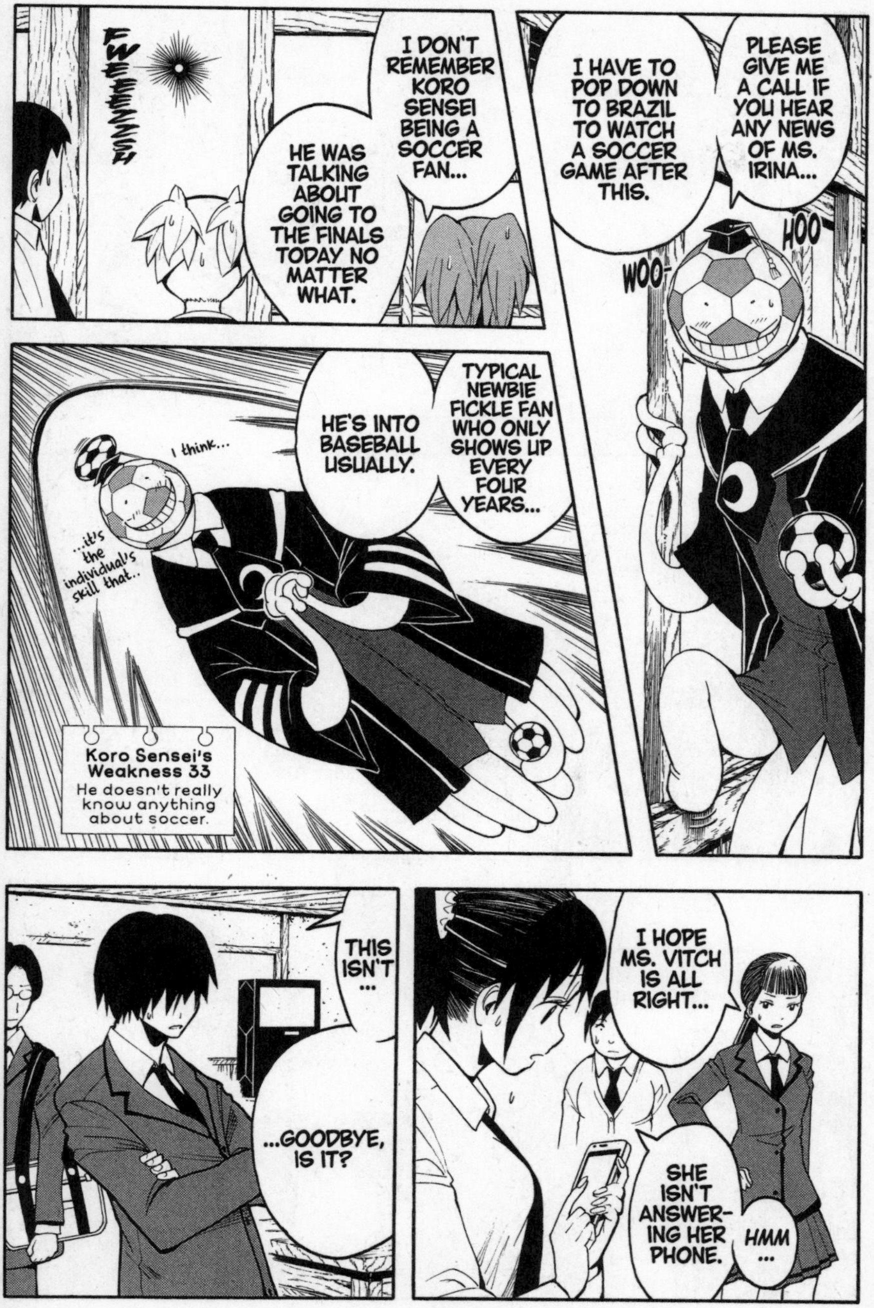
PLEASE GIVE ME A CALL IF YOU HEAR ANY NEWS OF MS. IRINA...
I HAVE TO POP DOWN TO BRAZIL TO WATCH A SOCCER GAME AFTER THIS.
HOO
WOO-
I DON'T REMEMBER KORO SENSEI BEING A SOCCER FAN...
HE WAS TALKING ABOUT GOING TO THE FINALS TODAY NO MATTER WHAT.
FWEEEZZSH
TYPICAL NEWBIE FICKLE FAN WHO ONLY SHOWS UP EVERY FOUR YEARS...
HE'S INTO BASEBALL USUALLY.
I think...
...it's the individual's skill that..
Koro Sensei's Weakness 33
He doesn't really know anything about soccer.
I HOPE MS. VITCH IS ALL RIGHT...
SHE ISN'T ANSWERING HER PHONE.
HMM ...
THIS ISN'T ...
...GOODBYE, IS IT?

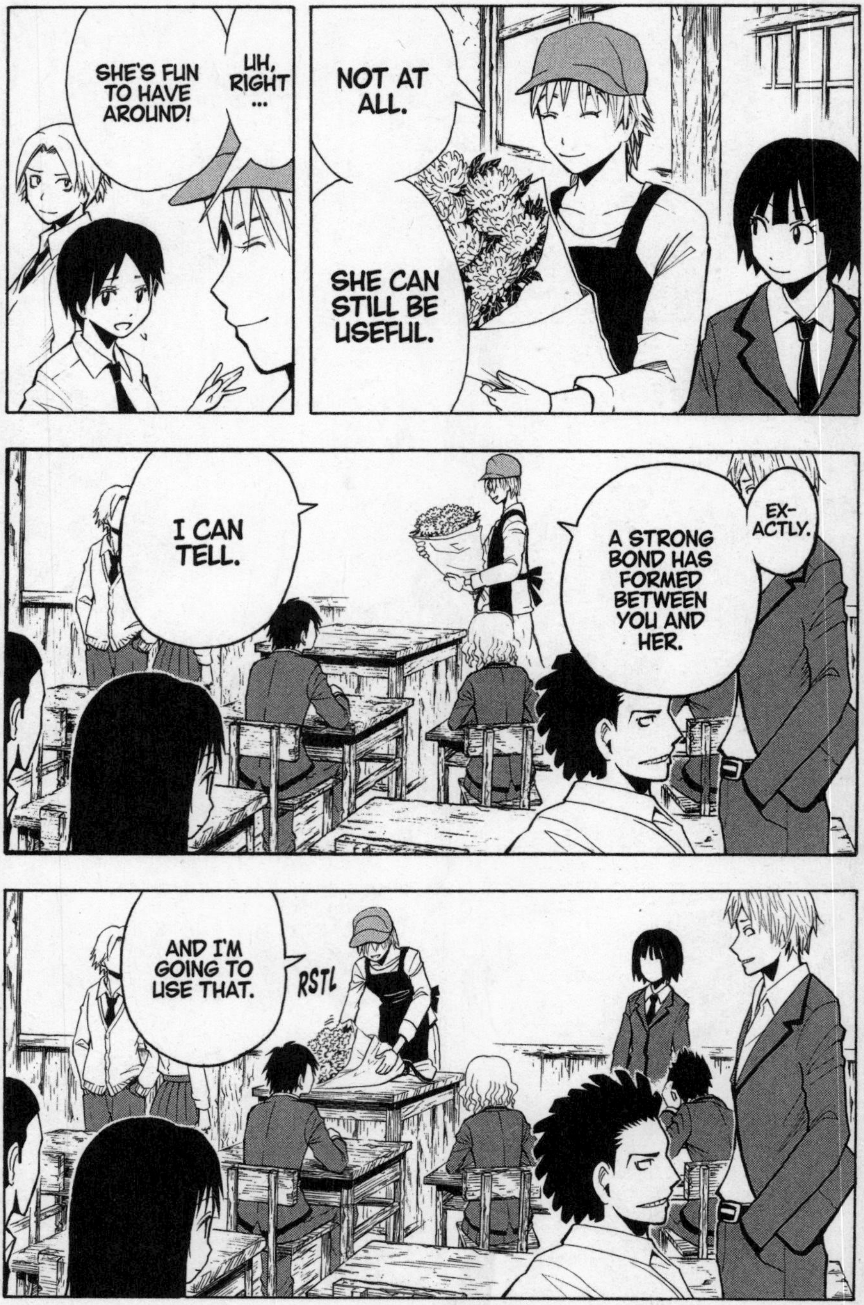
NOT AT ALL.
SHE CAN STILL BE USEFUL.
UH, RIGHT ...
SHE'S FUN TO HAVE AROUND!
EX-ACTLY.
A STRONG BOND HAS FORMED BETWEEN YOU AND HER.
I CAN TELL.
AND I'M GOING TO USE THAT.
RSTL

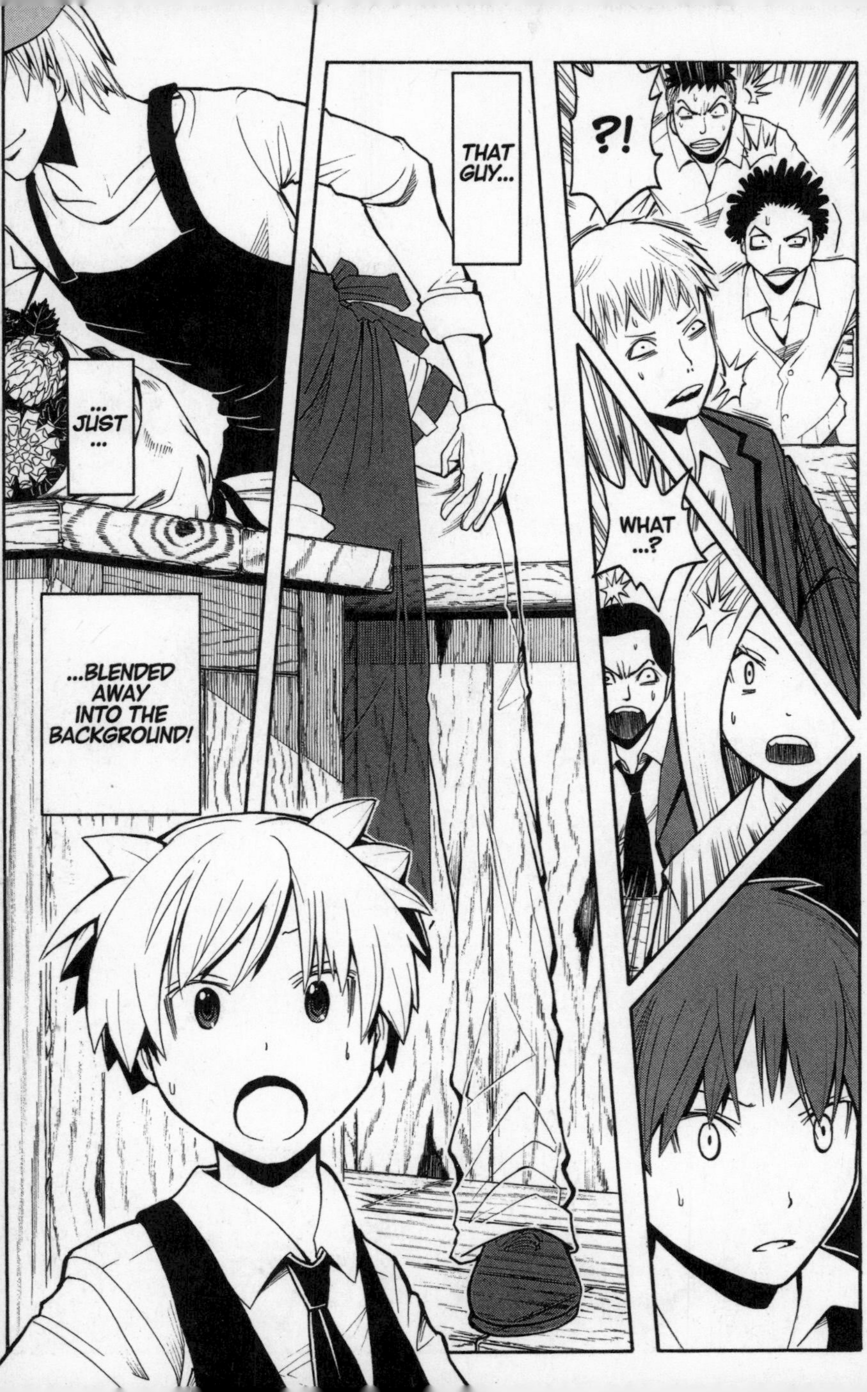
?!
WHAT ...?
THAT GUY...
...JUST...
...BLENDED AWAY INTO THE BACKGROUND!

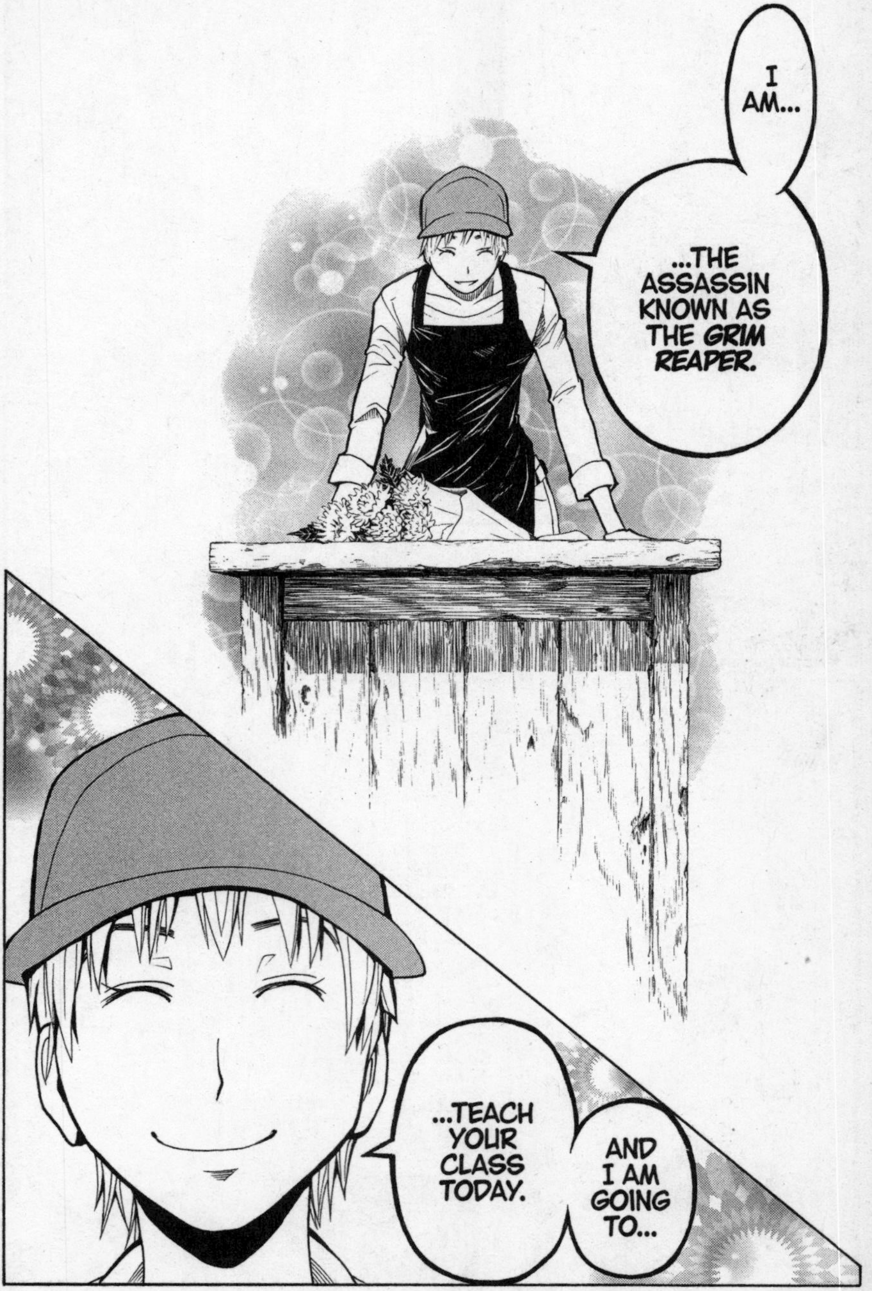
I AM...
...THE ASSASSIN KNOWN AS THE *GRIM REAPER.*
AND I AM GOING TO...
...TEACH YOUR CLASS TODAY.

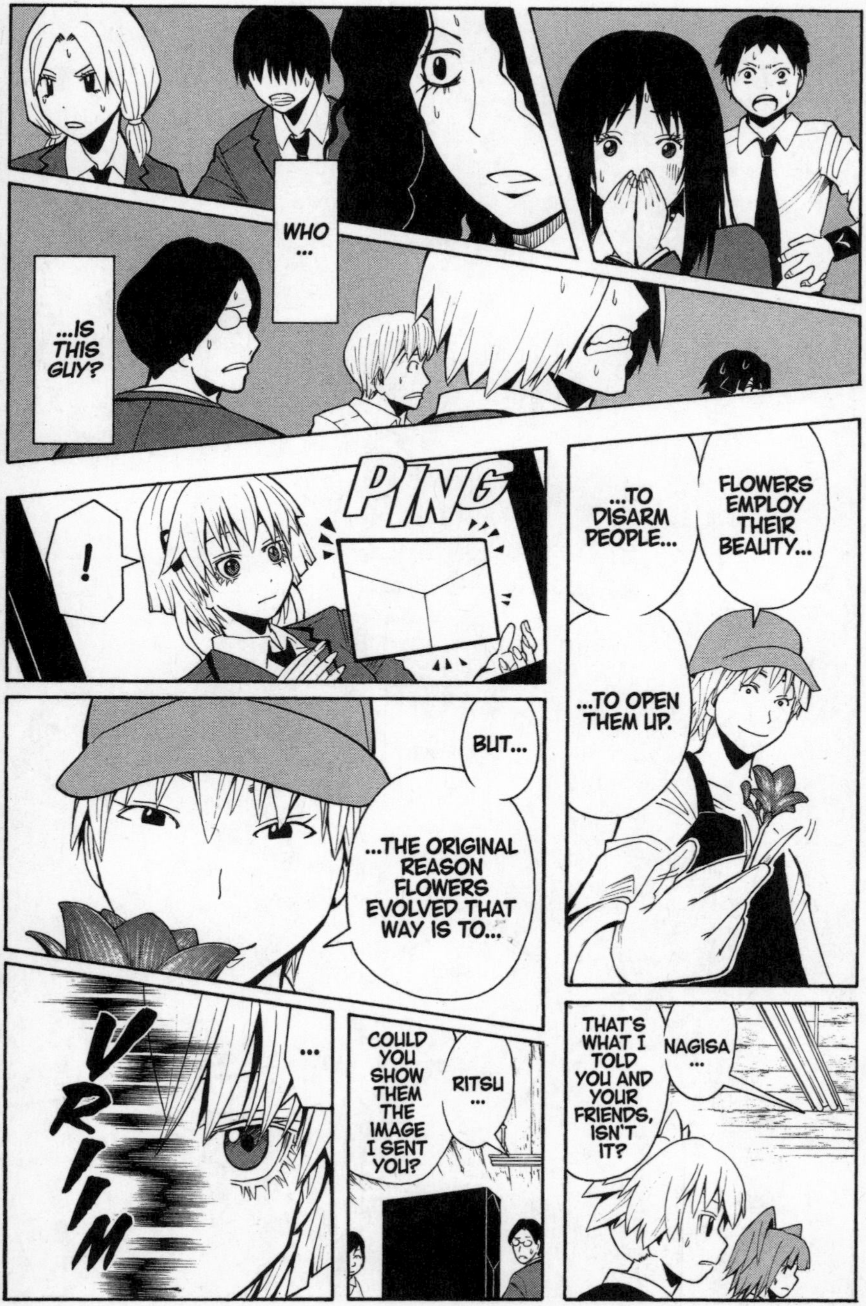
WHO...
...IS THIS GUY?
FLOWERS EMPLOY THEIR BEAUTY...
...TO DISARM PEOPLE...
...TO OPEN THEM UP.
PING
!
BUT...
...THE ORIGINAL REASON FLOWERS EVOLVED THAT WAY IS TO...
NAGISA...
THAT'S WHAT I TOLD YOU AND YOUR FRIENDS, ISN'T IT?
RITSU...
COULD YOU SHOW THEM THE IMAGE I SENT YOU?
...
VRIIM

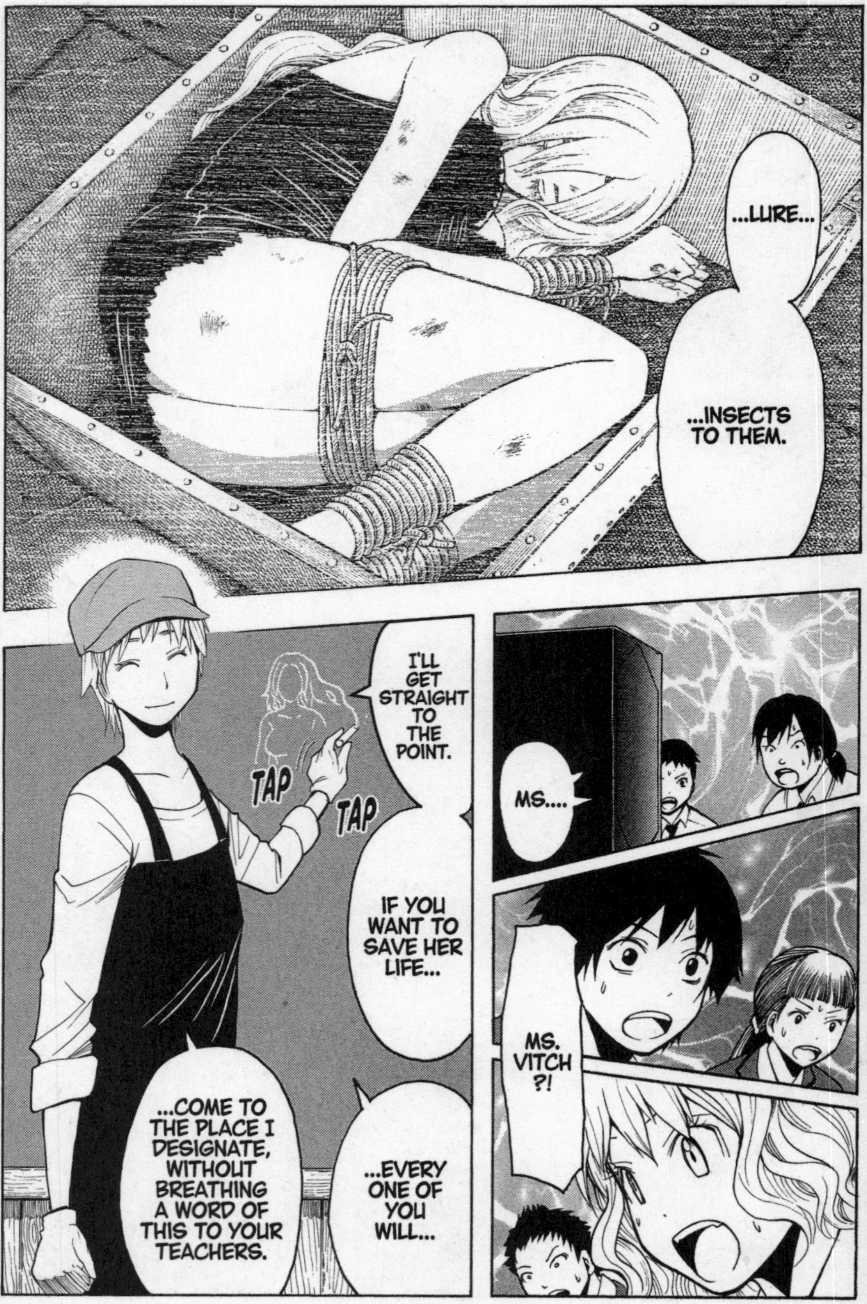
...LURE...
...INSECTS TO THEM.
MS....
MS. VITCH ?!
I'LL GET STRAIGHT TO THE POINT.
TAP
TAP
IF YOU WANT TO SAVE HER LIFE...
...EVERY ONE OF YOU WILL...
...COME TO THE PLACE I DESIGNATE, WITHOUT BREATHING A WORD OF THIS TO YOUR TEACHERS.

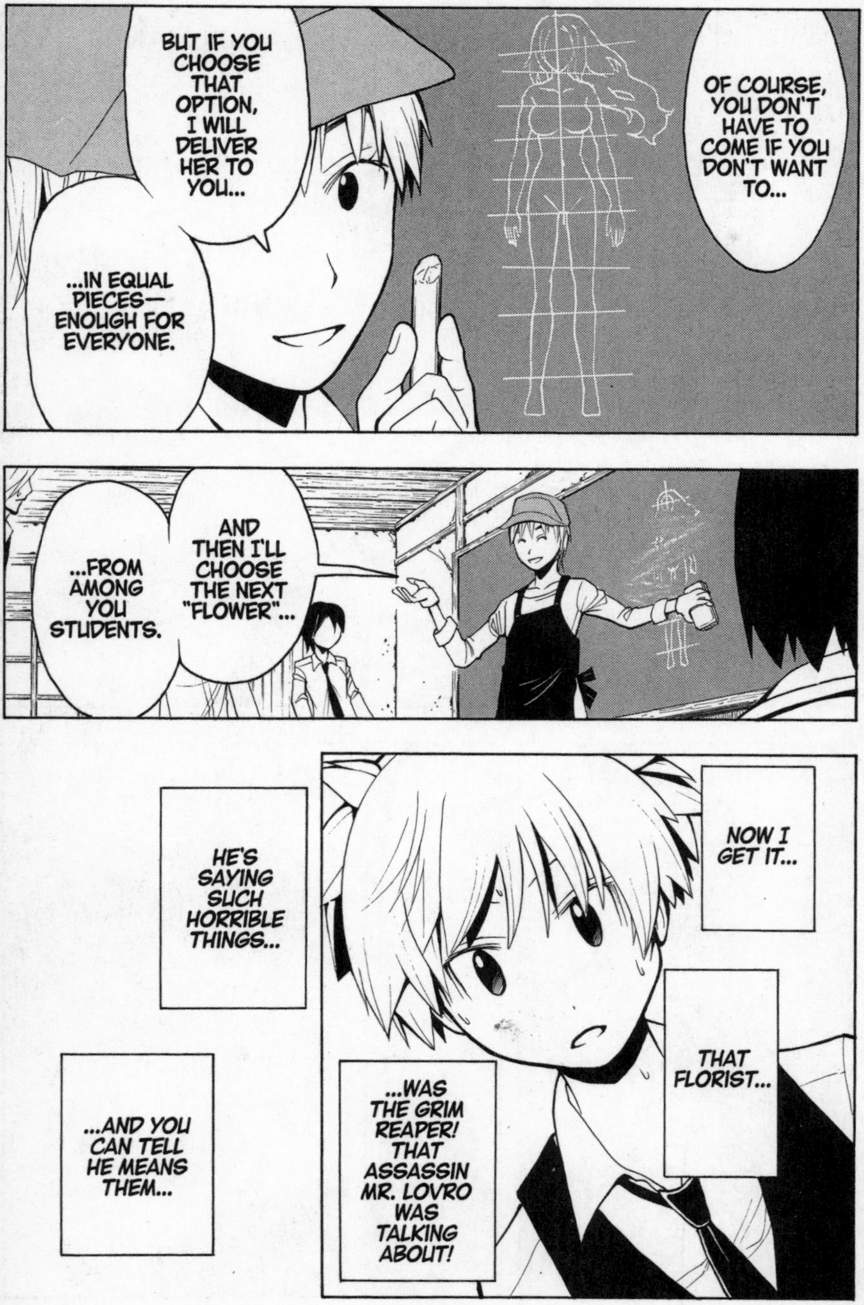
OF COURSE, YOU DON'T HAVE TO COME IF YOU DON'T WANT TO...
BUT IF YOU CHOOSE THAT OPTION, I WILL DELIVER HER TO YOU...
...IN EQUAL PIECES— ENOUGH FOR EVERYONE.
AND THEN I'LL CHOOSE THE NEXT "FLOWER"...
...FROM AMONG YOU STUDENTS.
NOW I GET IT...
THAT FLORIST...
...WAS THE GRIM REAPER! THAT ASSASSIN MR. LOVRO WAS TALKING ABOUT!
HE'S SAYING SUCH HORRIBLE THINGS...
...AND YOU CAN TELL HE MEANS THEM...

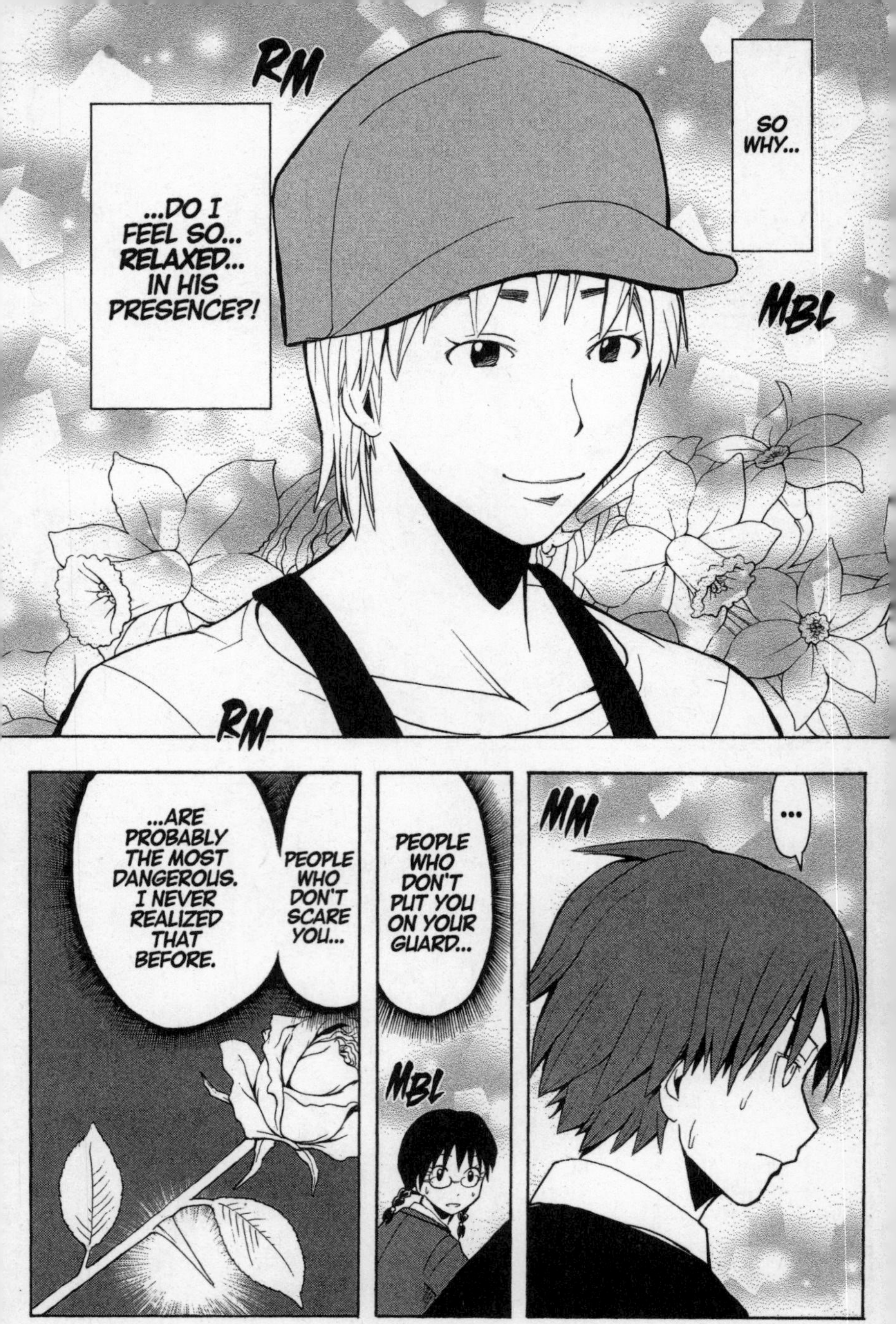
RM
SO WHY...
...DO I FEEL SO... RELAXED... IN HIS PRESENCE?!
MBL
RM
MM
...
PEOPLE WHO DON'T PUT YOU ON YOUR GUARD...
MBL
PEOPLE WHO DON'T SCARE YOU...
...ARE PROBABLY THE MOST DANGEROUS. I NEVER REALIZED THAT BEFORE.

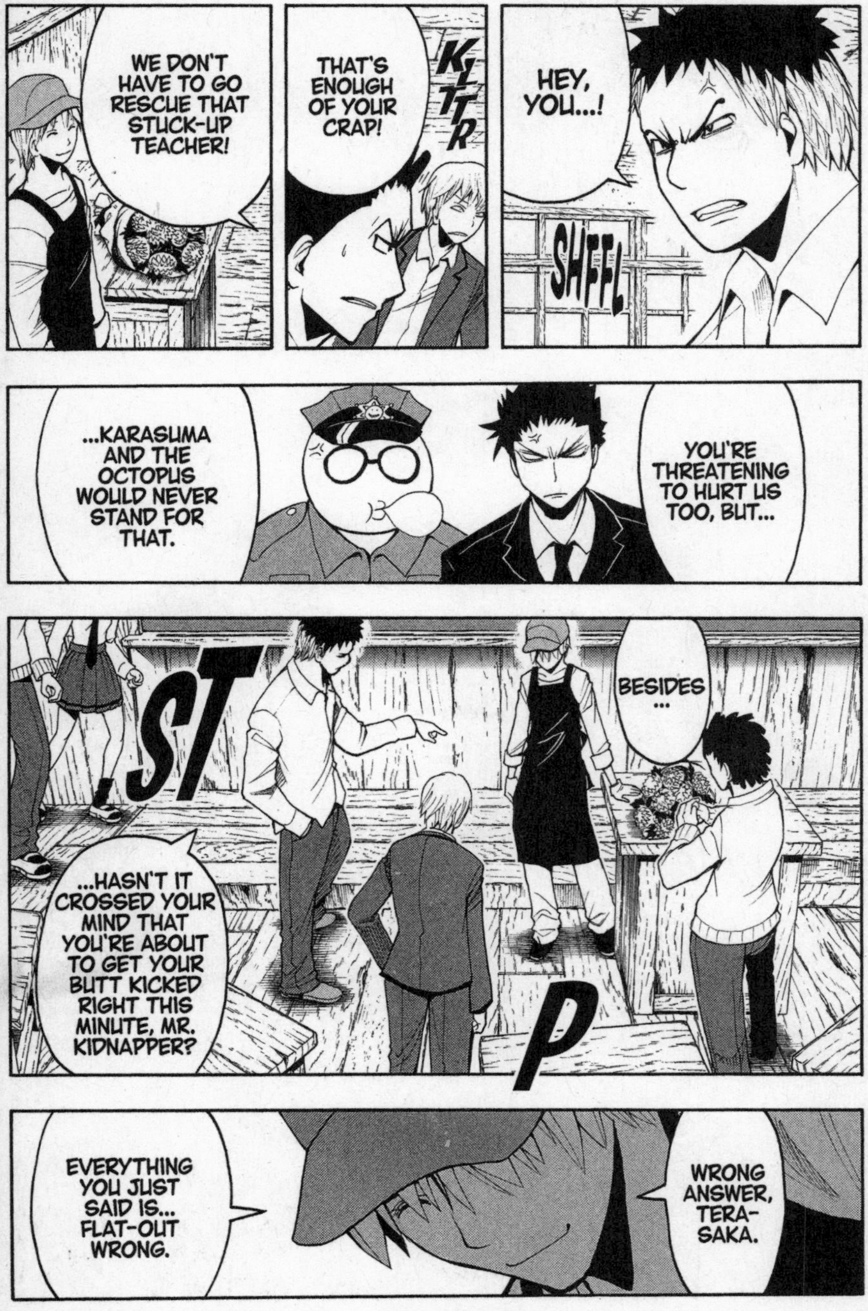
HEY, YOU...!
SHFFL
THAT'S ENOUGH OF YOUR CRAP!
KLTTR
WE DON'T HAVE TO GO RESCUE THAT STUCK-UP TEACHER!
YOU'RE THREATENING TO HURT US TOO, BUT...
...KARASUMA AND THE OCTOPUS WOULD NEVER STAND FOR THAT.
BESIDES...
ST
...HASN'T IT CROSSED YOUR MIND THAT YOU'RE ABOUT TO GET YOUR BUTT KICKED RIGHT THIS MINUTE, MR. KIDNAPPER?
P
WRONG ANSWER, TERA-SAKA.
EVERYTHING YOU JUST SAID IS... FLAT-OUT WRONG.

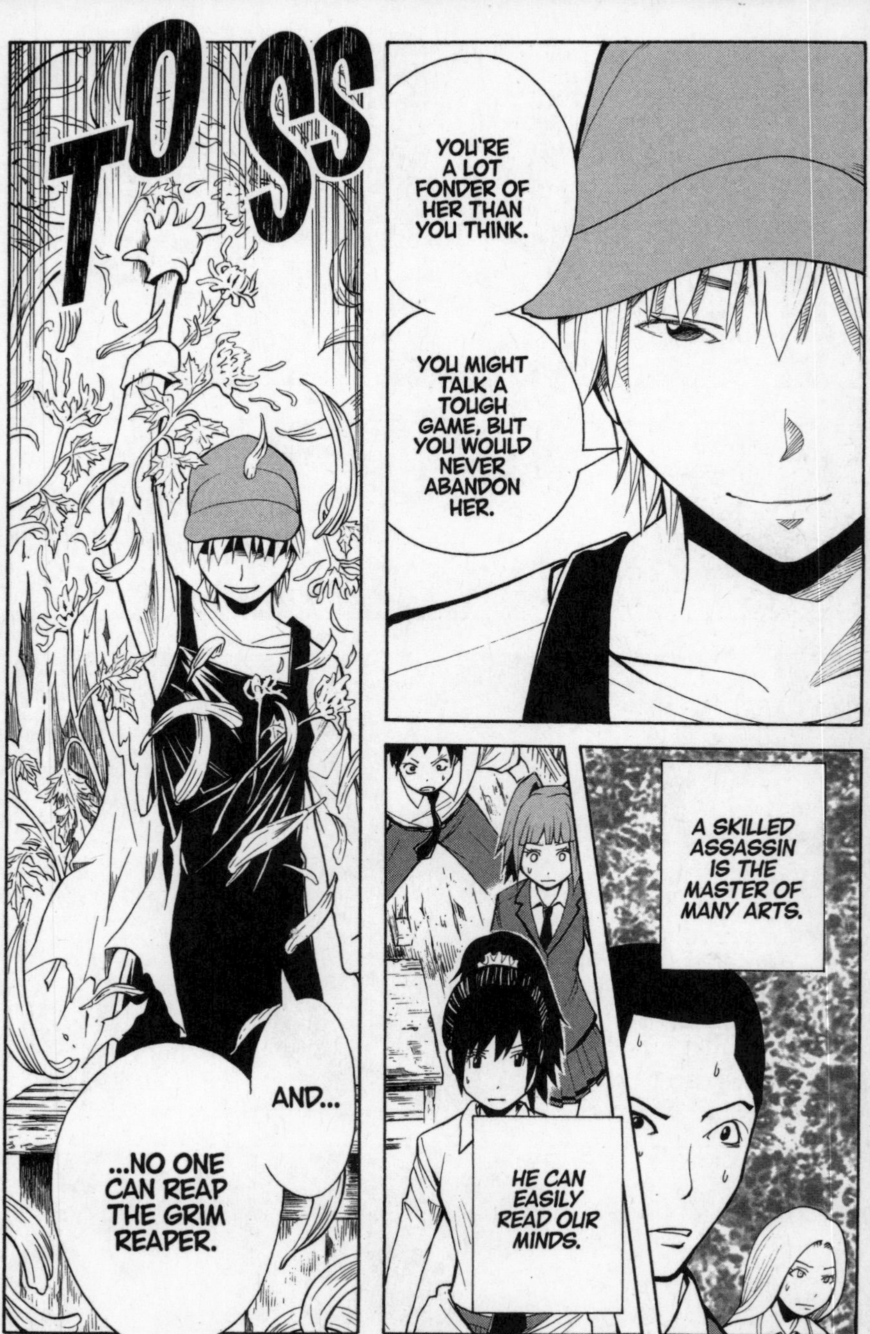
YOU'RE A LOT FONDER OF HER THAN YOU THINK.
YOU MIGHT TALK A TOUGH GAME, BUT YOU WOULD NEVER ABANDON HER.
A SKILLED ASSASSIN IS THE MASTER OF MANY ARTS.
HE CAN EASILY READ OUR MINDS.
TOSS
AND...
...NO ONE CAN REAP THE GRIM REAPER.

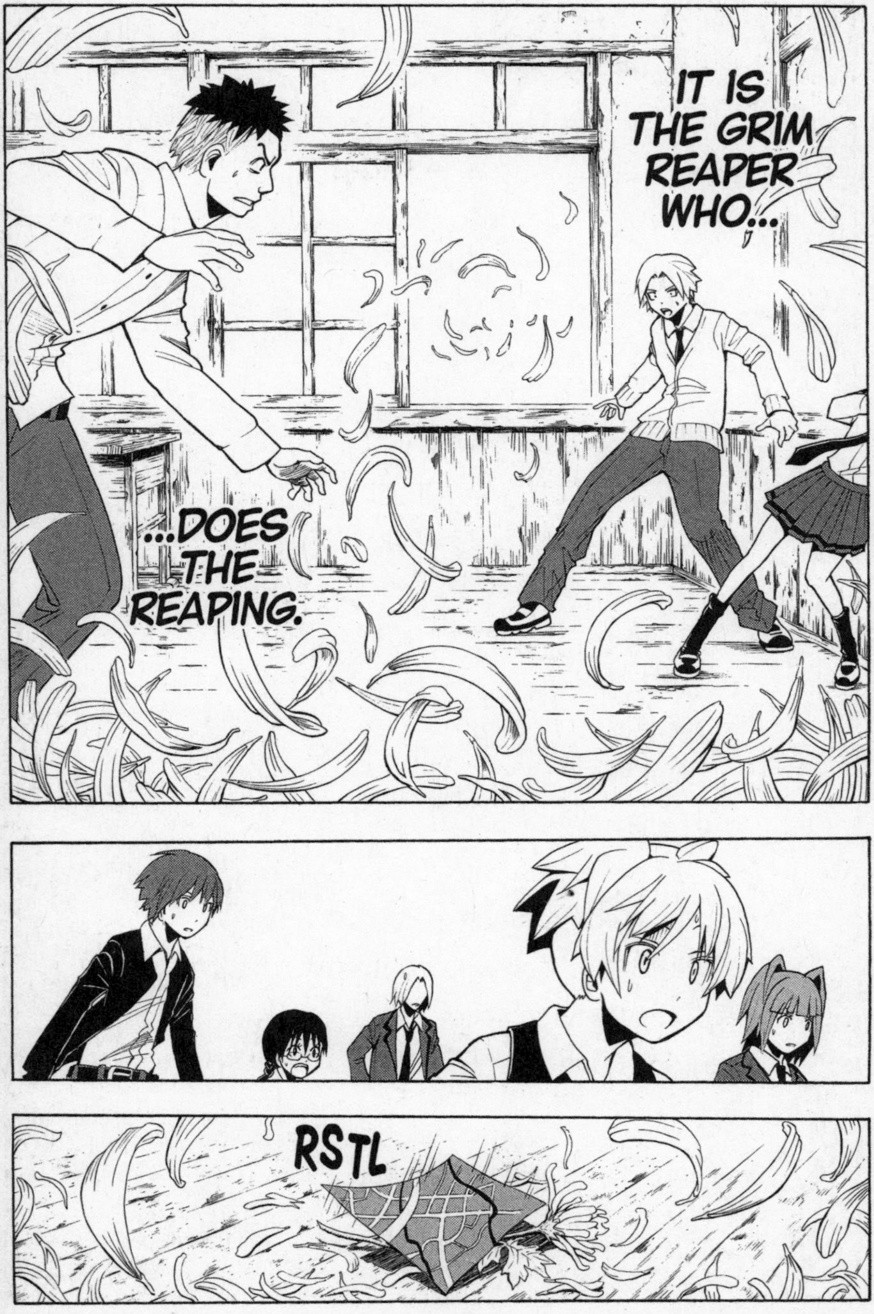
IT IS THE GRIM REAPER WHO...
...DOES THE REAPING.
RSTL

E-10 Hinano Kurahashi

- 😊 Birthday: October 23
- 😊 Height: 4' 11"
- 😊 Weight: 90 lbs.
- 😊 Favorite Subject: Biology
- 😊 Least Favorite Subject: Mathematics
- 😊 Hobby/Skill: Raising pets, collecting insects
- 😊 Future Goal: Zoologist
- 😊 Plans for the 100 million: Founding the Kurahashi Zoo
- 😊 Her type: Men eager to capture wild beasts

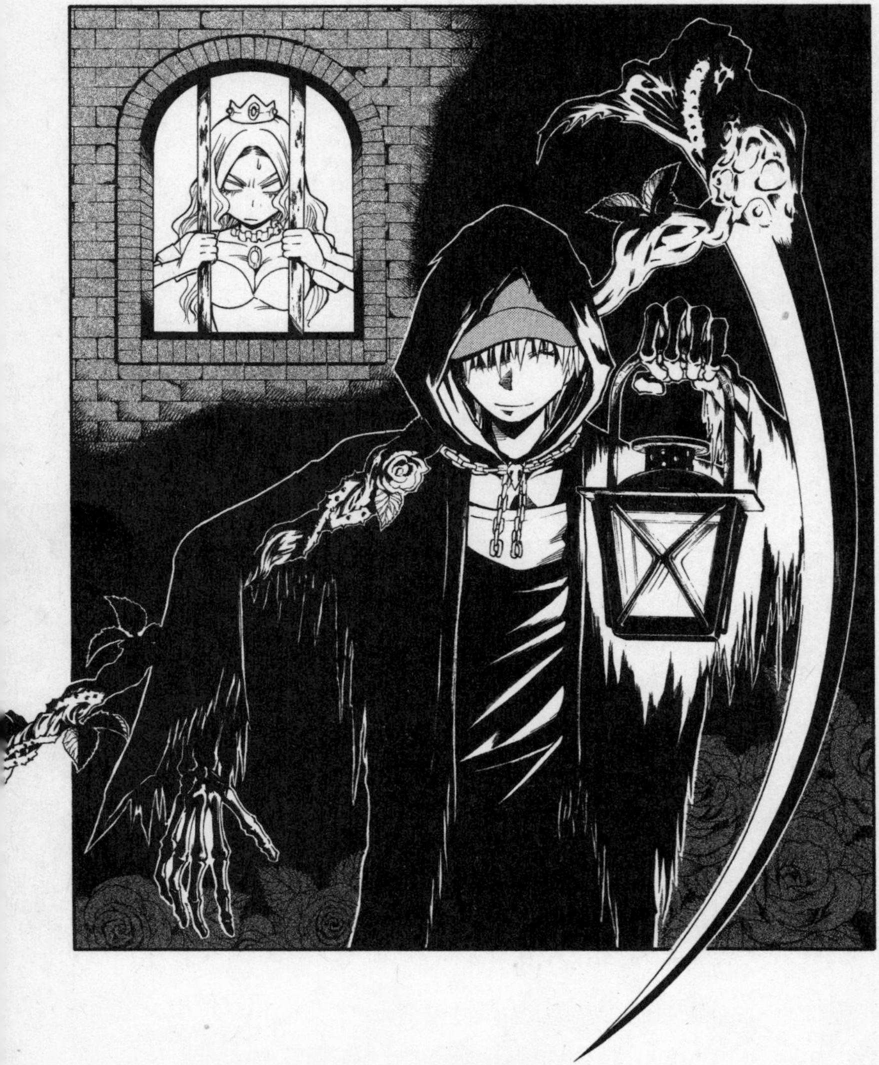

Class 101 Time for a Counterattack

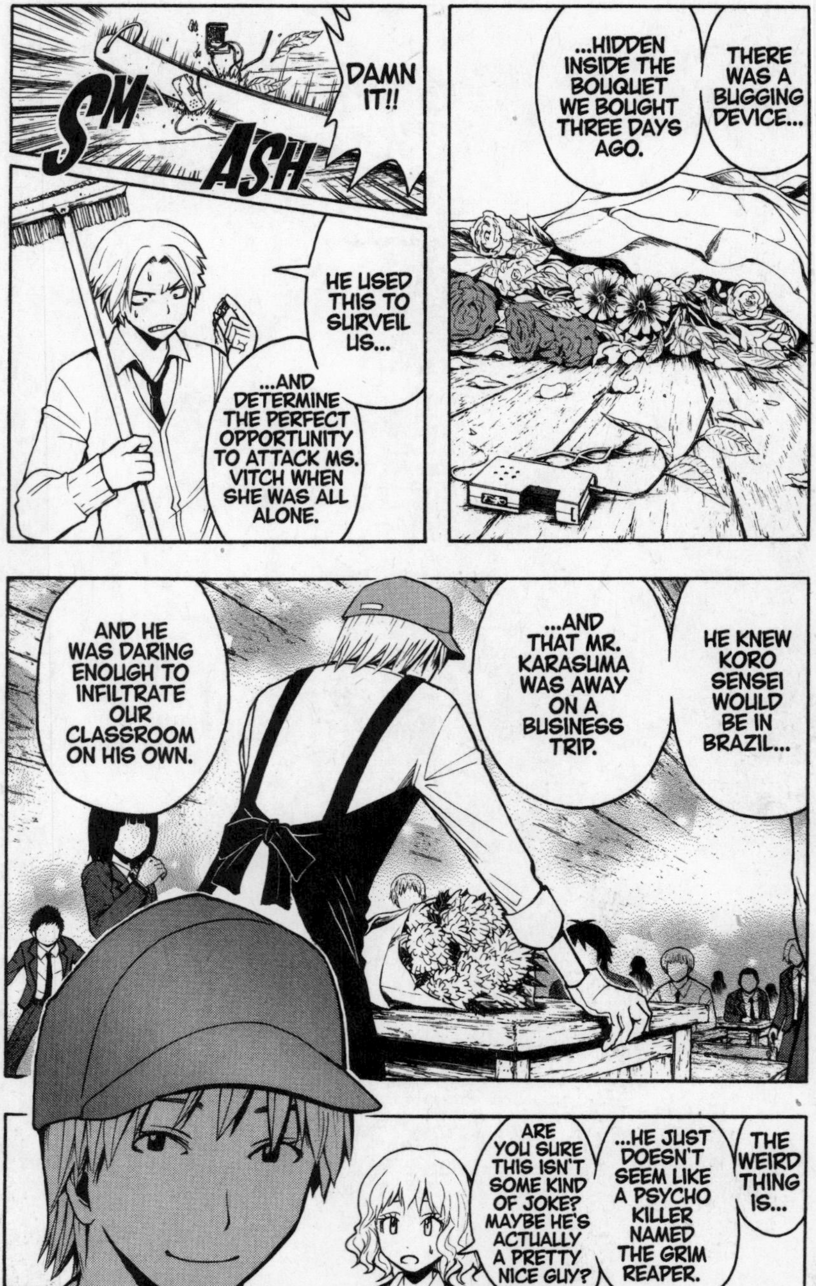
THERE WAS A BUGGING DEVICE...
...HIDDEN INSIDE THE BOUQUET WE BOUGHT THREE DAYS AGO.
DAMN IT!!
SMASH
HE USED THIS TO SURVEIL US...
...AND DETERMINE THE PERFECT OPPORTUNITY TO ATTACK MS. VITCH WHEN SHE WAS ALL ALONE.
HE KNEW KORO SENSEI WOULD BE IN BRAZIL...
...AND THAT MR. KARASUMA WAS AWAY ON A BUSINESS TRIP.
AND HE WAS DARING ENOUGH TO INFILTRATE OUR CLASSROOM ON HIS OWN.
THE WEIRD THING IS...
...HE JUST DOESN'T SEEM LIKE A PSYCHO KILLER NAMED THE GRIM REAPER.
ARE YOU SURE THIS ISN'T SOME KIND OF JOKE? MAYBE HE'S ACTUALLY A PRETTY NICE GUY?

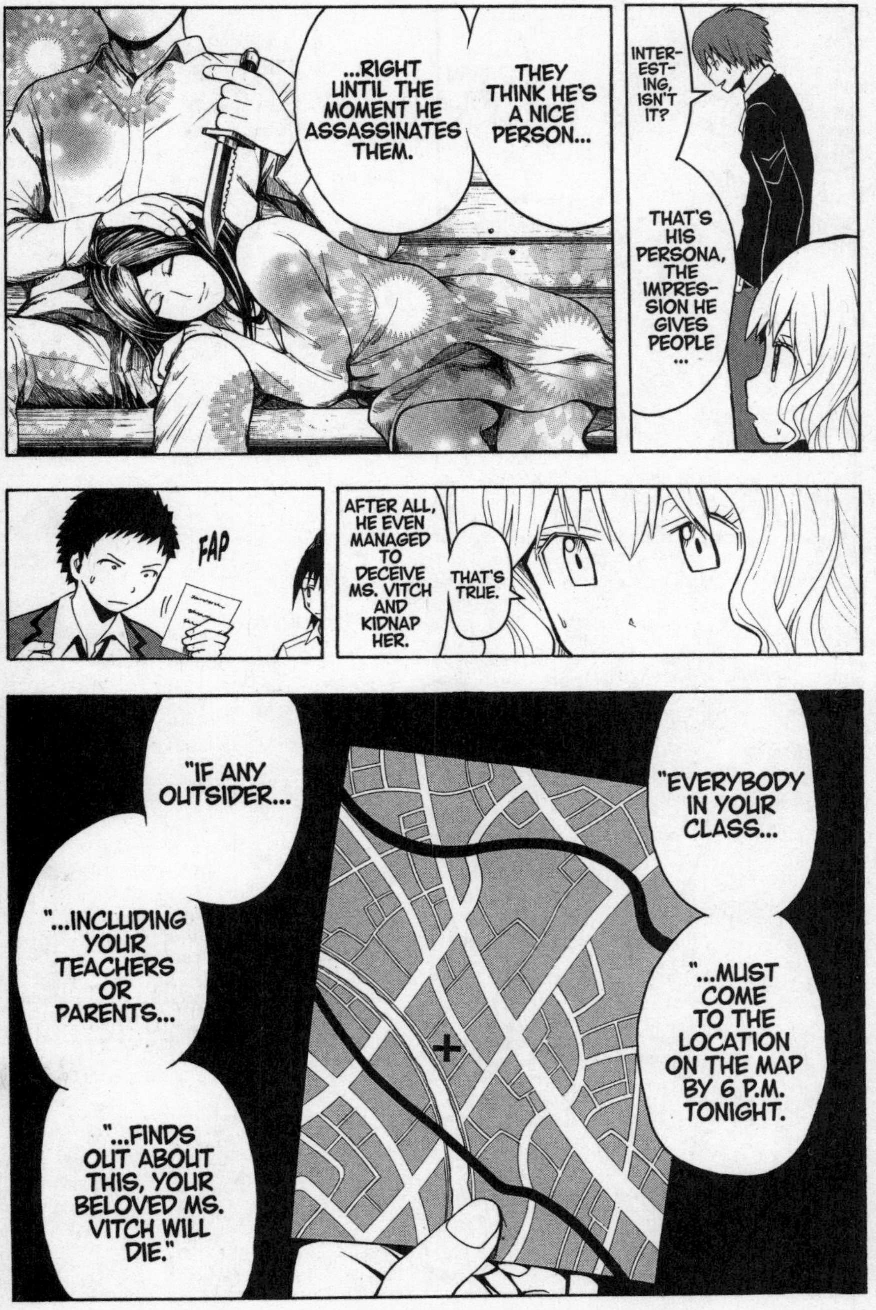
INTERESTING, ISN'T IT?
THAT'S HIS PERSONA, THE IMPRESSION HE GIVES PEOPLE...
THEY THINK HE'S A NICE PERSON...
...RIGHT UNTIL THE MOMENT HE ASSASSINATES THEM.
THAT'S TRUE.
AFTER ALL, HE EVEN MANAGED TO DECEIVE MS. VITCH AND KIDNAP HER.
FAP
"EVERYBODY IN YOUR CLASS...
"...MUST COME TO THE LOCATION ON THE MAP BY 6 P.M. TONIGHT.
"IF ANY OUTSIDER...
"...INCLUDING YOUR TEACHERS OR PARENTS...
"...FINDS OUT ABOUT THIS, YOUR BELOVED MS. VITCH WILL DIE."

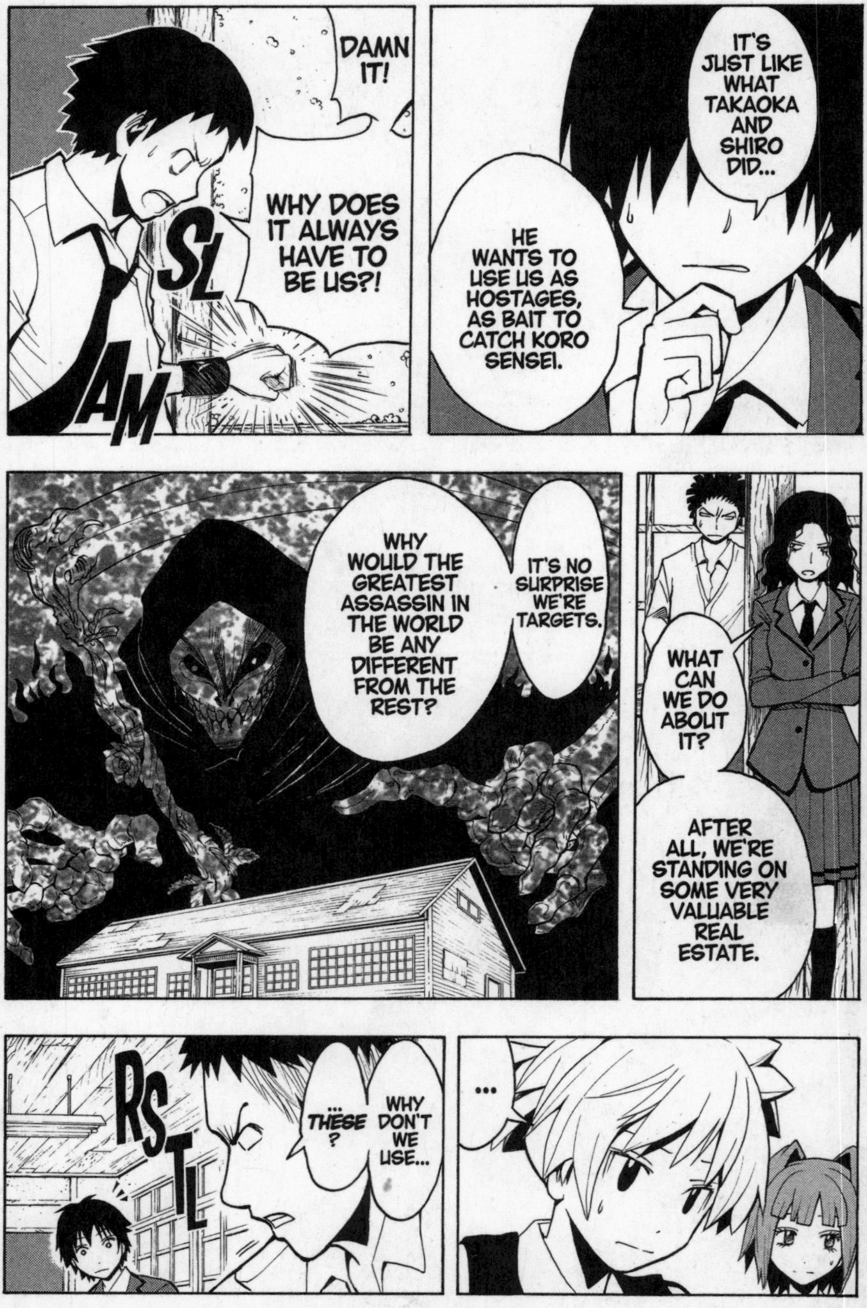
IT'S JUST LIKE WHAT TAKAOKA AND SHIRO DID...
HE WANTS TO USE US AS HOSTAGES, AS BAIT TO CATCH KORO SENSEI.
DAMN IT!
WHY DOES IT ALWAYS HAVE TO BE US?!
SLAM
WHAT CAN WE DO ABOUT IT?
AFTER ALL, WE'RE STANDING ON SOME VERY VALUABLE REAL ESTATE.
IT'S NO SURPRISE WE'RE TARGETS.
WHY WOULD THE GREATEST ASSASSIN IN THE WORLD BE ANY DIFFERENT FROM THE REST?
...
WHY DON'T WE USE...
...THESE?
RSTL

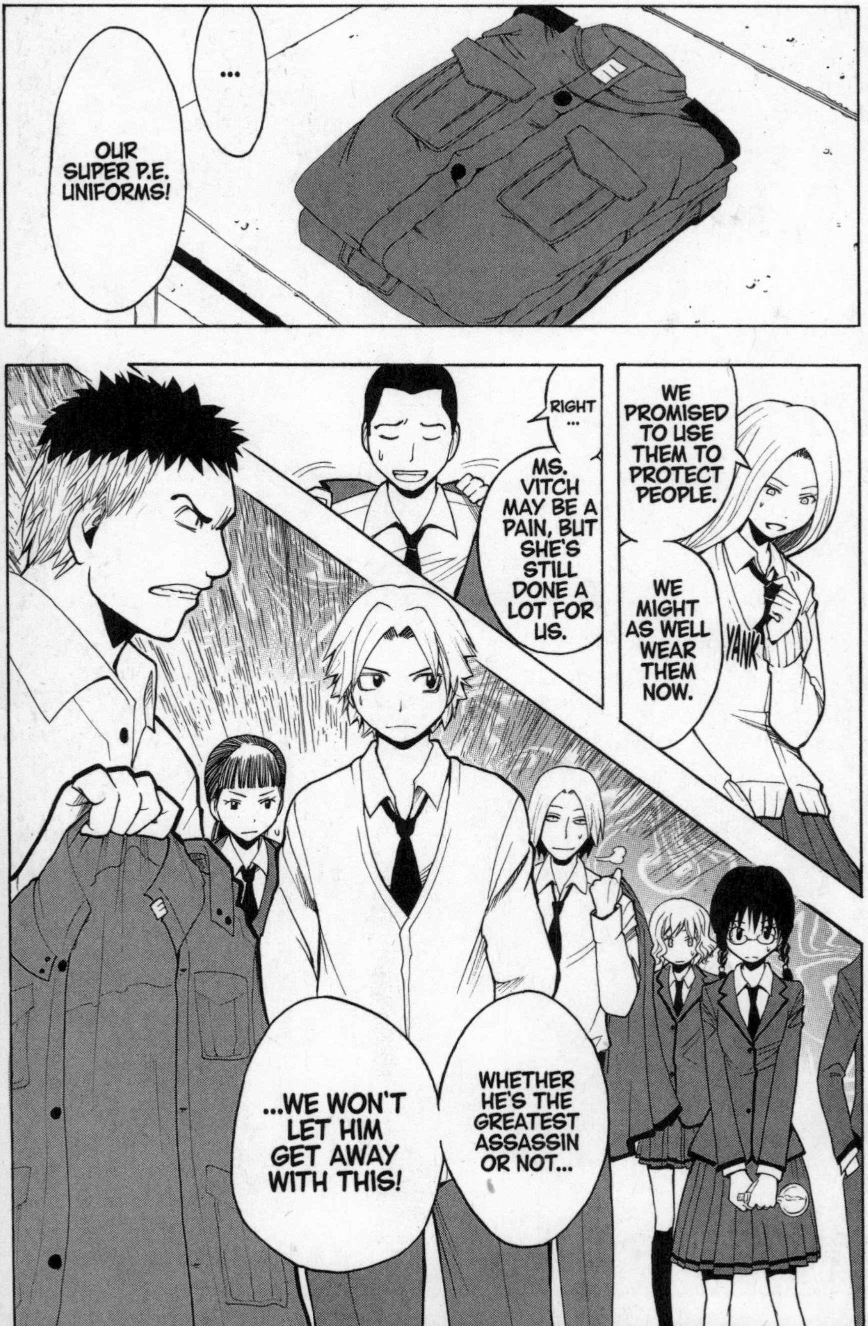
...
OUR SUPER P.E. UNIFORMS!
WE PROMISED TO USE THEM TO PROTECT PEOPLE.
WE MIGHT AS WELL WEAR THEM NOW.
YANK
RIGHT ...
MS. VITCH MAY BE A PAIN, BUT SHE'S STILL DONE A LOT FOR US.
WHETHER HE'S THE GREATEST ASSASSIN OR NOT...
...WE WON'T LET HIM GET AWAY WITH THIS!

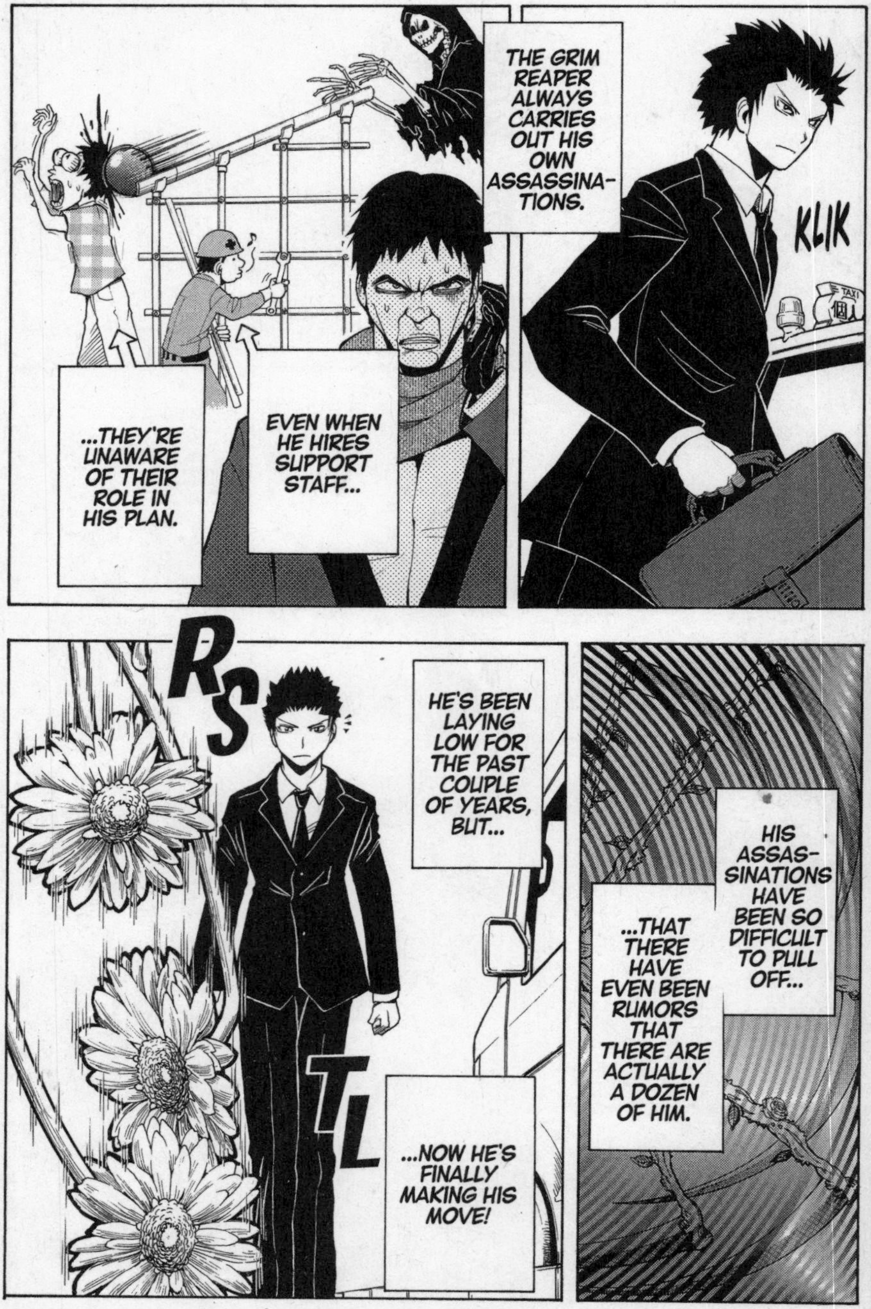
THE GRIM REAPER ALWAYS CARRIES OUT HIS OWN ASSASSINATIONS.
KLIK
TAXI
EVEN WHEN HE HIRES SUPPORT STAFF...
...THEY'RE UNAWARE OF THEIR ROLE IN HIS PLAN.
HIS ASSASSINATIONS HAVE BEEN SO DIFFICULT TO PULL OFF...
...THAT THERE HAVE EVEN BEEN RUMORS THAT THERE ARE ACTUALLY A DOZEN OF HIM.
RS
HE'S BEEN LAYING LOW FOR THE PAST COUPLE OF YEARS, BUT...
TL
...NOW HE'S FINALLY MAKING HIS MOVE!

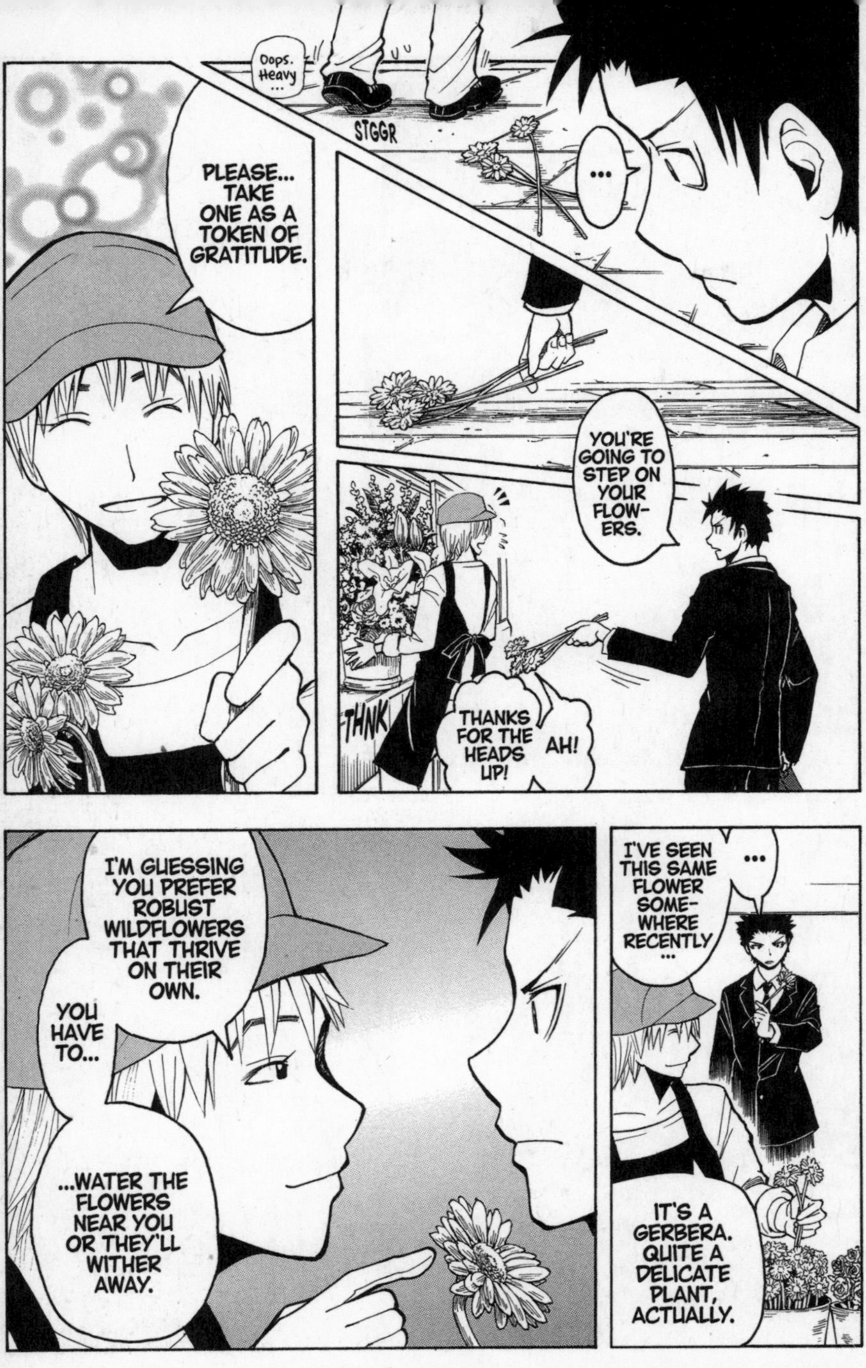

Oops. Heavy ...
STGGR
...
YOU'RE GOING TO STEP ON YOUR FLOW- ERS.
AH!
THANKS FOR THE HEADS UP!
THNK
PLEASE... TAKE ONE AS A TOKEN OF GRATITUDE.
...
I'VE SEEN THIS SAME FLOWER SOME- WHERE RECENTLY ...
IT'S A GERBERA. QUITE A DELICATE PLANT, ACTUALLY.
I'M GUESSING YOU PREFER ROBUST WILDFLOWERS THAT THRIVE ON THEIR OWN.
YOU HAVE TO...
...WATER THE FLOWERS NEAR YOU OR THEY'LL WITHER AWAY.

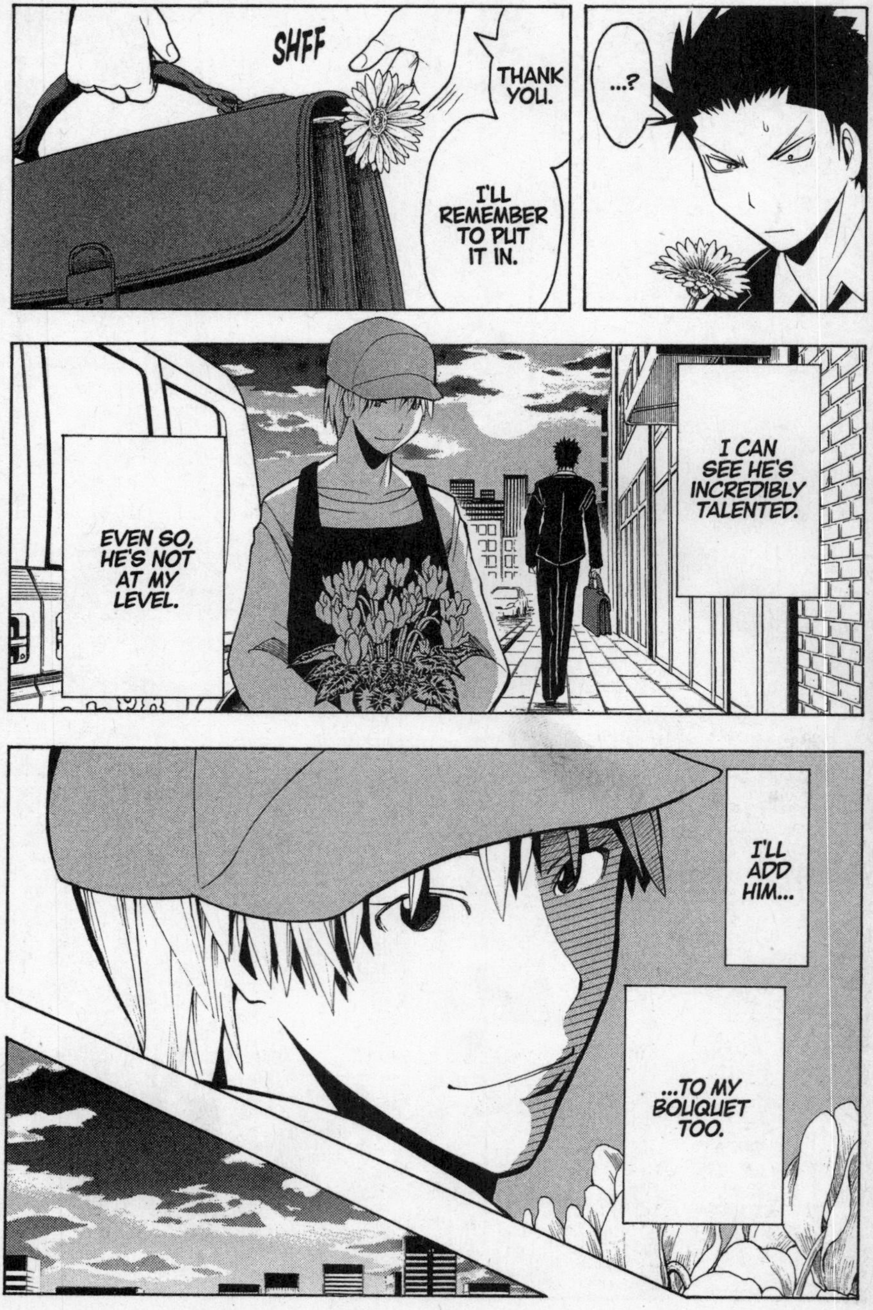
...?
SHFF
THANK YOU.
I'LL REMEMBER TO PUT IT IN.
I CAN SEE HE'S INCREDIBLY TALENTED.
EVEN SO, HE'S NOT AT MY LEVEL.
I'LL ADD HIM...
...TO MY BOUQUET TOO.

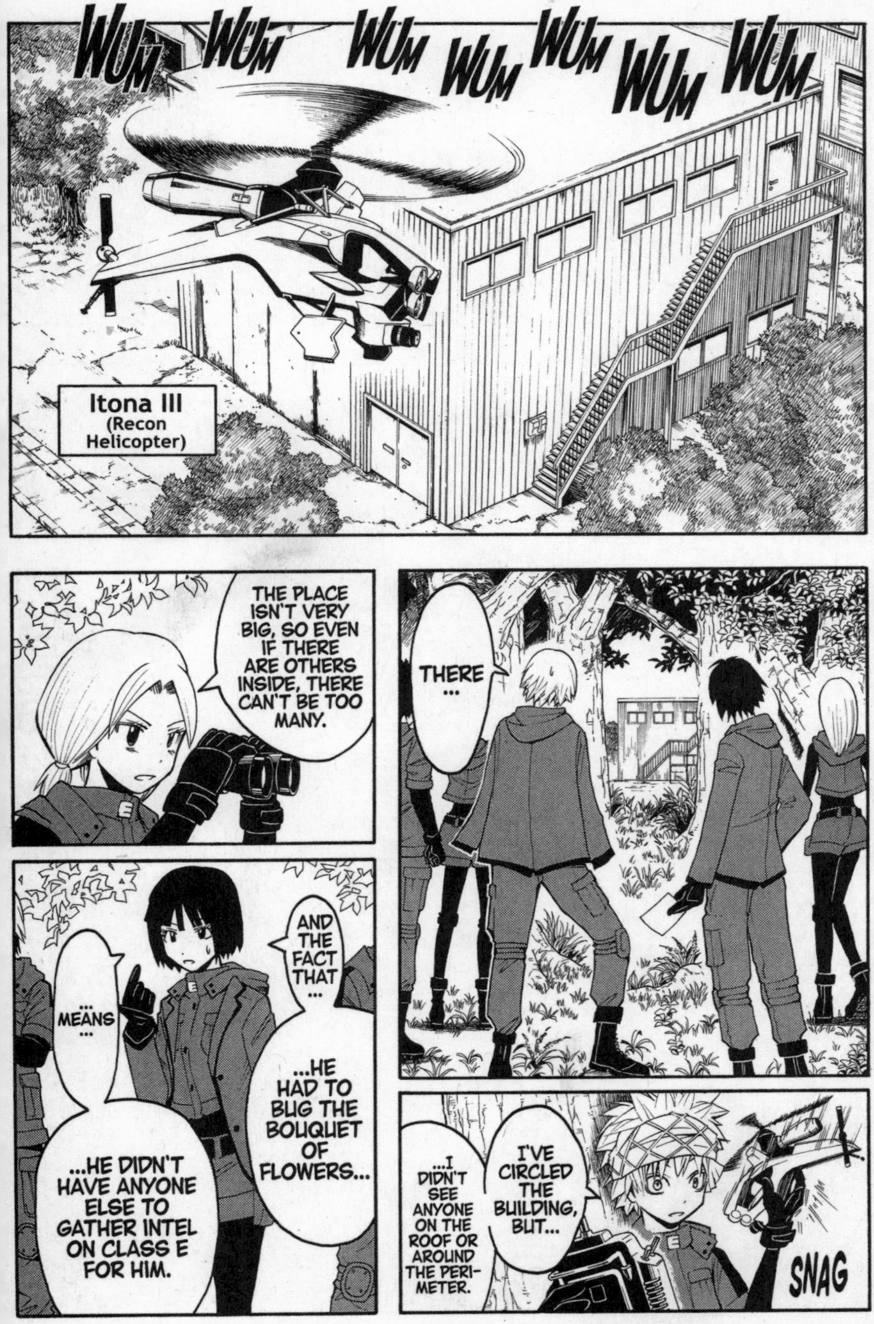
WUM WUM WUM WUM WUM WUM WUM
Itona III (Recon Helicopter)
THERE...
THE PLACE ISN'T VERY BIG, SO EVEN IF THERE ARE OTHERS INSIDE, THERE CAN'T BE TOO MANY.
I'VE CIRCLED THE BUILDING, BUT...
...I DIDN'T SEE ANYONE ON THE ROOF OR AROUND THE PERI-METER.
SNAG
AND THE FACT THAT...
...HE HAD TO BUG THE BOUQUET OF FLOWERS...
...MEANS...
...HE DIDN'T HAVE ANYONE ELSE TO GATHER INTEL ON CLASS E FOR HIM.

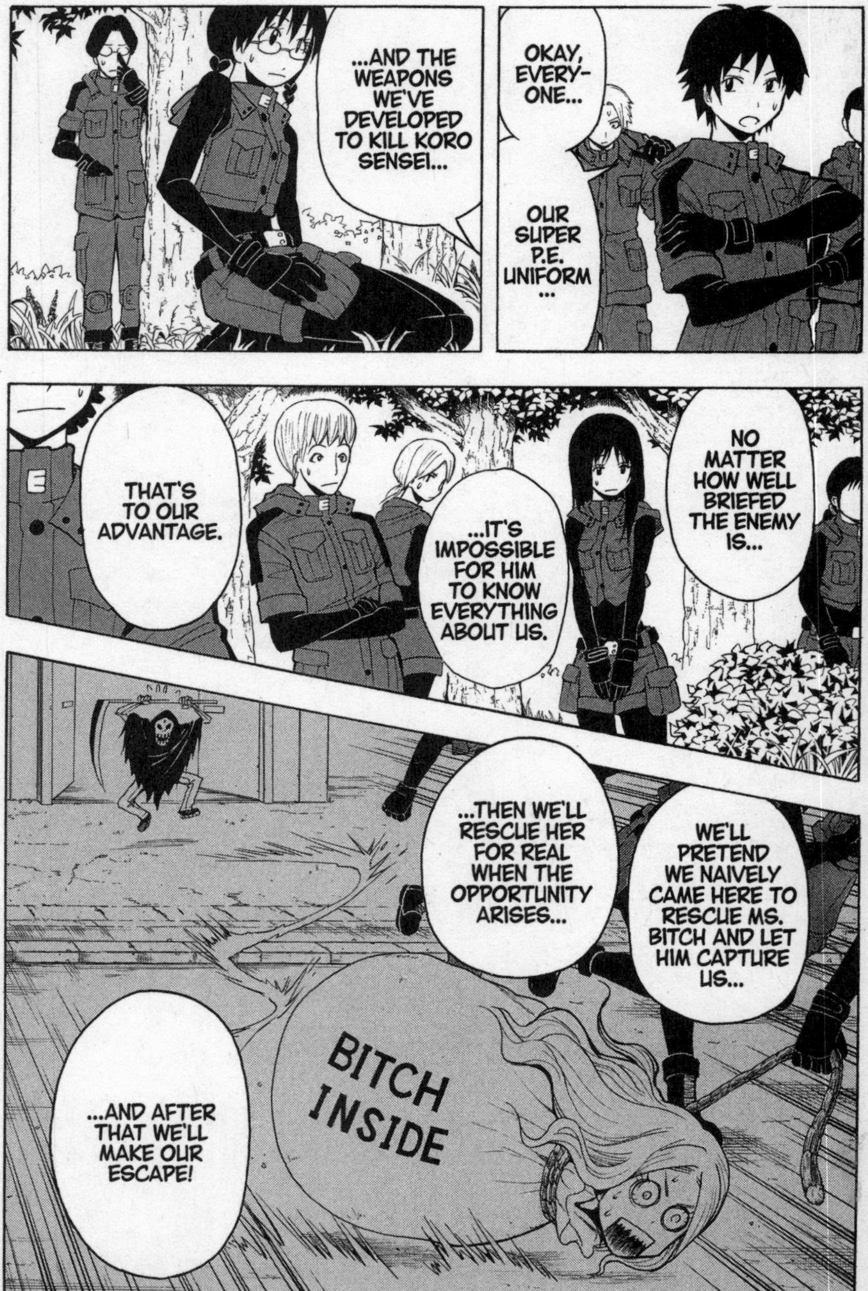
OKAY, EVERY-ONE...
OUR SUPER P.E. UNIFORM...
...AND THE WEAPONS WE'VE DEVELOPED TO KILL KORO SENSEI...
NO MATTER HOW WELL BRIEFED THE ENEMY IS...
...IT'S IMPOSSIBLE FOR HIM TO KNOW EVERYTHING ABOUT US.
THAT'S TO OUR ADVANTAGE.
WE'LL PRETEND WE NAIVELY CAME HERE TO RESCUE MS. BITCH AND LET HIM CAPTURE US...
...THEN WE'LL RESCUE HER FOR REAL WHEN THE OPPORTUNITY ARISES...
BITCH INSIDE
...AND AFTER THAT WE'LL MAKE OUR ESCAPE!

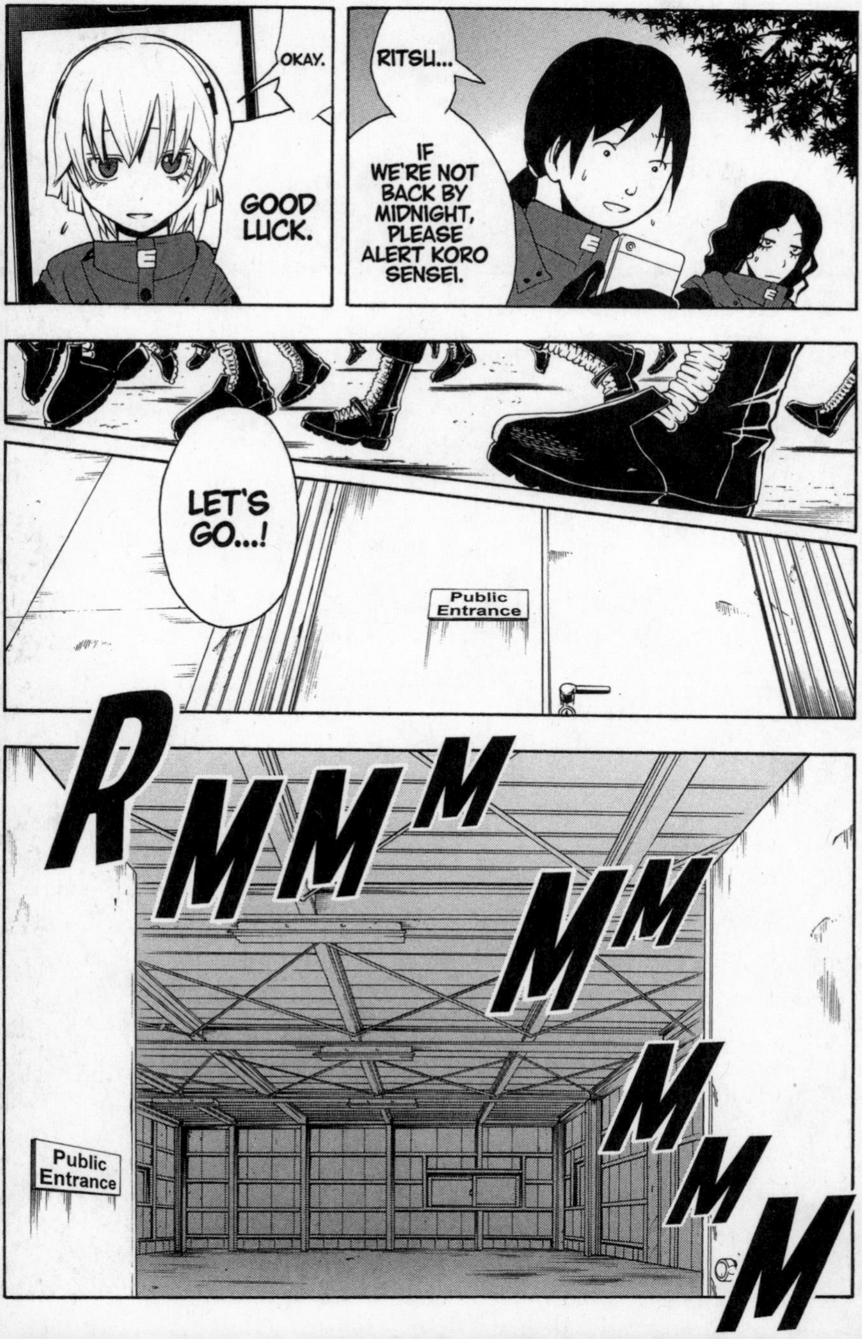
RITSU...
IF WE'RE NOT BACK BY MIDNIGHT, PLEASE ALERT KORO SENSEI.
OKAY.
GOOD LUCK.
LET'S GO...!
Public Entrance
RMMMMMMMMMMMM
Public Entrance

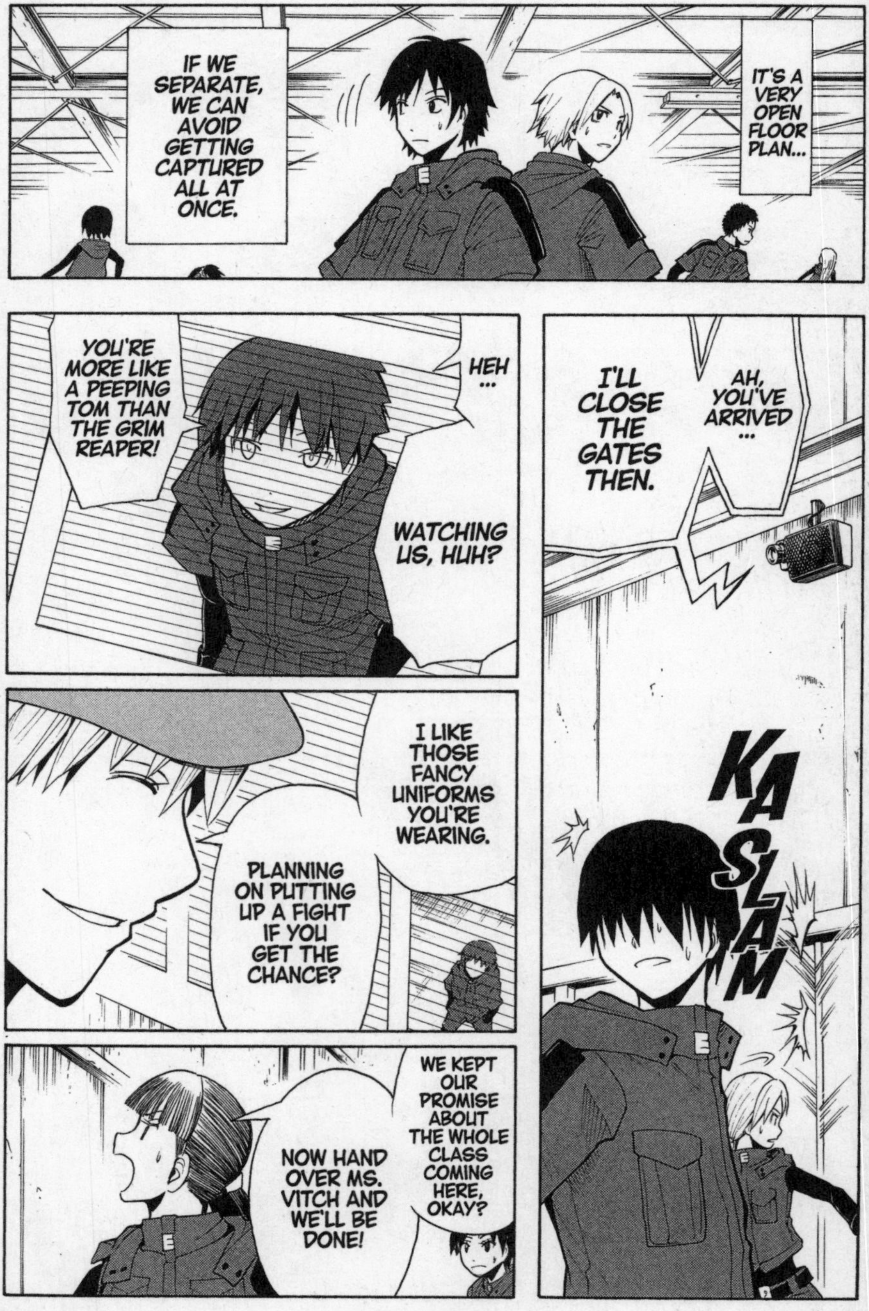
IT'S A VERY OPEN FLOOR PLAN...
IF WE SEPARATE, WE CAN AVOID GETTING CAPTURED ALL AT ONCE.
AH, YOU'VE ARRIVED ...
I'LL CLOSE THE GATES THEN.
KA SLAM
HEH ...
WATCHING US, HUH?
YOU'RE MORE LIKE A PEEPING TOM THAN THE GRIM REAPER!
I LIKE THOSE FANCY UNIFORMS YOU'RE WEARING.
PLANNING ON PUTTING UP A FIGHT IF YOU GET THE CHANCE?
WE KEPT OUR PROMISE ABOUT THE WHOLE CLASS COMING HERE, OKAY?
NOW HAND OVER MS. VITCH AND WE'LL BE DONE!

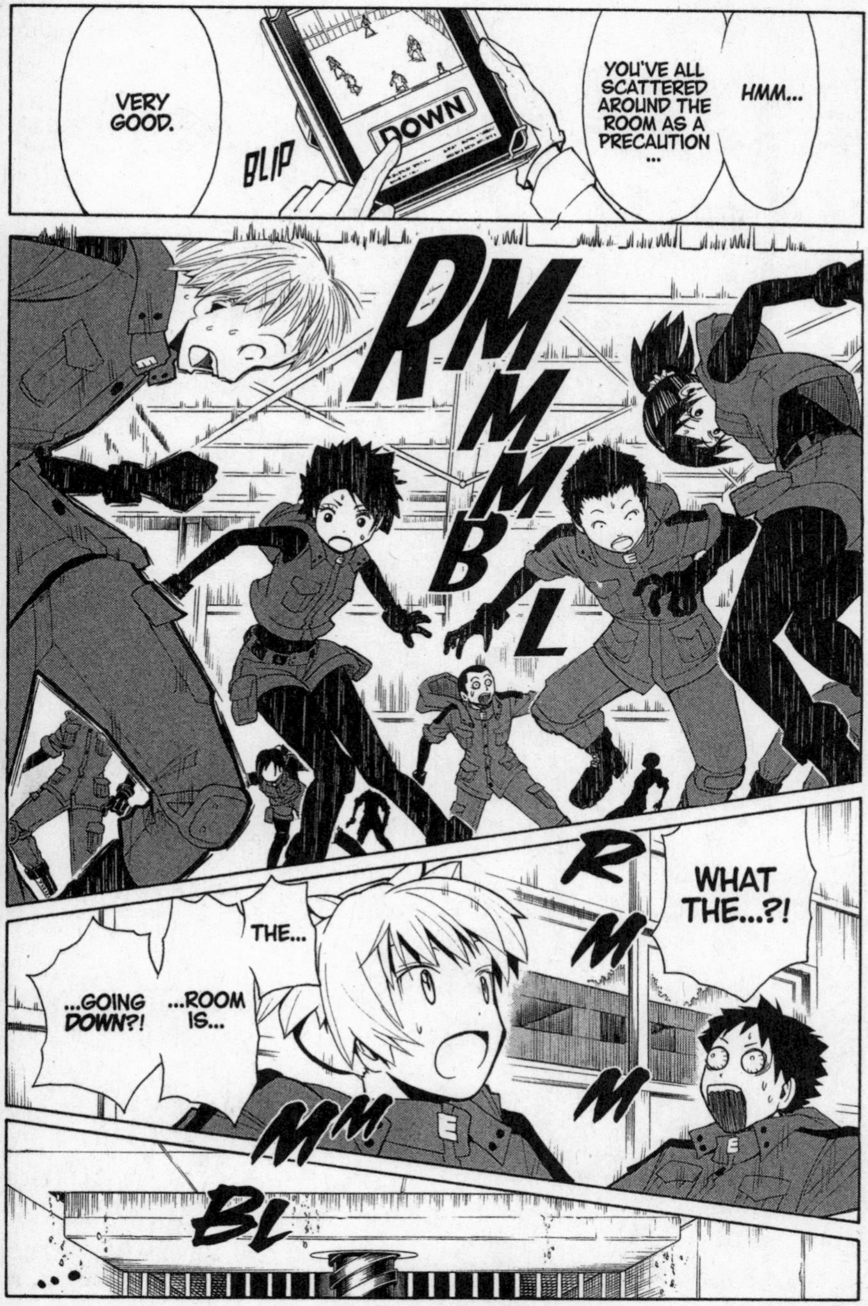
HMM...
YOU'VE ALL SCATTERED AROUND THE ROOM AS A PRECAUTION ...
DOWN
BLIP
VERY GOOD.
RMMMBL
R M M M
WHAT THE...?!
THE...
...ROOM IS...
...GOING DOWN?!
MM
BL

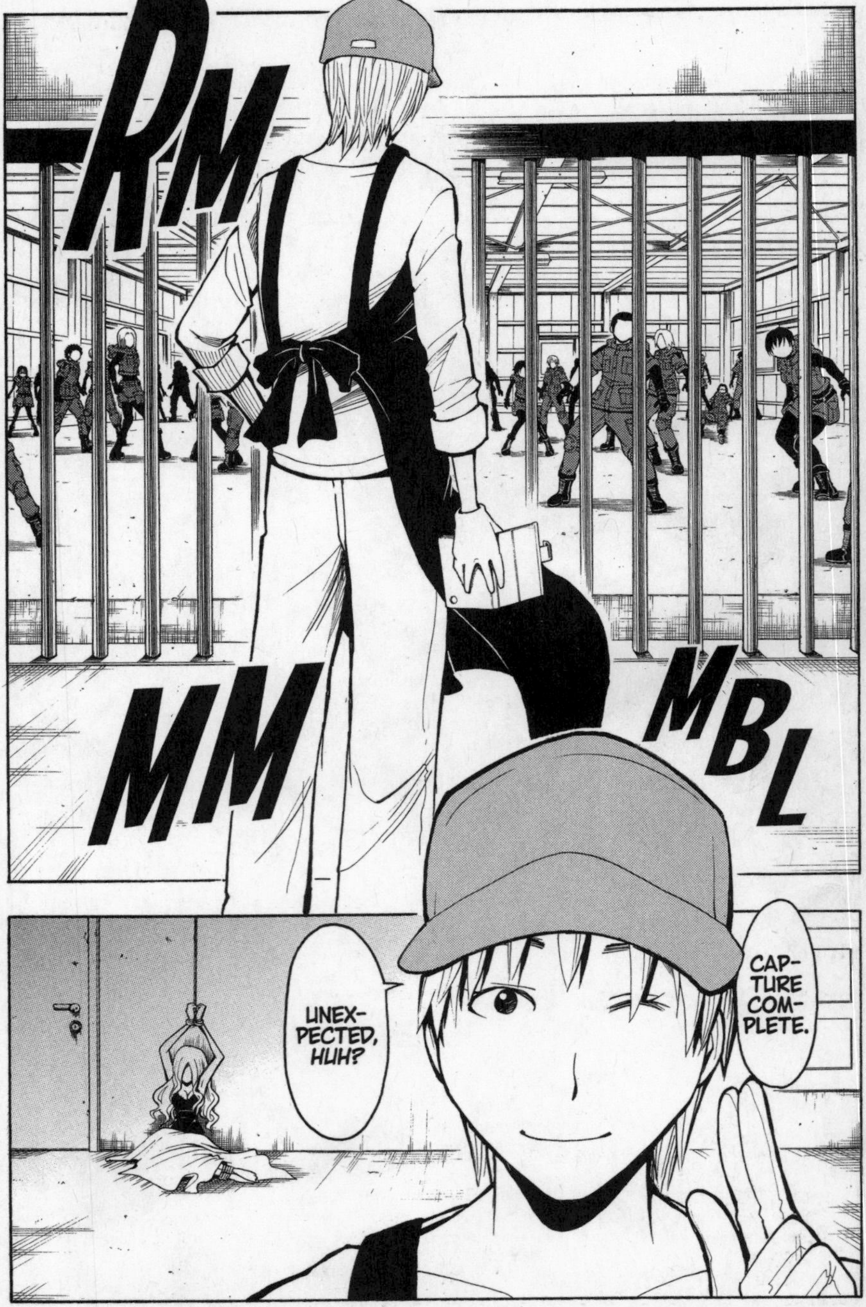
RM
MM
MBL
CAPTURE COMPLETE.
UNEXPECTED, HUH?

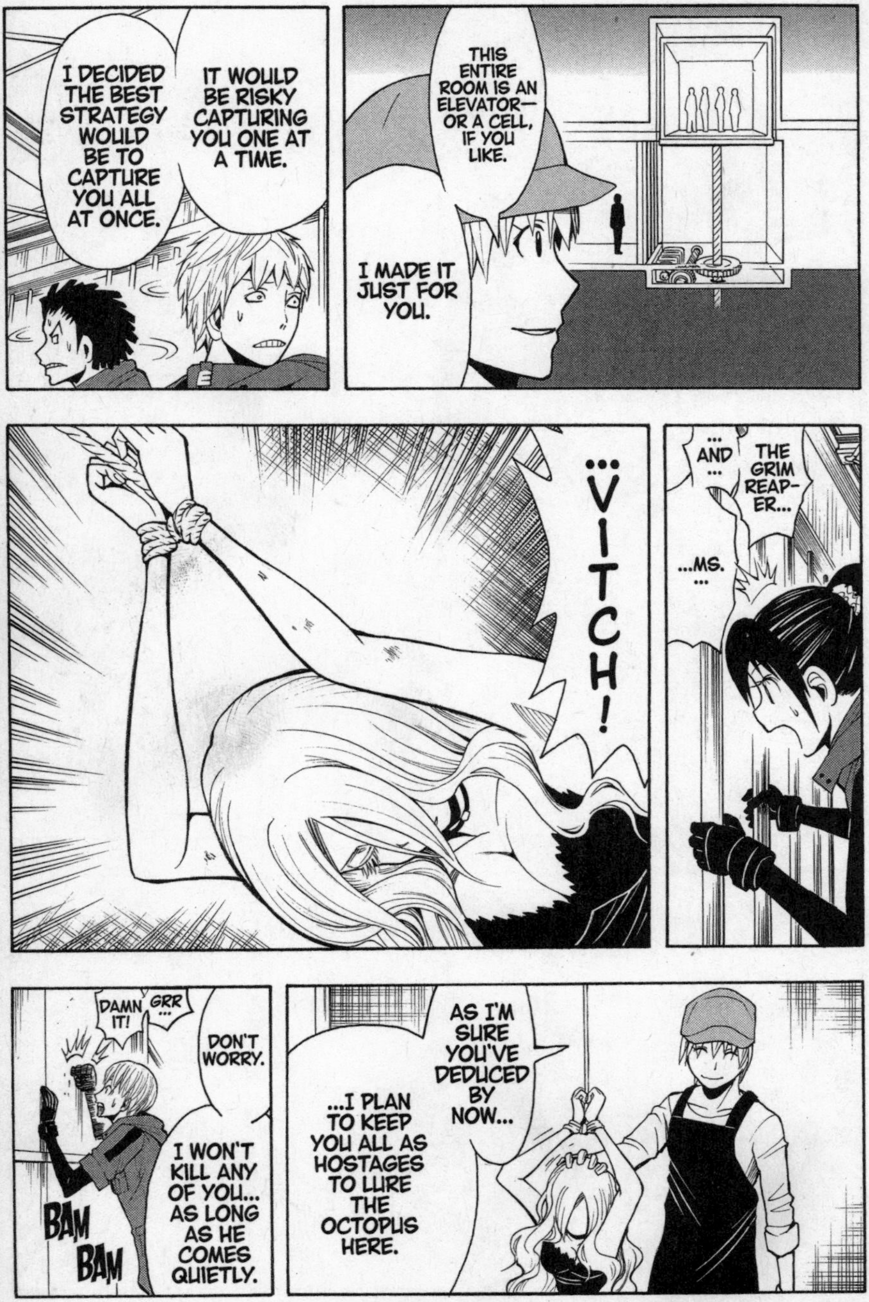
THIS ENTIRE ROOM IS AN ELEVATOR—OR A CELL, IF YOU LIKE.
I MADE IT JUST FOR YOU.
IT WOULD BE RISKY CAPTURING YOU ONE AT A TIME.
I DECIDED THE BEST STRATEGY WOULD BE TO CAPTURE YOU ALL AT ONCE.
THE GRIM REAPER...
...AND...
...MS. ...
...VITCH!
AS I'M SURE YOU'VE DEDUCED BY NOW...
...I PLAN TO KEEP YOU ALL AS HOSTAGES TO LURE THE OCTOPUS HERE.
DON'T WORRY.
I WON'T KILL ANY OF YOU... AS LONG AS HE COMES QUIETLY.
GRR...
DAMN IT!
BAM
BAM

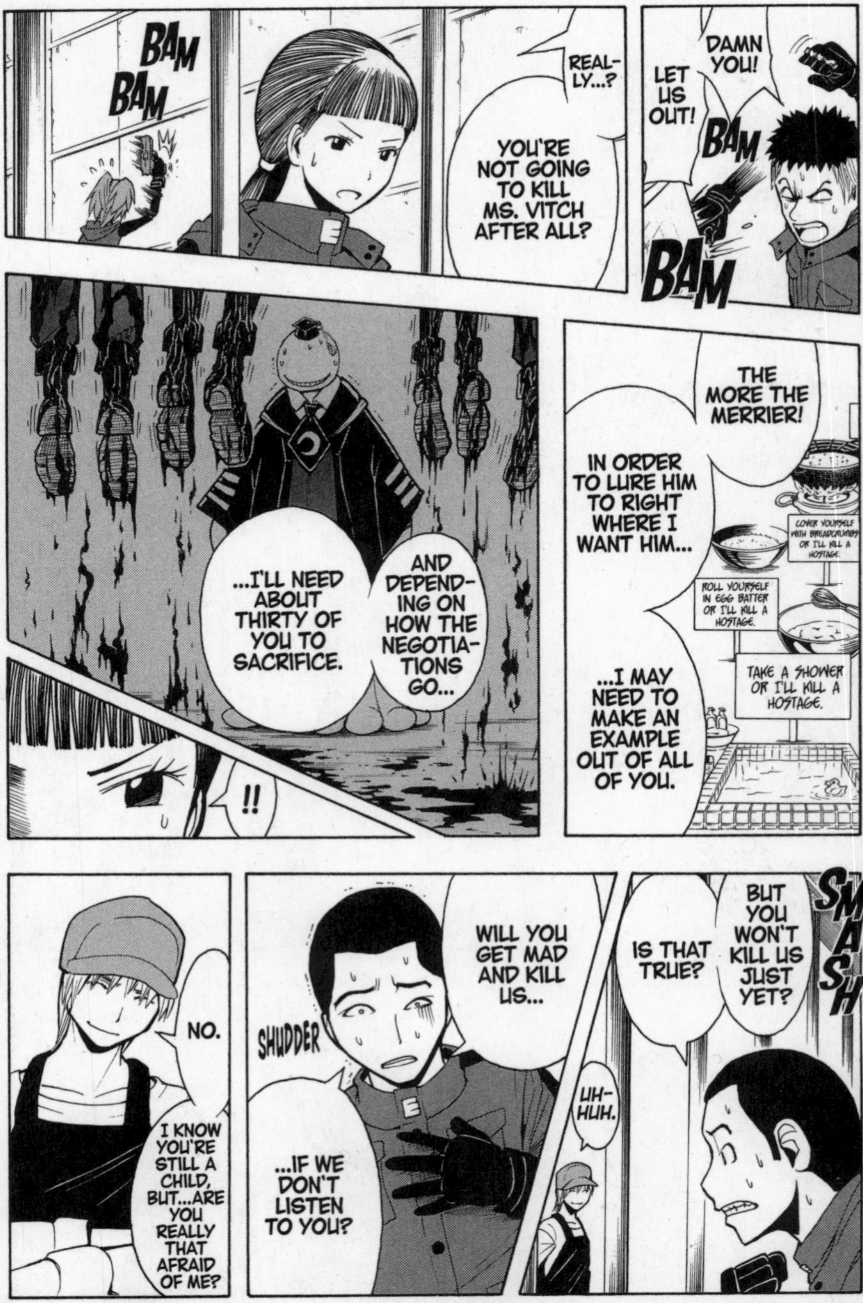
DAMN YOU!
LET US OUT!
BAM
BAM
REAL-LY...?
YOU'RE NOT GOING TO KILL MS. VITCH AFTER ALL?
BAM
BAM
THE MORE THE MERRIER!
IN ORDER TO LURE HIM TO RIGHT WHERE I WANT HIM...
COVER YOURSELF WITH BREADCRUMBS OR I'LL KILL A HOSTAGE.
ROLL YOURSELF IN EGG BATTER OR I'LL KILL A HOSTAGE.
TAKE A SHOWER OR I'LL KILL A HOSTAGE.
...I MAY NEED TO MAKE AN EXAMPLE OUT OF ALL OF YOU.
AND DEPENDING ON HOW THE NEGOTIATIONS GO...
...I'LL NEED ABOUT THIRTY OF YOU TO SACRIFICE.
!!
SMASH
BUT YOU WON'T KILL US JUST YET?
IS THAT TRUE?
UH-HUH.
WILL YOU GET MAD AND KILL US...
SHUDDER
...IF WE DON'T LISTEN TO YOU?
NO.
I KNOW YOU'RE STILL A CHILD, BUT...ARE YOU REALLY THAT AFRAID OF ME?

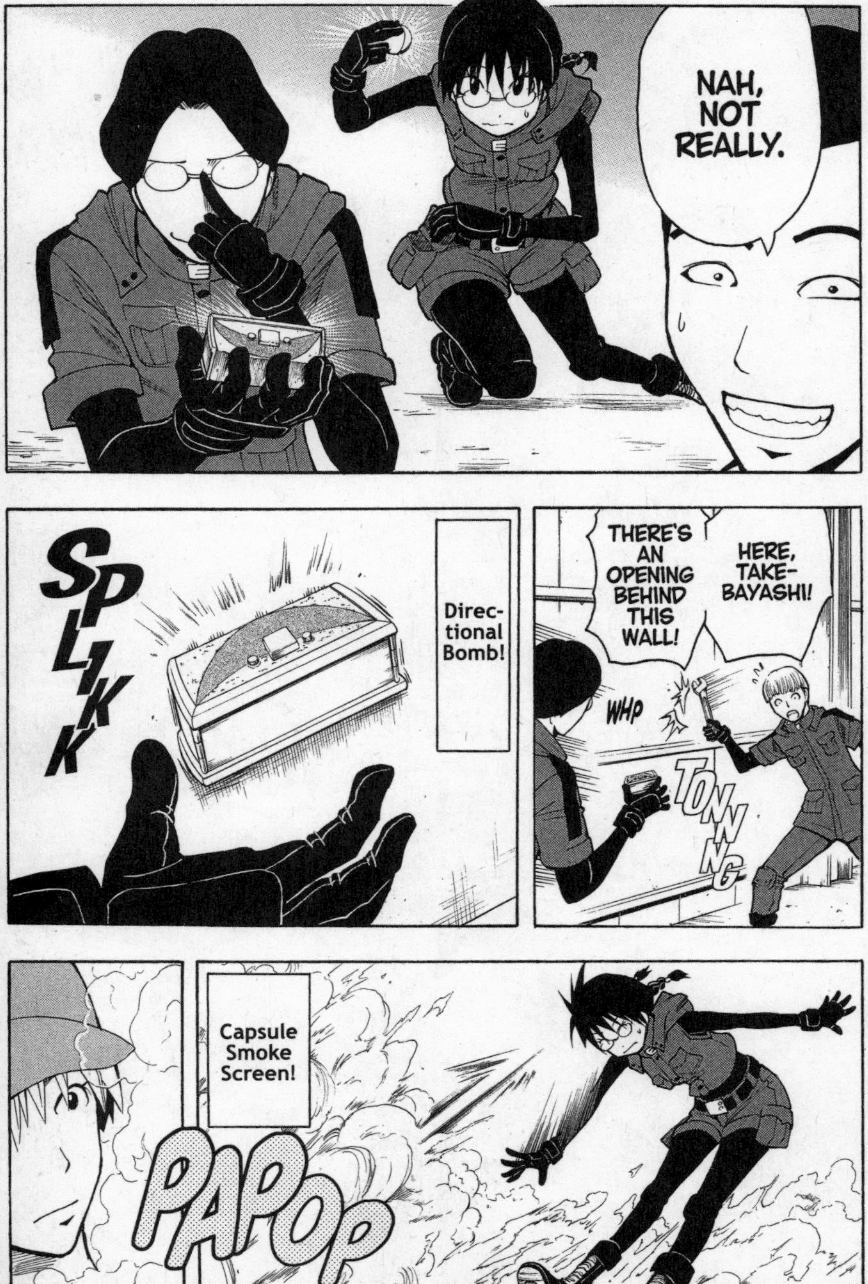
NAH, NOT REALLY.
HERE, TAKE-BAYASHI!
THERE'S AN OPENING BEHIND THIS WALL!
WHP
TONNNG
Directional Bomb!
SPLIKK
Capsule Smoke Screen!
PAPOP

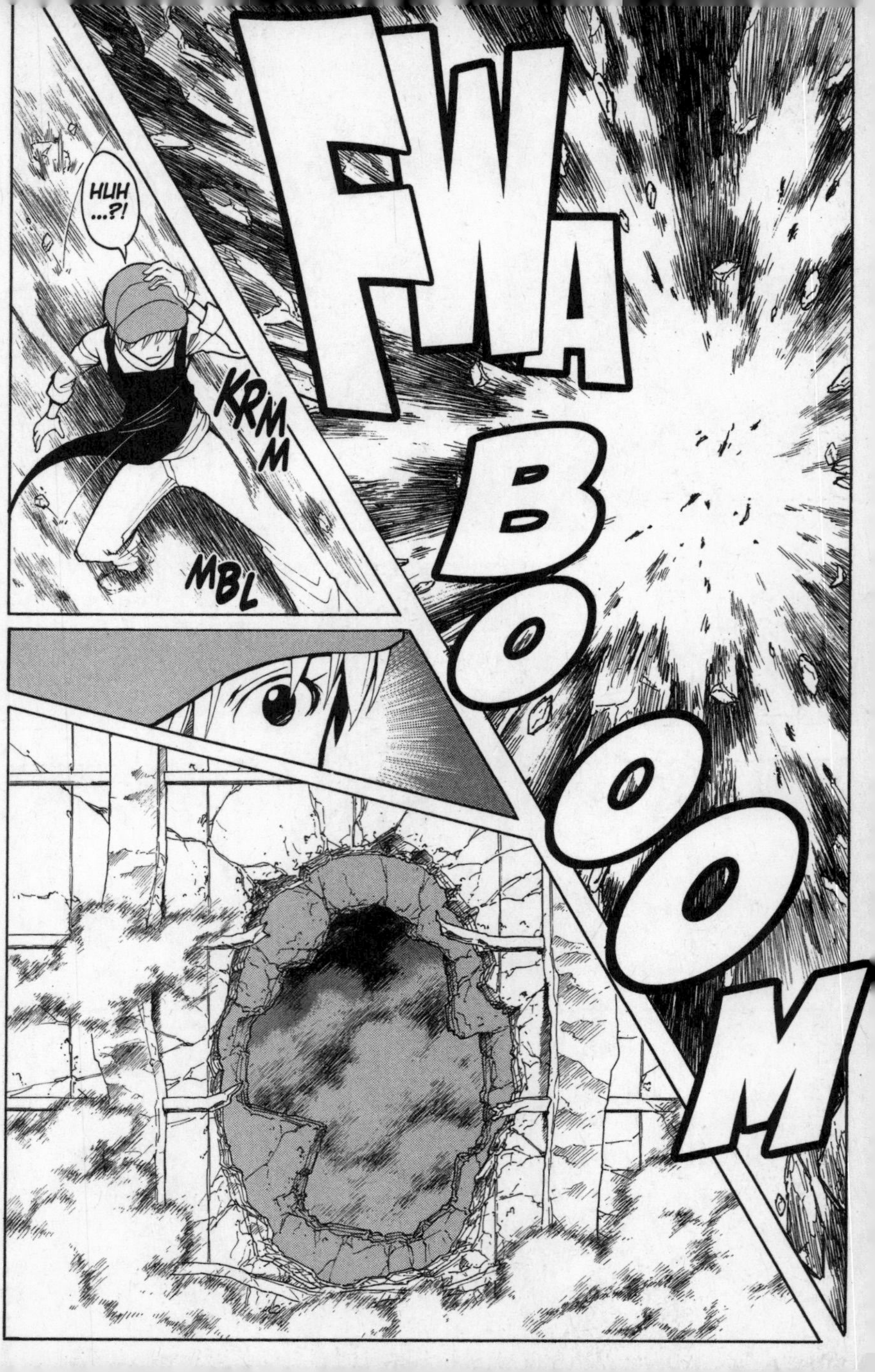
FWA
BOOOOM
HUH ...?!
KRMM
M
MBL

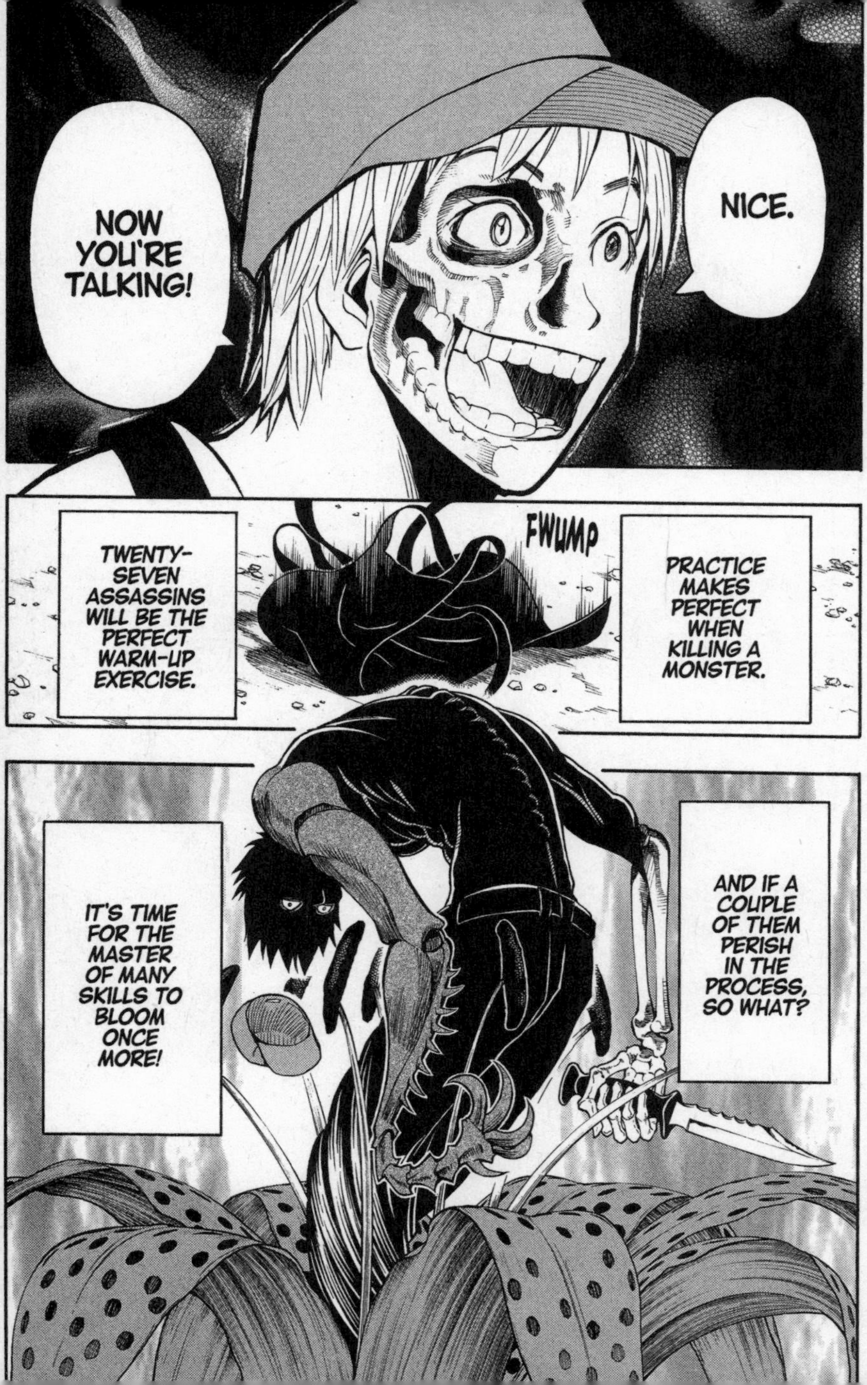
NICE.
NOW YOU'RE TALKING!
PRACTICE MAKES PERFECT WHEN KILLING A MONSTER.
FWUMP
TWENTY-SEVEN ASSASSINS WILL BE THE PERFECT WARM-UP EXERCISE.
AND IF A COUPLE OF THEM PERISH IN THE PROCESS, SO WHAT?
IT'S TIME FOR THE MASTER OF MANY SKILLS TO BLOOM ONCE MORE!

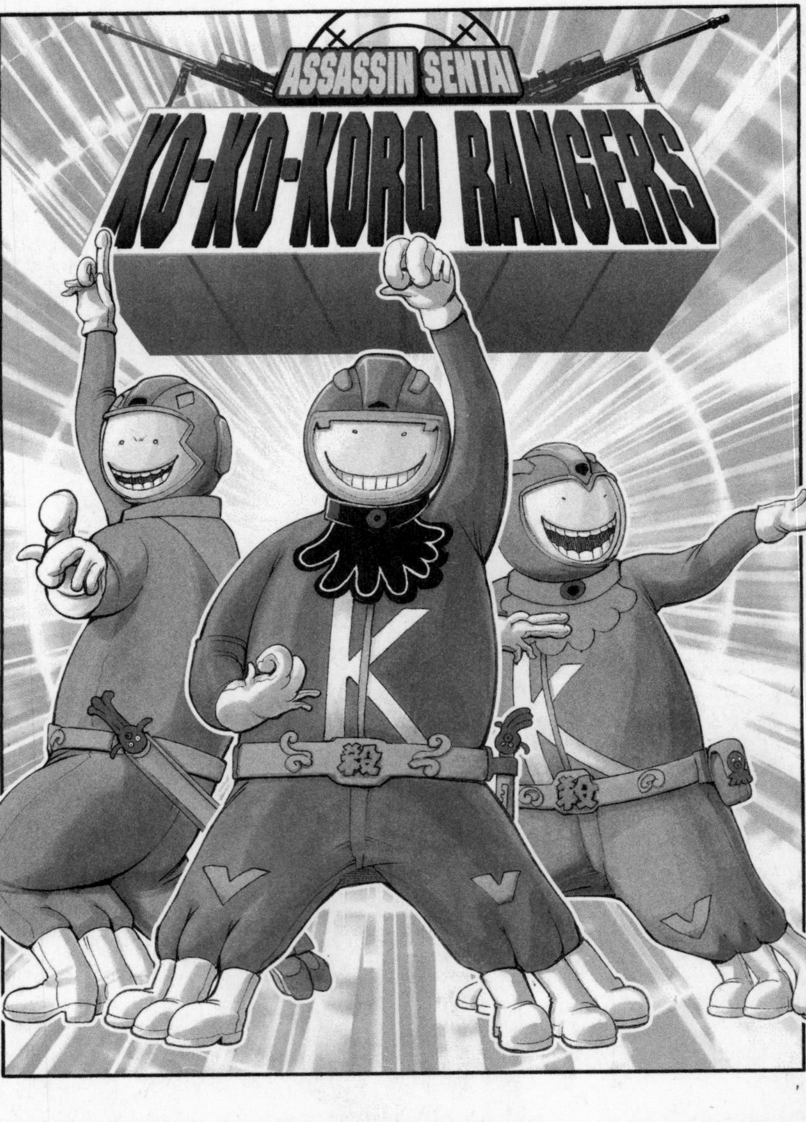
ASSASSIN SENTAI
KO-KO-KORO RANGERS
殺
殺

CLASS 102 TIME FOR THE GRIM REAPER–2ND PERIOD

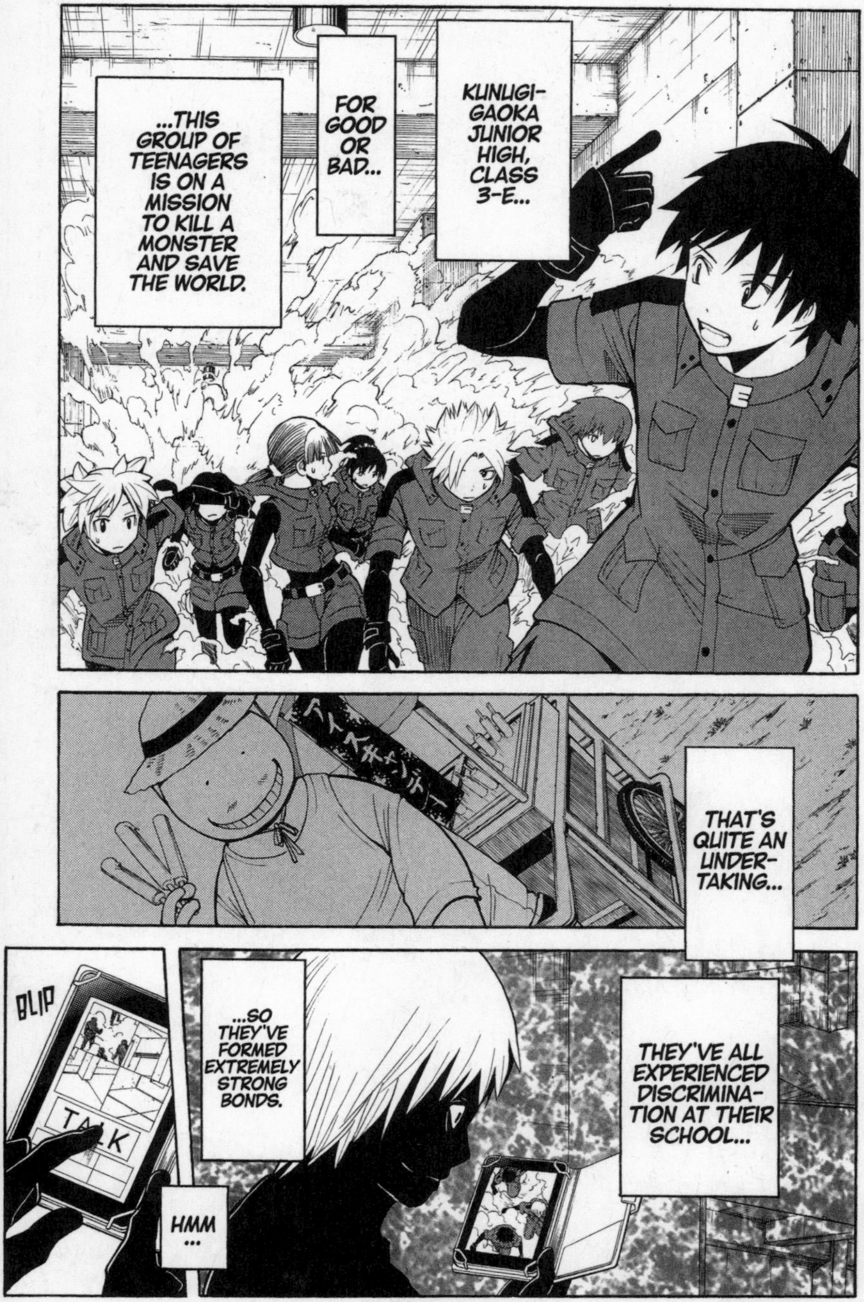
KUNUGI-GAOKA JUNIOR HIGH, CLASS 3-E...
FOR GOOD OR BAD...
...THIS GROUP OF TEENAGERS IS ON A MISSION TO KILL A MONSTER AND SAVE THE WORLD.
THAT'S QUITE AN UNDER-TAKING...
THEY'VE ALL EXPERIENCED DISCRIMINA-TION AT THEIR SCHOOL...
...SO THEY'VE FORMED EXTREMELY STRONG BONDS.
HMM...
BLIP
TALK

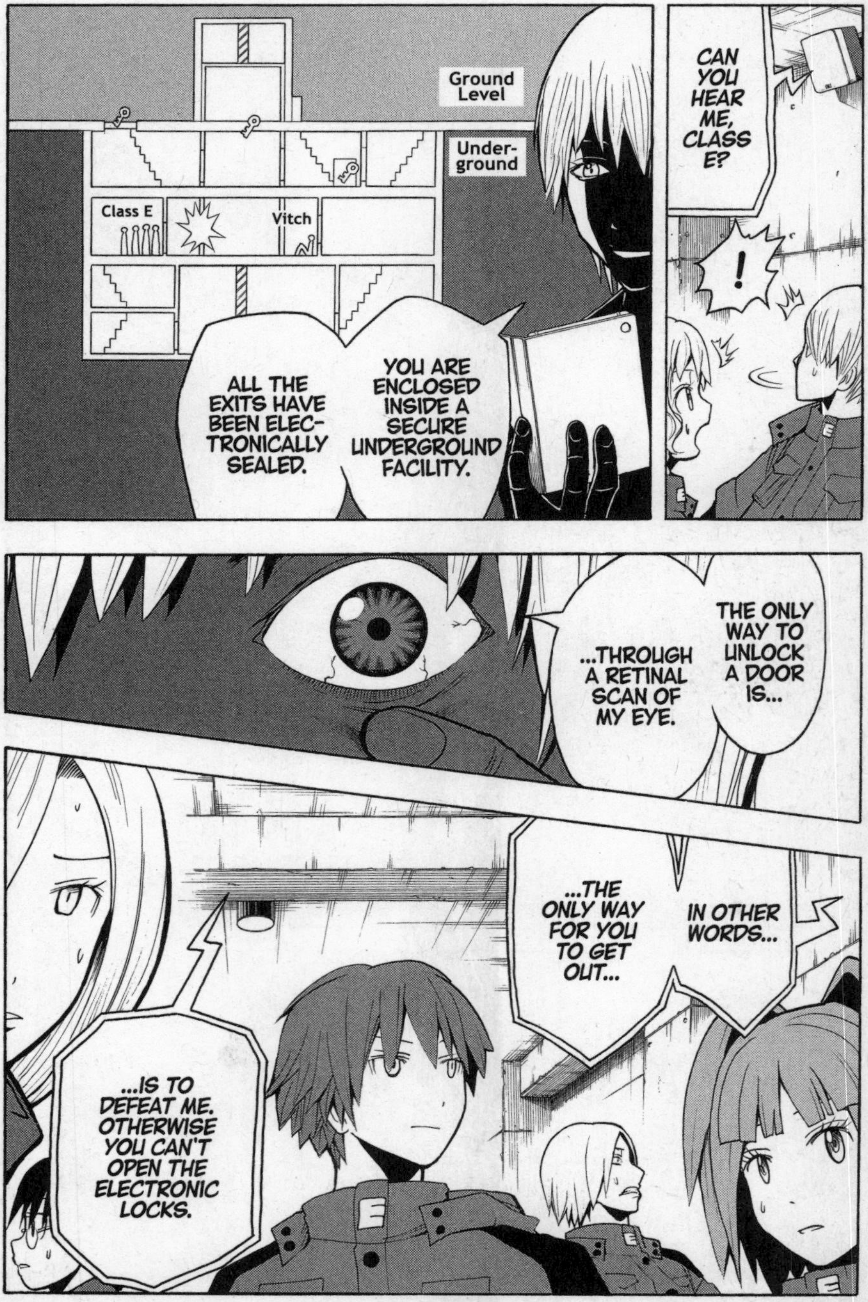
CAN YOU HEAR ME, CLASS E?
!
Ground Level
Underground
Class E
Vitch
YOU ARE ENCLOSED INSIDE A SECURE UNDERGROUND FACILITY.
ALL THE EXITS HAVE BEEN ELEC-TRONICALLY SEALED.
THE ONLY WAY TO UNLOCK A DOOR IS...
...THROUGH A RETINAL SCAN OF MY EYE.
IN OTHER WORDS...
...THE ONLY WAY FOR YOU TO GET OUT...
...IS TO DEFEAT ME. OTHERWISE YOU CAN'T OPEN THE ELECTRONIC LOCKS.

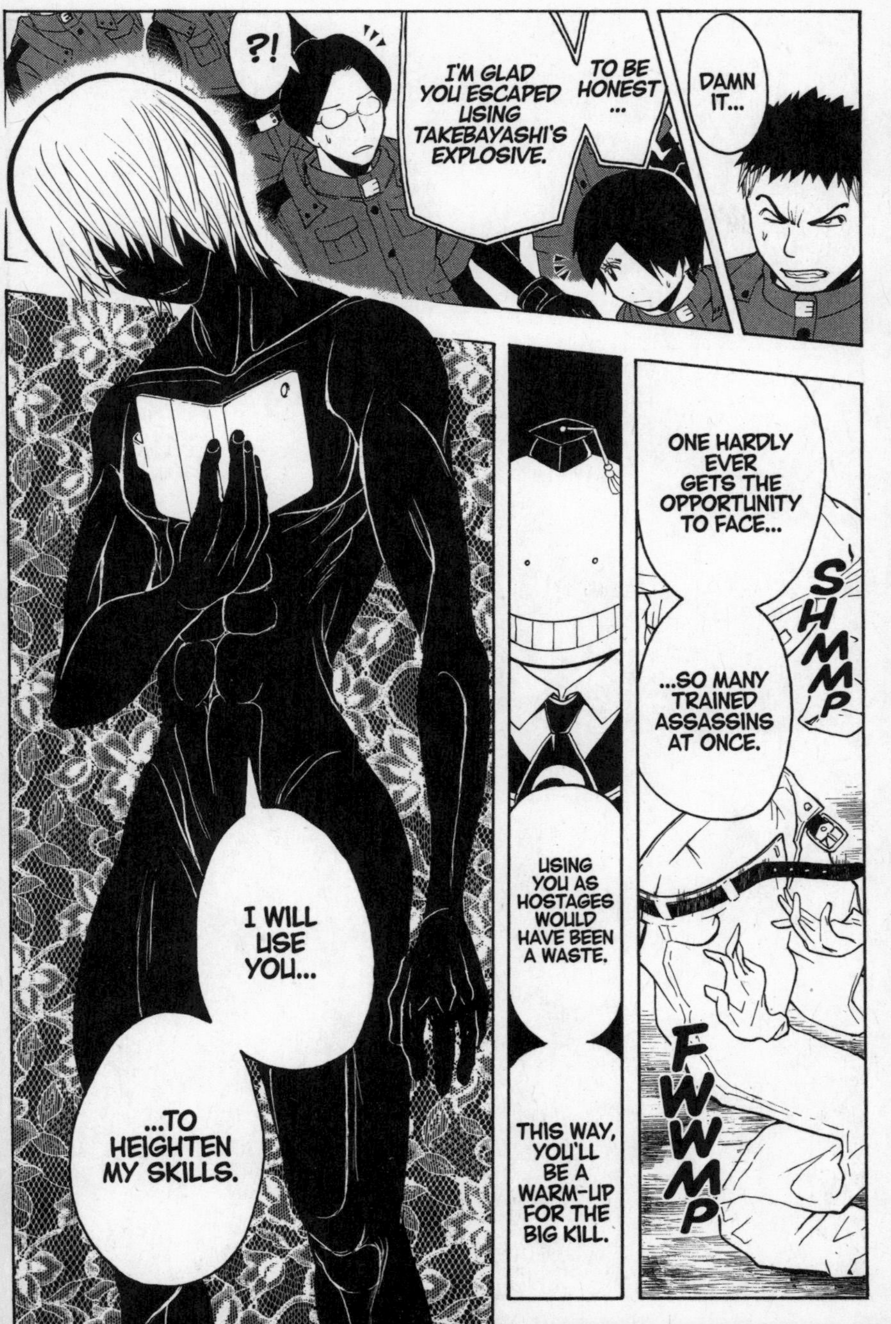
DAMN IT...
TO BE HONEST...
I'M GLAD YOU ESCAPED USING TAKEBAYASHI'S EXPLOSIVE.
?!
ONE HARDLY EVER GETS THE OPPORTUNITY TO FACE...
SHMMP
...SO MANY TRAINED ASSASSINS AT ONCE.
FWWMP
USING YOU AS HOSTAGES WOULD HAVE BEEN A WASTE.
THIS WAY, YOU'LL BE A WARM-UP FOR THE BIG KILL.
I WILL USE YOU...
...TO HEIGHTEN MY SKILLS.

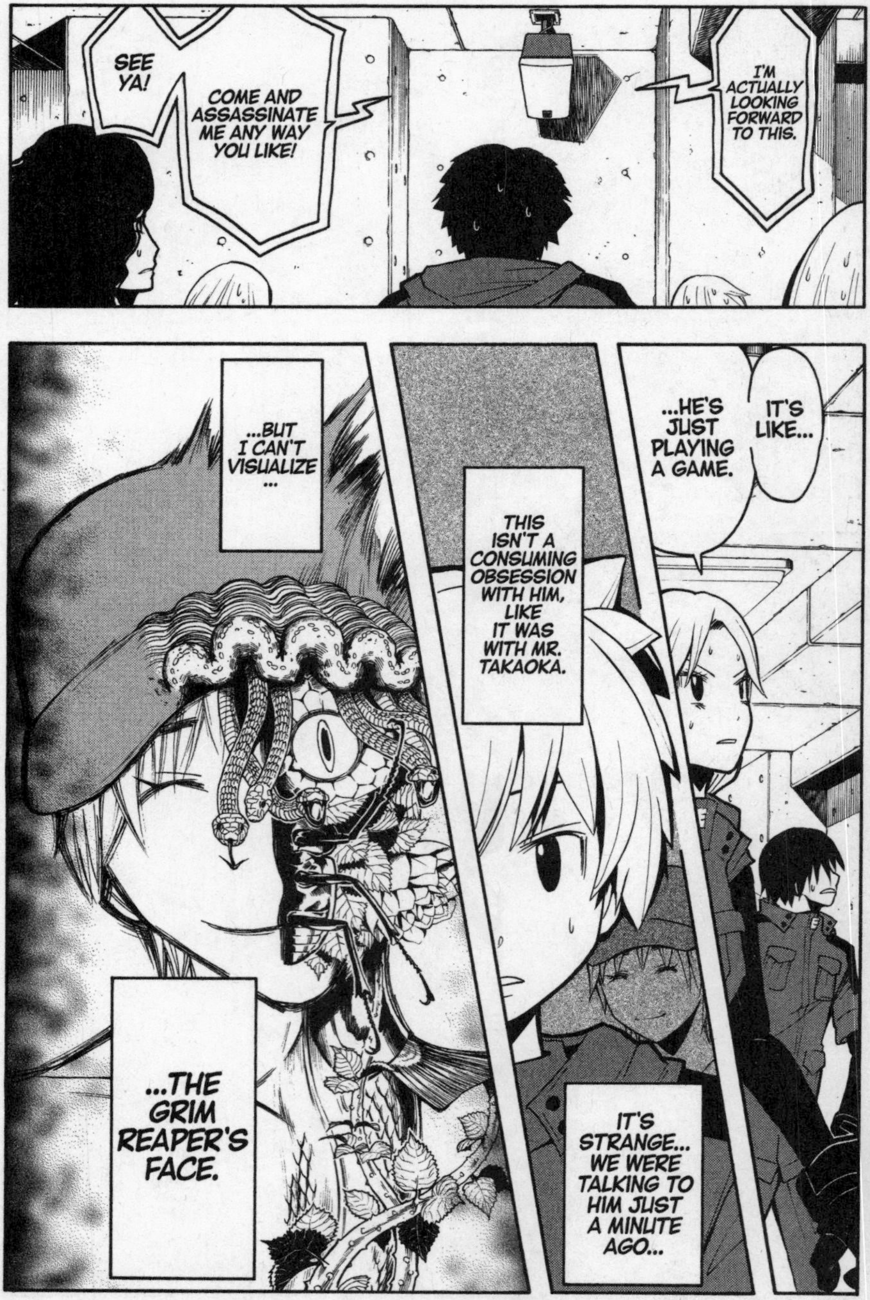
I'M ACTUALLY LOOKING FORWARD TO THIS.
COME AND ASSASSINATE ME ANY WAY YOU LIKE!
SEE YA!
IT'S LIKE...
...HE'S JUST PLAYING A GAME.
THIS ISN'T A CONSUMING OBSESSION WITH HIM, LIKE IT WAS WITH MR. TAKAOKA.
IT'S STRANGE... WE WERE TALKING TO HIM JUST A MINUTE AGO...
...BUT I CAN'T VISUALIZE ...
...THE GRIM REAPER'S FACE.

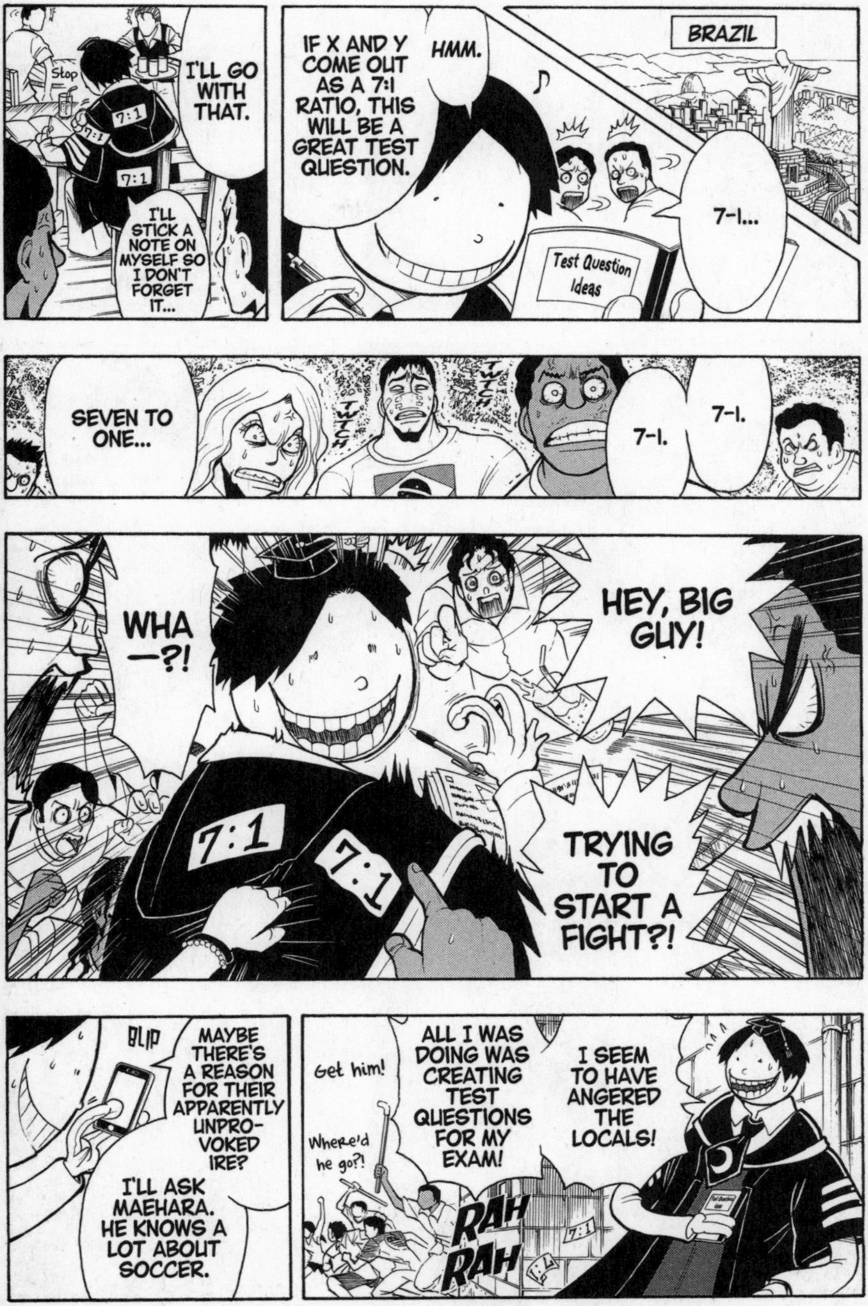
BRAZIL
7-1...
HMM.
IF X AND Y COME OUT AS A 7:1 RATIO, THIS WILL BE A GREAT TEST QUESTION.
Test Question Ideas
I'LL GO WITH THAT.
Stop
7:1
I'LL STICK A NOTE ON MYSELF SO I DON'T FORGET IT...
7-1.
7-1.
TWITCH
TWITCH
SEVEN TO ONE...
HEY, BIG GUY!
TRYING TO START A FIGHT?!
WHA—?!
7:1
7:1
I SEEM TO HAVE ANGERED THE LOCALS!
ALL I WAS DOING WAS CREATING TEST QUESTIONS FOR MY EXAM!
Get him!
Where'd he go?!
RAH RAH
BLIP
MAYBE THERE'S A REASON FOR THEIR APPARENTLY UNPRO-VOKED IRE?
I'LL ASK MAEHARA. HE KNOWS A LOT ABOUT SOCCER.

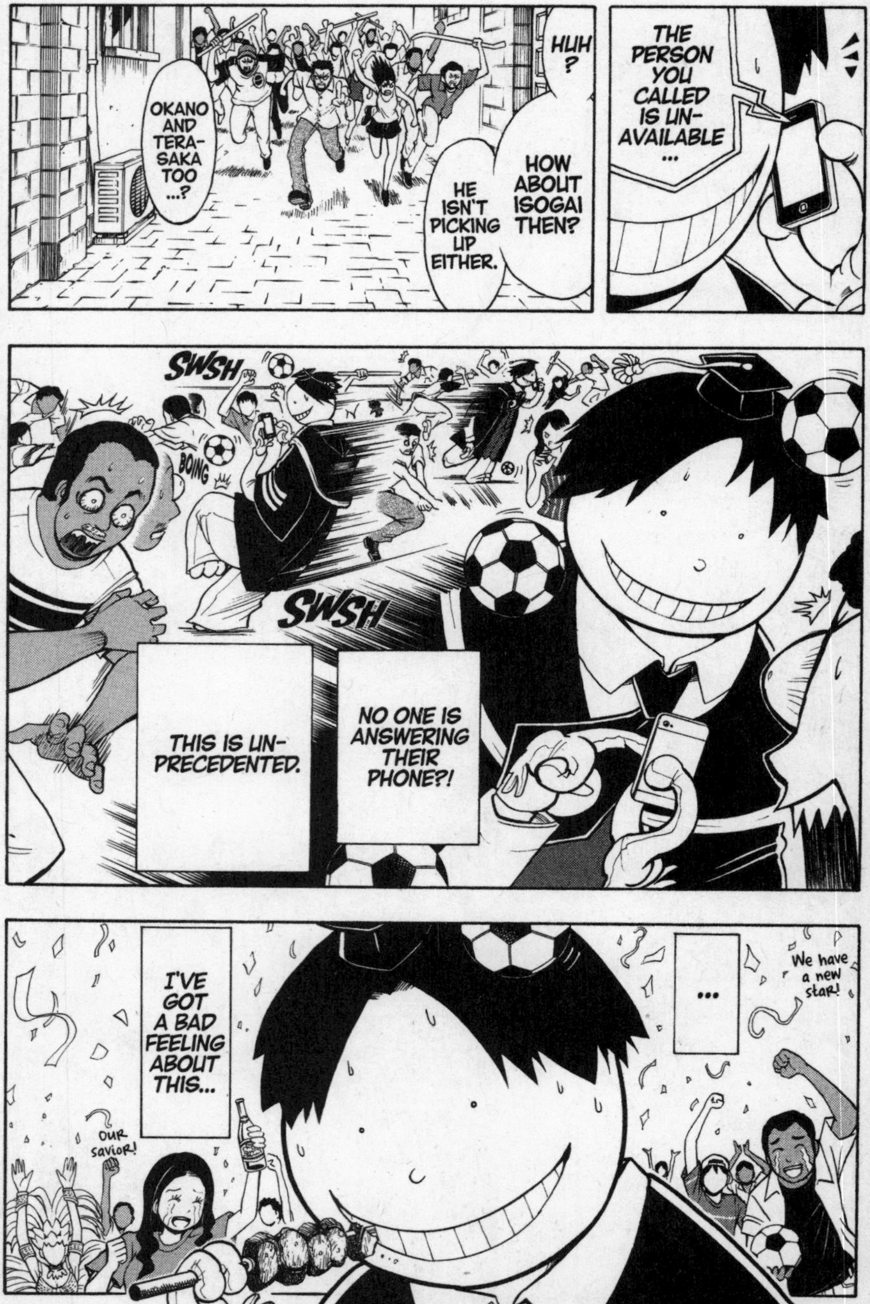
THE PERSON YOU CALLED IS UN-AVAILABLE ...
HUH?
HOW ABOUT ISOGAI THEN?
HE ISN'T PICKING UP EITHER.
OKANO AND TERA-SAKA TOO ...?
SWSH
BOING
SWSH
NO ONE IS ANSWERING THEIR PHONE?!
THIS IS UN-PRECEDENTED.
We have a new star!
...
I'VE GOT A BAD FEELING ABOUT THIS...
OUR savior!

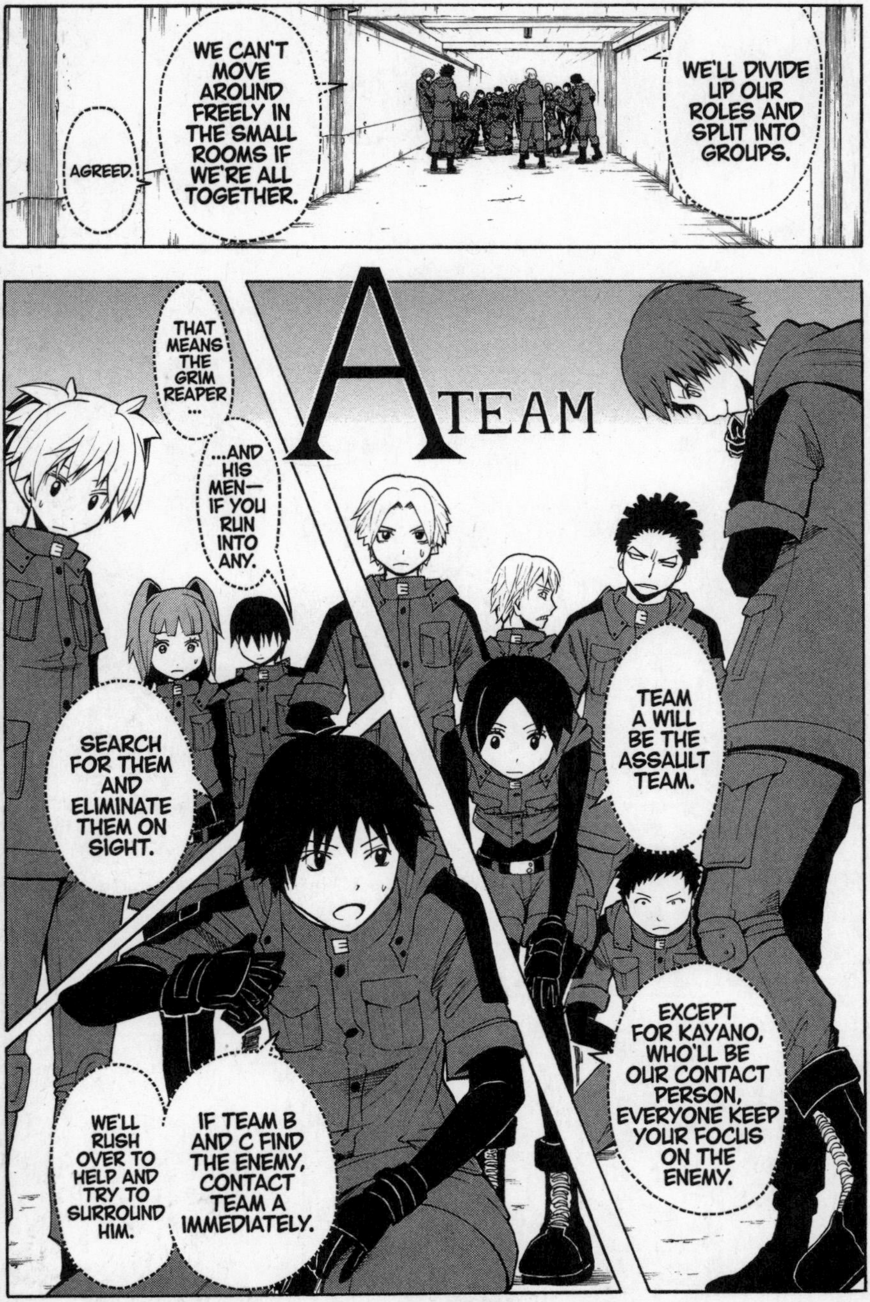
WE'LL DIVIDE UP OUR ROLES AND SPLIT INTO GROUPS.
WE CAN'T MOVE AROUND FREELY IN THE SMALL ROOMS IF WE'RE ALL TOGETHER.
AGREED.
A TEAM
TEAM A WILL BE THE ASSAULT TEAM.
EXCEPT FOR KAYANO, WHO'LL BE OUR CONTACT PERSON, EVERYONE KEEP YOUR FOCUS ON THE ENEMY.
THAT MEANS THE GRIM REAPER...
...AND HIS MEN—IF YOU RUN INTO ANY.
SEARCH FOR THEM AND ELIMINATE THEM ON SIGHT.
IF TEAM B AND C FIND THE ENEMY, CONTACT TEAM A IMMEDIATELY.
WE'LL RUSH OVER TO HELP AND TRY TO SURROUND HIM.

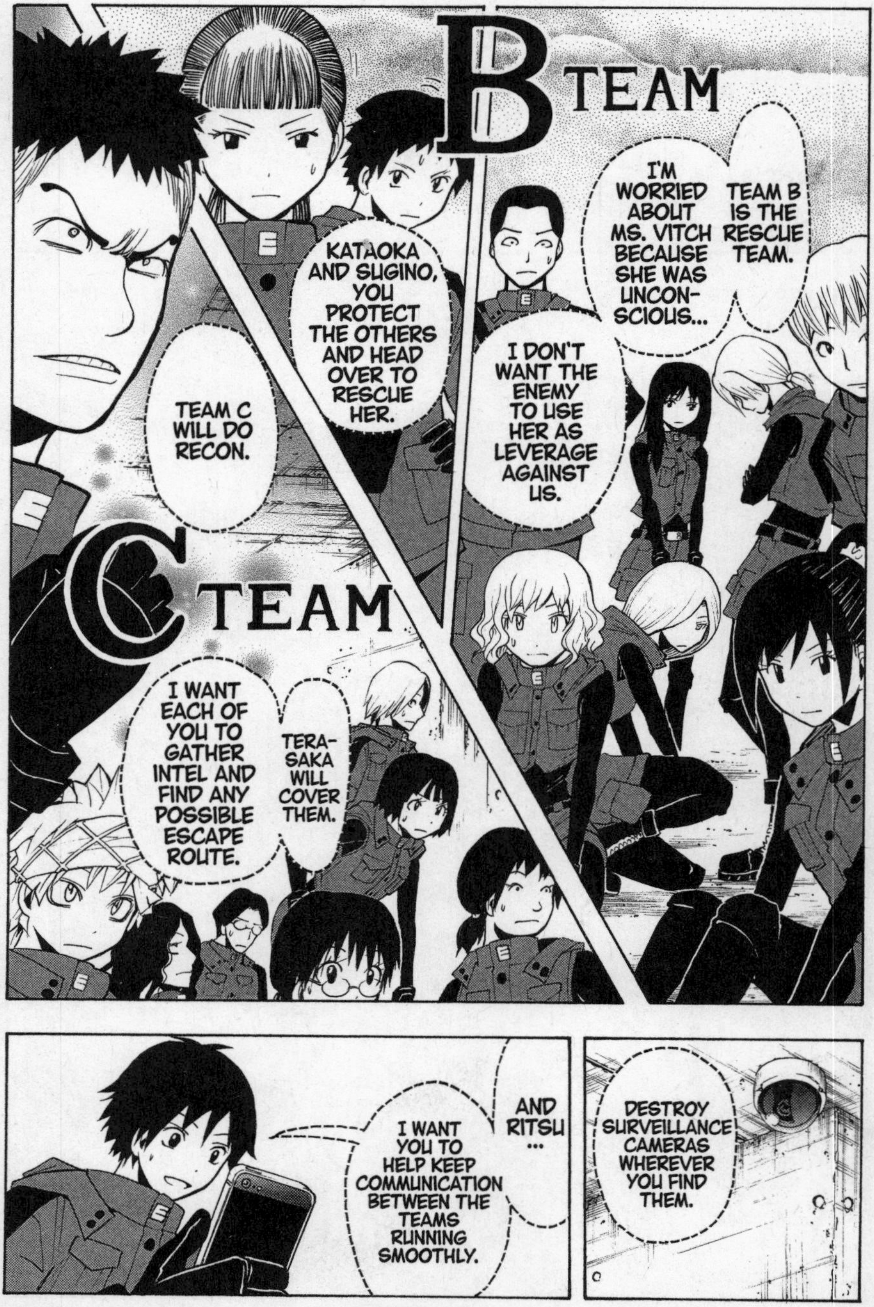
B TEAM
TEAM B IS THE RESCUE TEAM.
I'M WORRIED ABOUT MS. VITCH BECAUSE SHE WAS UNCONSCIOUS...
I DON'T WANT THE ENEMY TO USE HER AS LEVERAGE AGAINST US.
KATAOKA AND SUGINO, YOU PROTECT THE OTHERS AND HEAD OVER TO RESCUE HER.
TEAM C WILL DO RECON.
C TEAM
TERA-SAKA WILL COVER THEM.
I WANT EACH OF YOU TO GATHER INTEL AND FIND ANY POSSIBLE ESCAPE ROUTE.
DESTROY SURVEILLANCE CAMERAS WHEREVER YOU FIND THEM.
AND RITSU ...
I WANT YOU TO HELP KEEP COMMUNICATION BETWEEN THE TEAMS RUNNING SMOOTHLY.

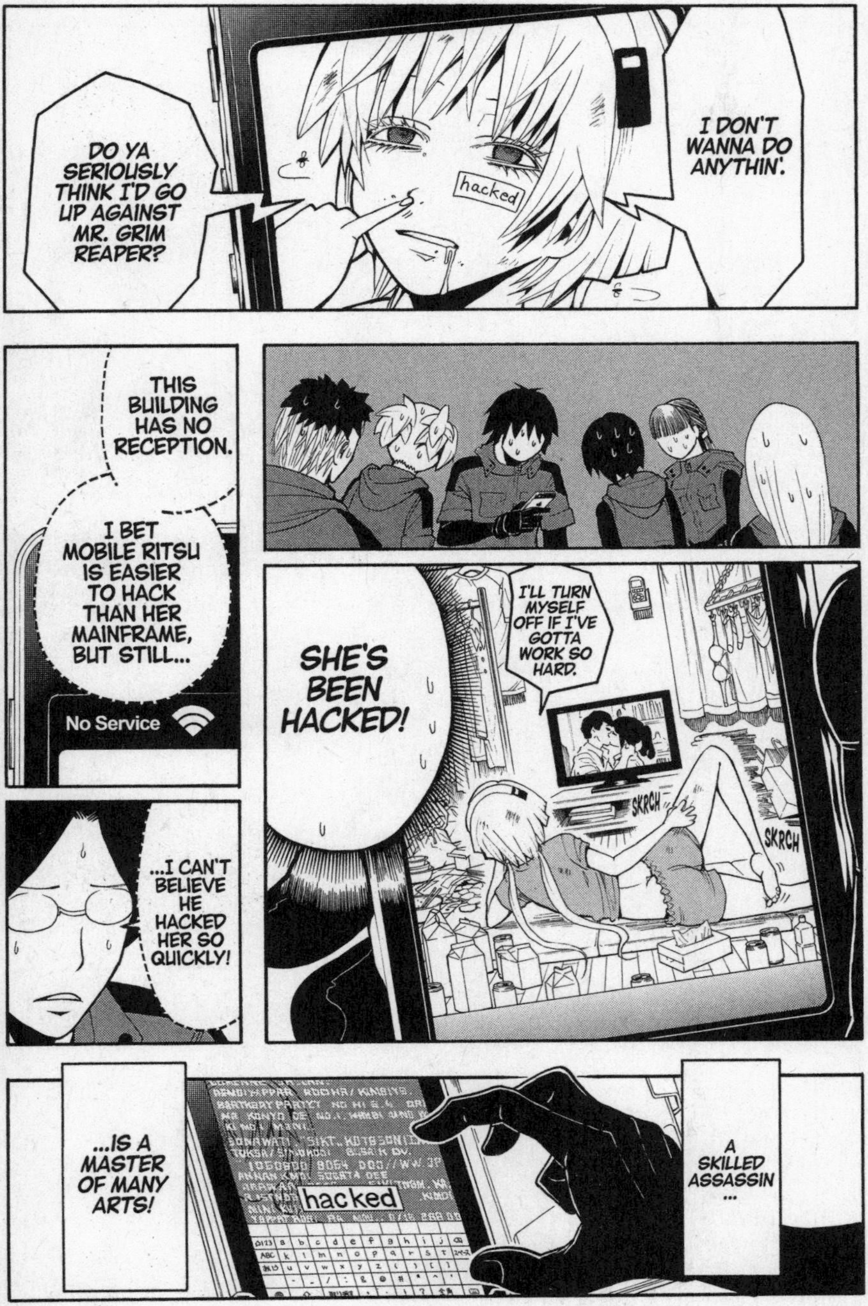
I DON'T WANNA DO ANYTHIN'.
hacked
DO YA SERIOUSLY THINK I'D GO UP AGAINST MR. GRIM REAPER?
THIS BUILDING HAS NO RECEPTION.
I BET MOBILE RITSU IS EASIER TO HACK THAN HER MAINFRAME, BUT STILL...
No Service
I'LL TURN MYSELF OFF IF I'VE GOTTA WORK SO HARD.
SKRCH
SKRCH
SHE'S BEEN HACKED!
...I CAN'T BELIEVE HE HACKED HER SO QUICKLY!
A SKILLED ASSASSIN ...
hacked
...IS A MASTER OF MANY ARTS!

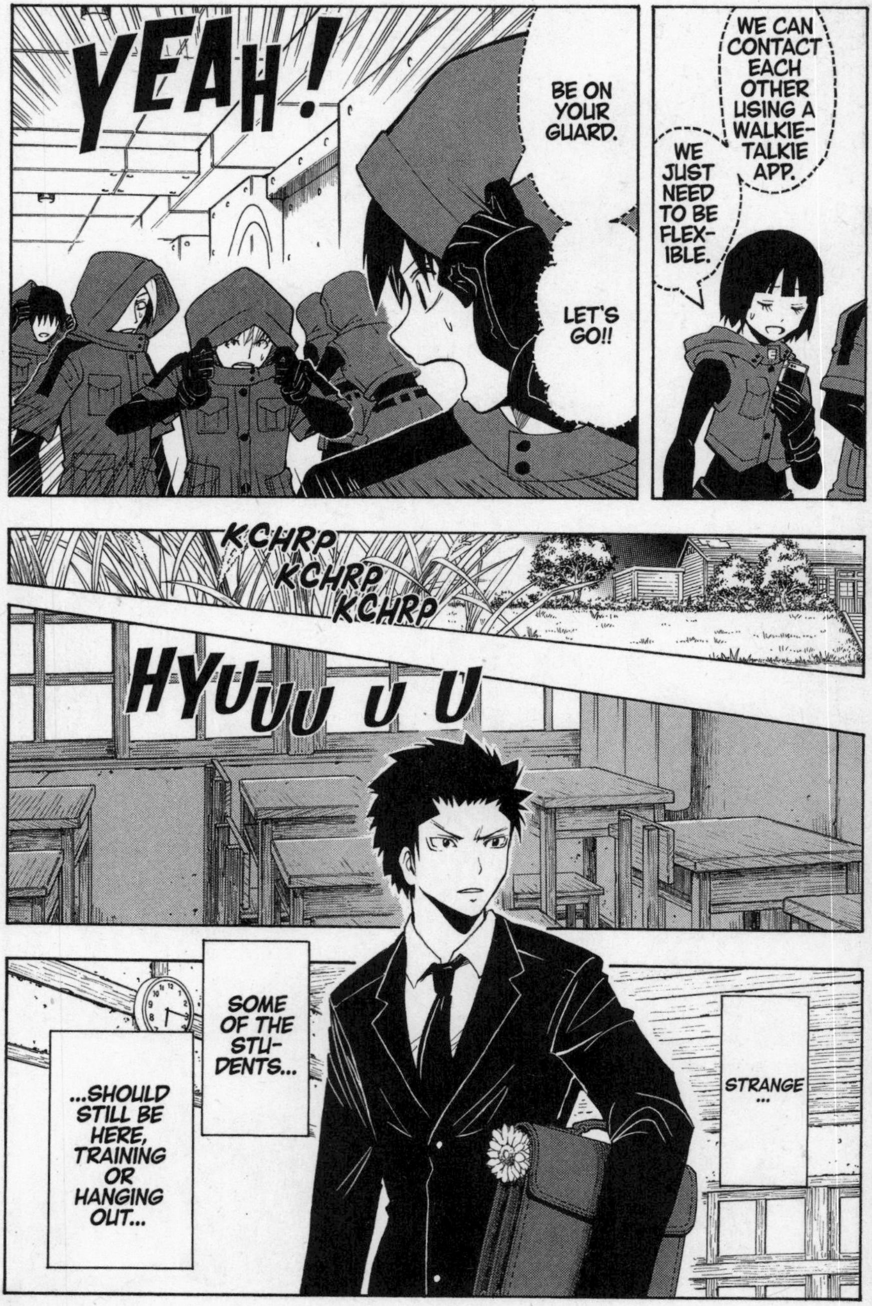
WE CAN CONTACT EACH OTHER USING A WALKIE-TALKIE APP.
WE JUST NEED TO BE FLEX-IBLE.
BE ON YOUR GUARD.
LET'S GO!!
YEAH!
KCHRP
KCHRP
KCHRP
HYUUUU U U
STRANGE...
SOME OF THE STU-DENTS...
...SHOULD STILL BE HERE, TRAINING OR HANGING OUT...

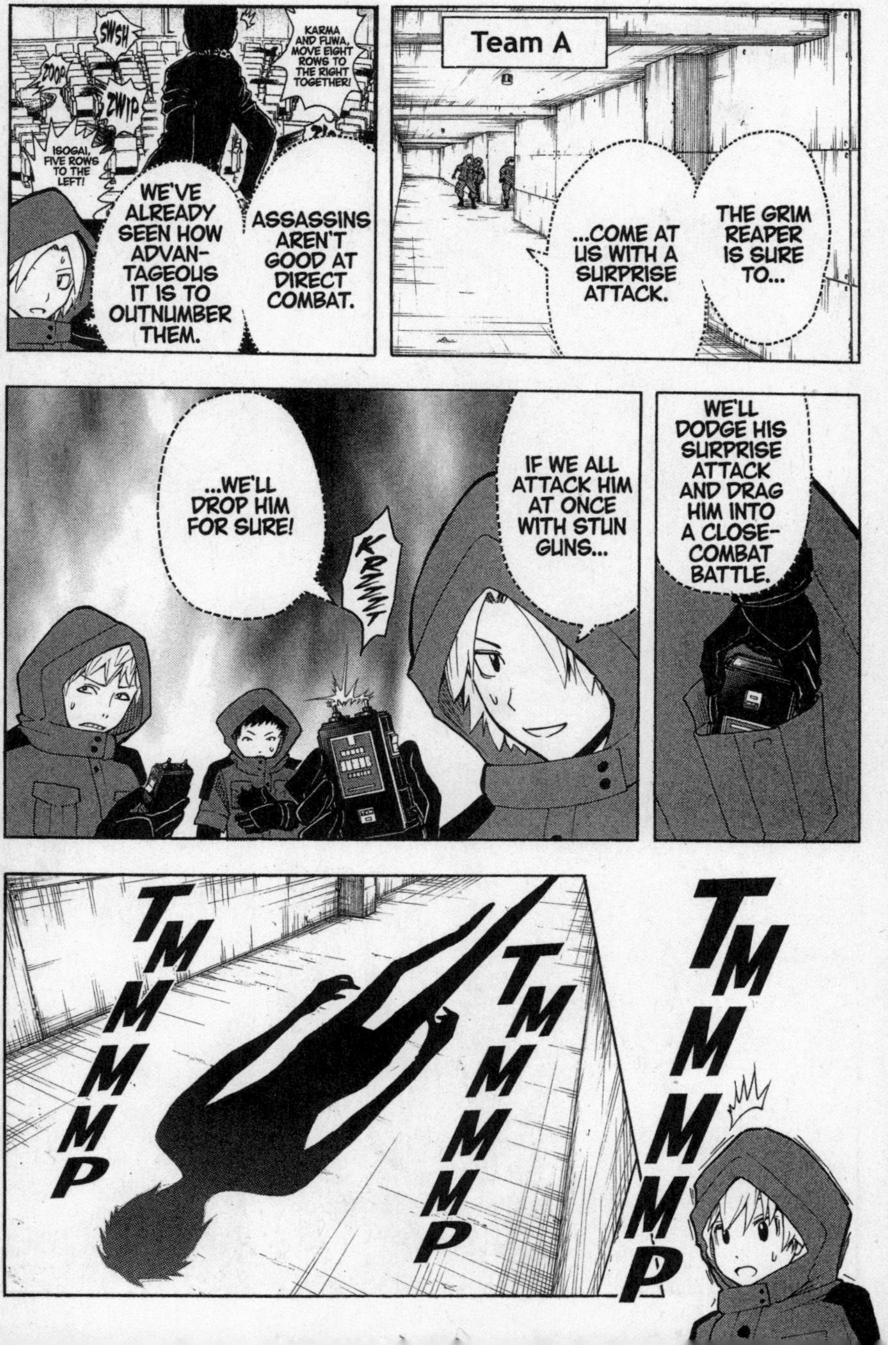
Team A
THE GRIM REAPER IS SURE TO...
...COME AT US WITH A SURPRISE ATTACK.
KARMA AND FUWA, MOVE EIGHT ROWS TO THE RIGHT TOGETHER!
SWSH
ZOOP
ZWIP
ISOGAI, FIVE ROWS TO THE LEFT!
ASSASSINS AREN'T GOOD AT DIRECT COMBAT.
WE'VE ALREADY SEEN HOW ADVAN-TAGEOUS IT IS TO OUTNUMBER THEM.
WE'LL DODGE HIS SURPRISE ATTACK AND DRAG HIM INTO A CLOSE-COMBAT BATTLE.
IF WE ALL ATTACK HIM AT ONCE WITH STUN GUNS...
KRZZZT
...WE'LL DROP HIM FOR SURE!
TMMMMP
TMMMMP
TMMMMP

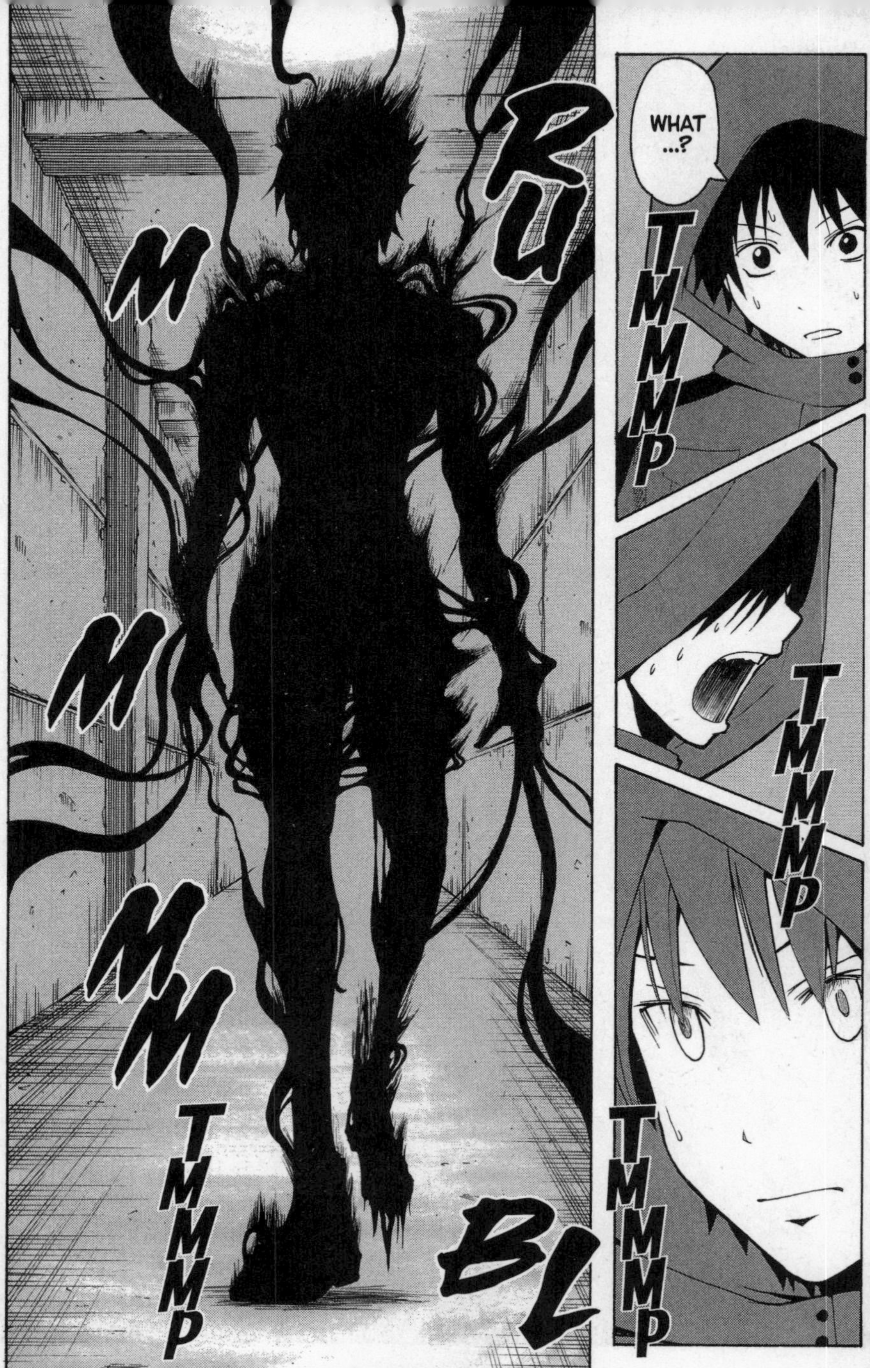
WHAT ...?
TMMMP
TMMMP
TMMMP
RU
M
M
MM
BL
TMMMP

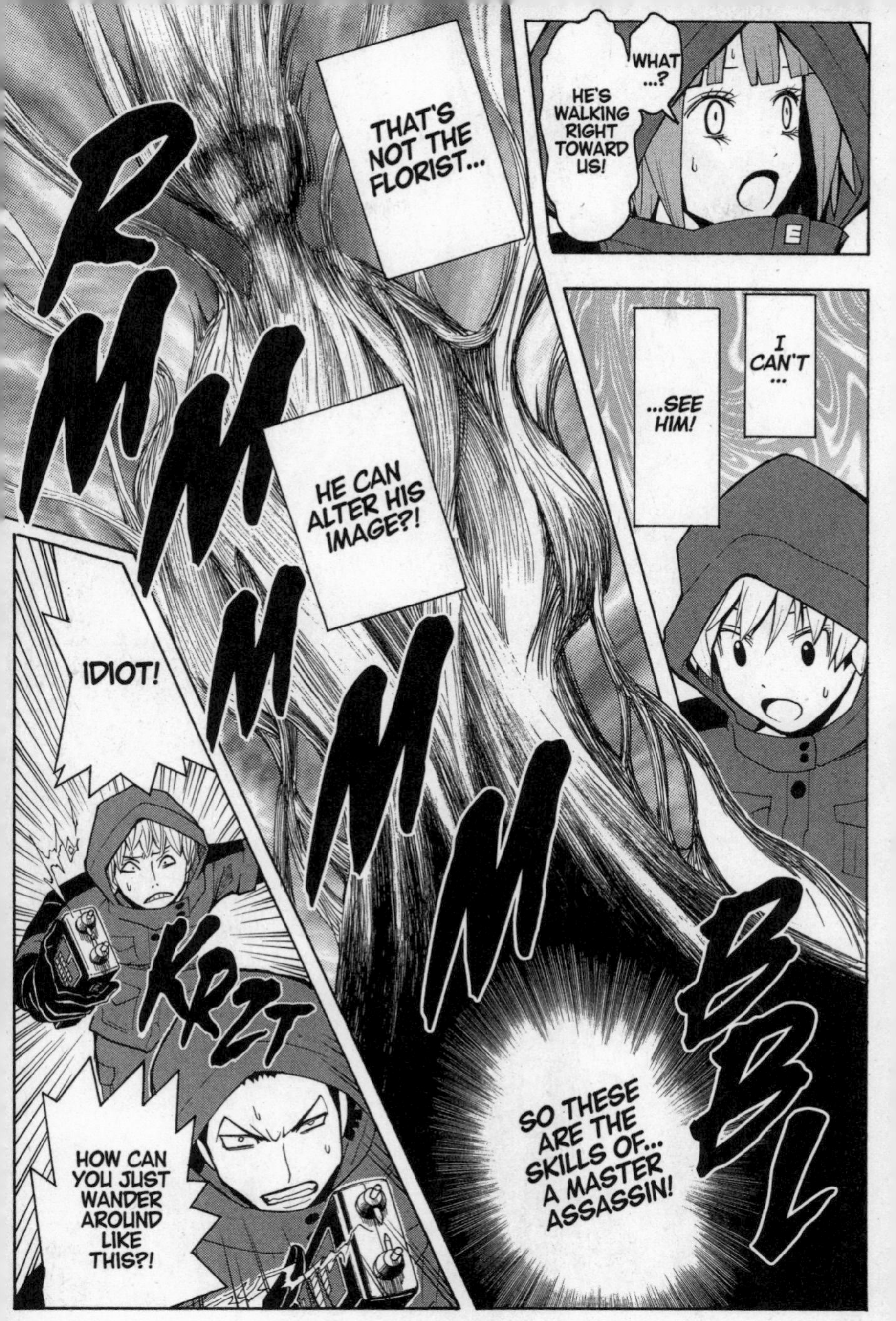

WHAT ...?
HE'S WALKING RIGHT TOWARD US!
THAT'S NOT THE FLORIST...
HE CAN ALTER HIS IMAGE?!
I CAN'T ...
...SEE HIM!
SO THESE ARE THE SKILLS OF... A MASTER ASSASSIN!
IDIOT!
KRZT
HOW CAN YOU JUST WANDER AROUND LIKE THIS?!

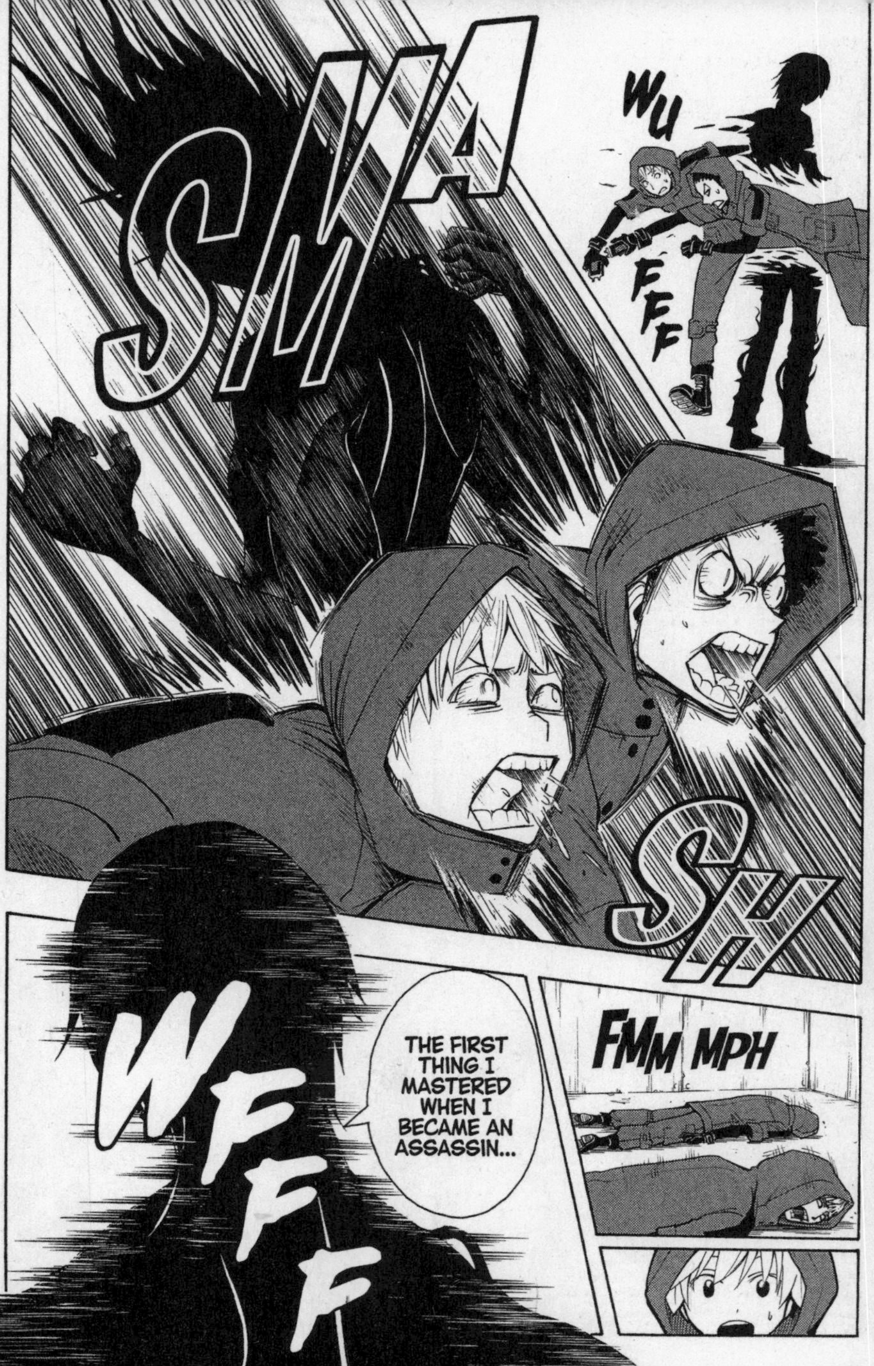
WU
FFF
SMA
SH
FMM MPH
THE FIRST THING I MASTERED WHEN I BECAME AN ASSASSIN...
WFFF

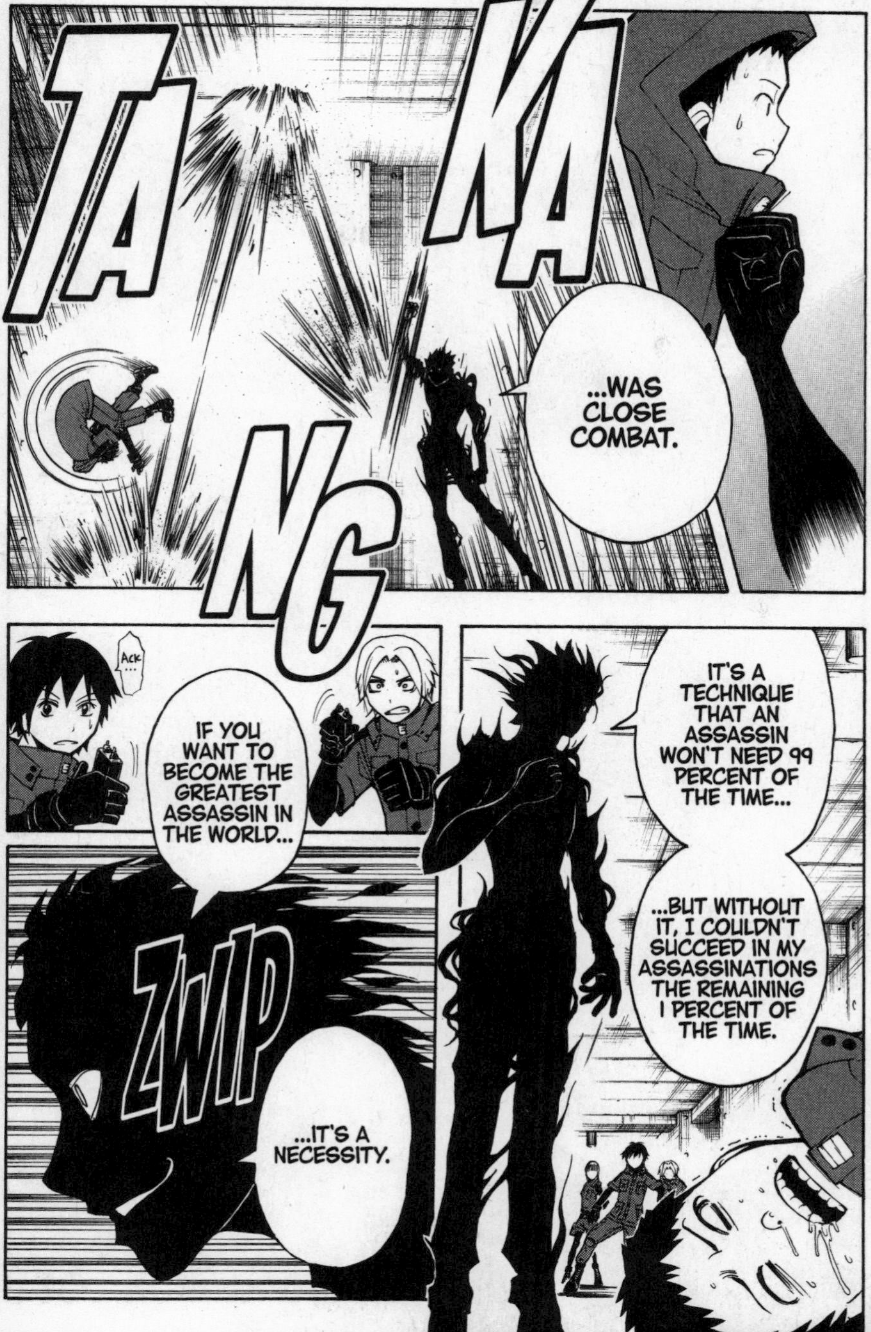
TAKANG
...WAS CLOSE COMBAT.
IT'S A TECHNIQUE THAT AN ASSASSIN WON'T NEED 99 PERCENT OF THE TIME...
...BUT WITHOUT IT, I COULDN'T SUCCEED IN MY ASSASSINATIONS THE REMAINING 1 PERCENT OF THE TIME.
IF YOU WANT TO BECOME THE GREATEST ASSASSIN IN THE WORLD...
ACK...
ZWIP
...IT'S A NECESSITY.

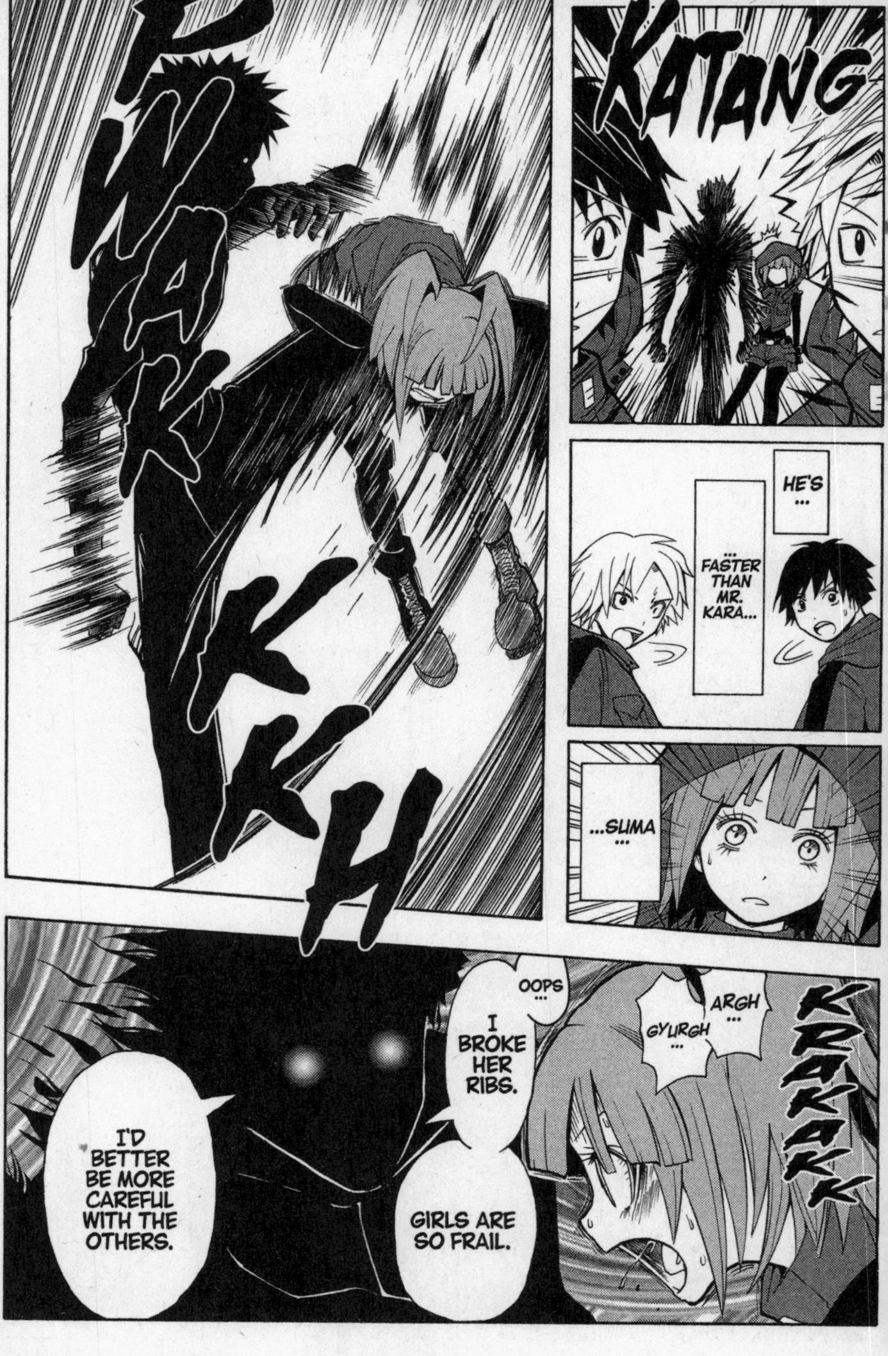
KATANG
HE'S...
...FASTER THAN MR. KARA...
...SUMA...
WAKKKH
KRAKAKK
ARGH...
GYURGH...
OOPS...
I BROKE HER RIBS.
GIRLS ARE SO FRAIL.
I'D BETTER BE MORE CAREFUL WITH THE OTHERS.

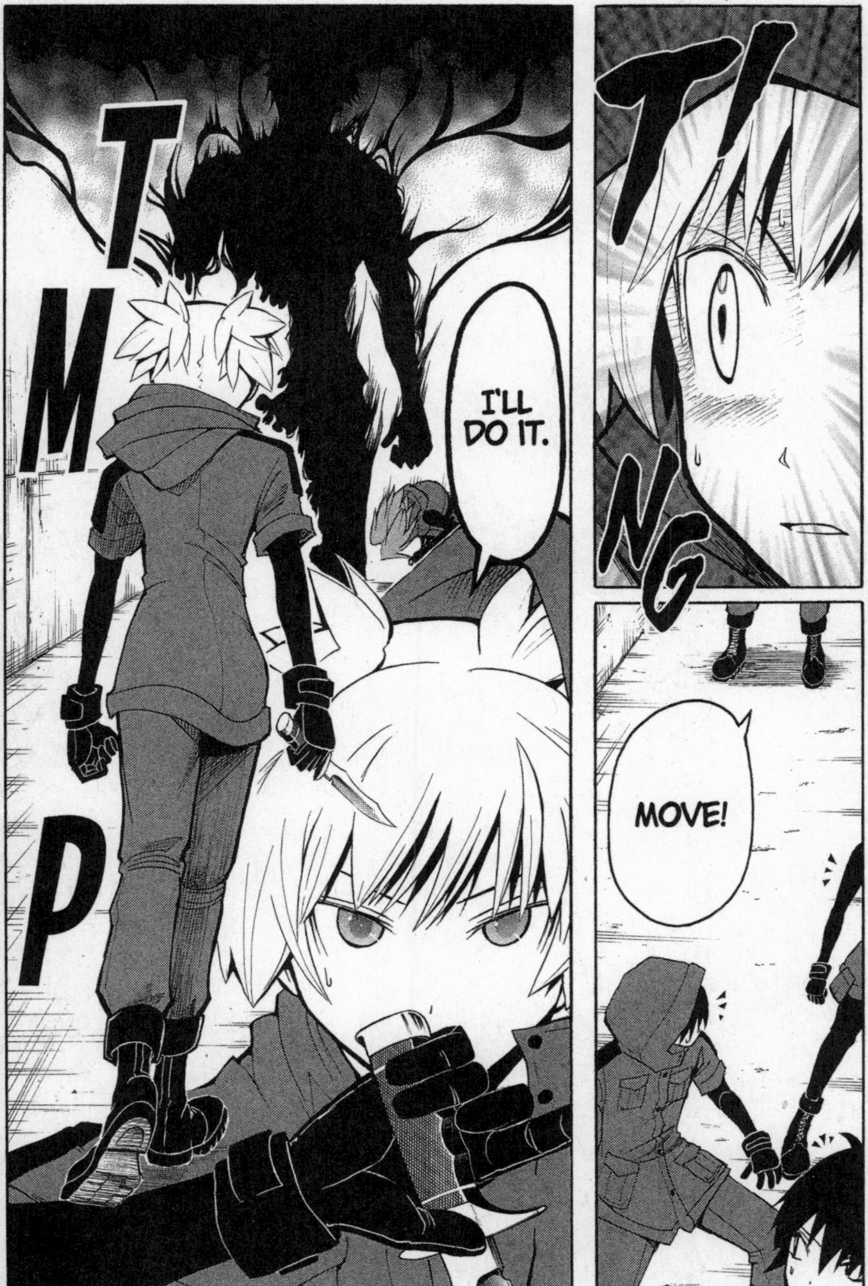
TING
MOVE!
TMP
I'LL DO IT.

Hacked-Ritsu's New Feature

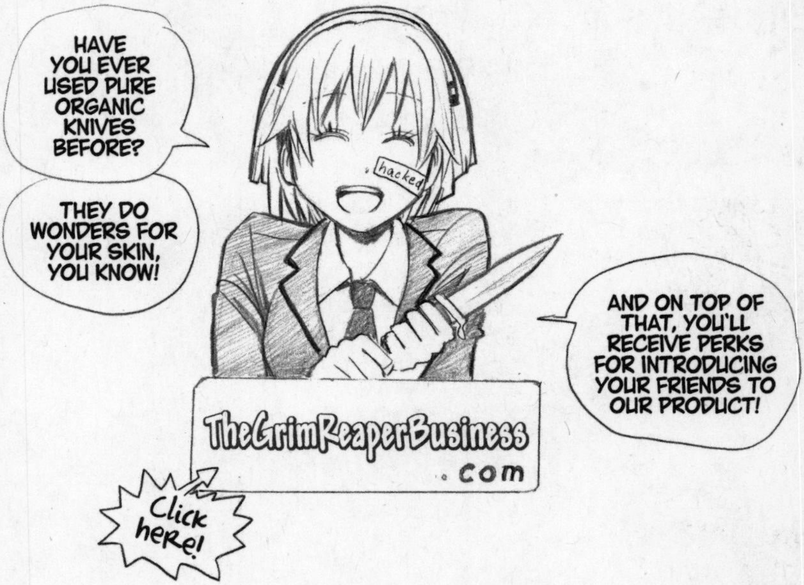
HAVE YOU EVER USED PURE ORGANIC KNIVES BEFORE?
THEY DO WONDERS FOR YOUR SKIN, YOU KNOW!
AND ON TOP OF THAT, YOU'LL RECEIVE PERKS FOR INTRODUCING YOUR FRIENDS TO OUR PRODUCT!
hacked
TheGrimReaperBusiness.com
Click here!

She's become an illegal spambot.

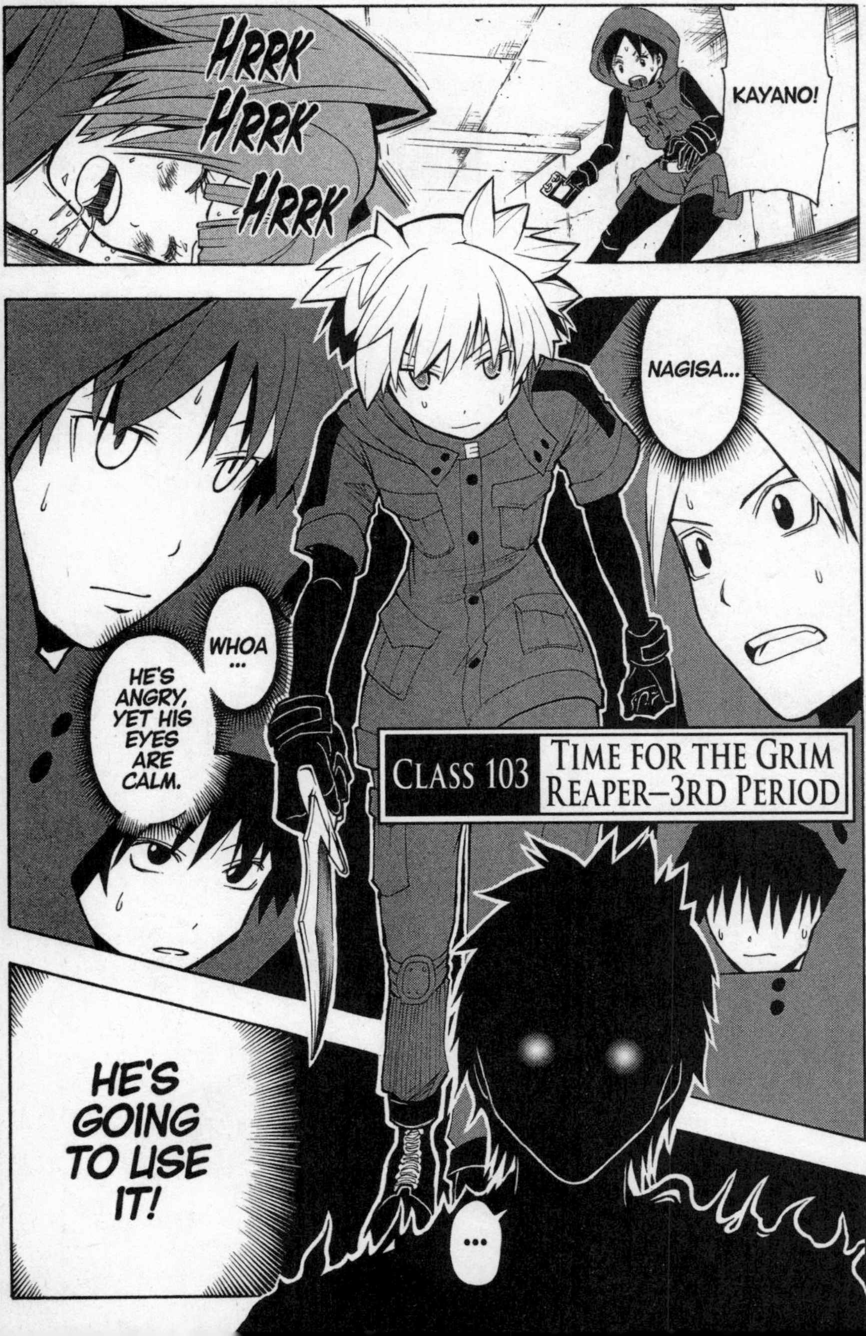
KAYANO!
HRRK HRRK HRRK
NAGISA...
CLASS 103 TIME FOR THE GRIM REAPER—3RD PERIOD
WHOA ...
HE'S ANGRY, YET HIS EYES ARE CALM.
HE'S GOING TO USE IT!
...

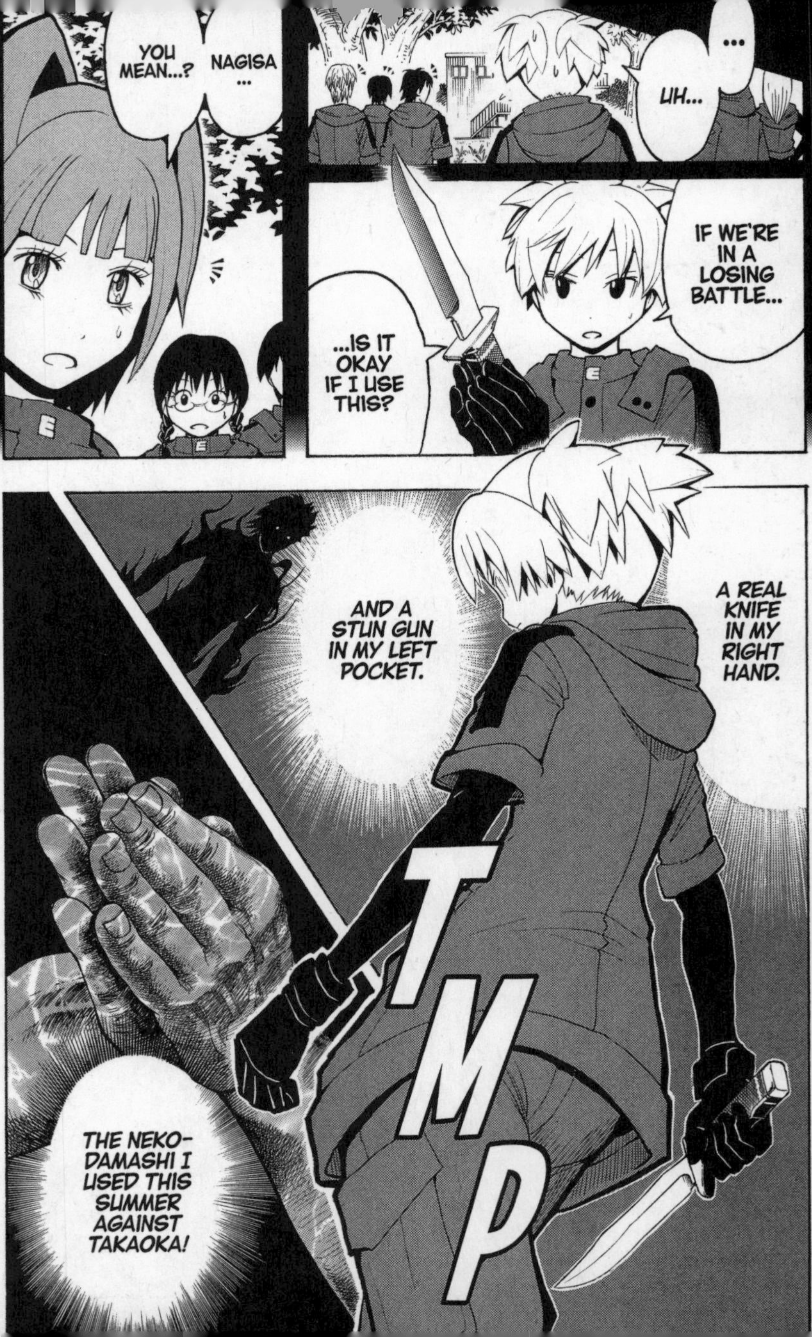
...
UH...
IF WE'RE IN A LOSING BATTLE...
...IS IT OKAY IF I USE THIS?
NAGISA...
YOU MEAN...?
A REAL KNIFE IN MY RIGHT HAND.
AND A STUN GUN IN MY LEFT POCKET.
TMP
THE NEKO-DAMASHI I USED THIS SUMMER AGAINST TAKAOKA!

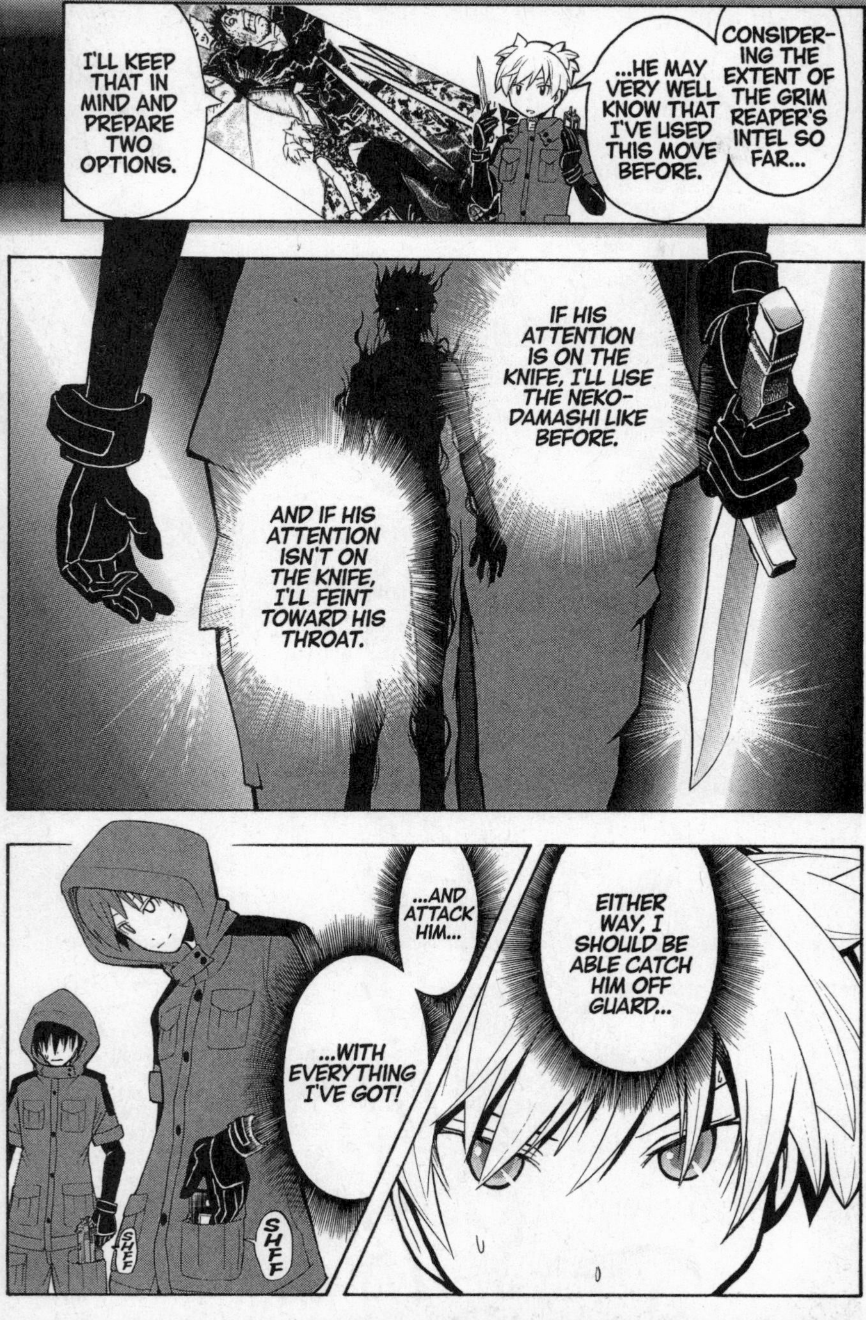
CONSIDERING THE EXTENT OF THE GRIM REAPER'S INTEL SO FAR...
...HE MAY VERY WELL KNOW THAT I'VE USED THIS MOVE BEFORE.
I'LL KEEP THAT IN MIND AND PREPARE TWO OPTIONS.
IF HIS ATTENTION IS ON THE KNIFE, I'LL USE THE NEKO-DAMASHI LIKE BEFORE.
AND IF HIS ATTENTION ISN'T ON THE KNIFE, I'LL FEINT TOWARD HIS THROAT.
EITHER WAY, I SHOULD BE ABLE CATCH HIM OFF GUARD...
...AND ATTACK HIM...
...WITH EVERYTHING I'VE GOT!
SHFF
SHFF

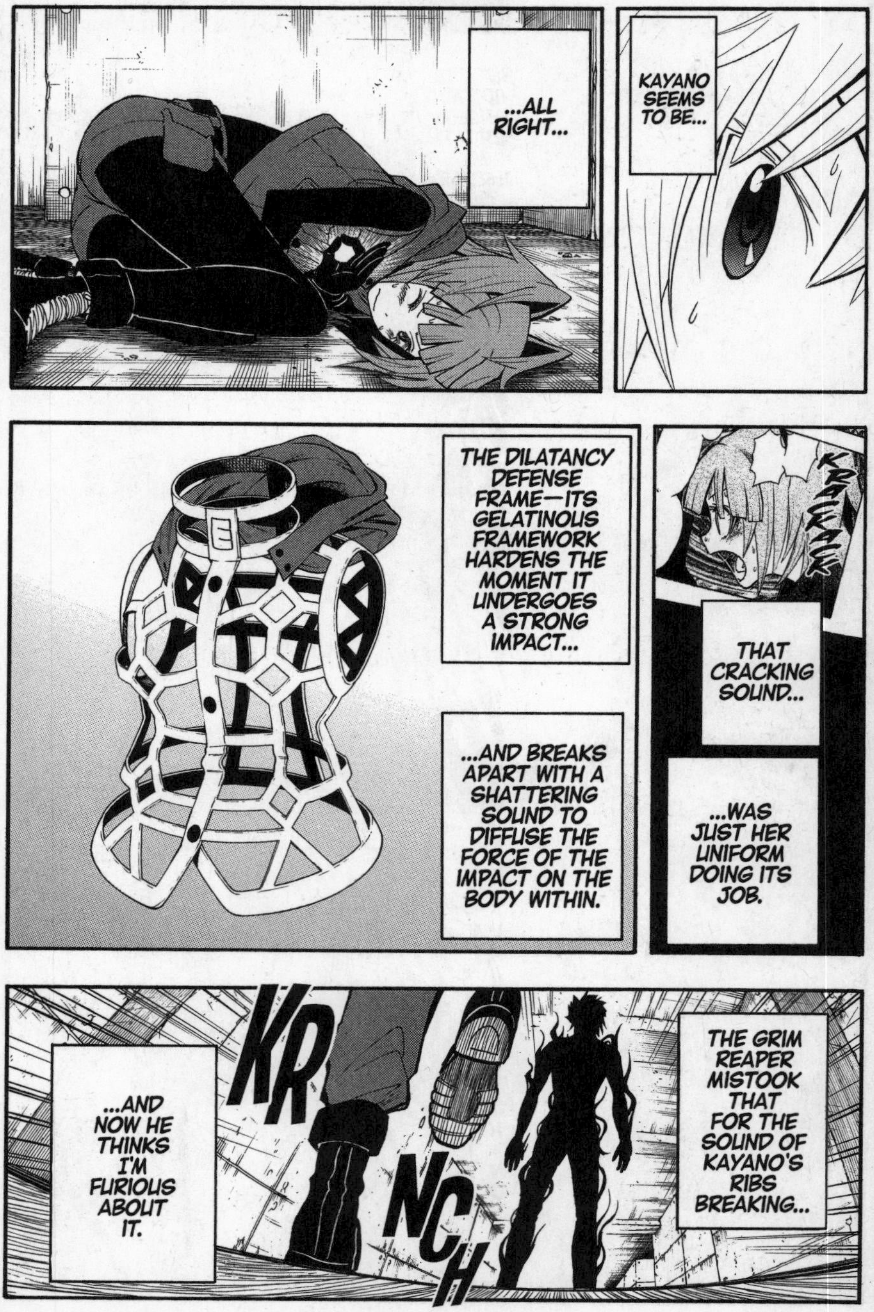
KAYANO SEEMS TO BE...
...ALL RIGHT...
KRACKACK
THAT CRACKING SOUND...
...WAS JUST HER UNIFORM DOING ITS JOB.
THE DILATANCY DEFENSE FRAME—ITS GELATINOUS FRAMEWORK HARDENS THE MOMENT IT UNDERGOES A STRONG IMPACT...
...AND BREAKS APART WITH A SHATTERING SOUND TO DIFFUSE THE FORCE OF THE IMPACT ON THE BODY WITHIN.
THE GRIM REAPER MISTOOK THAT FOR THE SOUND OF KAYANO'S RIBS BREAKING...
KRNCH
...AND NOW HE THINKS I'M FURIOUS ABOUT IT.

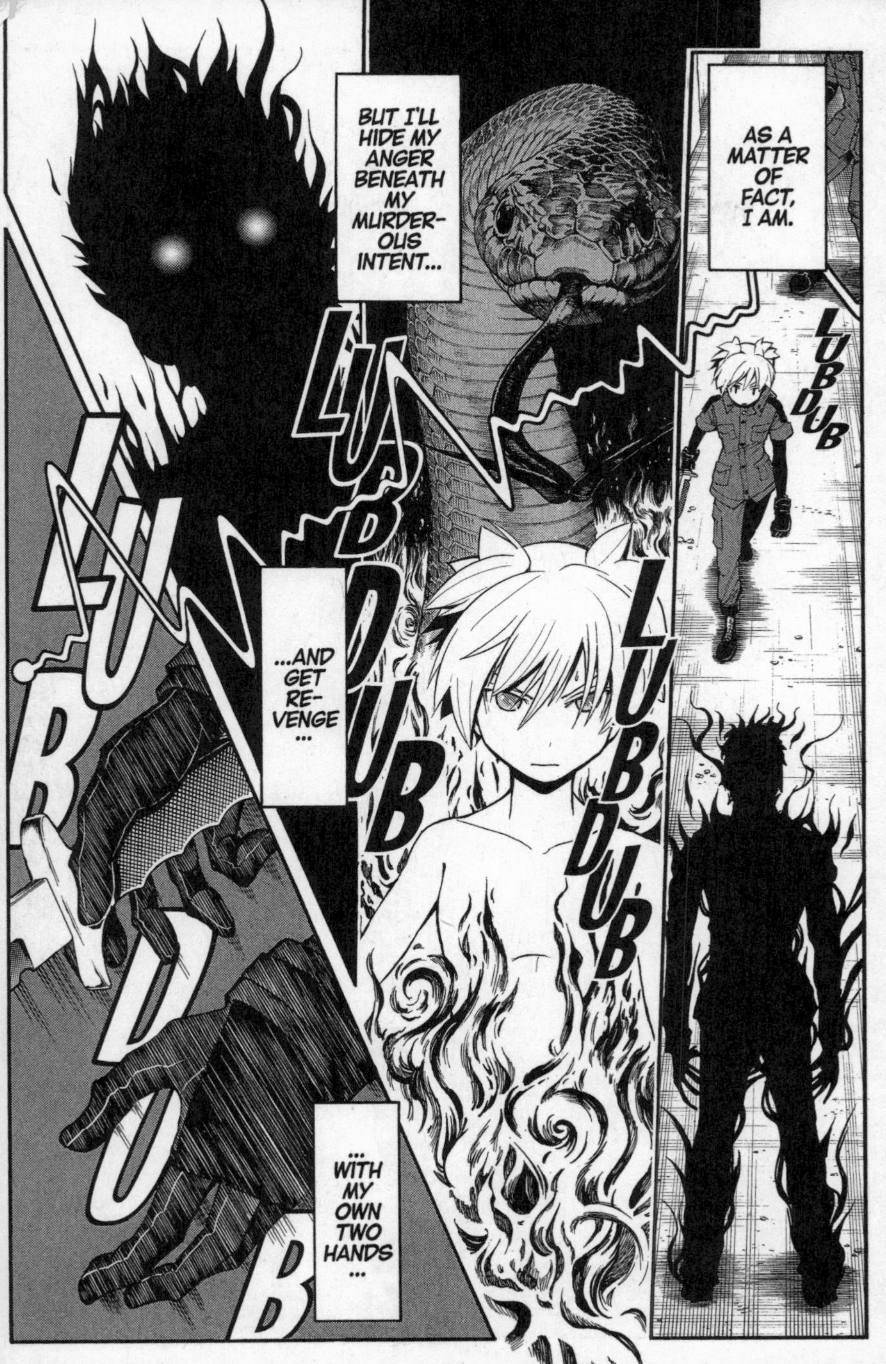
AS A MATTER OF FACT, I AM.
LUB DUB
LUB DUB
BUT I'LL HIDE MY ANGER BENEATH MY MURDEROUS INTENT...
LUB DUB
...AND GET REVENGE...
LUB DUB
...WITH MY OWN TWO HANDS...

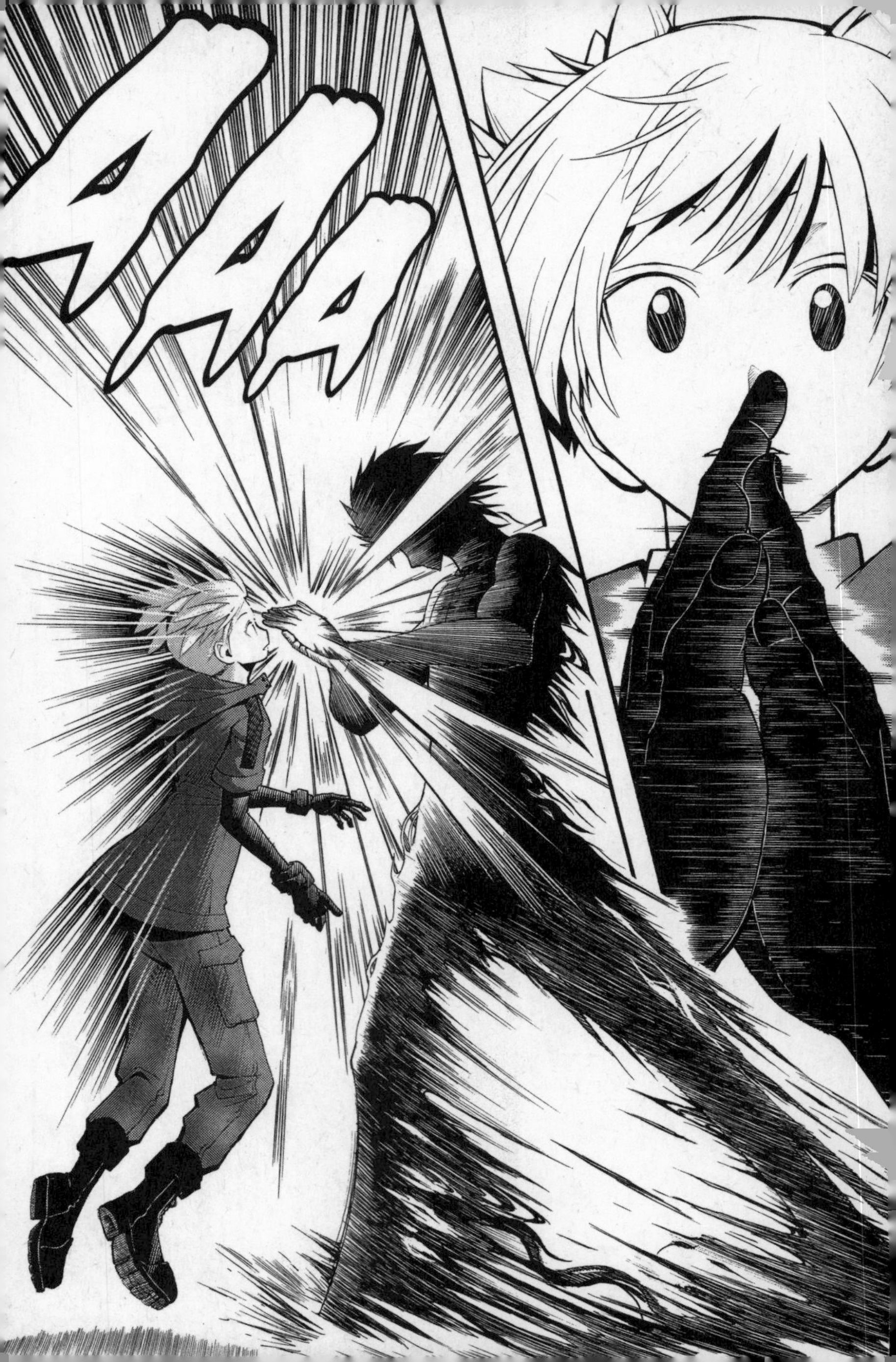

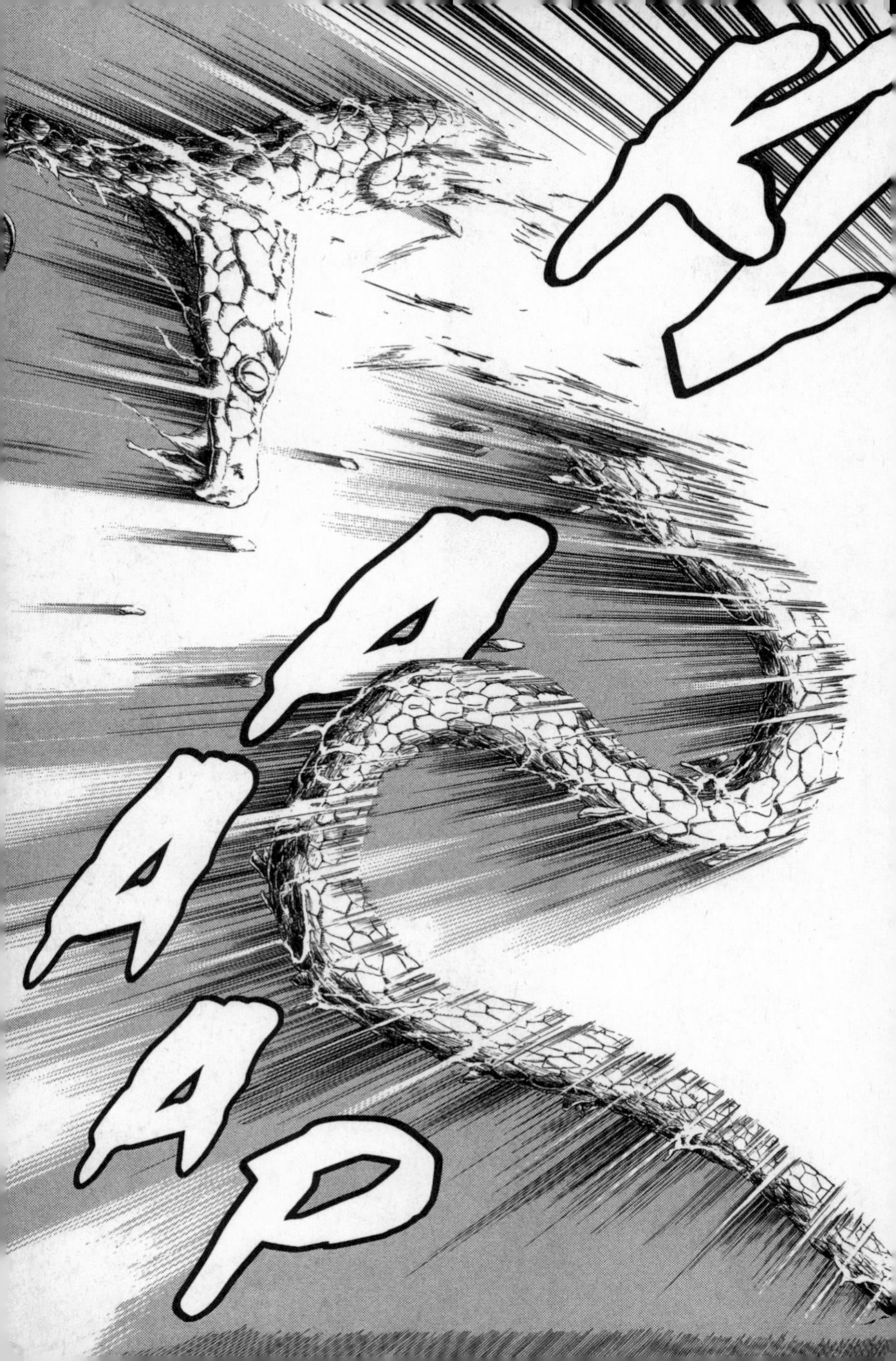
AAAP

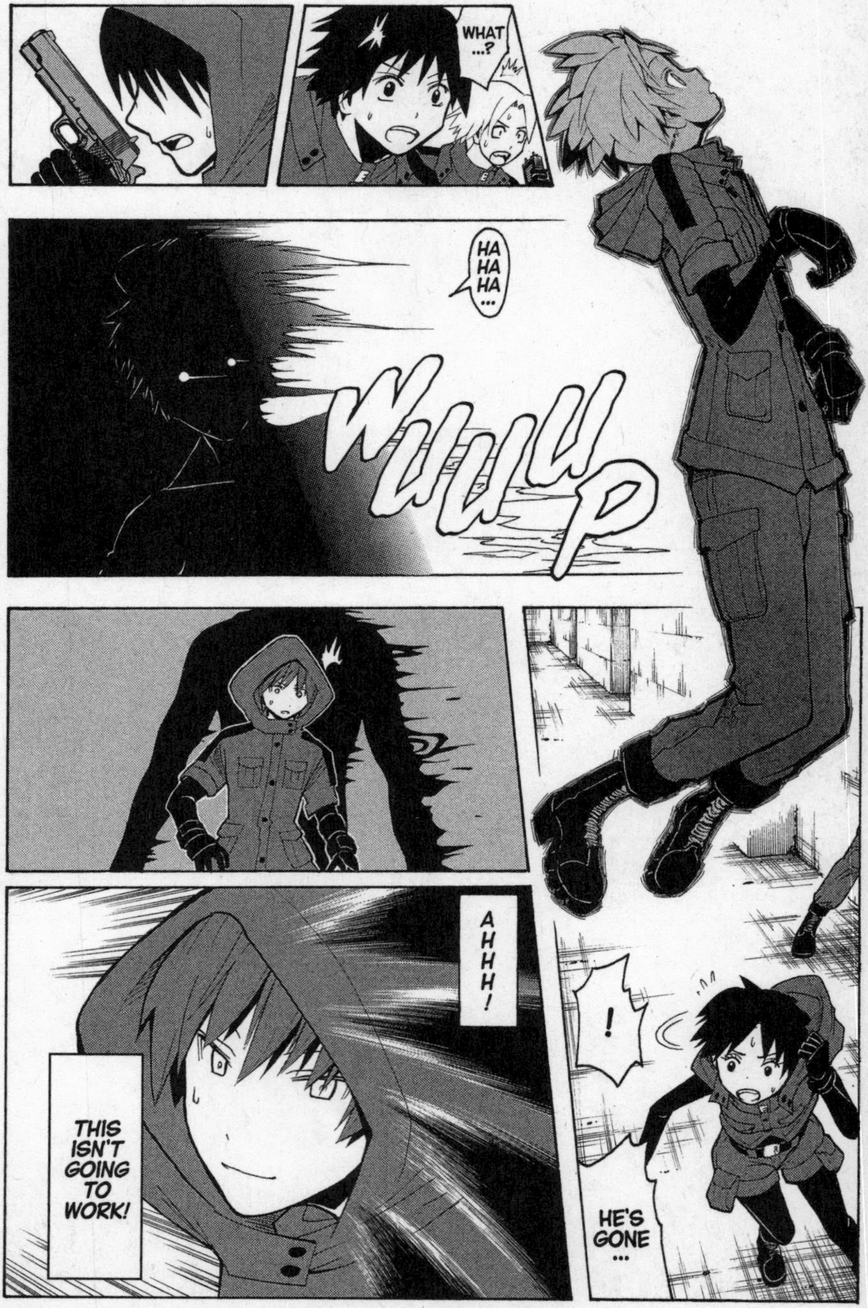
WHAT ...?
HA HA HA ...
WUUUP
!
HE'S GONE ...
AHHHH!
THIS ISN'T GOING TO WORK!

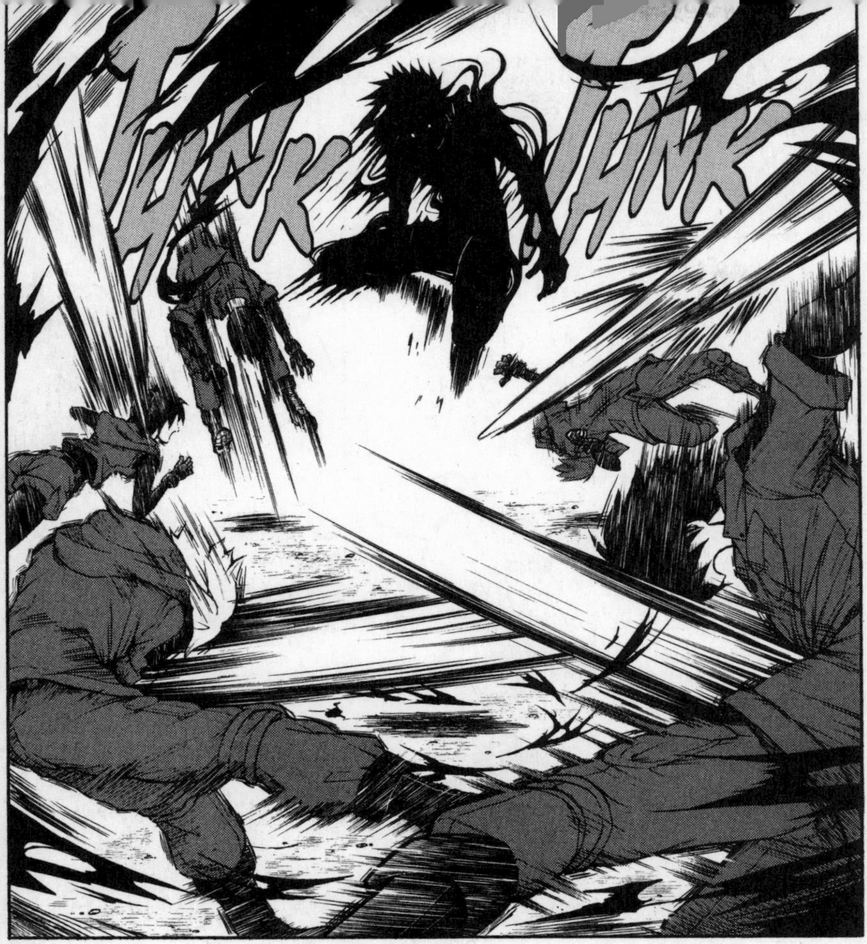

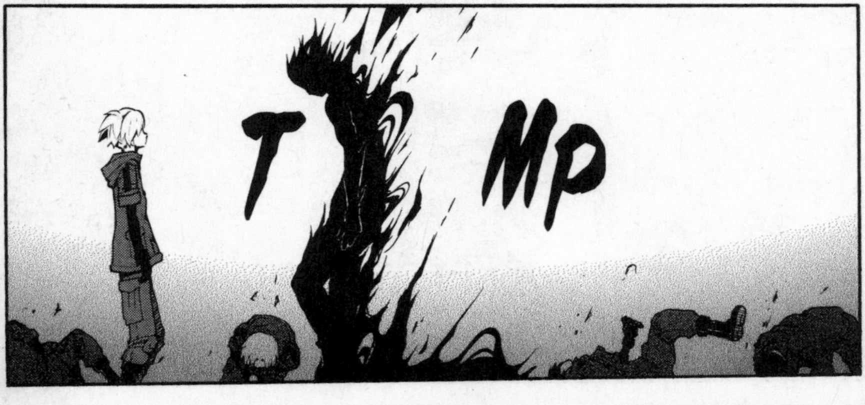
T
MP

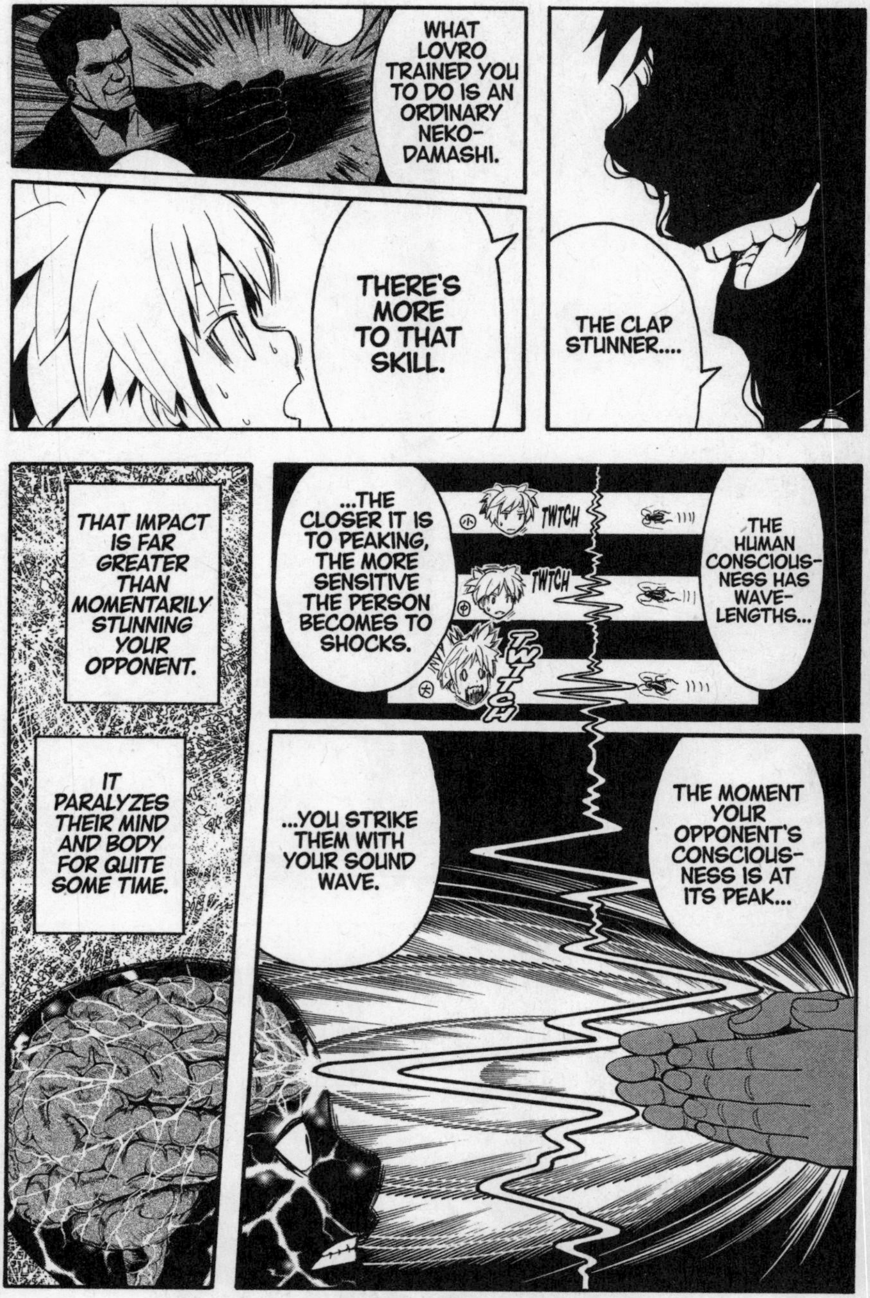
THE CLAP STUNNER....
WHAT LOVRO TRAINED YOU TO DO IS AN ORDINARY NEKO-DAMASHI.
THERE'S MORE TO THAT SKILL.
THE HUMAN CONSCIOUSNESS HAS WAVELENGTHS...
TWTCH
小
TWTCH
中
TWITCH
大
...THE CLOSER IT IS TO PEAKING, THE MORE SENSITIVE THE PERSON BECOMES TO SHOCKS.
THE MOMENT YOUR OPPONENT'S CONSCIOUSNESS IS AT ITS PEAK...
...YOU STRIKE THEM WITH YOUR SOUND WAVE.
THAT IMPACT IS FAR GREATER THAN MOMENTARILY STUNNING YOUR OPPONENT.
IT PARALYZES THEIR MIND AND BODY FOR QUITE SOME TIME.

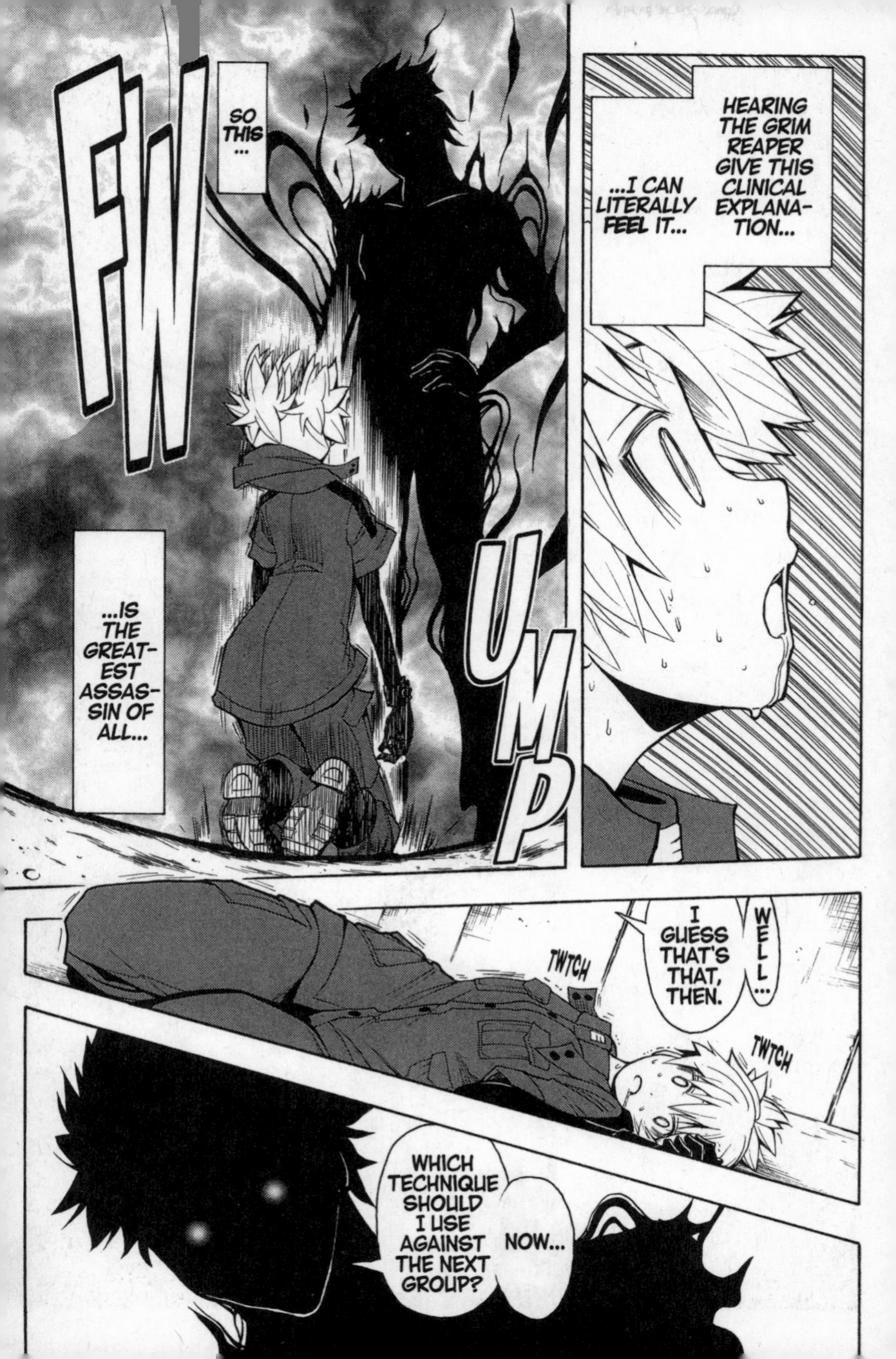
HEARING THE GRIM REAPER GIVE THIS CLINICAL EXPLANATION...
...I CAN LITERALLY FEEL IT...
SO THIS...
FW
UMP
...IS THE GREATEST ASSASSIN OF ALL...
WELL...
I GUESS THAT'S THAT, THEN.
TWTCH
TWTCH
NOW...
WHICH TECHNIQUE SHOULD I USE AGAINST THE NEXT GROUP?

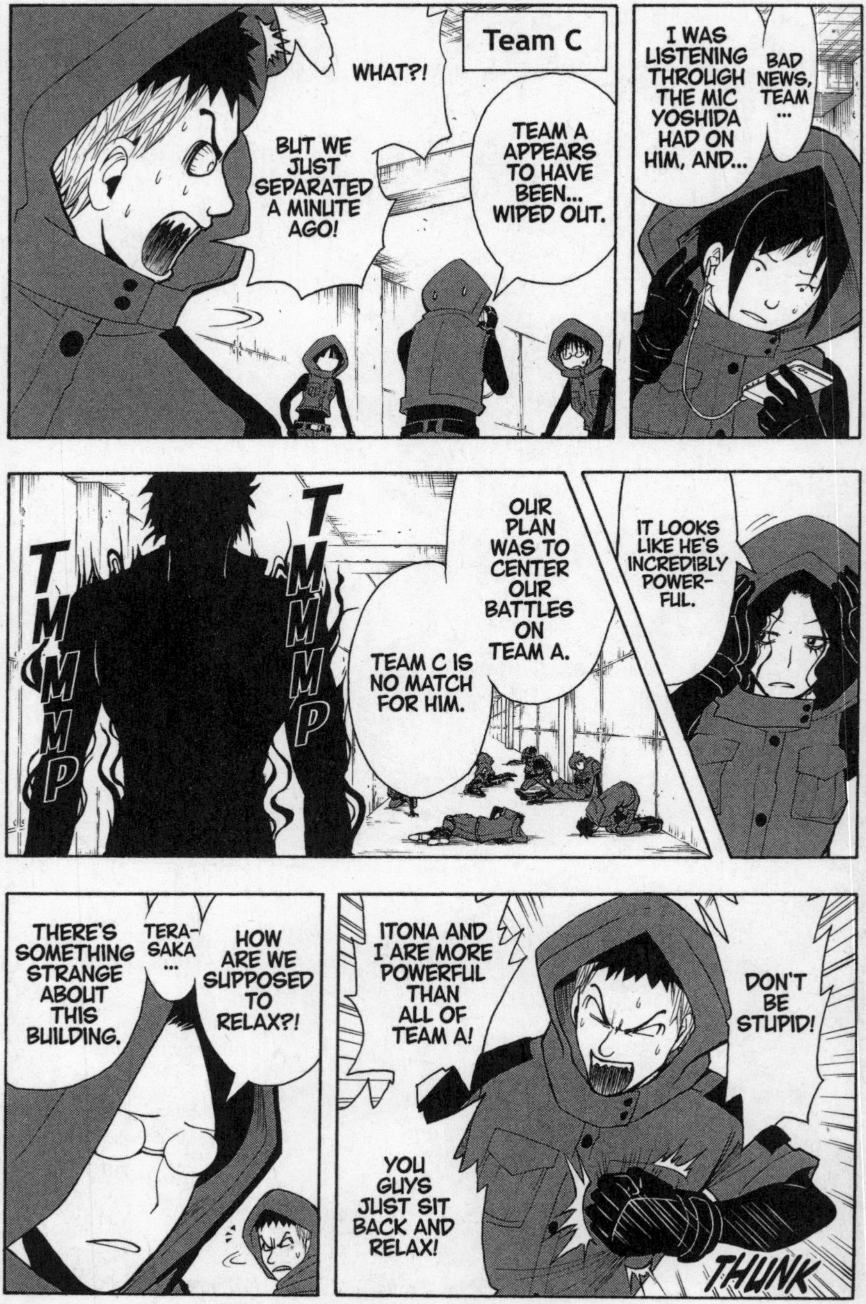
BAD NEWS, TEAM ...
I WAS LISTENING THROUGH THE MIC YOSHIDA HAD ON HIM, AND...
Team C
TEAM A APPEARS TO HAVE BEEN... WIPED OUT.
WHAT?!
BUT WE JUST SEPARATED A MINUTE AGO!
IT LOOKS LIKE HE'S INCREDIBLY POWER-FUL.
OUR PLAN WAS TO CENTER OUR BATTLES ON TEAM A.
TEAM C IS NO MATCH FOR HIM.
TMMMP
TMMMP
DON'T BE STUPID!
ITONA AND I ARE MORE POWERFUL THAN ALL OF TEAM A!
YOU GUYS JUST SIT BACK AND RELAX!
THUNK
HOW ARE WE SUPPOSED TO RELAX?!
TERA-SAKA ...
THERE'S SOMETHING STRANGE ABOUT THIS BUILDING.

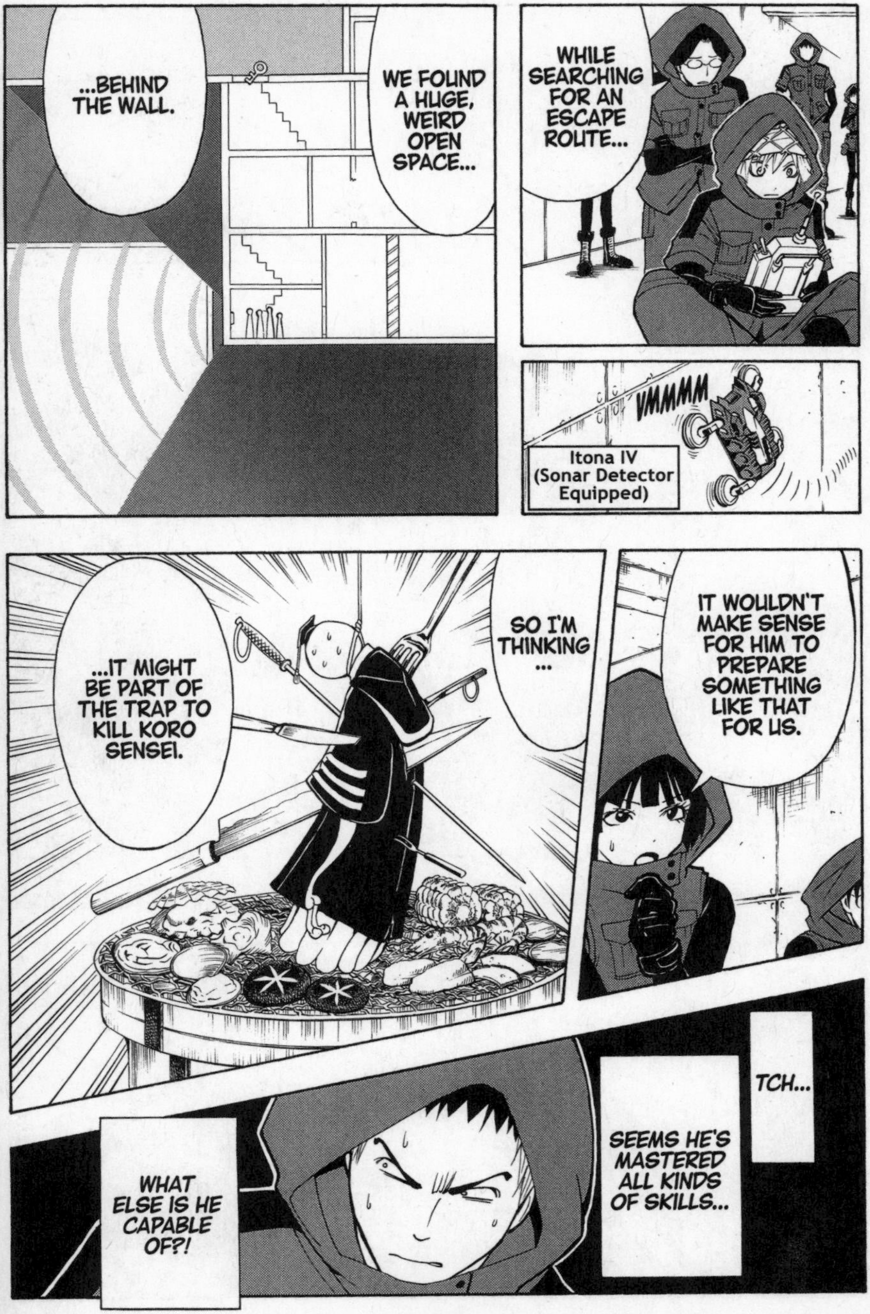
WHILE SEARCHING FOR AN ESCAPE ROUTE...
VMMMM
Itona IV (Sonar Detector Equipped)
WE FOUND A HUGE, WEIRD OPEN SPACE...
...BEHIND THE WALL.
IT WOULDN'T MAKE SENSE FOR HIM TO PREPARE SOMETHING LIKE THAT FOR US.
SO I'M THINKING ...
...IT MIGHT BE PART OF THE TRAP TO KILL KORO SENSEI.
TCH...
SEEMS HE'S MASTERED ALL KINDS OF SKILLS...
WHAT ELSE IS HE CAPABLE OF?!

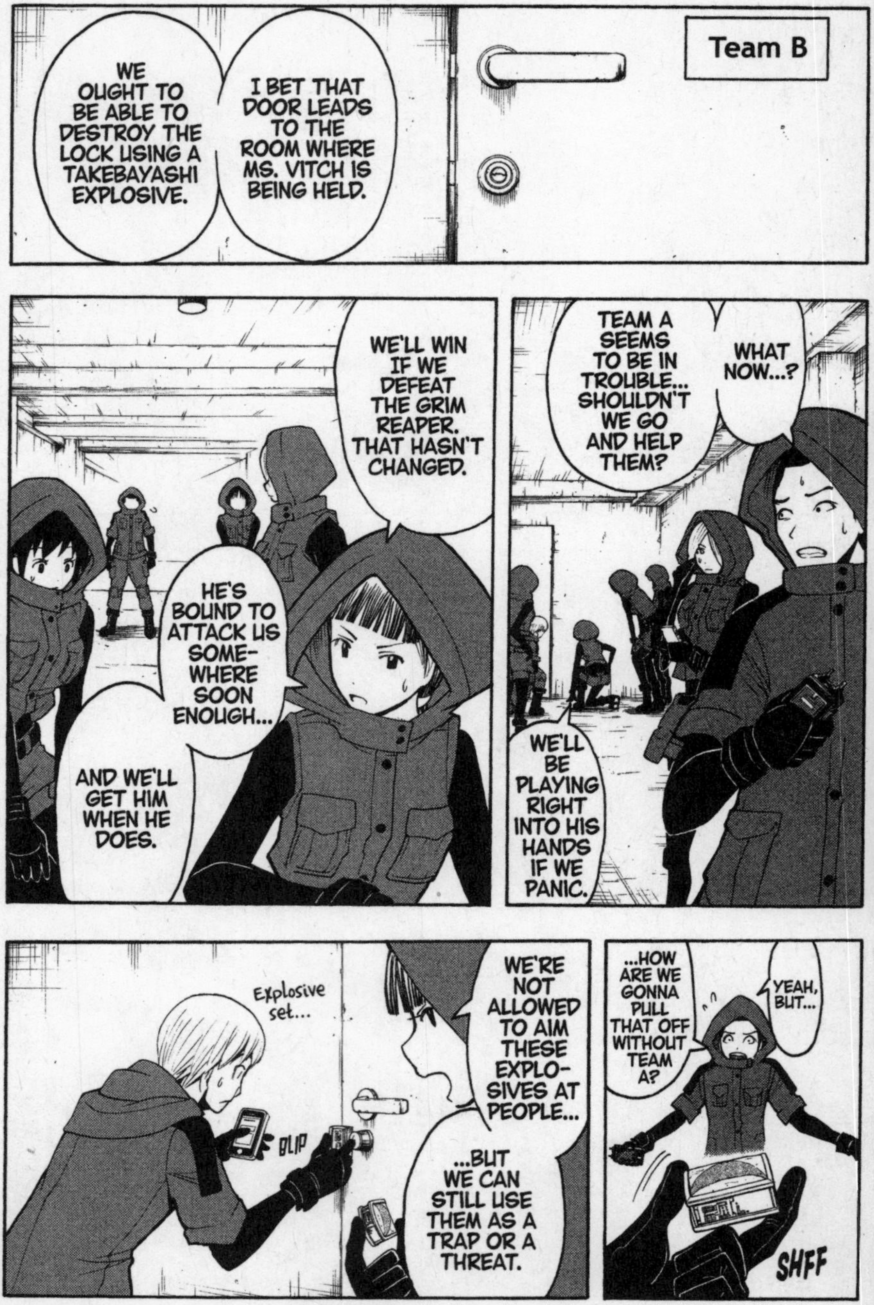
Team B
I BET THAT DOOR LEADS TO THE ROOM WHERE MS. VITCH IS BEING HELD.
WE OUGHT TO BE ABLE TO DESTROY THE LOCK USING A TAKEBAYASHI EXPLOSIVE.
WHAT NOW...?
TEAM A SEEMS TO BE IN TROUBLE... SHOULDN'T WE GO AND HELP THEM?
WE'LL BE PLAYING RIGHT INTO HIS HANDS IF WE PANIC.
WE'LL WIN IF WE DEFEAT THE GRIM REAPER. THAT HASN'T CHANGED.
HE'S BOUND TO ATTACK US SOME-WHERE SOON ENOUGH...
AND WE'LL GET HIM WHEN HE DOES.
YEAH, BUT...
...HOW ARE WE GONNA PULL THAT OFF WITHOUT TEAM A?
SHFF
WE'RE NOT ALLOWED TO AIM THESE EXPLO-SIVES AT PEOPLE...
Explosive set...
BLIP
...BUT WE CAN STILL USE THEM AS A TRAP OR A THREAT.

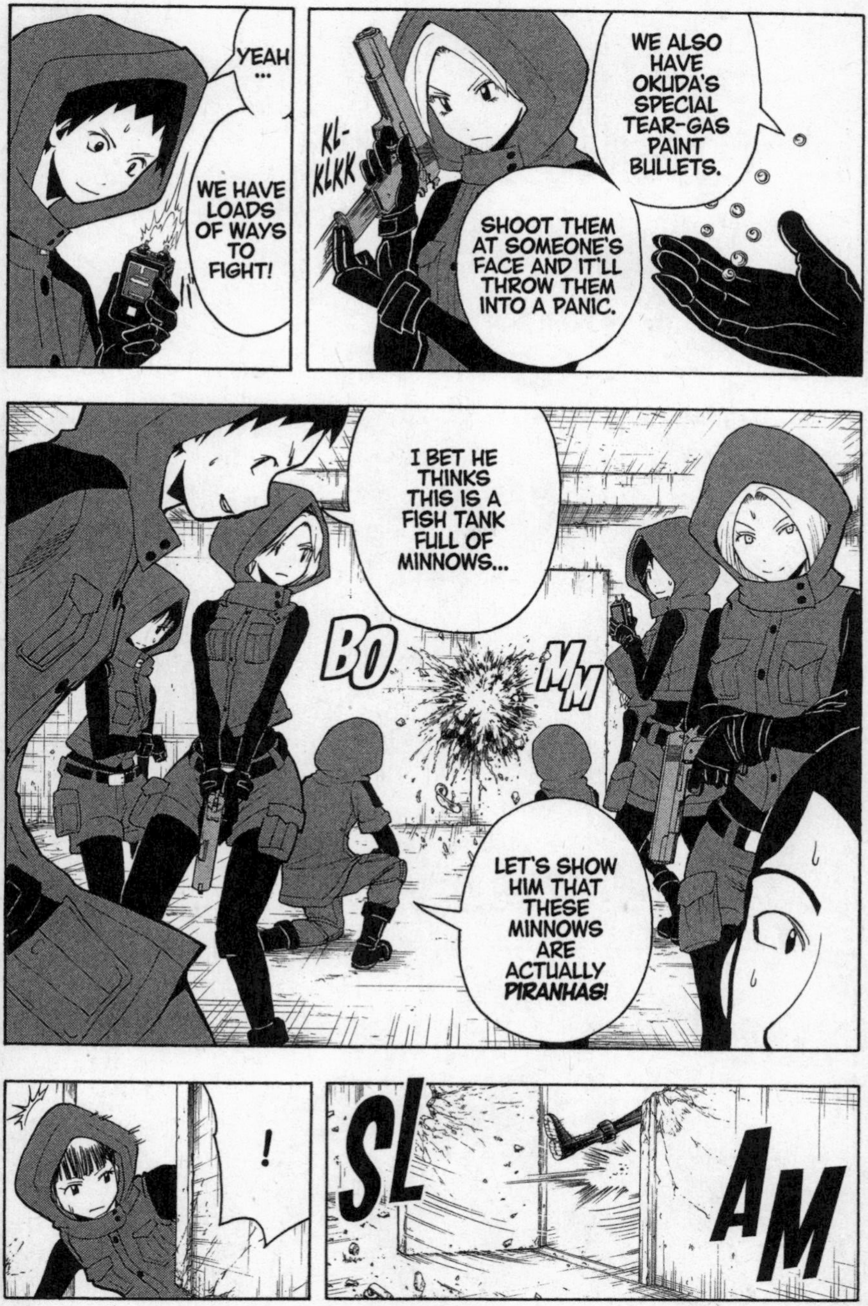
WE ALSO HAVE OKUDA'S SPECIAL TEAR-GAS PAINT BULLETS.
SHOOT THEM AT SOMEONE'S FACE AND IT'LL THROW THEM INTO A PANIC.
KL-KLKK
YEAH ...
WE HAVE LOADS OF WAYS TO FIGHT!
I BET HE THINKS THIS IS A FISH TANK FULL OF MINNOWS...
BOMM
LET'S SHOW HIM THAT THESE MINNOWS ARE ACTUALLY PIRANHAS!
SLAM
!

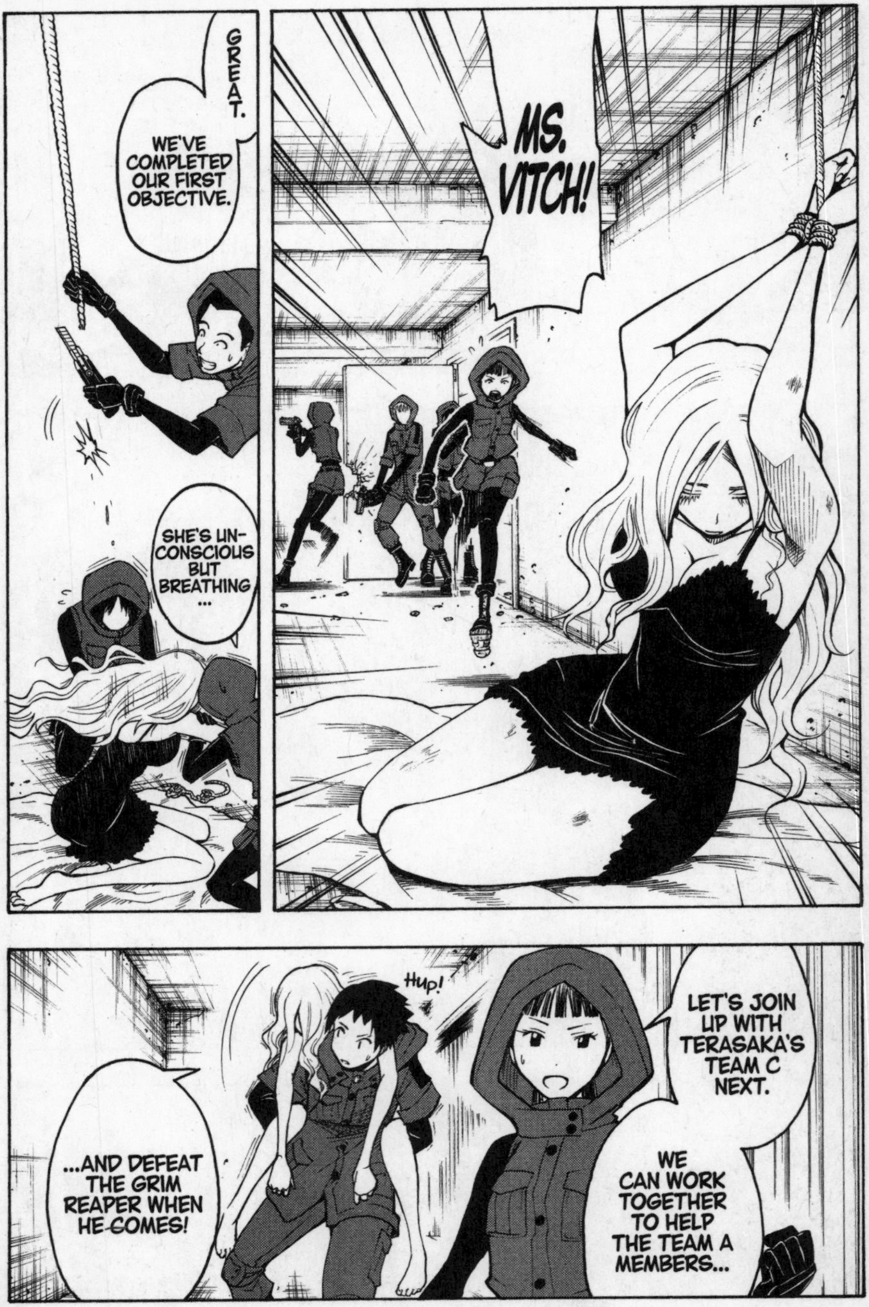
MS. VITCH!
GREAT.
WE'VE COMPLETED OUR FIRST OBJECTIVE.
SHE'S UN-CONSCIOUS BUT BREATHING ...
LET'S JOIN UP WITH TERASAKA'S TEAM C NEXT.
WE CAN WORK TOGETHER TO HELP THE TEAM A MEMBERS...
Hup!
...AND DEFEAT THE GRIM REAPER WHEN HE COMES!

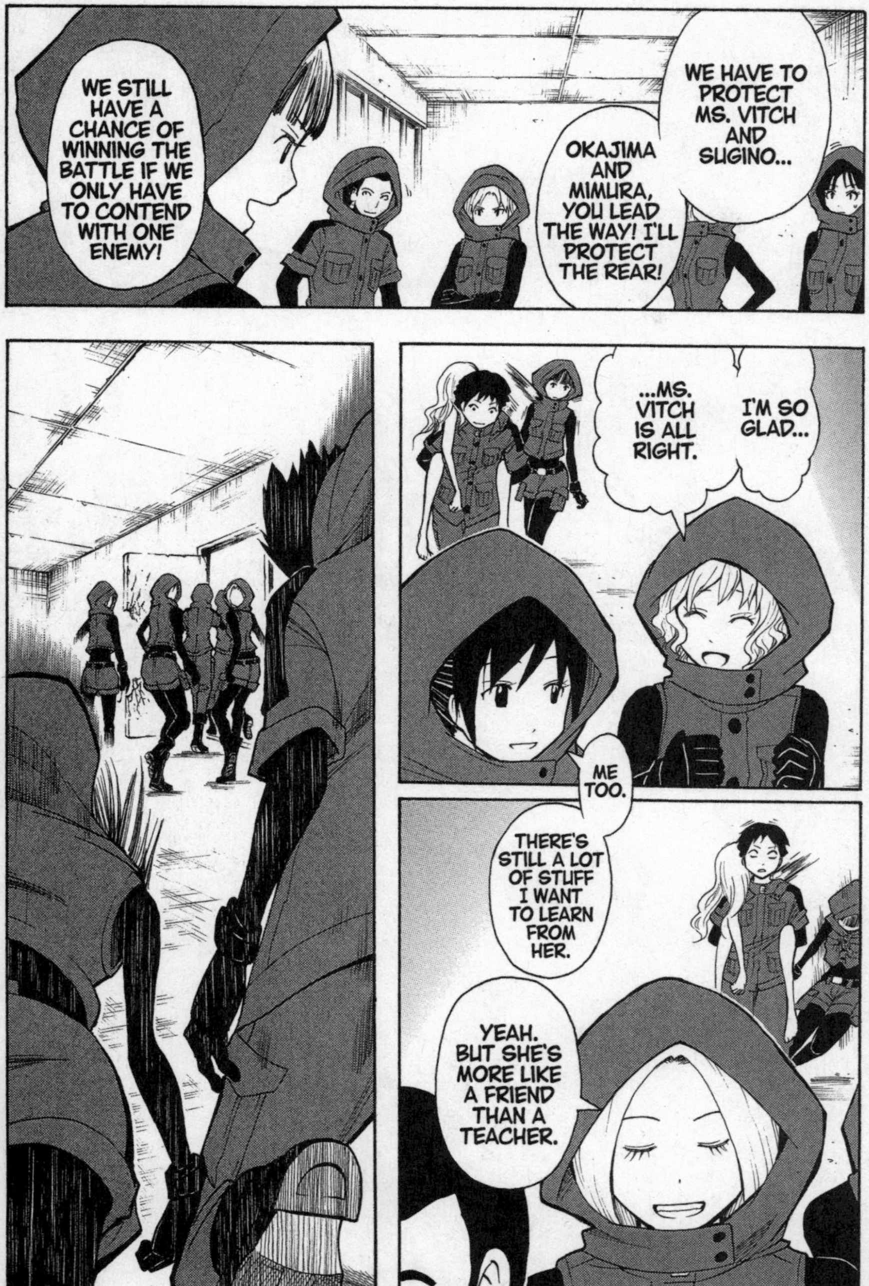
WE HAVE TO PROTECT MS. VITCH AND SUGINO...
OKAJIMA AND MIMURA, YOU LEAD THE WAY! I'LL PROTECT THE REAR!
WE STILL HAVE A CHANCE OF WINNING THE BATTLE IF WE ONLY HAVE TO CONTEND WITH ONE ENEMY!
I'M SO GLAD...
...MS. VITCH IS ALL RIGHT.
ME TOO.
THERE'S STILL A LOT OF STUFF I WANT TO LEARN FROM HER.
YEAH. BUT SHE'S MORE LIKE A FRIEND THAN A TEACHER.

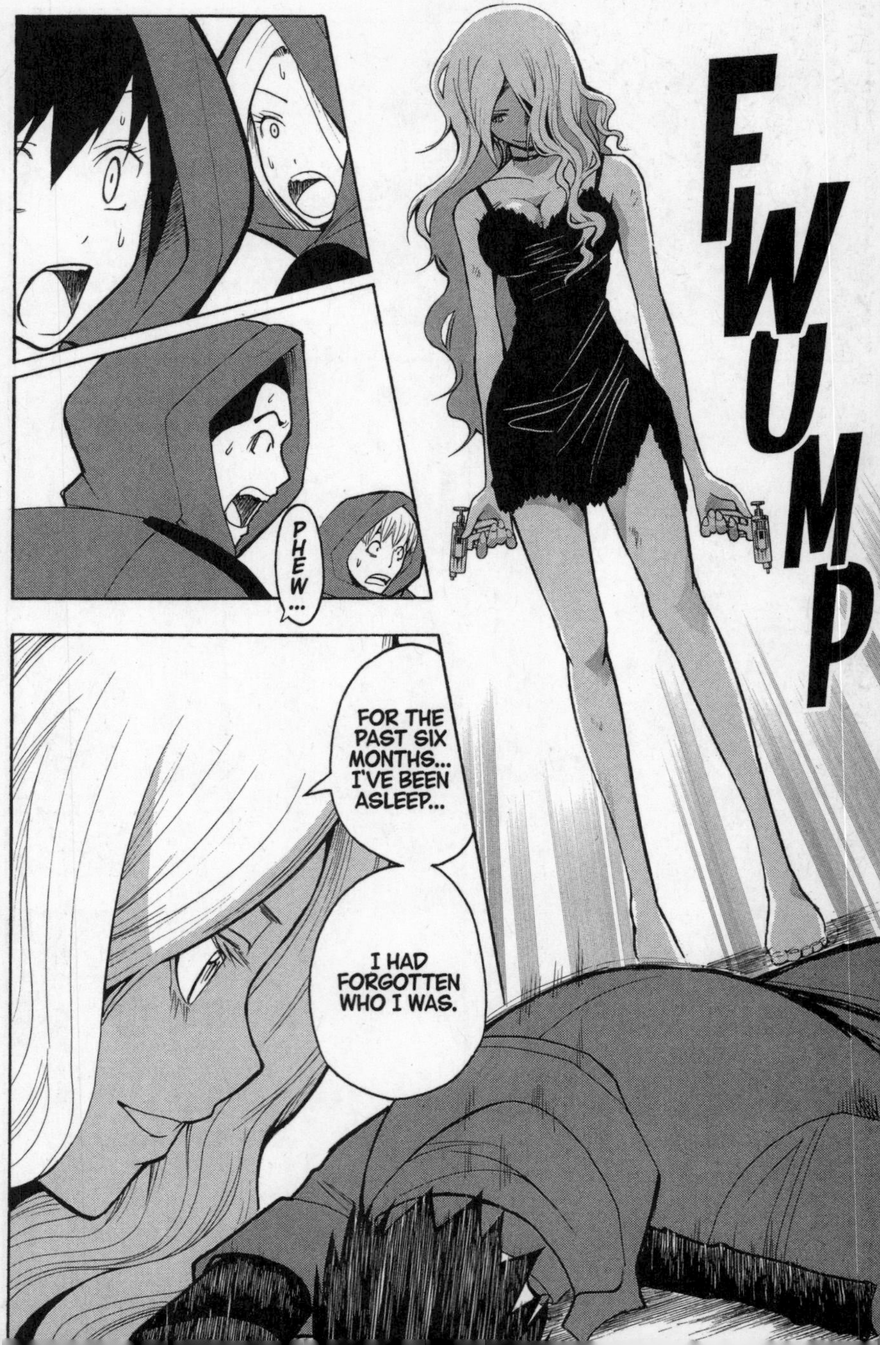
FWUMP
PHEW...
FOR THE PAST SIX MONTHS... I'VE BEEN ASLEEP...
I HAD FORGOTTEN WHO I WAS.

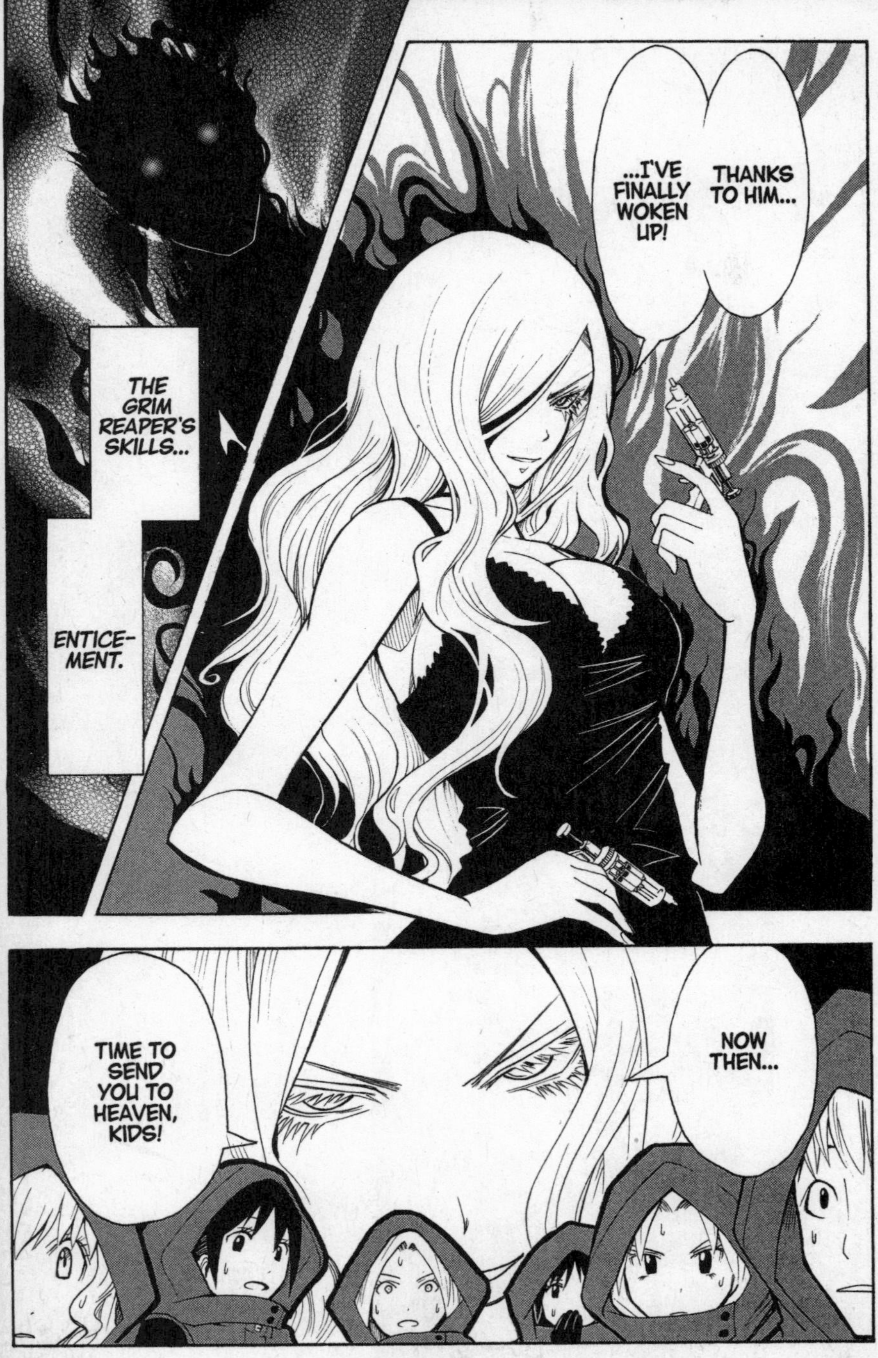
THANKS TO HIM...
...I'VE FINALLY WOKEN UP!
THE GRIM REAPER'S SKILLS...
ENTICEMENT.
NOW THEN...
TIME TO SEND YOU TO HEAVEN, KIDS!

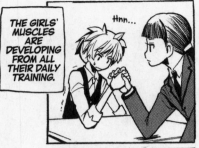

Spasmodic Funnies

Arm Wrestling

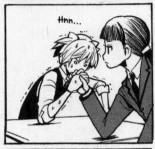

Hnn...
THE GIRLS' MUSCLES ARE DEVELOPING FROM ALL THEIR DAILY TRAINING.
Hnn...
Hnn...
Hnn...
Hnn...
MY ARM WON'T BUDGE...
Hnn...
NO ONE WANTS TO GO UP AGAINST NAGISA BECAUSE EVERYONE FEELS SORRY FOR HIM.

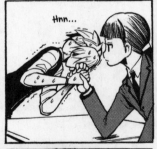

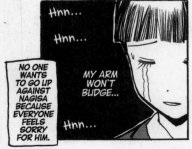

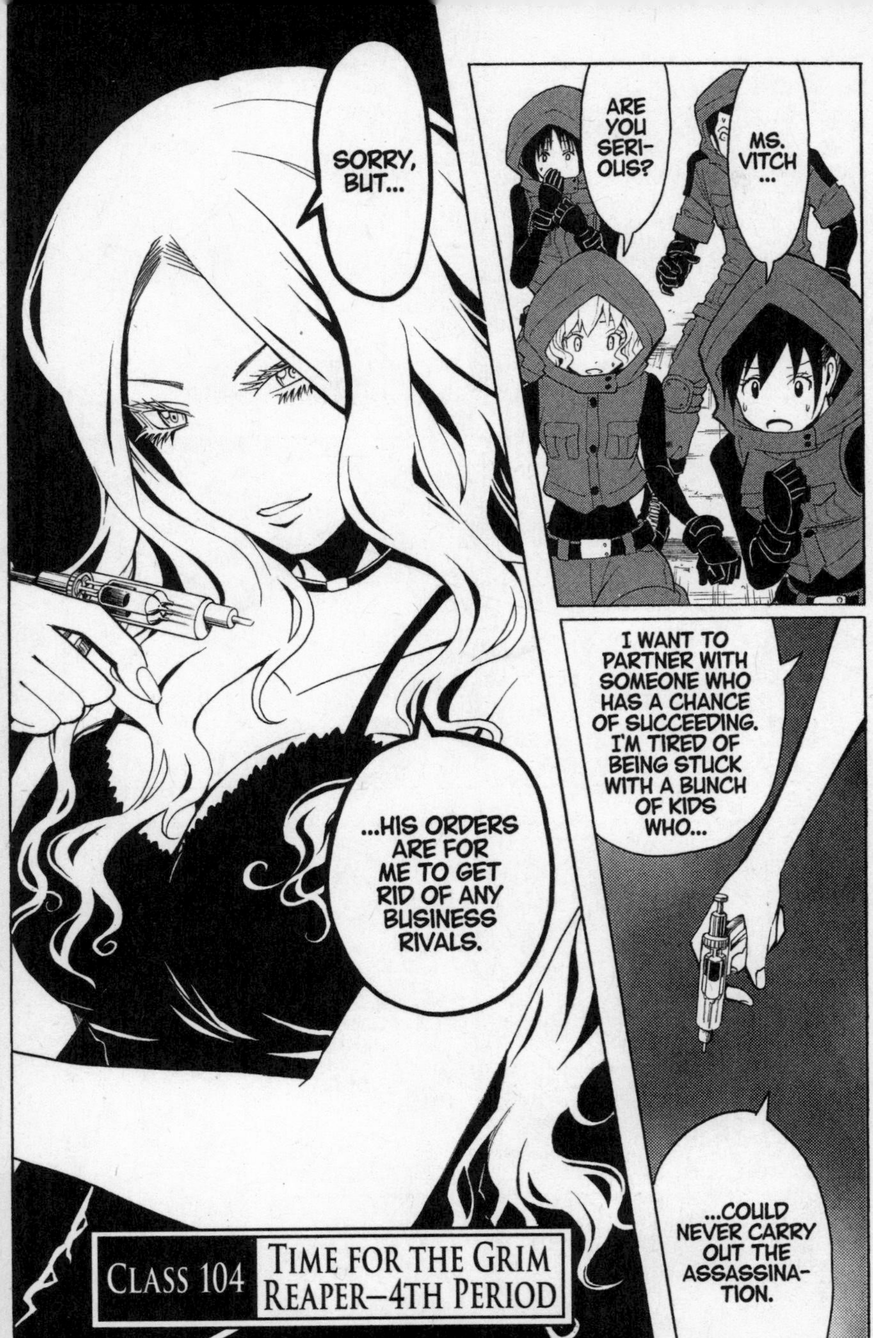
MS. VITCH...
ARE YOU SERIOUS?
I WANT TO PARTNER WITH SOMEONE WHO HAS A CHANCE OF SUCCEEDING. I'M TIRED OF BEING STUCK WITH A BUNCH OF KIDS WHO...
...COULD NEVER CARRY OUT THE ASSASSINATION.
SORRY, BUT...
...HIS ORDERS ARE FOR ME TO GET RID OF ANY BUSINESS RIVALS.
CLASS 104 TIME FOR THE GRIM REAPER—4TH PERIOD

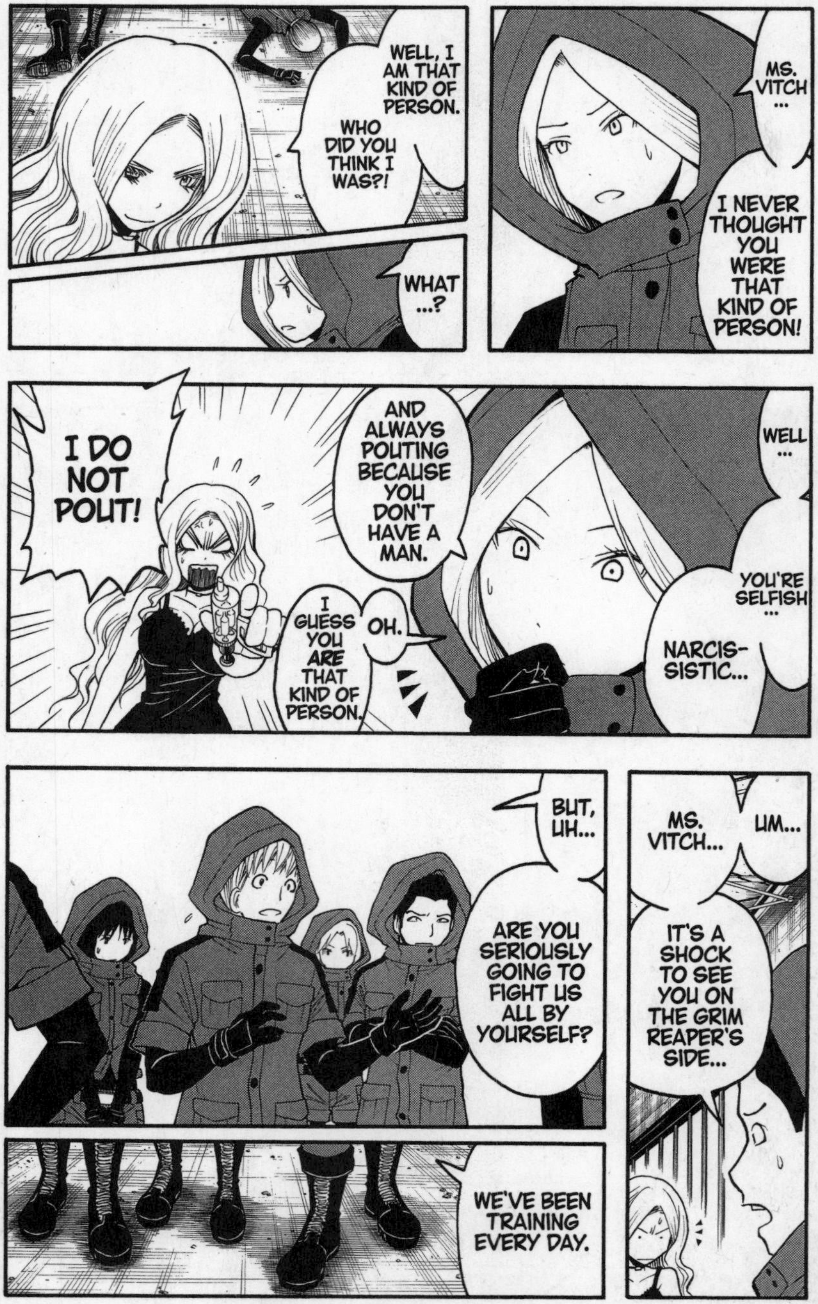
MS. VITCH ...
I NEVER THOUGHT YOU WERE THAT KIND OF PERSON!
WELL, I AM THAT KIND OF PERSON.
WHO DID YOU THINK I WAS?!
WHAT ...?
WELL ...
YOU'RE SELFISH ...
NARCIS-SISTIC...
AND ALWAYS POUTING BECAUSE YOU DON'T HAVE A MAN.
OH.
I GUESS YOU ARE THAT KIND OF PERSON.
I DO NOT POUT!
UM...
MS. VITCH...
IT'S A SHOCK TO SEE YOU ON THE GRIM REAPER'S SIDE...
BUT, UH...
ARE YOU SERIOUSLY GOING TO FIGHT US ALL BY YOURSELF?
WE'VE BEEN TRAINING EVERY DAY.

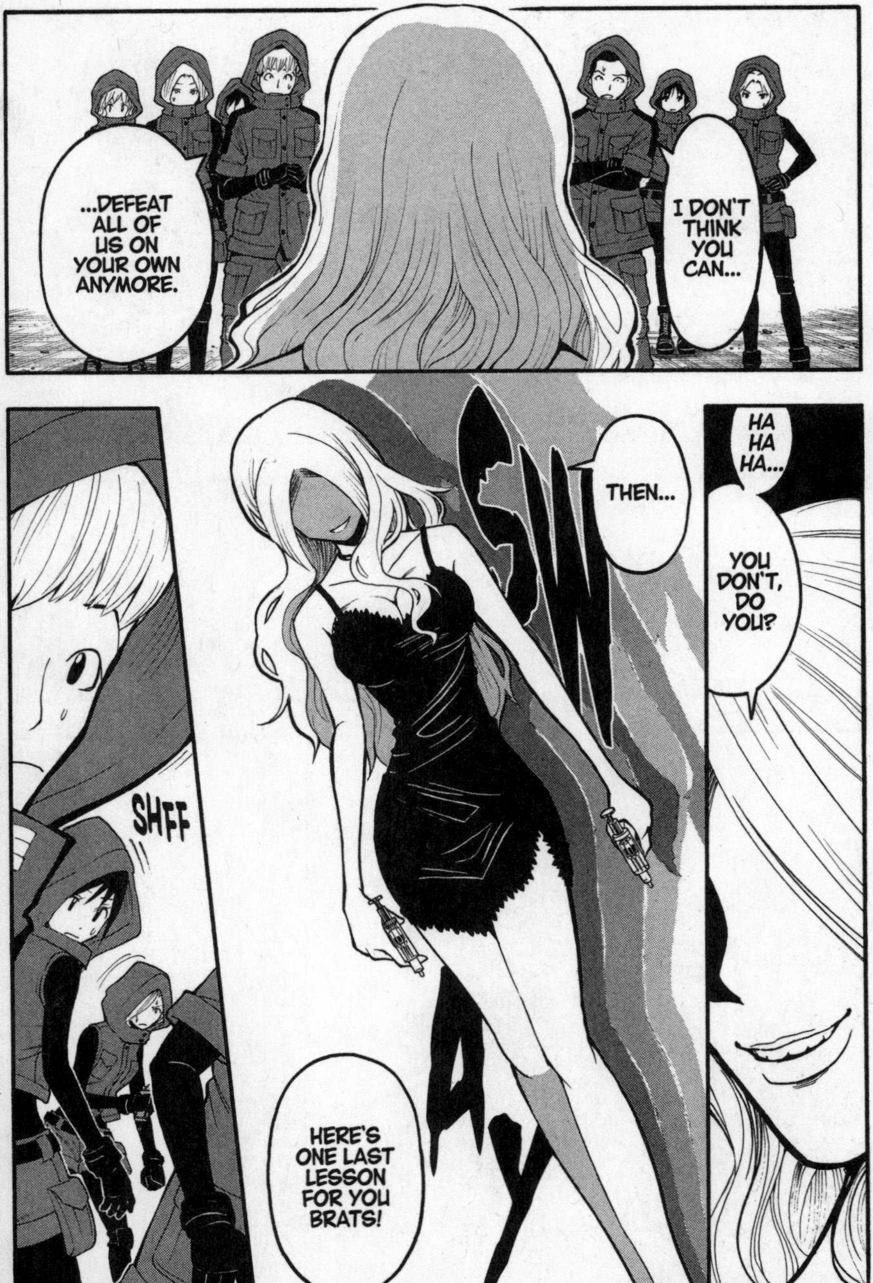
I DON'T THINK YOU CAN...
...DEFEAT ALL OF US ON YOUR OWN ANYMORE.
HA HA HA...
YOU DON'T, DO YOU?
THEN...
HERE'S ONE LAST LESSON FOR YOU BRATS!
SHFF

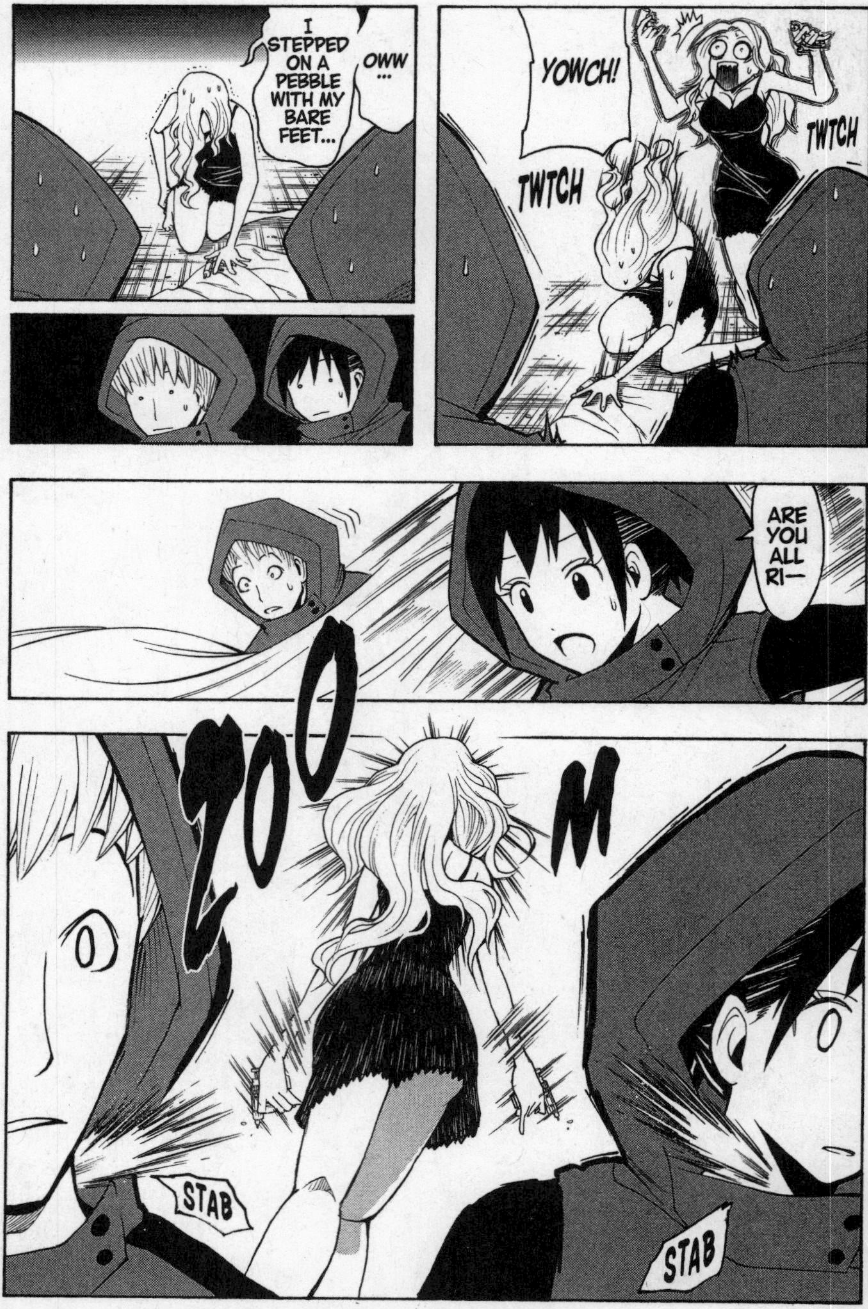
YOWCH!
TWTCH
TWTCH
OWW ...
I STEPPED ON A PEBBLE WITH MY BARE FEET...
ARE YOU ALL RI—
ZOOOM
STAB
STAB

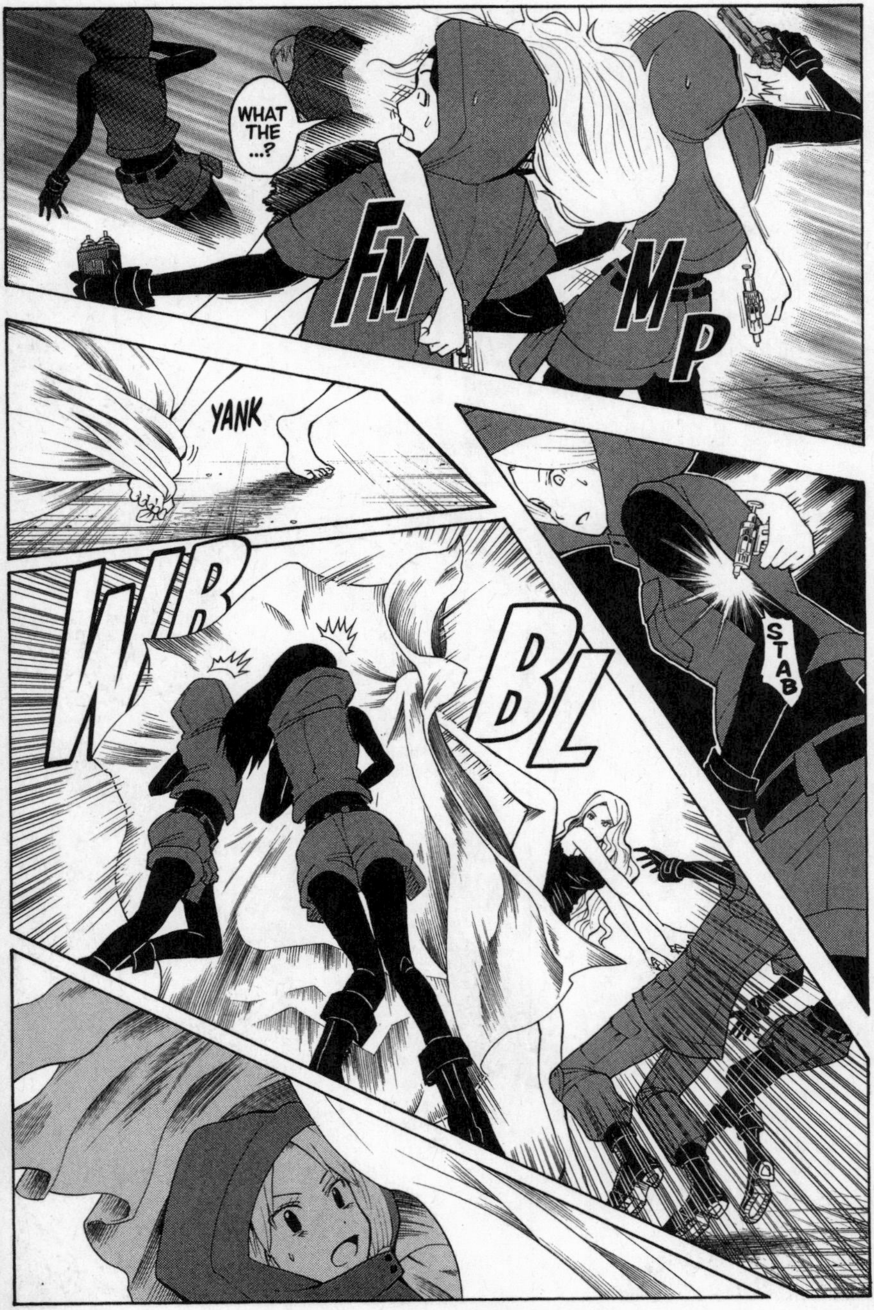
WHAT THE ...?
FM
MP
STAB
YANK
WB
BL

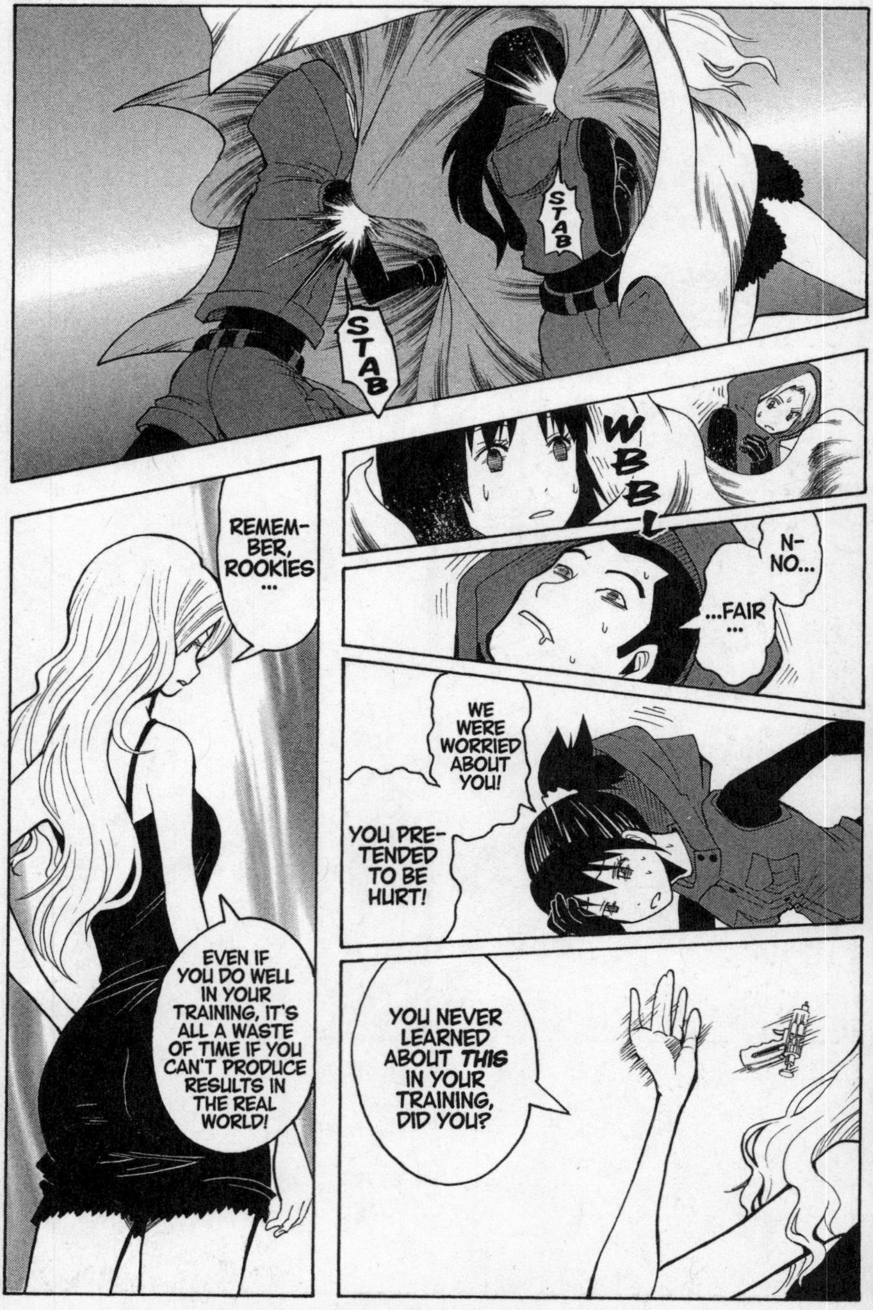
STAB
STAB
WBBL
N-NO...
...FAIR...
WE WERE WORRIED ABOUT YOU!
YOU PRETENDED TO BE HURT!
YOU NEVER LEARNED ABOUT *THIS* IN YOUR TRAINING, DID YOU?
REMEMBER, ROOKIES...
EVEN IF YOU DO WELL IN YOUR TRAINING, IT'S ALL A WASTE OF TIME IF YOU CAN'T PRODUCE RESULTS IN THE REAL WORLD!

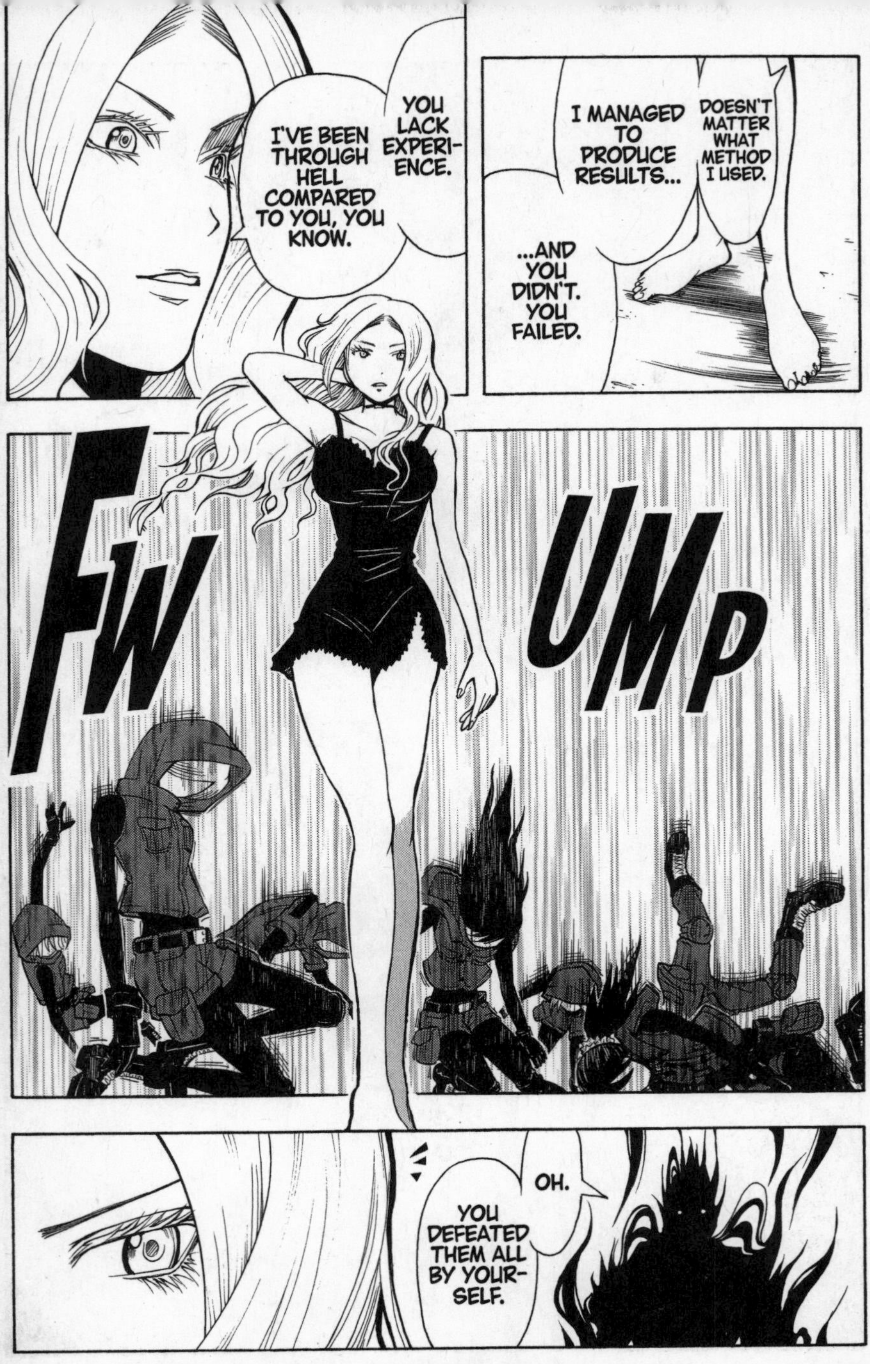
DOESN'T MATTER WHAT METHOD I USED.
I MANAGED TO PRODUCE RESULTS...
...AND YOU DIDN'T. YOU FAILED.
YOU LACK EXPERIENCE.
I'VE BEEN THROUGH HELL COMPARED TO YOU, YOU KNOW.
FWUMP
OH.
YOU DEFEATED THEM ALL BY YOURSELF.

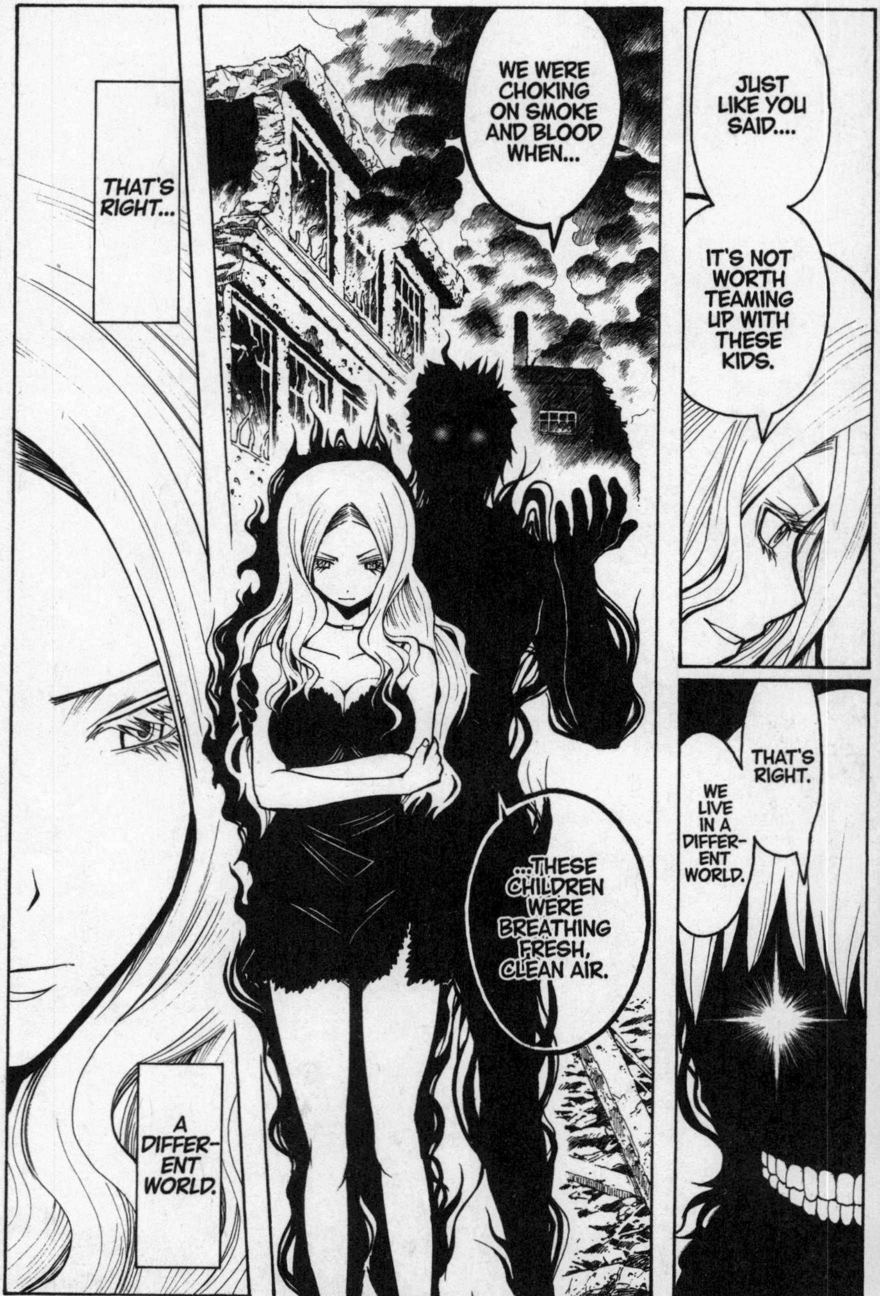
JUST LIKE YOU SAID....
IT'S NOT WORTH TEAMING UP WITH THESE KIDS.
THAT'S RIGHT.
WE LIVE IN A DIFFER-ENT WORLD.
WE WERE CHOKING ON SMOKE AND BLOOD WHEN...
...THESE CHILDREN WERE BREATHING FRESH, CLEAN AIR.
THAT'S RIGHT...
A DIFFER-ENT WORLD.

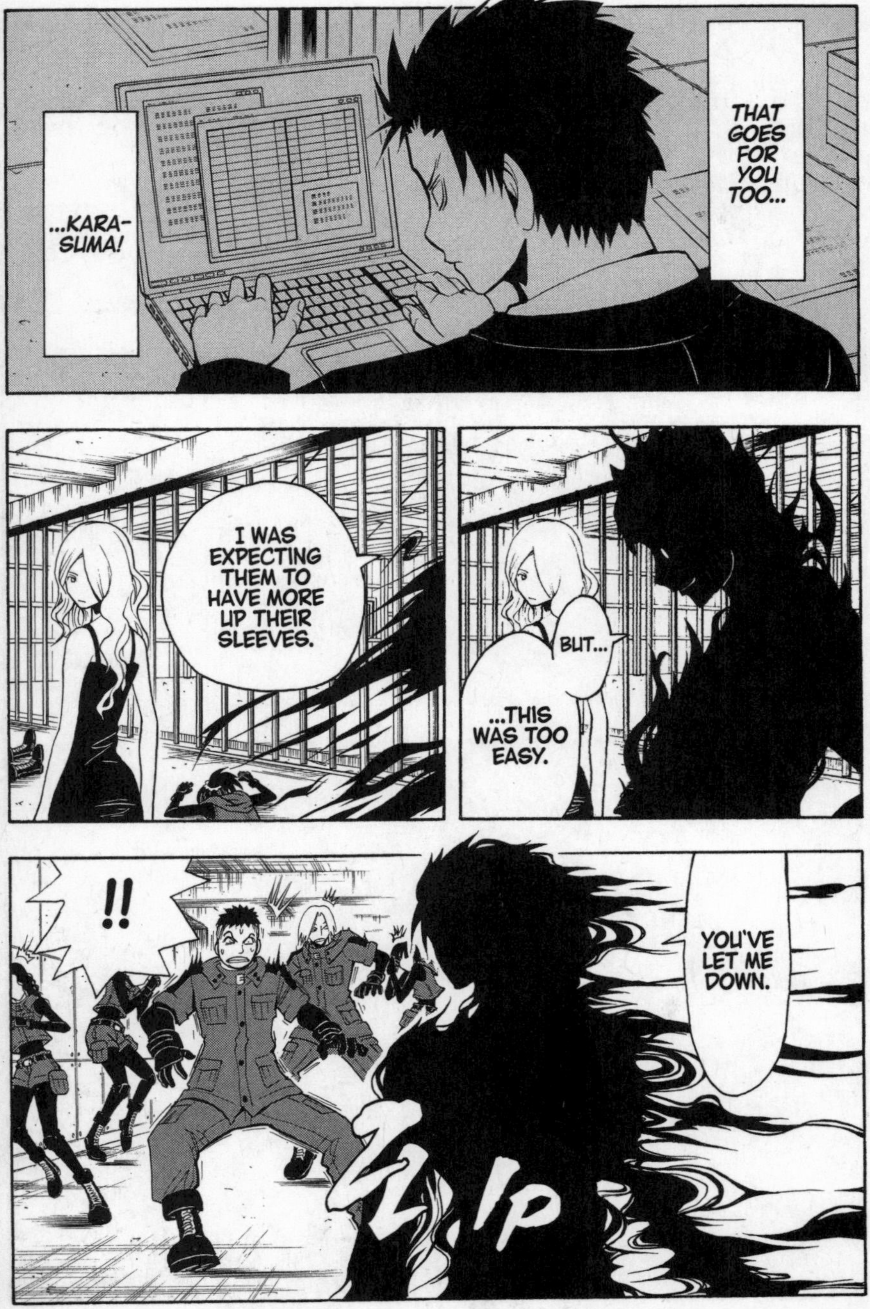
THAT GOES FOR YOU TOO...
...KARA-SUMA!
BUT...
...THIS WAS TOO EASY.
I WAS EXPECTING THEM TO HAVE MORE UP THEIR SLEEVES.
YOU'VE LET ME DOWN.
!!

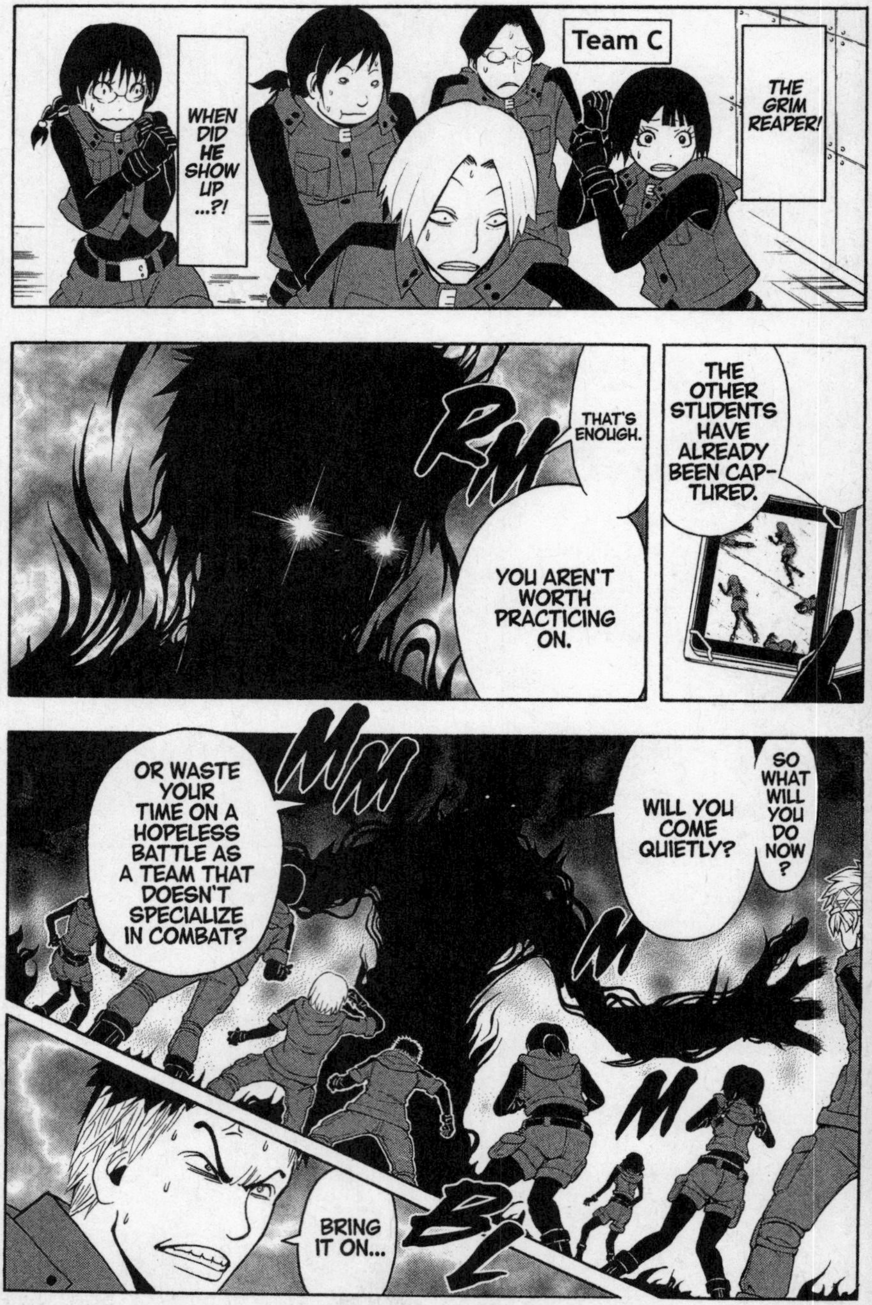
Team C
THE GRIM REAPER!
WHEN DID HE SHOW UP ...?!
THE OTHER STUDENTS HAVE ALREADY BEEN CAPTURED.
RM
THAT'S ENOUGH.
YOU AREN'T WORTH PRACTICING ON.
SO WHAT WILL YOU DO NOW?
WILL YOU COME QUIETLY?
MM
OR WASTE YOUR TIME ON A HOPELESS BATTLE AS A TEAM THAT DOESN'T SPECIALIZE IN COMBAT?
M
M
BRING IT ON...
BL

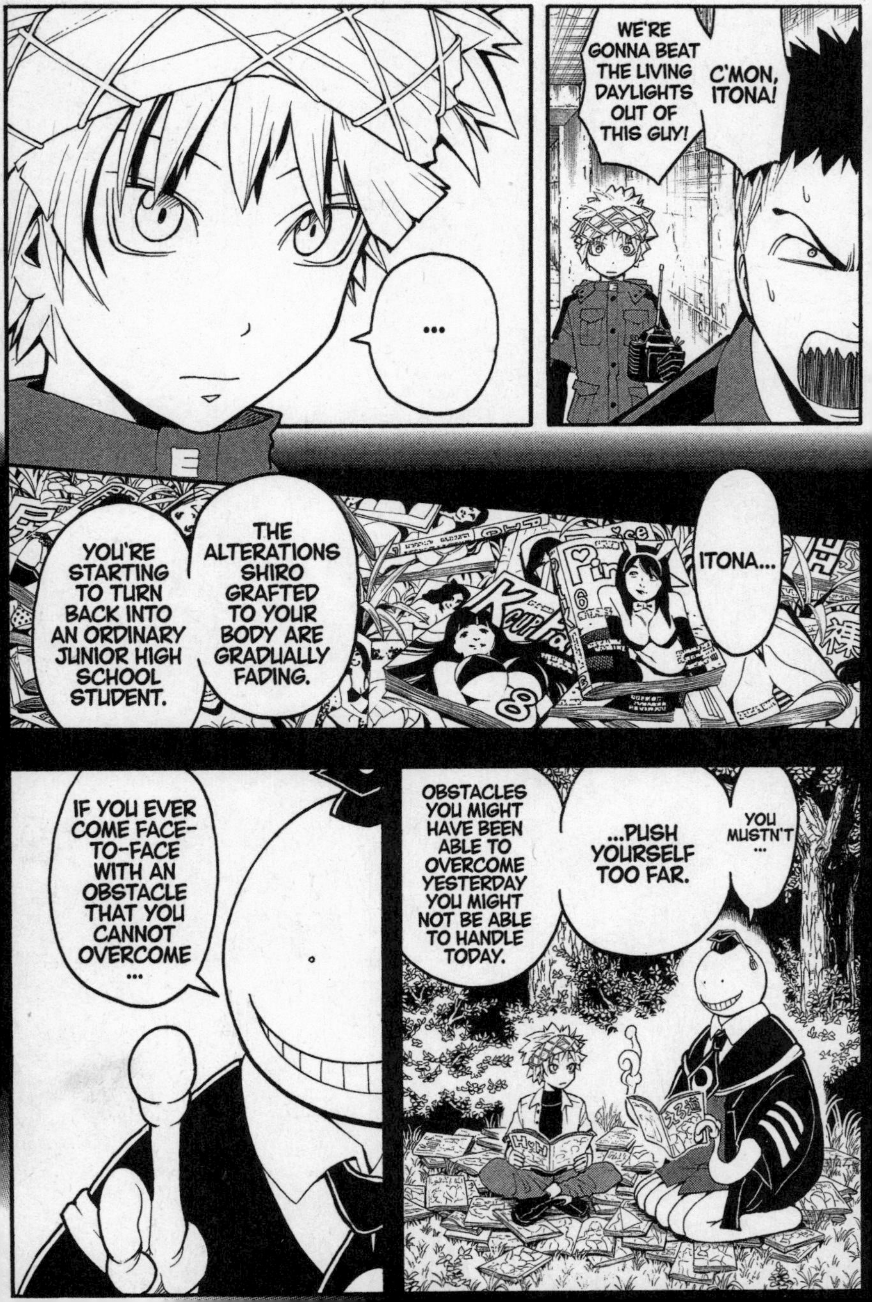
C'MON, ITONA!
WE'RE GONNA BEAT THE LIVING DAYLIGHTS OUT OF THIS GUY!
...
ITONA...
THE ALTERATIONS SHIRO GRAFTED TO YOUR BODY ARE GRADUALLY FADING.
YOU'RE STARTING TO TURN BACK INTO AN ORDINARY JUNIOR HIGH SCHOOL STUDENT.
YOU MUSTN'T ...
...PUSH YOURSELF TOO FAR.
OBSTACLES YOU MIGHT HAVE BEEN ABLE TO OVERCOME YESTERDAY YOU MIGHT NOT BE ABLE TO HANDLE TODAY.
IF YOU EVER COME FACE-TO-FACE WITH AN OBSTACLE THAT YOU CANNOT OVERCOME ...

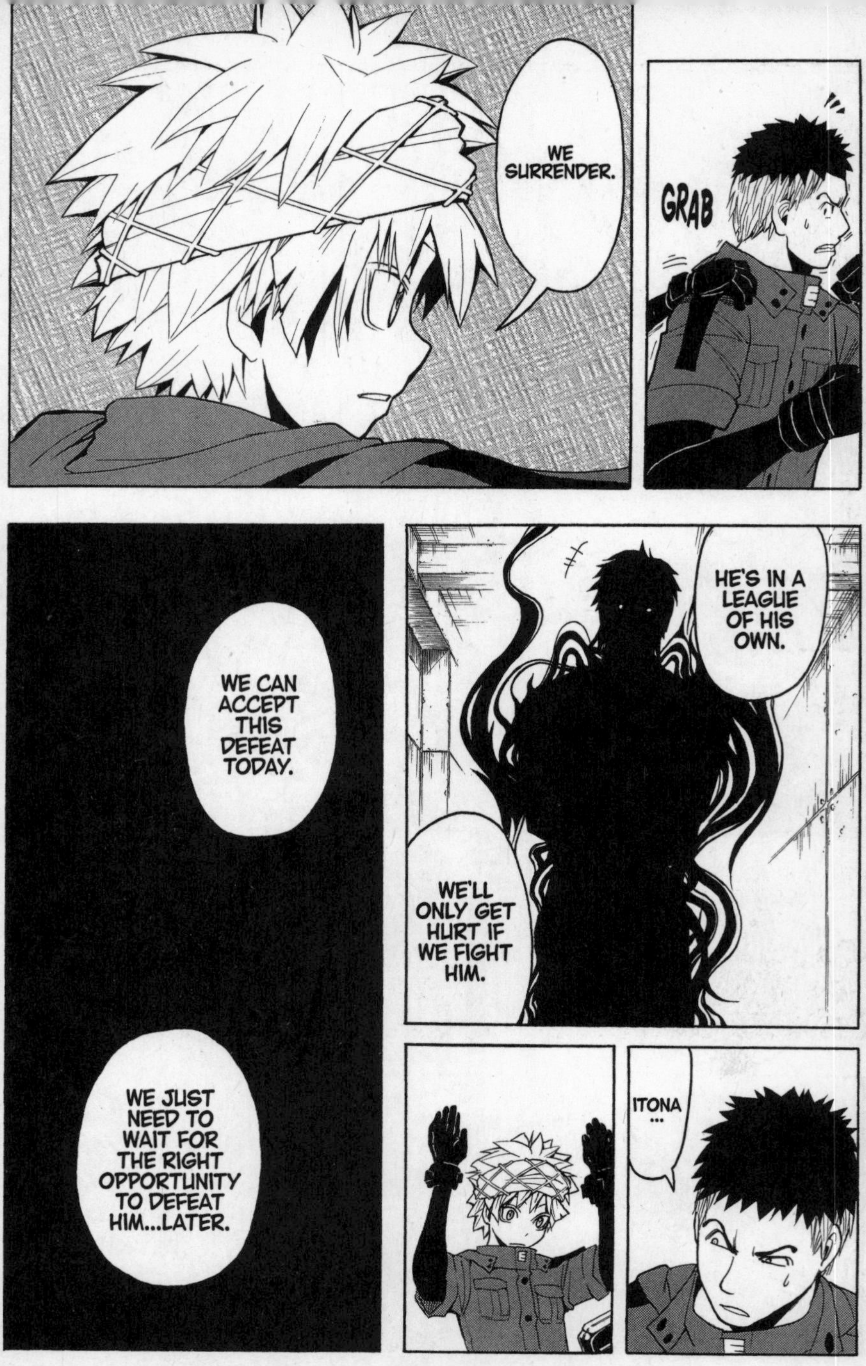
GRAB
WE SURRENDER.
HE'S IN A LEAGUE OF HIS OWN.
WE'LL ONLY GET HURT IF WE FIGHT HIM.
ITONA...
WE CAN ACCEPT THIS DEFEAT TODAY.
WE JUST NEED TO WAIT FOR THE RIGHT OPPORTUNITY TO DEFEAT HIM...LATER.

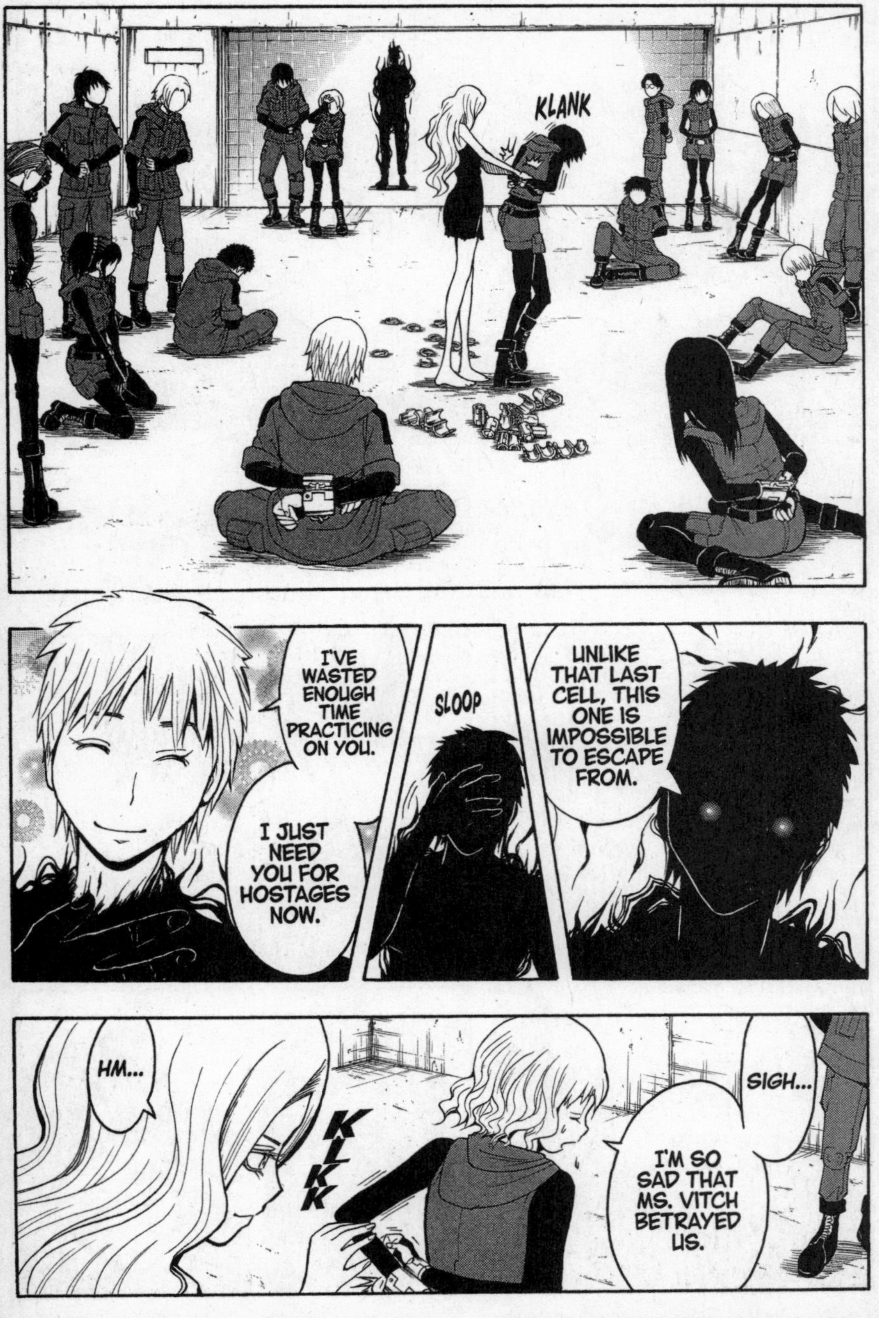
KLANK
UNLIKE THAT LAST CELL, THIS ONE IS IMPOSSIBLE TO ESCAPE FROM.
SLOOP
I'VE WASTED ENOUGH TIME PRACTICING ON YOU.
I JUST NEED YOU FOR HOSTAGES NOW.
SIGH...
I'M SO SAD THAT MS. VITCH BETRAYED US.
KLIKK
HM...

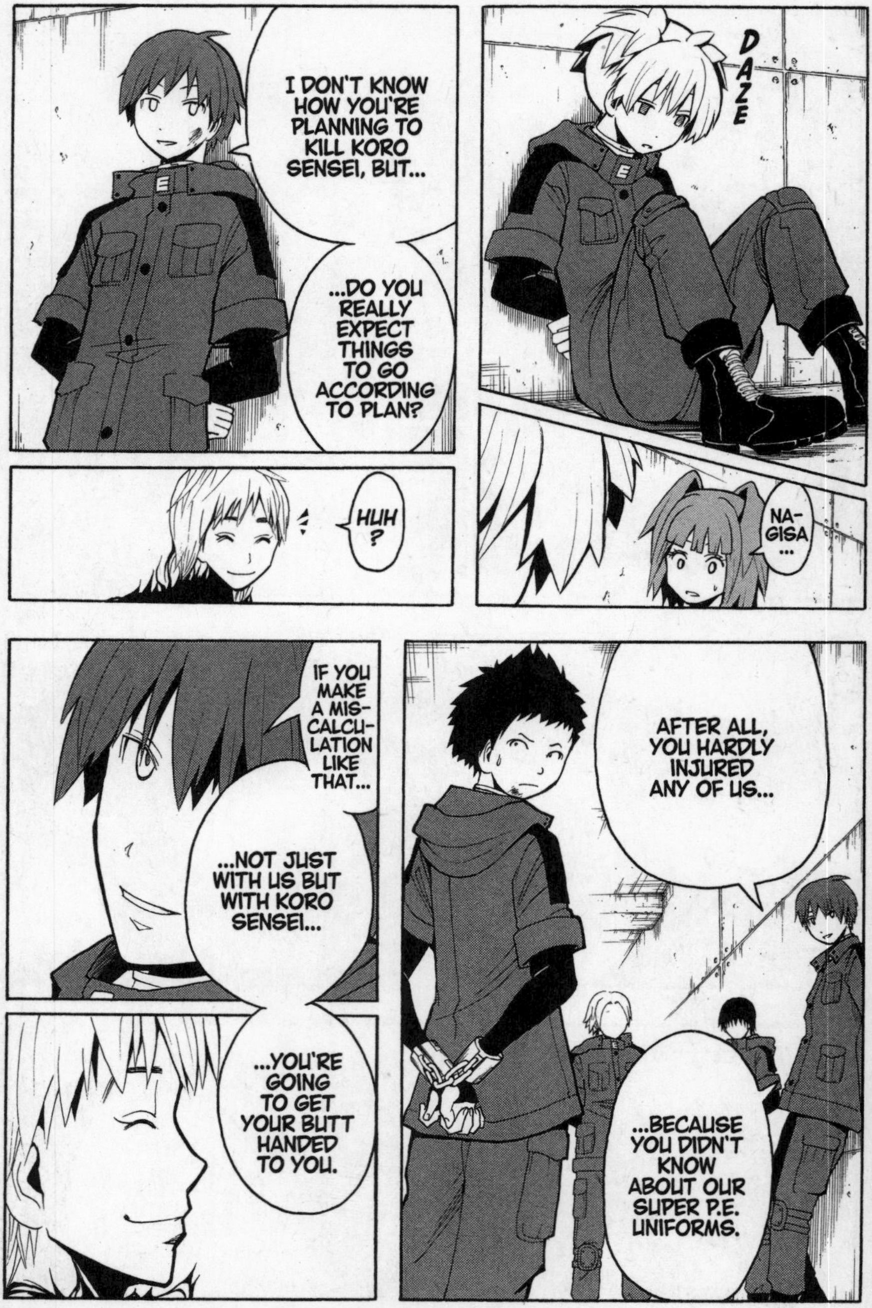
DAZE
I DON'T KNOW HOW YOU'RE PLANNING TO KILL KORO SENSEI, BUT...
...DO YOU REALLY EXPECT THINGS TO GO ACCORDING TO PLAN?
NA-GISA...
HUH?
AFTER ALL, YOU HARDLY INJURED ANY OF US...
...BECAUSE YOU DIDN'T KNOW ABOUT OUR SUPER P.E. UNIFORMS.
IF YOU MAKE A MIS-CALCU-LATION LIKE THAT...
...NOT JUST WITH US BUT WITH KORO SENSEI...
...YOU'RE GOING TO GET YOUR BUTT HANDED TO YOU.

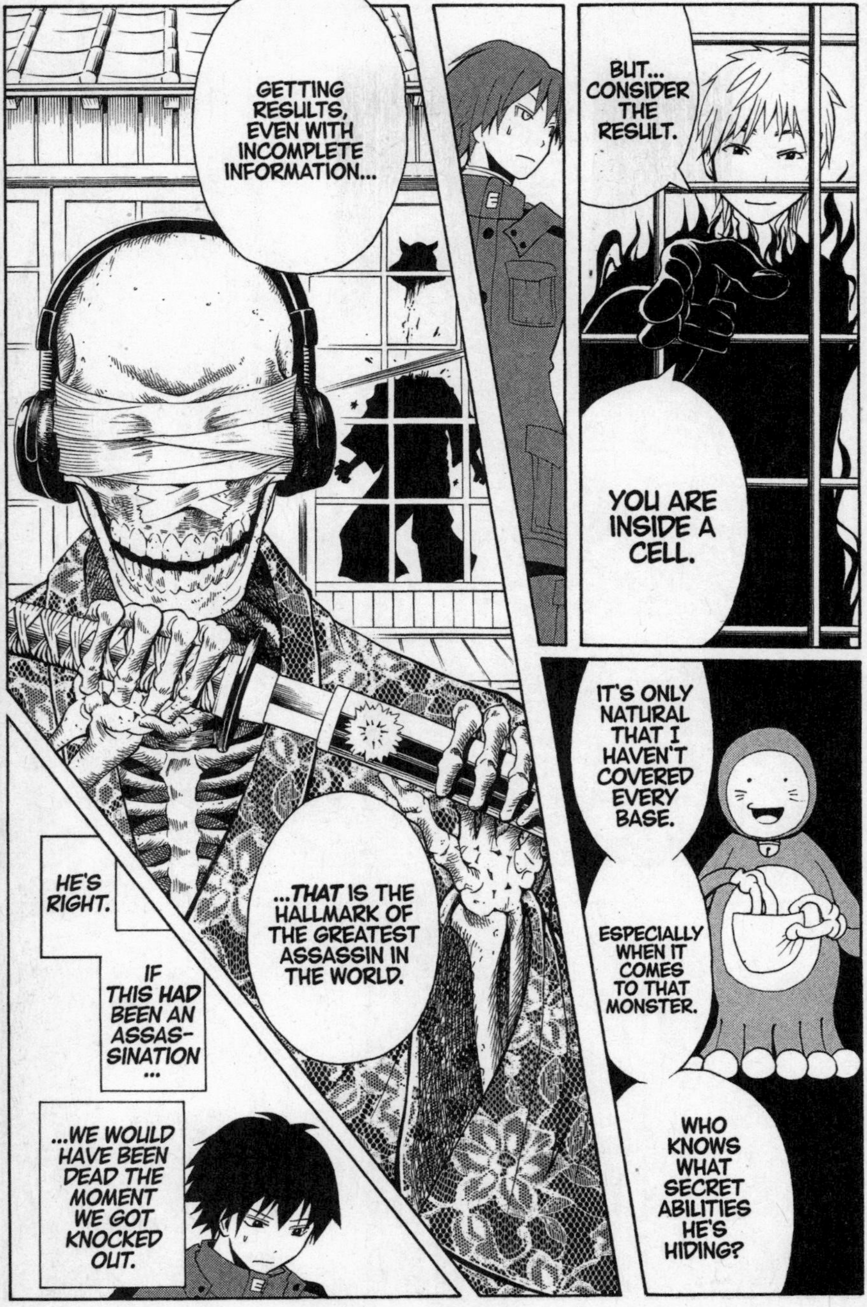
BUT... CONSIDER THE RESULT.
YOU ARE INSIDE A CELL.
GETTING RESULTS, EVEN WITH INCOMPLETE INFORMATION...
...*THAT* IS THE HALLMARK OF THE GREATEST ASSASSIN IN THE WORLD.
IT'S ONLY NATURAL THAT I HAVEN'T COVERED EVERY BASE.
ESPECIALLY WHEN IT COMES TO THAT MONSTER.
WHO KNOWS WHAT SECRET ABILITIES HE'S HIDING?
HE'S RIGHT.
IF THIS HAD BEEN AN ASSAS-SINATION...
...WE WOULD HAVE BEEN DEAD THE MOMENT WE GOT KNOCKED OUT.

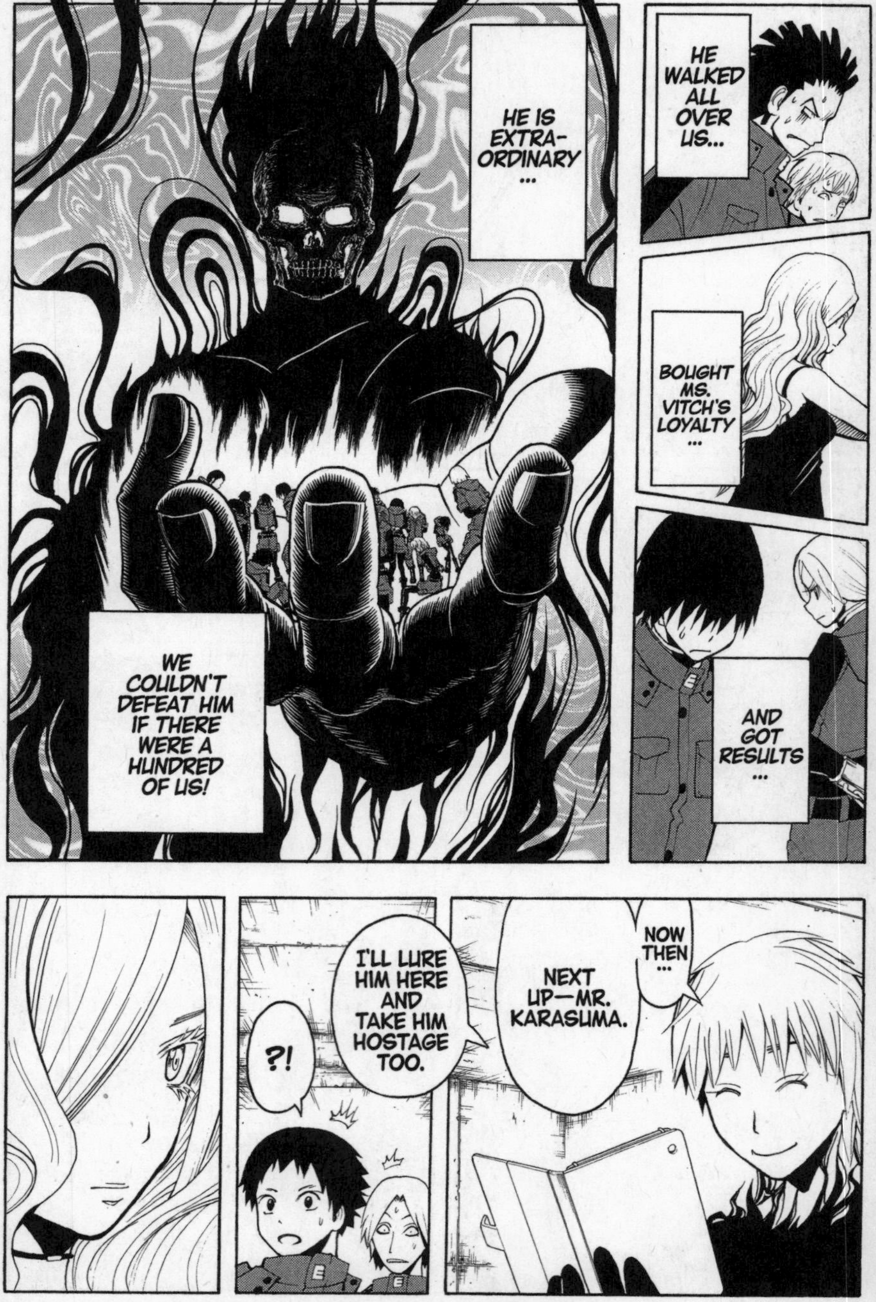
HE WALKED ALL OVER US...
BOUGHT MS. VITCH'S LOYALTY...
AND GOT RESULTS...
HE IS EXTRA-ORDINARY...
WE COULDN'T DEFEAT HIM IF THERE WERE A HUNDRED OF US!
NOW THEN...
NEXT UP—MR. KARASUMA.
I'LL LURE HIM HERE AND TAKE HIM HOSTAGE TOO.
?!

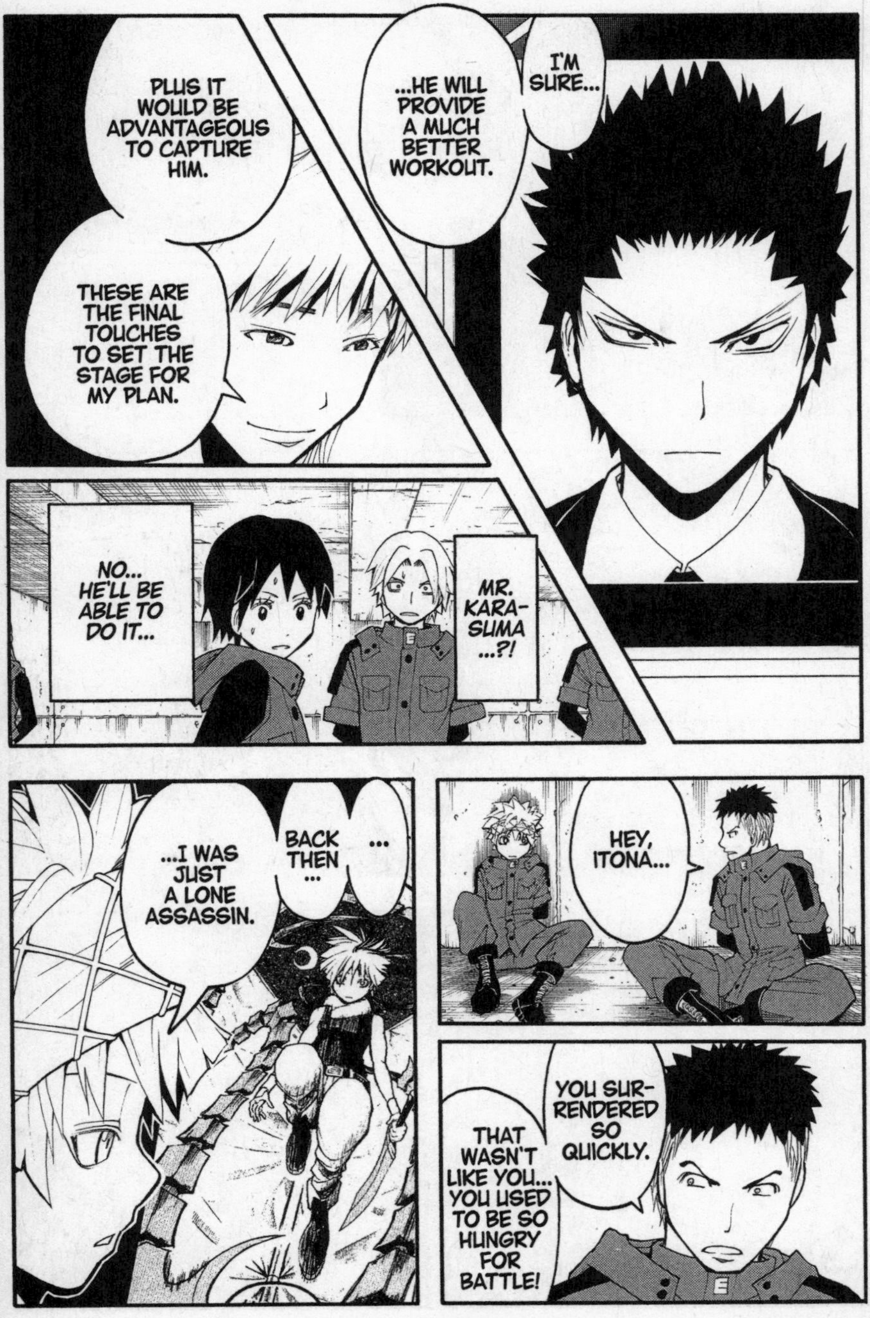
I'M SURE...
...HE WILL PROVIDE A MUCH BETTER WORKOUT.
PLUS IT WOULD BE ADVANTAGEOUS TO CAPTURE HIM.
THESE ARE THE FINAL TOUCHES TO SET THE STAGE FOR MY PLAN.
MR. KARA-SUMA ...?!
NO... HE'LL BE ABLE TO DO IT...
HEY, ITONA...
YOU SUR-RENDERED SO QUICKLY.
THAT WASN'T LIKE YOU... YOU USED TO BE SO HUNGRY FOR BATTLE!
...
BACK THEN ...
...I WAS JUST A LONE ASSASSIN.

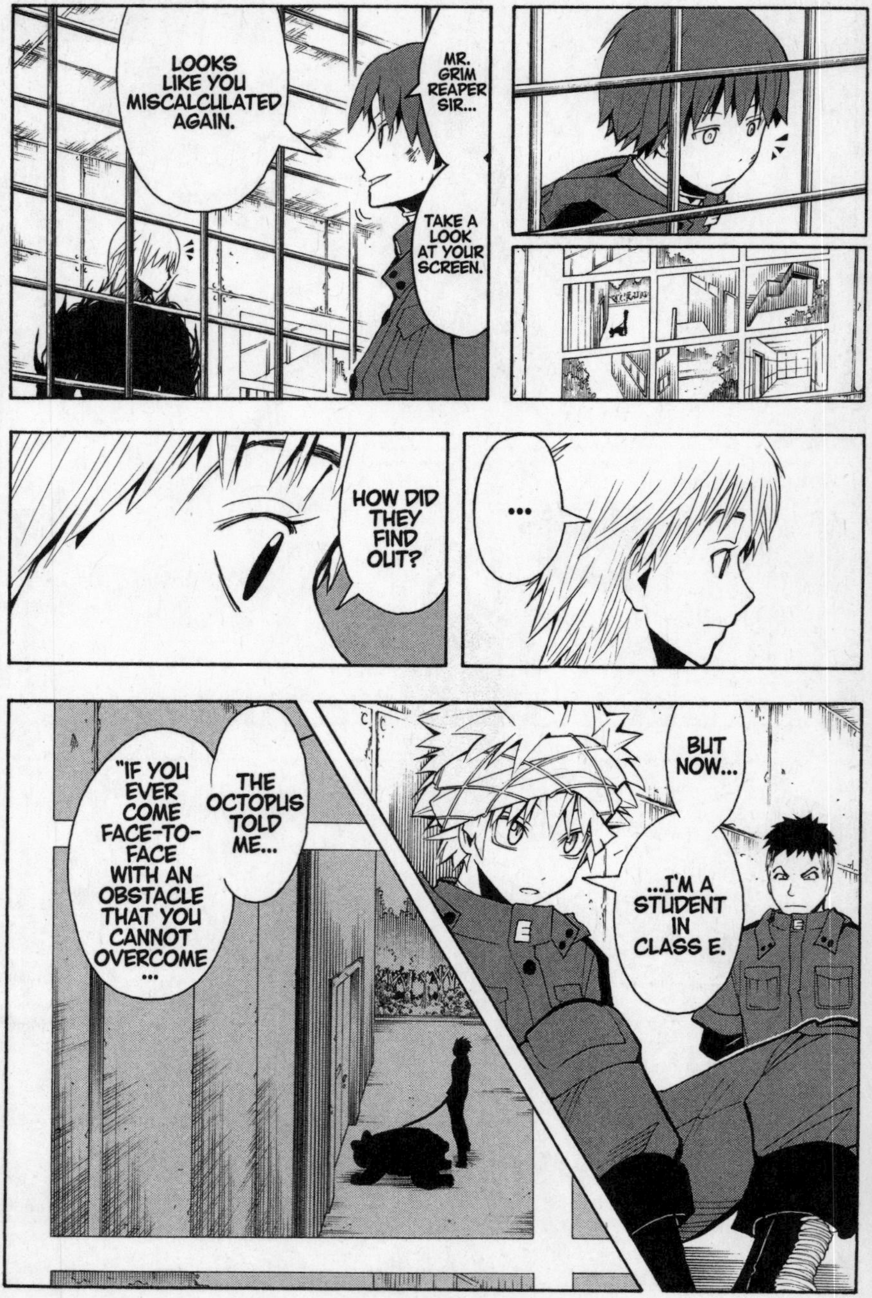
MR. GRIM REAPER SIR...
LOOKS LIKE YOU MISCALCULATED AGAIN.
TAKE A LOOK AT YOUR SCREEN.
...
HOW DID THEY FIND OUT?
BUT NOW...
...I'M A STUDENT IN CLASS E.
THE OCTOPUS TOLD ME...
"IF YOU EVER COME FACE-TO-FACE WITH AN OBSTACLE THAT YOU CANNOT OVERCOME...

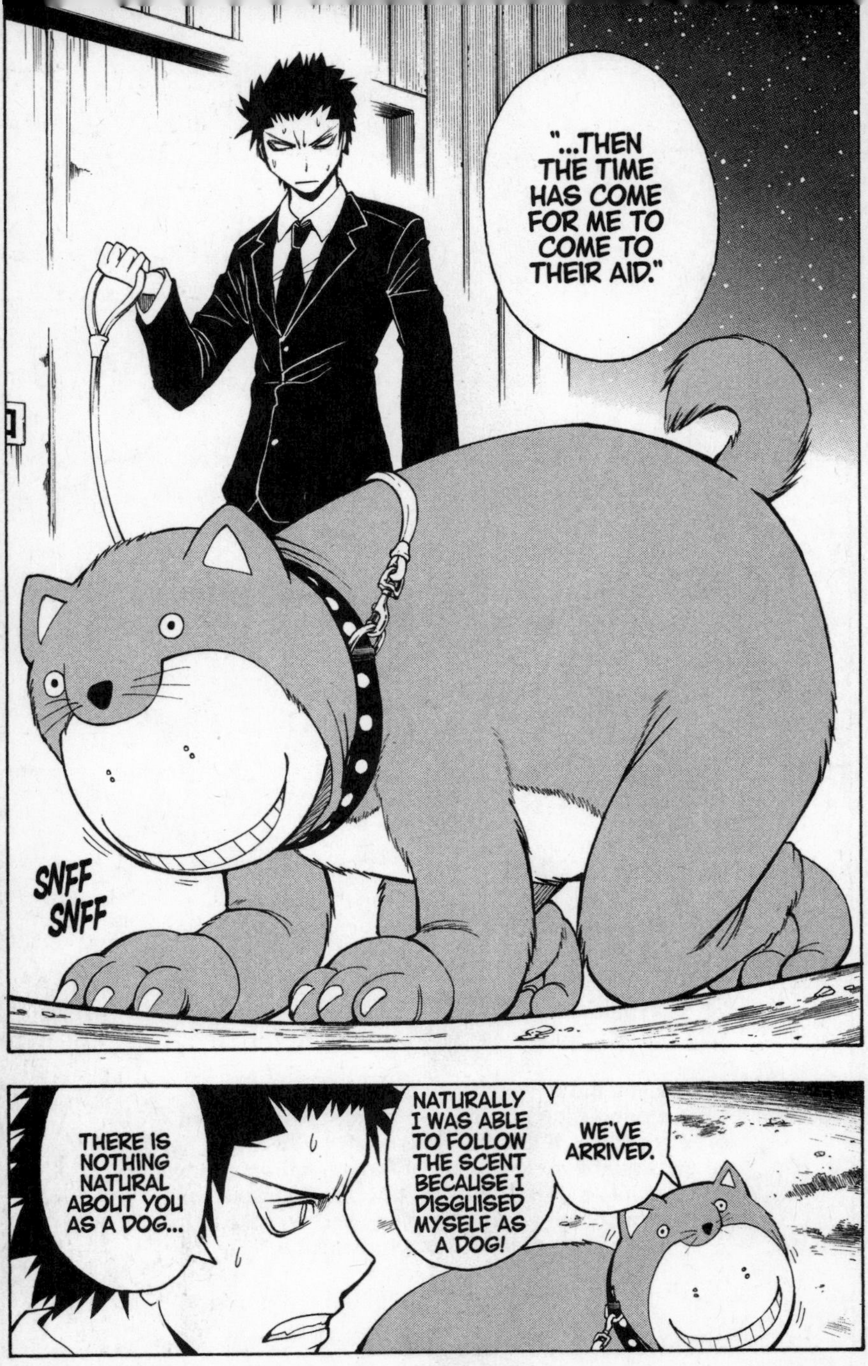
"...THEN THE TIME HAS COME FOR ME TO COME TO THEIR AID."
SNFF SNFF
WE'VE ARRIVED.
NATURALLY I WAS ABLE TO FOLLOW THE SCENT BECAUSE I DISGUISED MYSELF AS A DOG!
THERE IS NOTHING NATURAL ABOUT YOU AS A DOG...

Ms. Vitch's Super Amazing Technique Series③
-Acting Like an Idiot-

Duuuuh.

A daring move which she only resorts to when
the timing is right. She can act out 48 different
types of idiots if she believes that it will lower her
target's guard. At a glance, she may embarrassingly
appear like a genuine idiot, but she'll regain your
respect when she explains, "You should take pride
in your results, not your means."

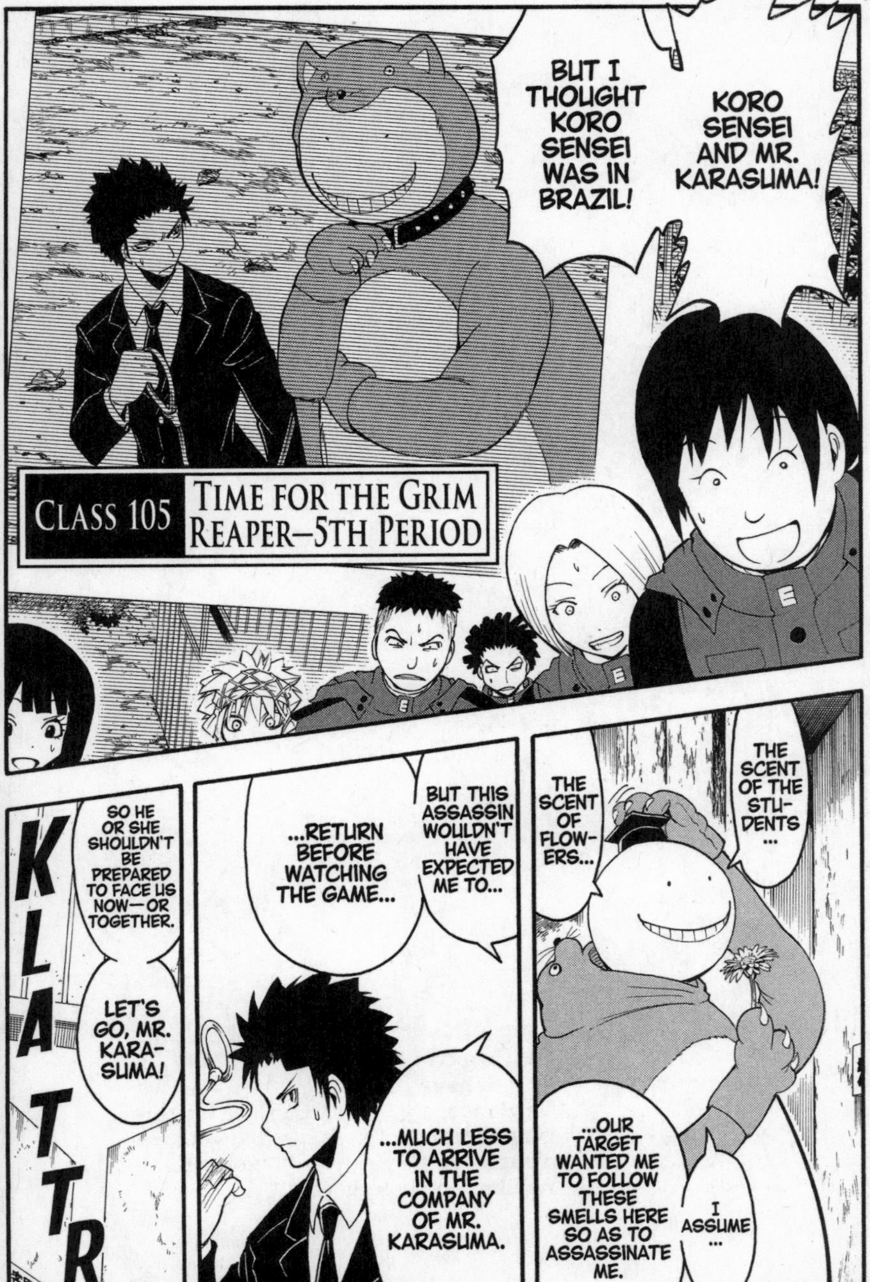
KORO SENSEI AND MR. KARASUMA!
BUT I THOUGHT KORO SENSEI WAS IN BRAZIL!
CLASS 105 TIME FOR THE GRIM REAPER—5TH PERIOD
THE SCENT OF THE STUDENTS...
THE SCENT OF FLOWERS...
...OUR TARGET WANTED ME TO FOLLOW THESE SMELLS HERE SO AS TO ASSASSINATE ME.
I ASSUME...
BUT THIS ASSASSIN WOULDN'T HAVE EXPECTED ME TO...
...RETURN BEFORE WATCHING THE GAME...
...MUCH LESS TO ARRIVE IN THE COMPANY OF MR. KARASUMA.
SO HE OR SHE SHOULDN'T BE PREPARED TO FACE US NOW—OR TOGETHER.
LET'S GO, MR. KARASUMA!
KLATTR

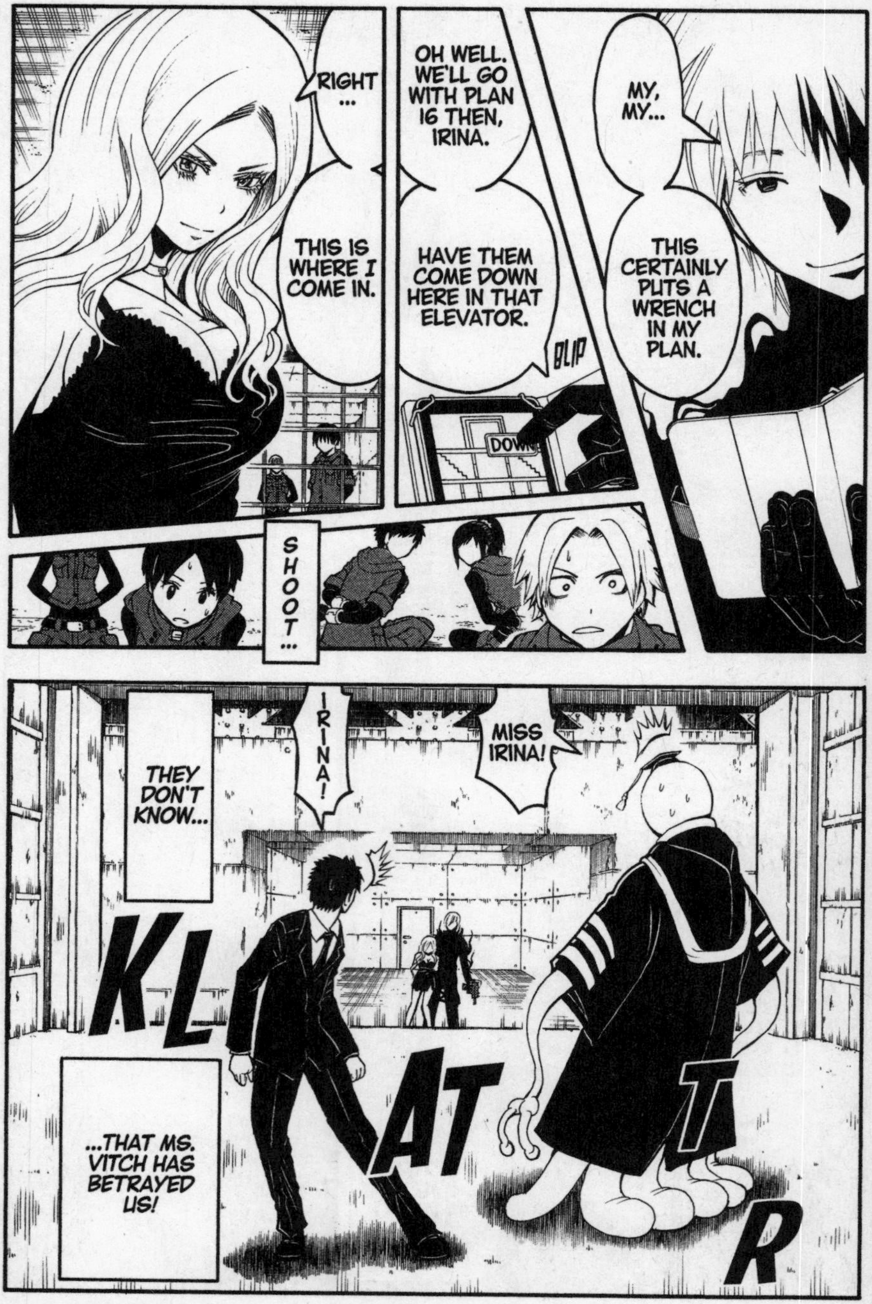
MY, MY...
THIS CERTAINLY PUTS A WRENCH IN MY PLAN.
OH WELL. WE'LL GO WITH PLAN 16 THEN, IRINA.
HAVE THEM COME DOWN HERE IN THAT ELEVATOR.
BLIP
DOWN
RIGHT ...
THIS IS WHERE I COME IN.
SHOOT ...
MISS IRINA!
IRINA!
THEY DON'T KNOW...
...THAT MS. VITCH HAS BETRAYED US!
KLATTR

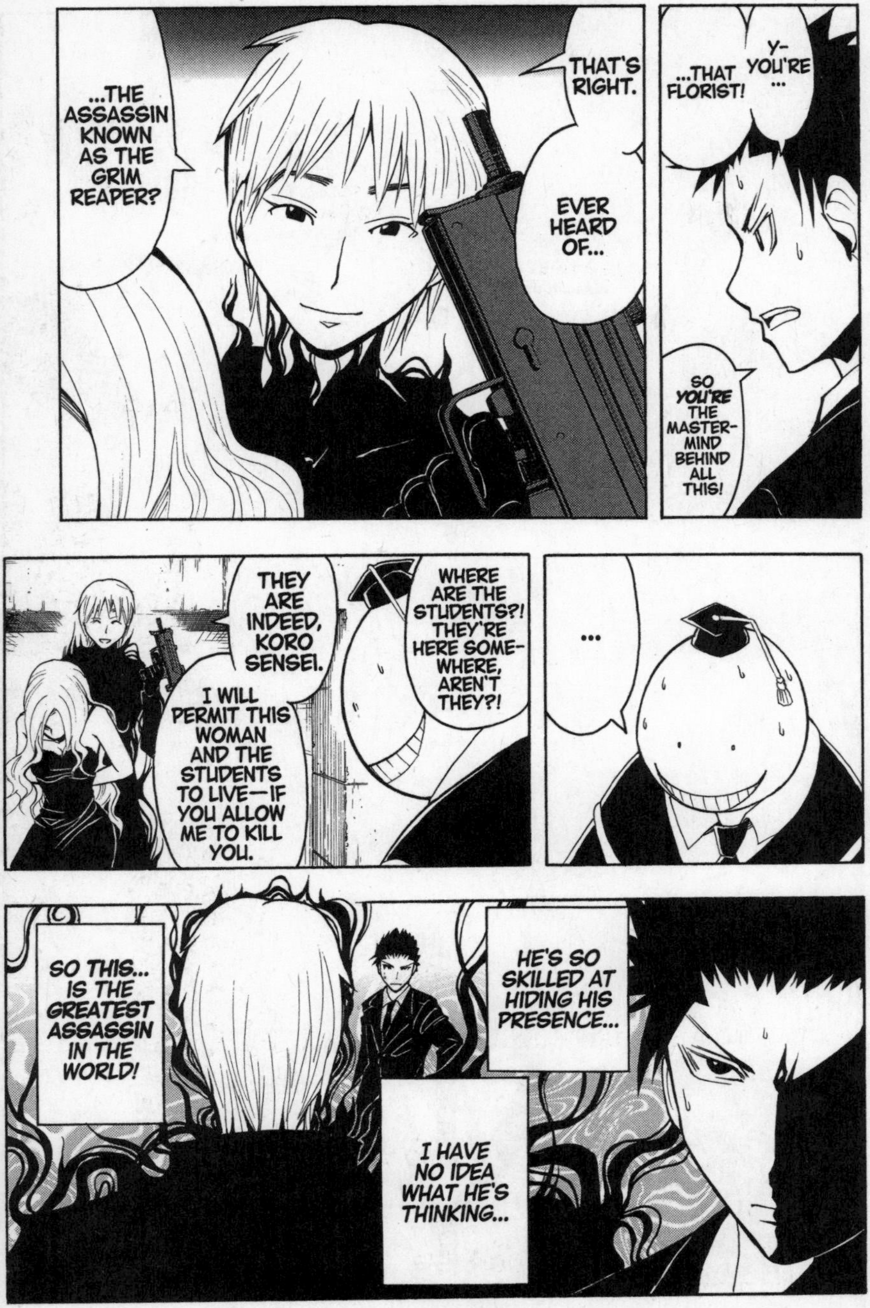
Y-YOU'RE...
...THAT FLORIST!
SO *YOU'RE* THE MASTERMIND BEHIND ALL THIS!
THAT'S RIGHT.
EVER HEARD OF...
...THE ASSASSIN KNOWN AS THE GRIM REAPER?
...
WHERE ARE THE STUDENTS?! THEY'RE HERE SOMEWHERE, AREN'T THEY?!
THEY ARE INDEED, KORO SENSEI.
I WILL PERMIT THIS WOMAN AND THE STUDENTS TO LIVE—IF YOU ALLOW ME TO KILL YOU.
HE'S SO SKILLED AT HIDING HIS PRESENCE...
SO THIS... IS THE GREATEST ASSASSIN IN THE WORLD!
I HAVE NO IDEA WHAT HE'S THINKING...

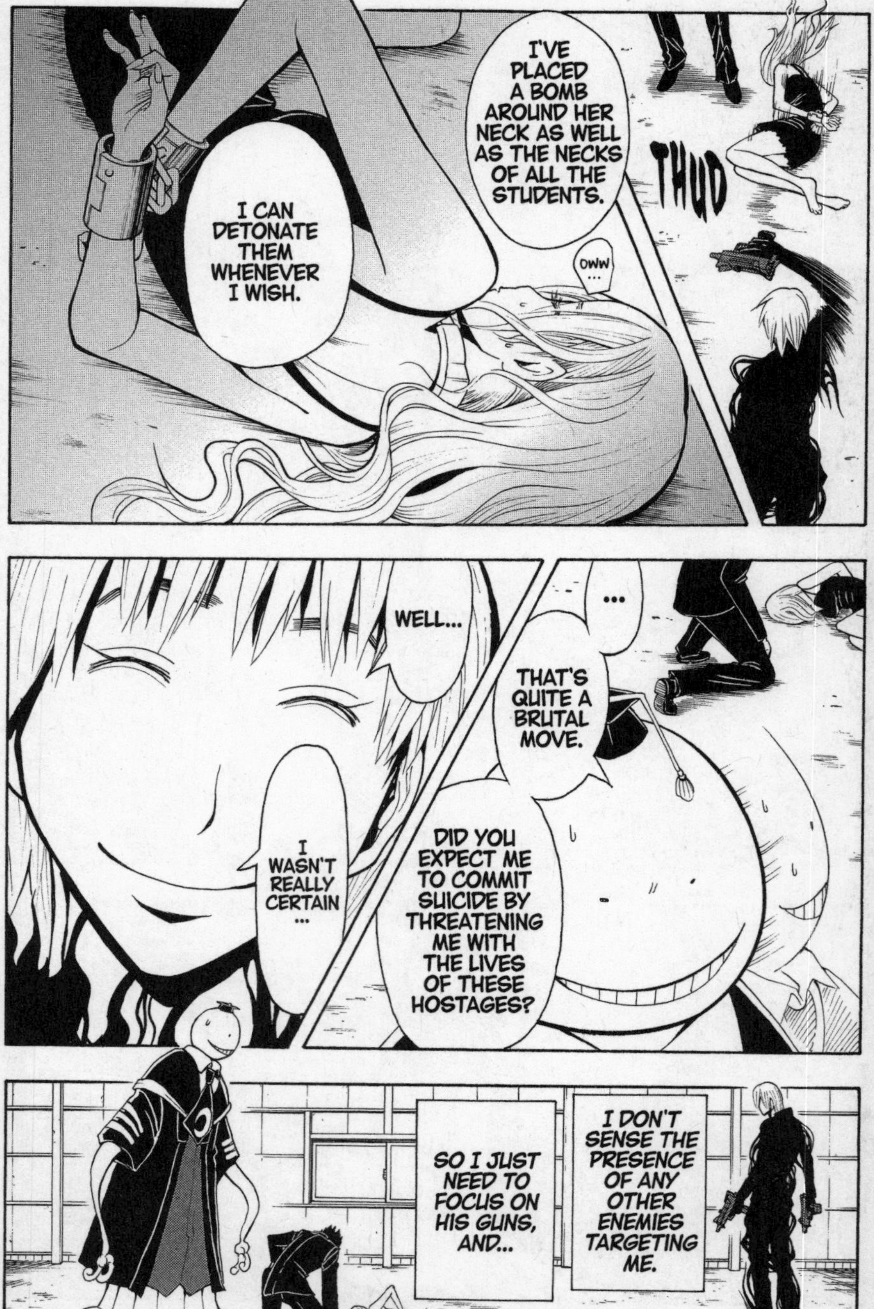
THUD
I'VE PLACED A BOMB AROUND HER NECK AS WELL AS THE NECKS OF ALL THE STUDENTS.
I CAN DETONATE THEM WHENEVER I WISH.
OWW...
...
THAT'S QUITE A BRUTAL MOVE.
DID YOU EXPECT ME TO COMMIT SUICIDE BY THREATENING ME WITH THE LIVES OF THESE HOSTAGES?
WELL...
I WASN'T REALLY CERTAIN...
I DON'T SENSE THE PRESENCE OF ANY OTHER ENEMIES TARGETING ME.
SO I JUST NEED TO FOCUS ON HIS GUNS, AND...

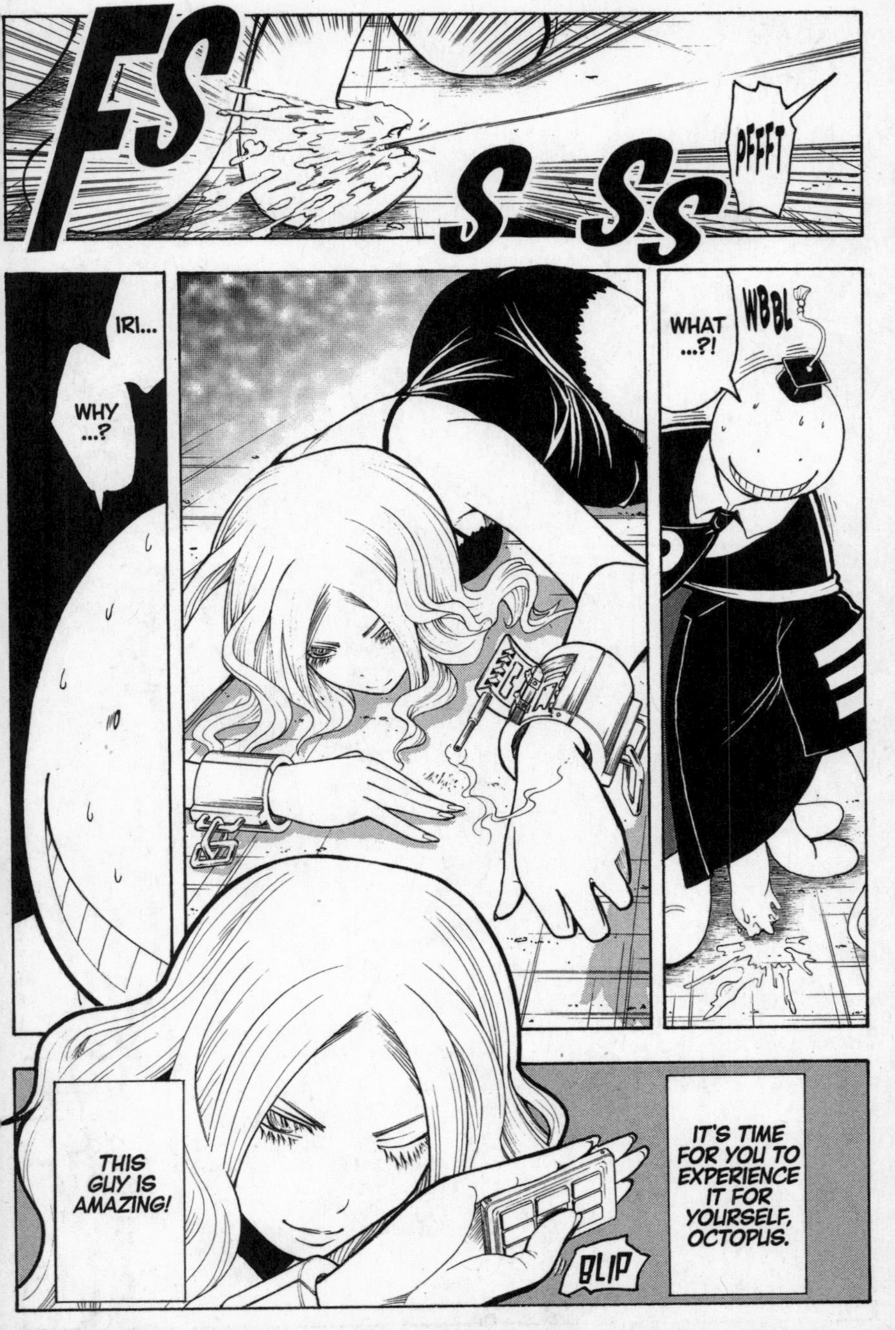
PFFFT
FS
S S S
WBBL
WHAT ...?!
IRI...
WHY ...?
IT'S TIME FOR YOU TO EXPERIENCE IT FOR YOURSELF, OCTOPUS.
BLIP
THIS GUY IS AMAZING!

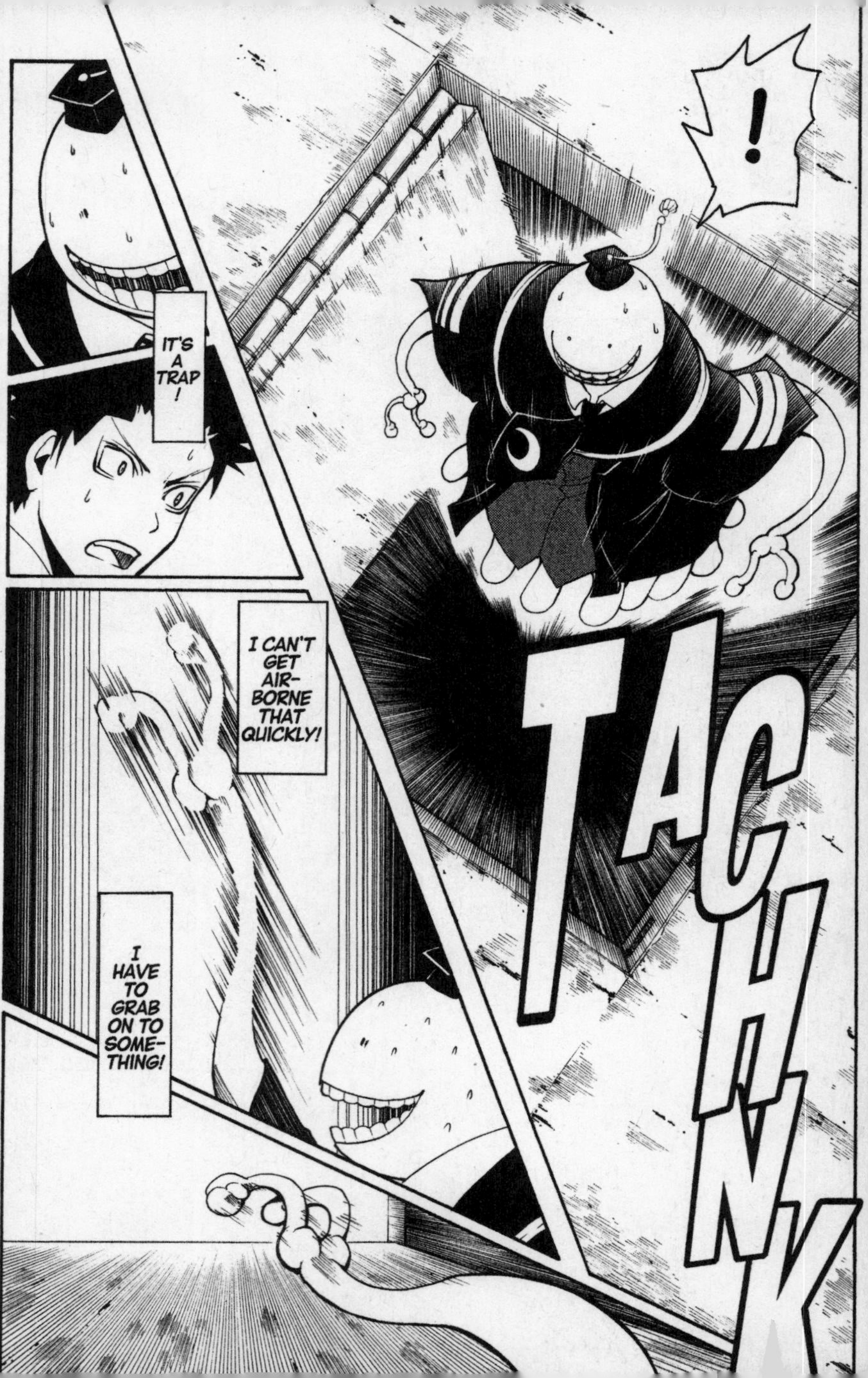
!
TACHNK
IT'S A TRAP!
I CAN'T GET AIRBORNE THAT QUICKLY!
I HAVE TO GRAB ON TO SOMETHING!

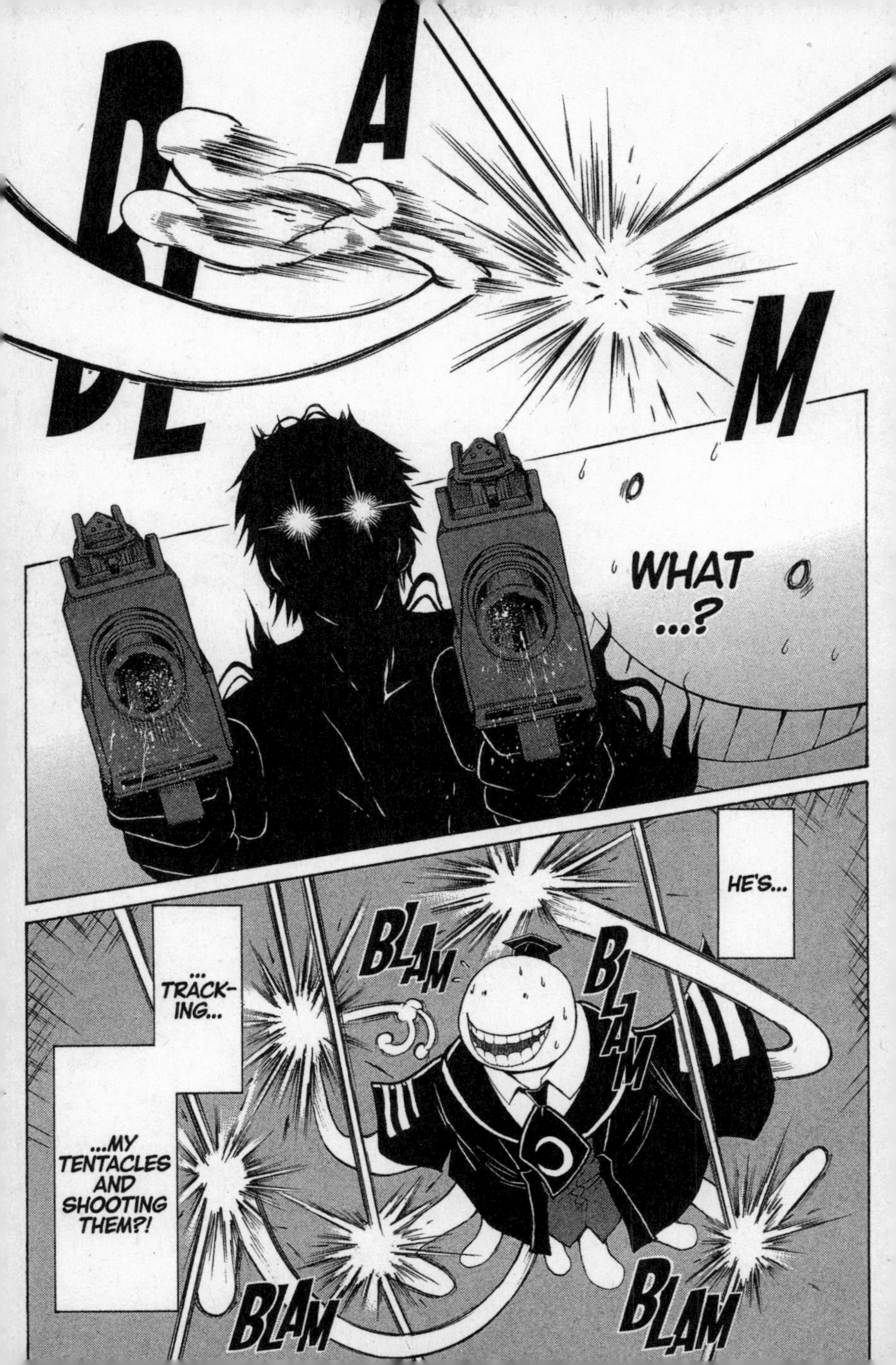
BLAM
WHAT ...?
HE'S...
BLAM
BLAM
... TRACKING...
...MY TENTACLES AND SHOOTING THEM?!
BLAM
BLAM

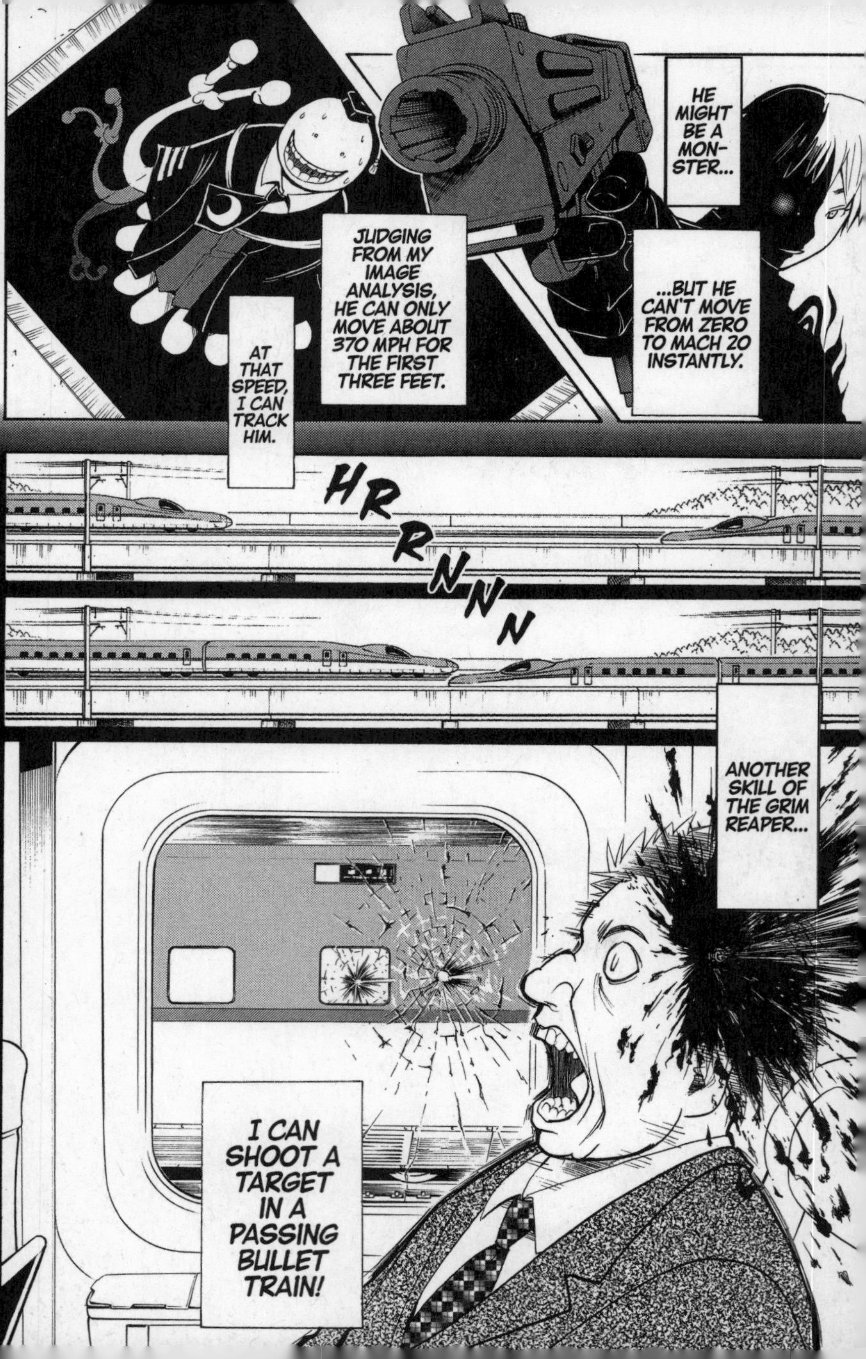
HE MIGHT BE A MONSTER...
...BUT HE CAN'T MOVE FROM ZERO TO MACH 20 INSTANTLY.
JUDGING FROM MY IMAGE ANALYSIS, HE CAN ONLY MOVE ABOUT 370 MPH FOR THE FIRST THREE FEET.
AT THAT SPEED, I CAN TRACK HIM.
HRRNNNN
ANOTHER SKILL OF THE GRIM REAPER...
I CAN SHOOT A TARGET IN A PASSING BULLET TRAIN!

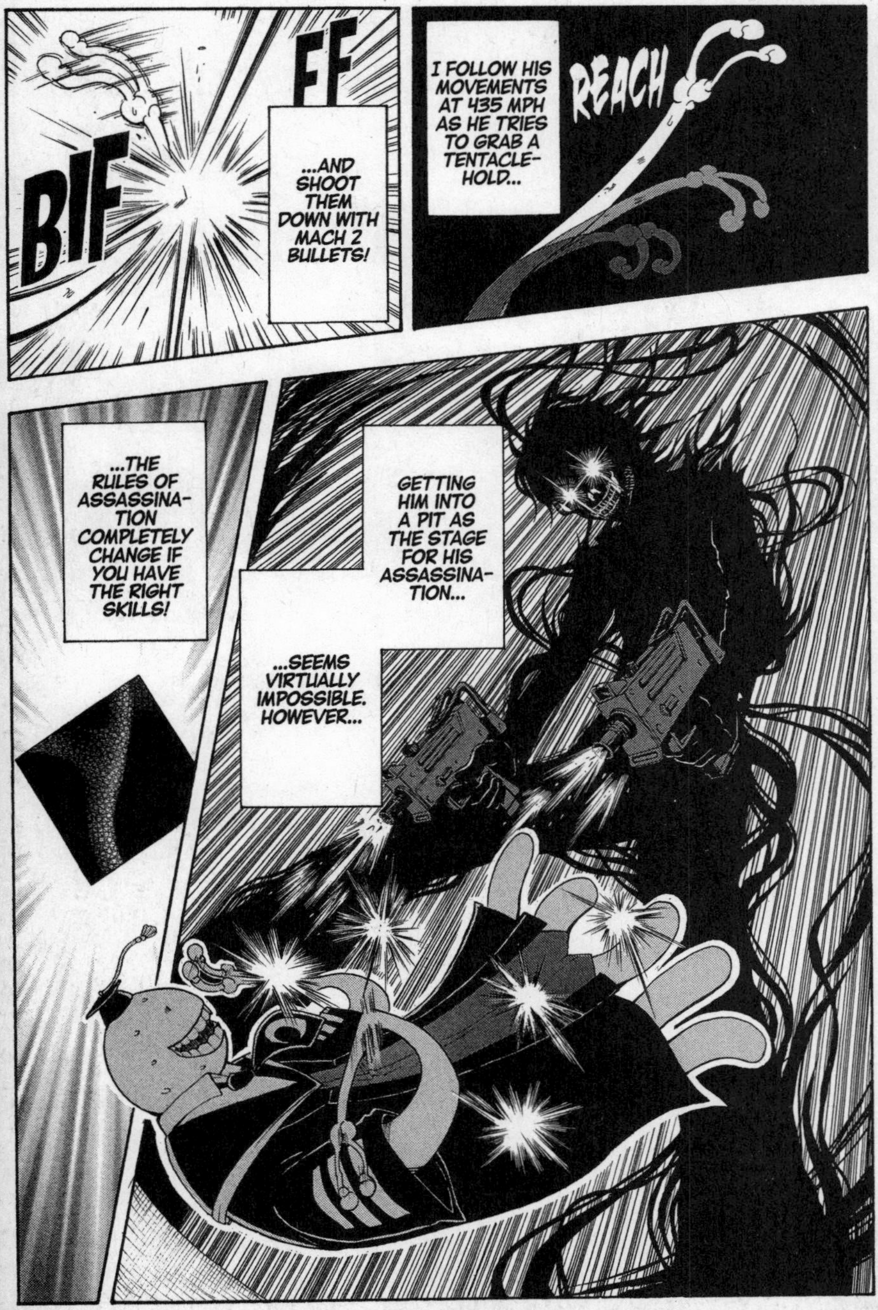
I FOLLOW HIS MOVEMENTS AT 435 MPH AS HE TRIES TO GRAB A TENTACLE-HOLD...
REACH
FF
...AND SHOOT THEM DOWN WITH MACH 2 BULLETS!
BIF
GETTING HIM INTO A PIT AS THE STAGE FOR HIS ASSASSINATION...
...SEEMS VIRTUALLY IMPOSSIBLE. HOWEVER...
...THE RULES OF ASSASSINATION COMPLETELY CHANGE IF YOU HAVE THE RIGHT SKILLS!

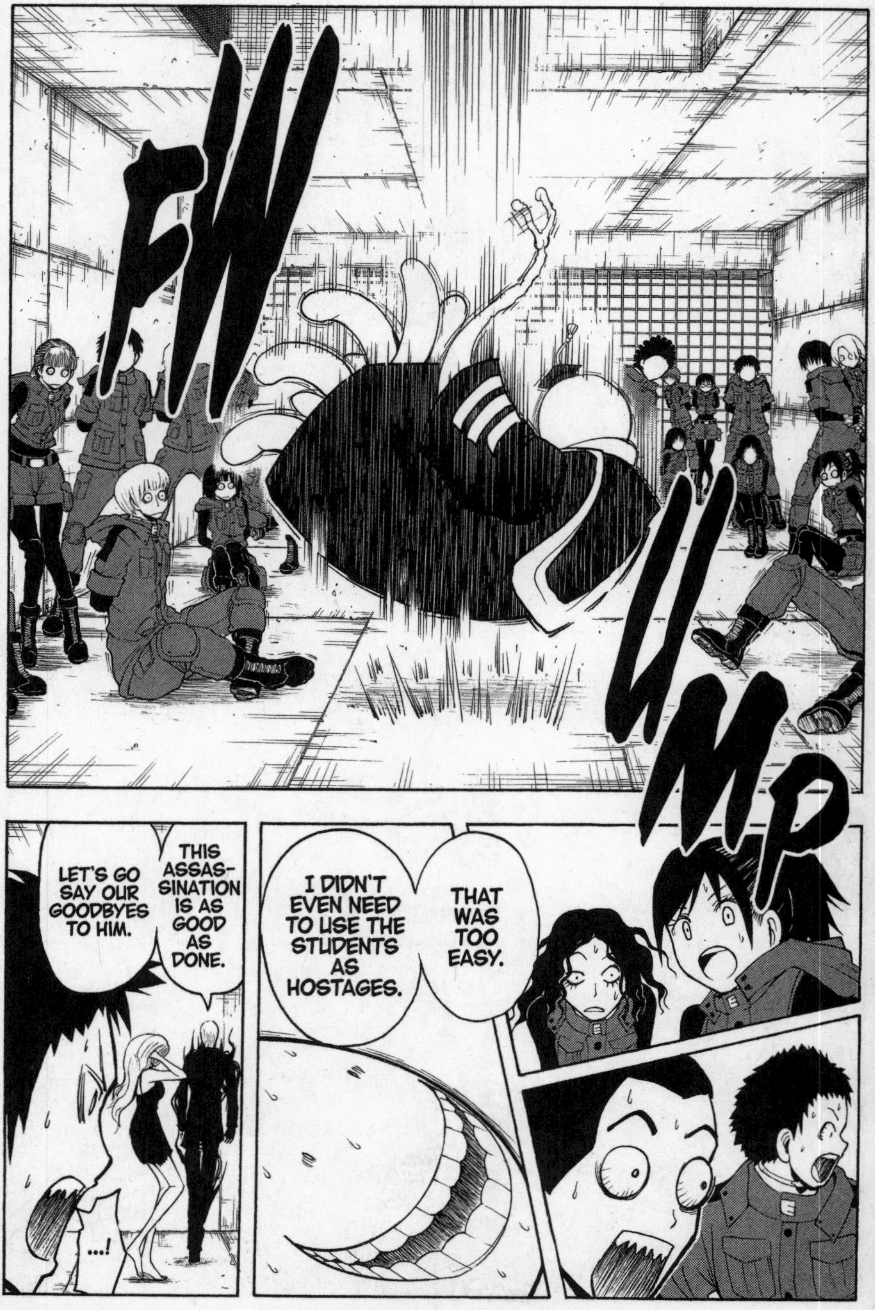
FWUMP
THAT WAS TOO EASY.
I DIDN'T EVEN NEED TO USE THE STUDENTS AS HOSTAGES.
THIS ASSAS-SINATION IS AS GOOD AS DONE.
LET'S GO SAY OUR GOODBYES TO HIM.
...!

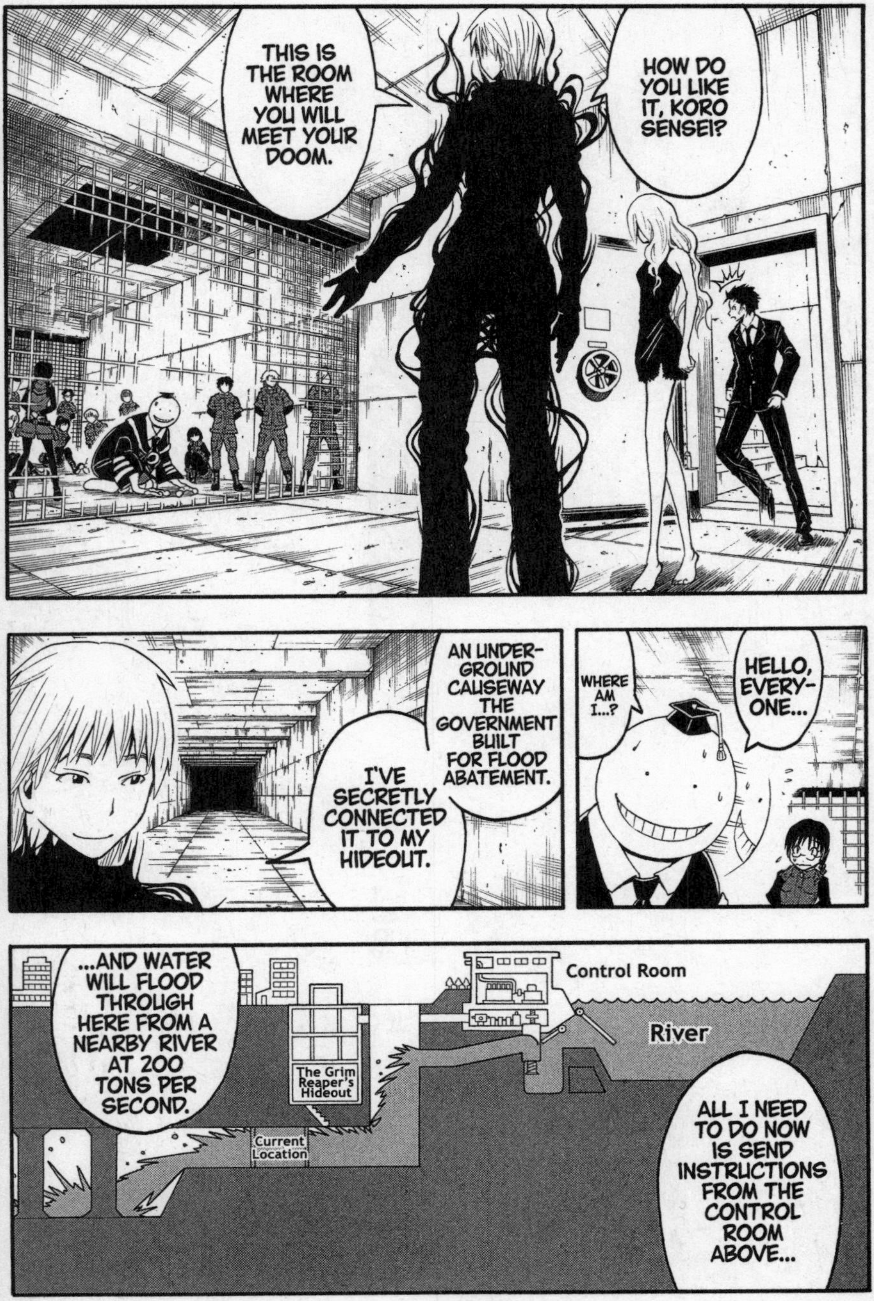
HOW DO YOU LIKE IT, KORO SENSEI?
THIS IS THE ROOM WHERE YOU WILL MEET YOUR DOOM.
HELLO, EVERY-ONE...
WHERE AM I...?
AN UNDER-GROUND CAUSEWAY THE GOVERNMENT BUILT FOR FLOOD ABATEMENT.
I'VE SECRETLY CONNECTED IT TO MY HIDEOUT.
Control Room
River
ALL I NEED TO DO NOW IS SEND INSTRUCTIONS FROM THE CONTROL ROOM ABOVE...
The Grim Reaper's Hideout
...AND WATER WILL FLOOD THROUGH HERE FROM A NEARBY RIVER AT 200 TONS PER SECOND.
Current Location

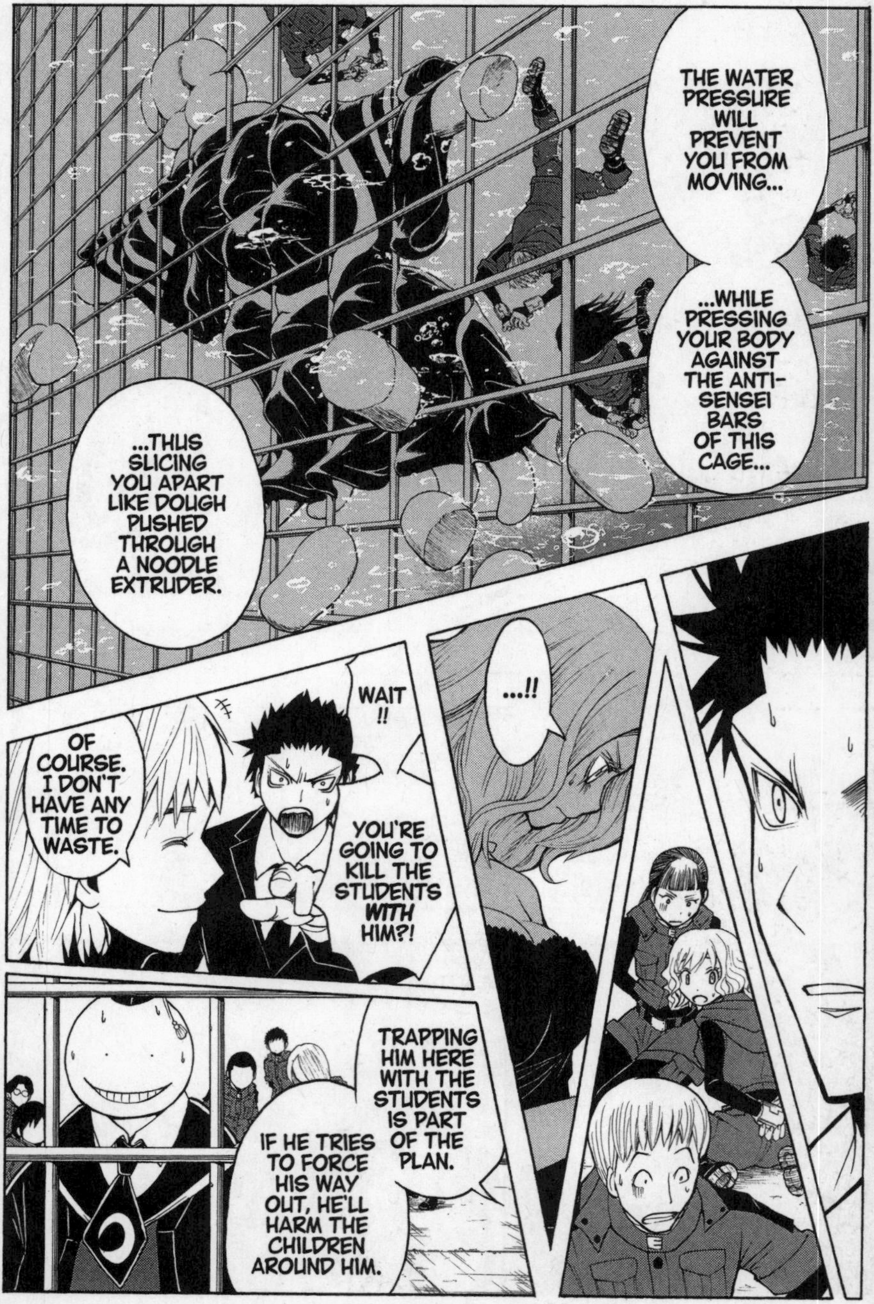
THE WATER PRESSURE WILL PREVENT YOU FROM MOVING...
...WHILE PRESSING YOUR BODY AGAINST THE ANTI-SENSEI BARS OF THIS CAGE...
...THUS SLICING YOU APART LIKE DOUGH PUSHED THROUGH A NOODLE EXTRUDER.
...!!
WAIT !!
YOU'RE GOING TO KILL THE STUDENTS *WITH* HIM?!
OF COURSE. I DON'T HAVE ANY TIME TO WASTE.
TRAPPING HIM HERE WITH THE STUDENTS IS PART OF THE PLAN.
IF HE TRIES TO FORCE HIS WAY OUT, HE'LL HARM THE CHILDREN AROUND HIM.

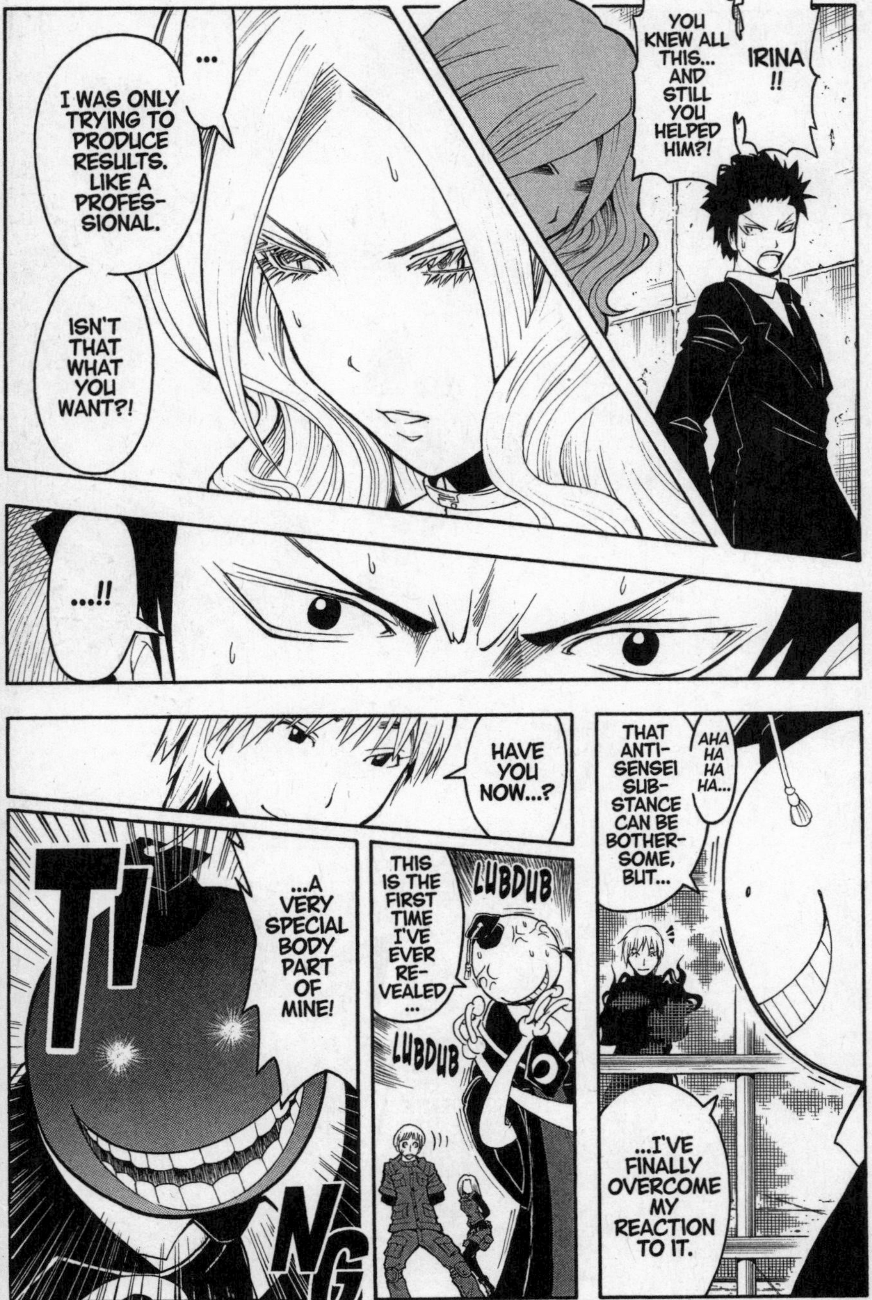
IRINA!!
YOU KNEW ALL THIS... AND STILL YOU HELPED HIM?!
...
I WAS ONLY TRYING TO PRODUCE RESULTS. LIKE A PROFESSIONAL.
ISN'T THAT WHAT YOU WANT?!
...!!
AHA HA HA HA...
THAT ANTI-SENSEI SUBSTANCE CAN BE BOTHERSOME, BUT...
...I'VE FINALLY OVERCOME MY REACTION TO IT.
HAVE YOU NOW...?
LUBDUB
THIS IS THE FIRST TIME I'VE EVER REVEALED...
LUBDUB
...A VERY SPECIAL BODY PART OF MINE!
TING

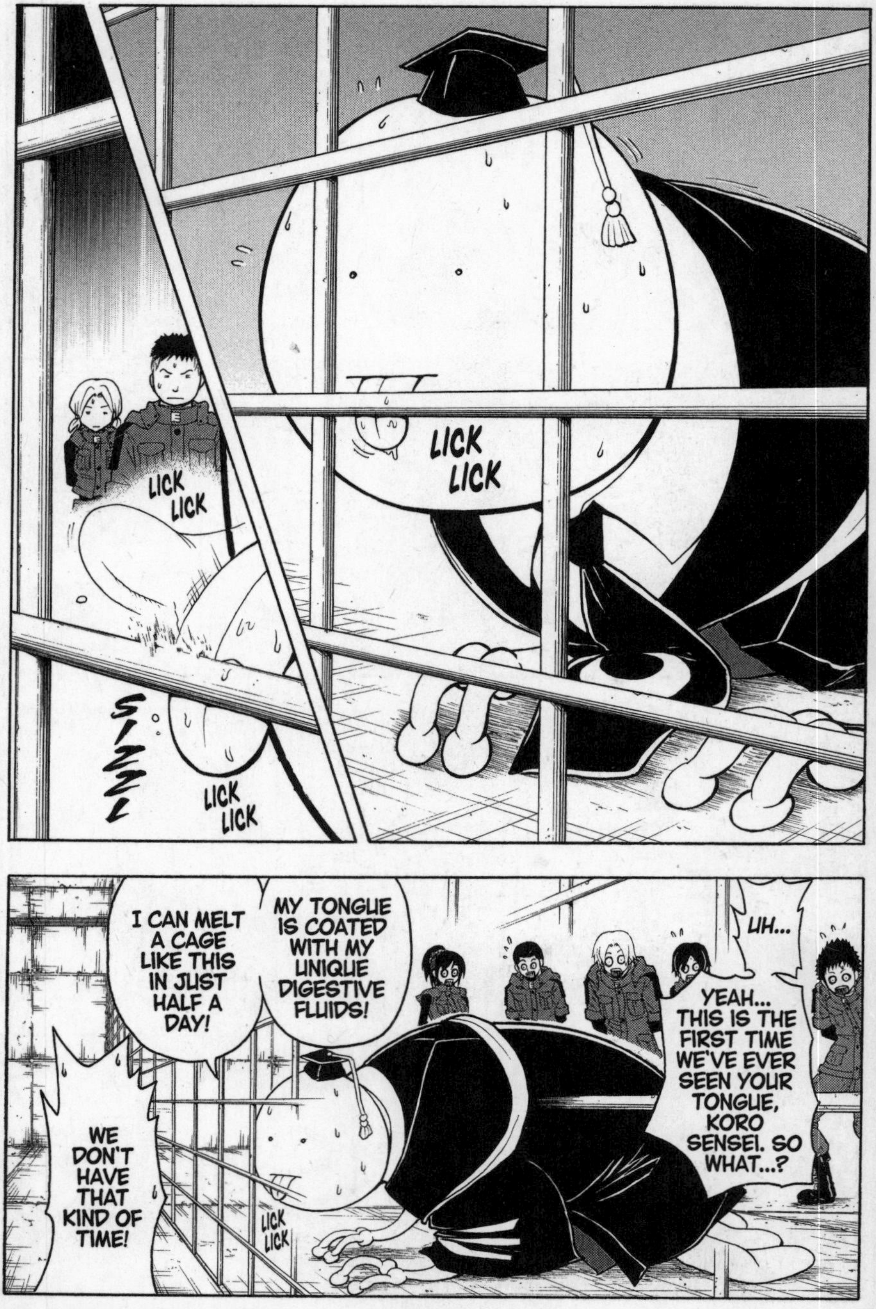
LICK LICK
LICK LICK
SIZZZL
LICK LICK
UH...
YEAH... THIS IS THE FIRST TIME WE'VE EVER SEEN YOUR TONGUE, KORO SENSEI. SO WHAT...?
MY TONGUE IS COATED WITH MY UNIQUE DIGESTIVE FLUIDS!
I CAN MELT A CAGE LIKE THIS IN JUST HALF A DAY!
WE DON'T HAVE THAT KIND OF TIME!
LICK LICK

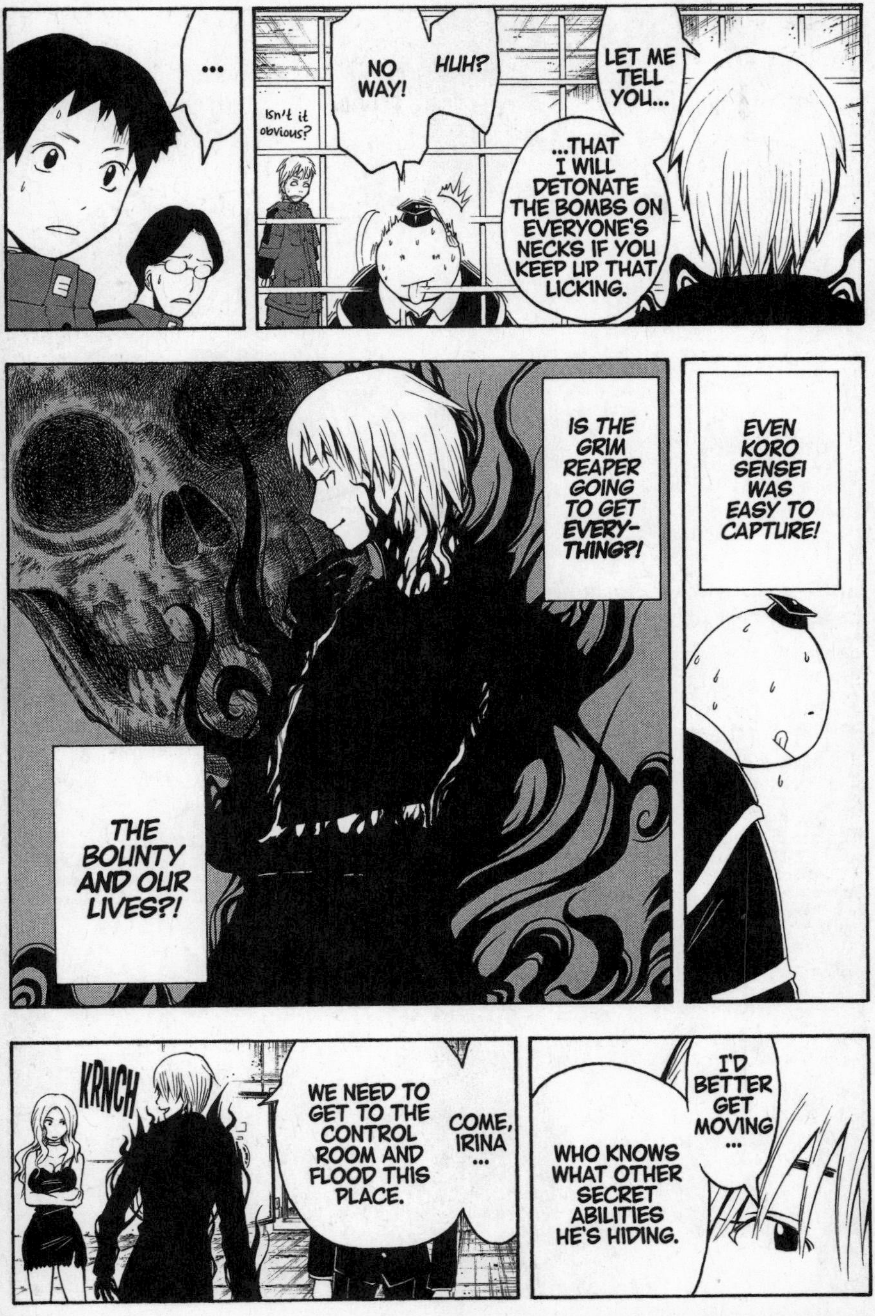
LET ME TELL YOU...
...THAT I WILL DETONATE THE BOMBS ON EVERYONE'S NECKS IF YOU KEEP UP THAT LICKING.
HUH?
NO WAY!
Isn't it obvious?
...
EVEN KORO SENSEI WAS EASY TO CAPTURE!
IS THE GRIM REAPER GOING TO GET EVERYTHING?!
THE BOUNTY AND OUR LIVES?!
I'D BETTER GET MOVING...
WHO KNOWS WHAT OTHER SECRET ABILITIES HE'S HIDING.
COME, IRINA...
WE NEED TO GET TO THE CONTROL ROOM AND FLOOD THIS PLACE.
KRNCH

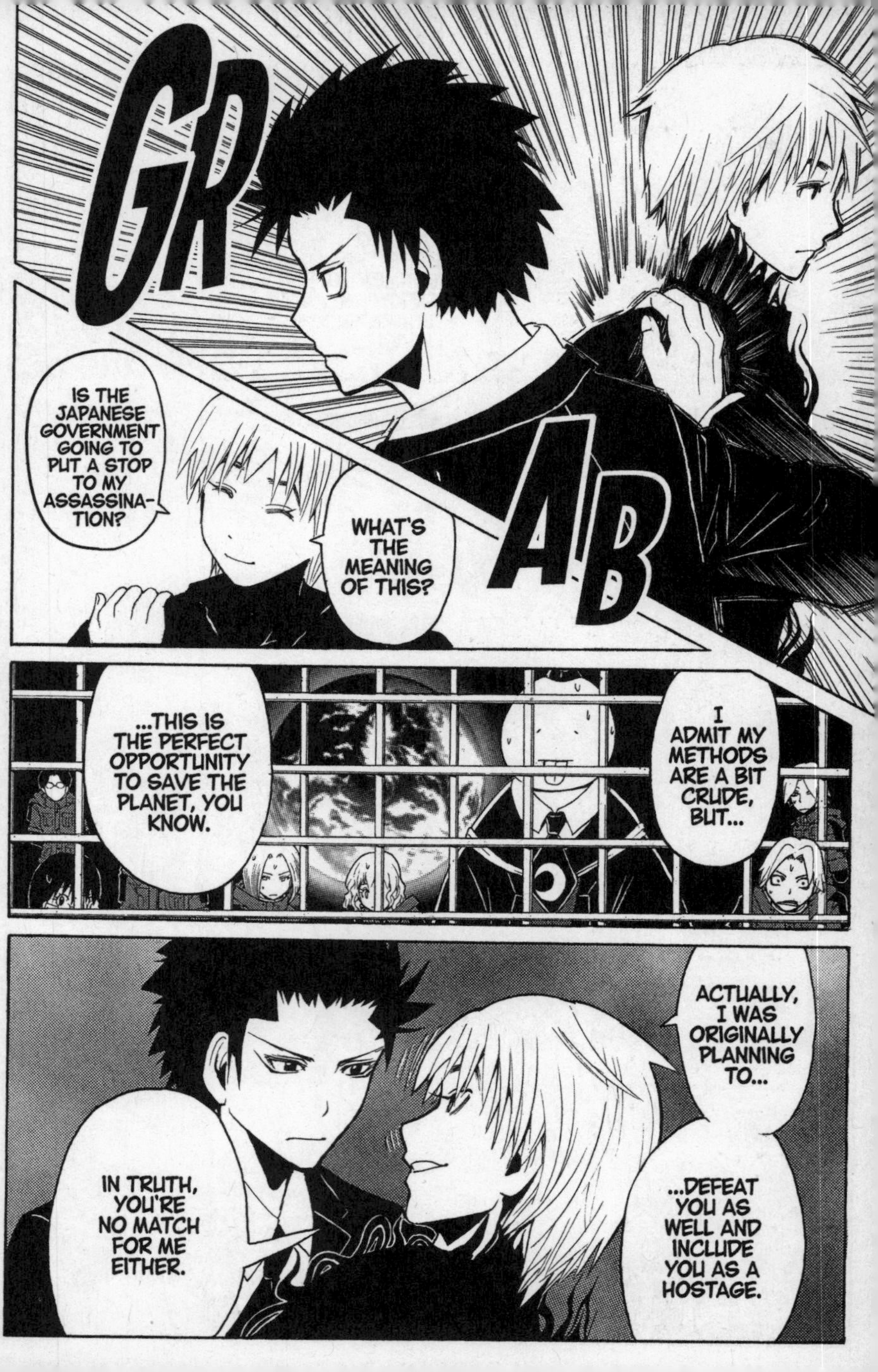
GR
AB
WHAT'S THE MEANING OF THIS?
IS THE JAPANESE GOVERNMENT GOING TO PUT A STOP TO MY ASSASSINA-TION?
I ADMIT MY METHODS ARE A BIT CRUDE, BUT...
...THIS IS THE PERFECT OPPORTUNITY TO SAVE THE PLANET, YOU KNOW.
ACTUALLY, I WAS ORIGINALLY PLANNING TO...
...DEFEAT YOU AS WELL AND INCLUDE YOU AS A HOSTAGE.
IN TRUTH, YOU'RE NO MATCH FOR ME EITHER.

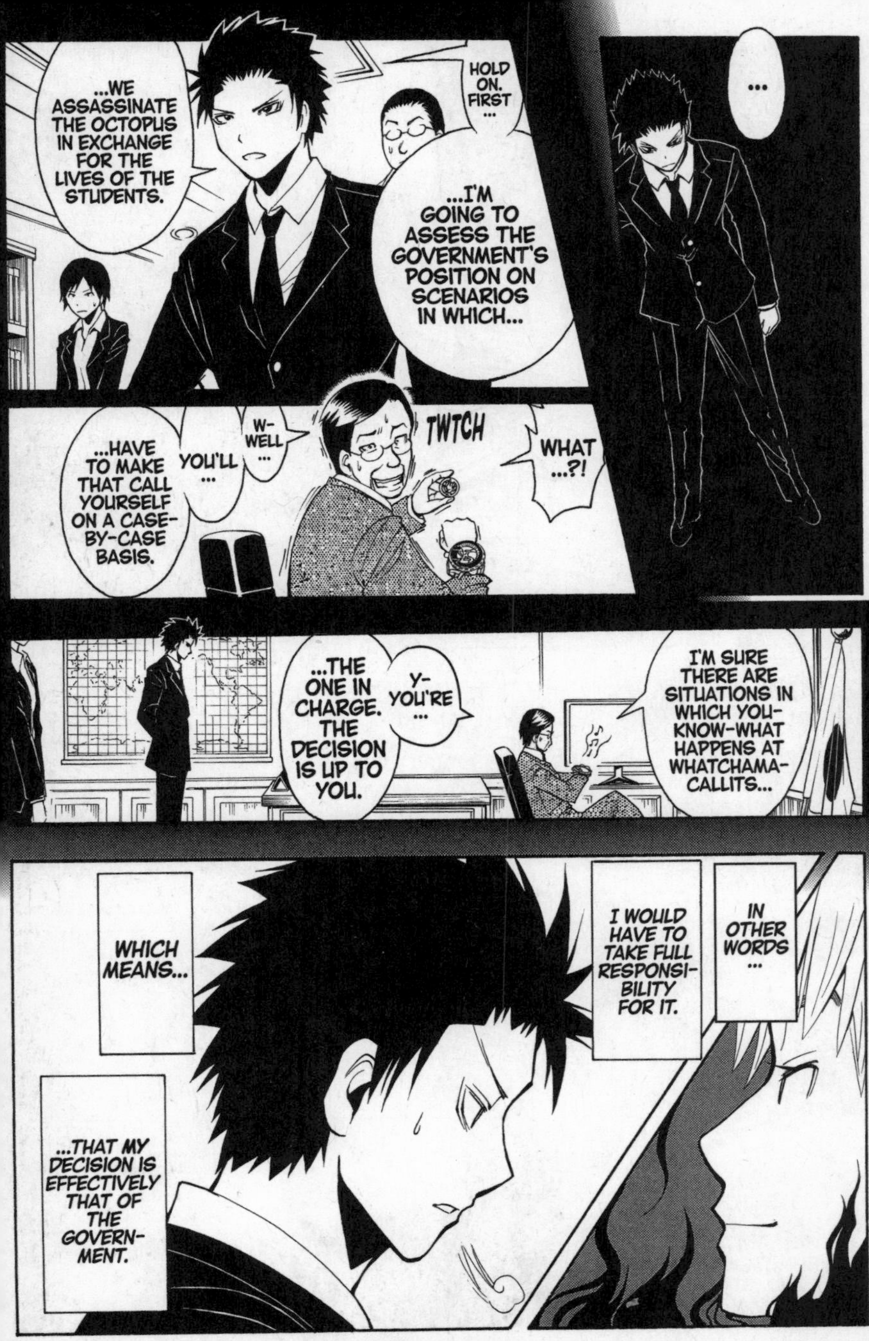
...
HOLD ON. FIRST ...
...I'M GOING TO ASSESS THE GOVERNMENT'S POSITION ON SCENARIOS IN WHICH...
...WE ASSASSINATE THE OCTOPUS IN EXCHANGE FOR THE LIVES OF THE STUDENTS.
WHAT ...?!
TWTCH
W-WELL ...
YOU'LL ...
...HAVE TO MAKE THAT CALL YOURSELF ON A CASE-BY-CASE BASIS.
I'M SURE THERE ARE SITUATIONS IN WHICH YOU-KNOW-WHAT HAPPENS AT WHATCHAMA-CALLITS...
Y-YOU'RE ...
...THE ONE IN CHARGE. THE DECISION IS UP TO YOU.
IN OTHER WORDS ...
I WOULD HAVE TO TAKE FULL RESPONSI-BILITY FOR IT.
WHICH MEANS...
...THAT MY DECISION IS EFFECTIVELY THAT OF THE GOVERN-MENT.

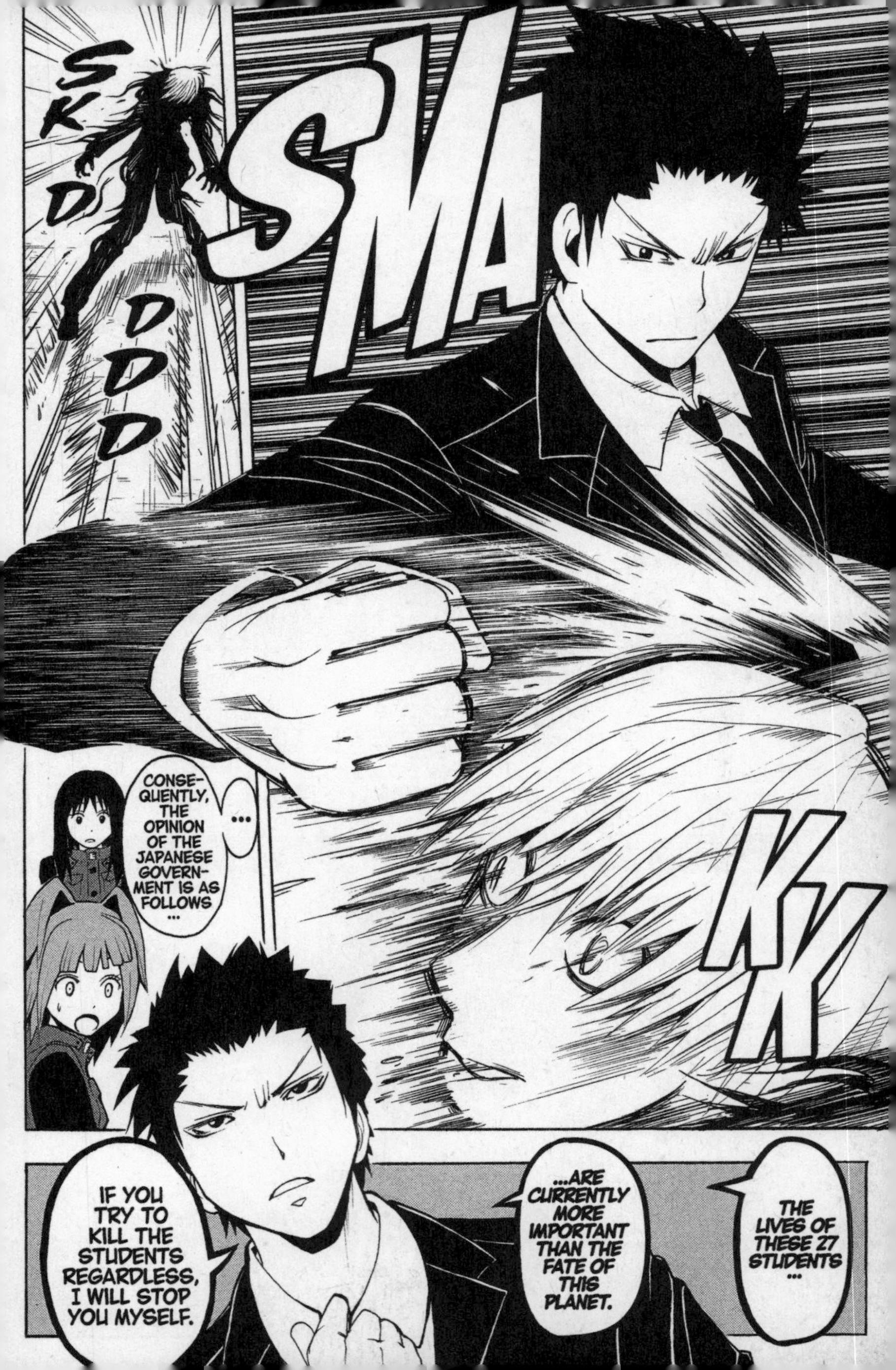
SMA
KK
SKD
DDDD
CONSE-QUENTLY, THE OPINION OF THE JAPANESE GOVERN-MENT IS AS FOLLOWS ...
...
THE LIVES OF THESE 27 STUDENTS ...
...ARE CURRENTLY MORE IMPORTANT THAN THE FATE OF THIS PLANET.
IF YOU TRY TO KILL THE STUDENTS REGARDLESS, I WILL STOP YOU MYSELF.

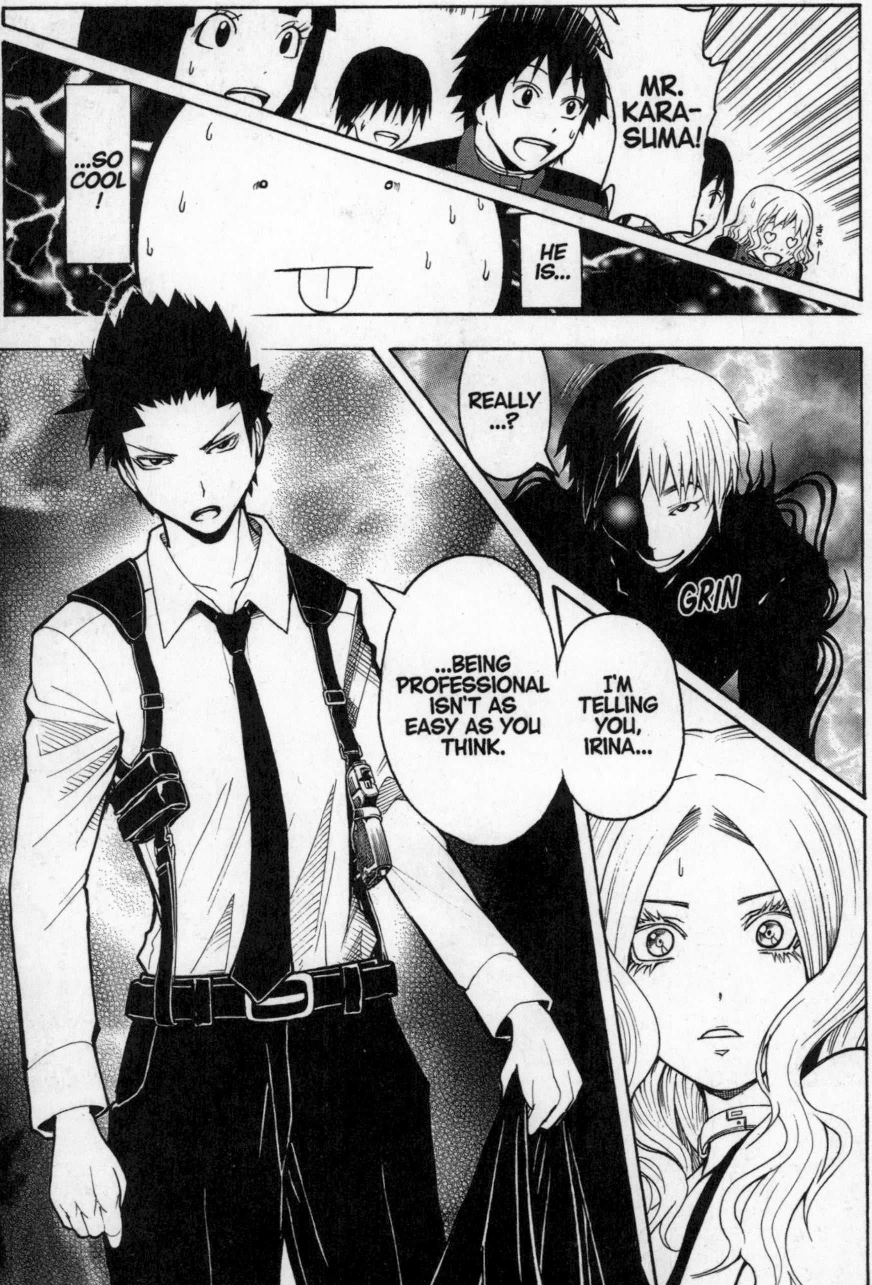
MR. KARA-SUMA!
きゃー
HE IS...
...SO COOL!
REALLY ...?
GRIN
I'M TELLING YOU, IRINA...
...BEING PROFESSIONAL ISN'T AS EASY AS YOU THINK.

Oh, but you mustn't do you-know-what during a you-know-what!

The you-know-what are...

And the whatcha-macallits can be annoying...

GOKI ONAGA

- 🙂 BIRTHDAY: DECEMBER 8 (59 YEARS OLD)

- 🙂 HEIGHT: 5' 8"

- 🙂 WEIGHT: 176 LBS.

- 🙂 CAREER HISTORY: CHIEF OF STAFF → CHIEF OF INTER SERVICES INTELLIGENCE

- 🙂 HOBBY/SKILLS: PLAYING WITH HIS SON'S OLD TOYS.

- 🙂 MOTTO: DEFEAT DOES NOT ARISE FROM NATURAL CAUSES BUT THE FAULTS OF THE GENERAL.

- 🙂 UNOFFICIAL NICKNAME GIVEN BY SUBORDINATES: "CHIEF YOU-KNOW-WHAT."

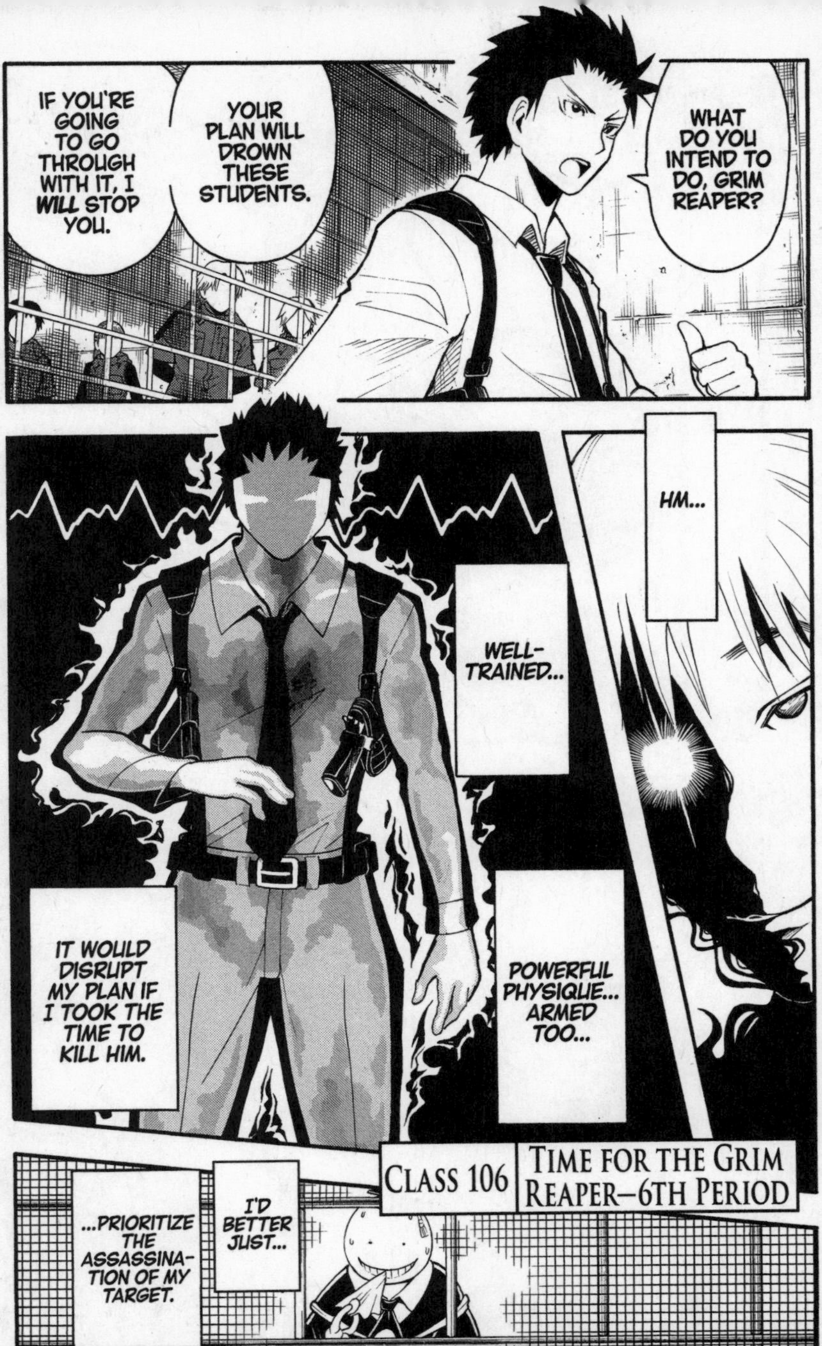
WHAT DO YOU INTEND TO DO, GRIM REAPER?
YOUR PLAN WILL DROWN THESE STUDENTS.
IF YOU'RE GOING TO GO THROUGH WITH IT, I WILL STOP YOU.
HM...
WELL-TRAINED...
POWERFUL PHYSIQUE... ARMED TOO...
IT WOULD DISRUPT MY PLAN IF I TOOK THE TIME TO KILL HIM.
CLASS 106
TIME FOR THE GRIM REAPER—6TH PERIOD
I'D BETTER JUST...
...PRIORITIZE THE ASSASSINATION OF MY TARGET.

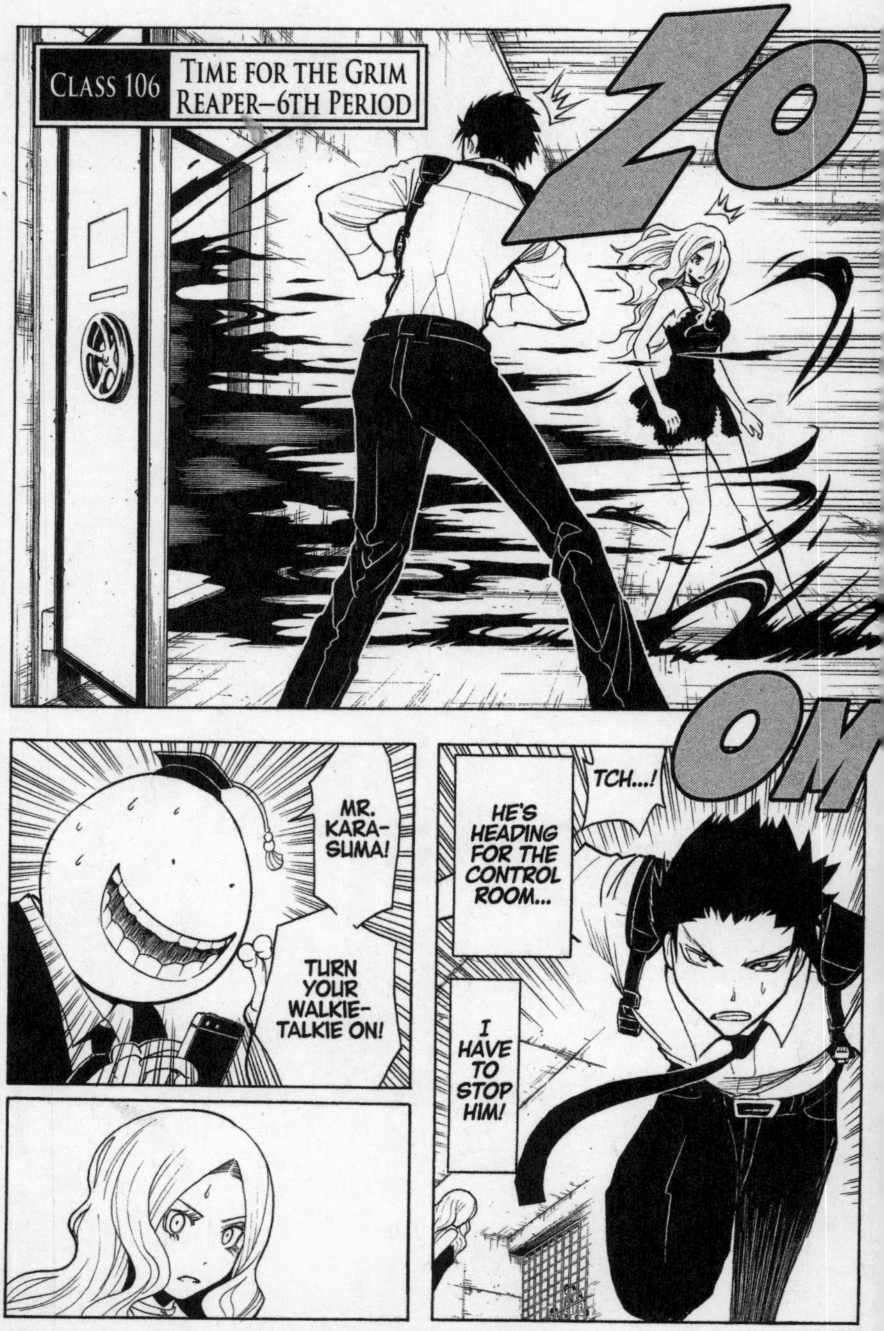
Class 106
Time for the Grim Reaper—6th Period
ZO
OM
TCH...!
HE'S HEADING FOR THE CONTROL ROOM...
I HAVE TO STOP HIM!
MR. KARASUMA!
TURN YOUR WALKIE-TALKIE ON!

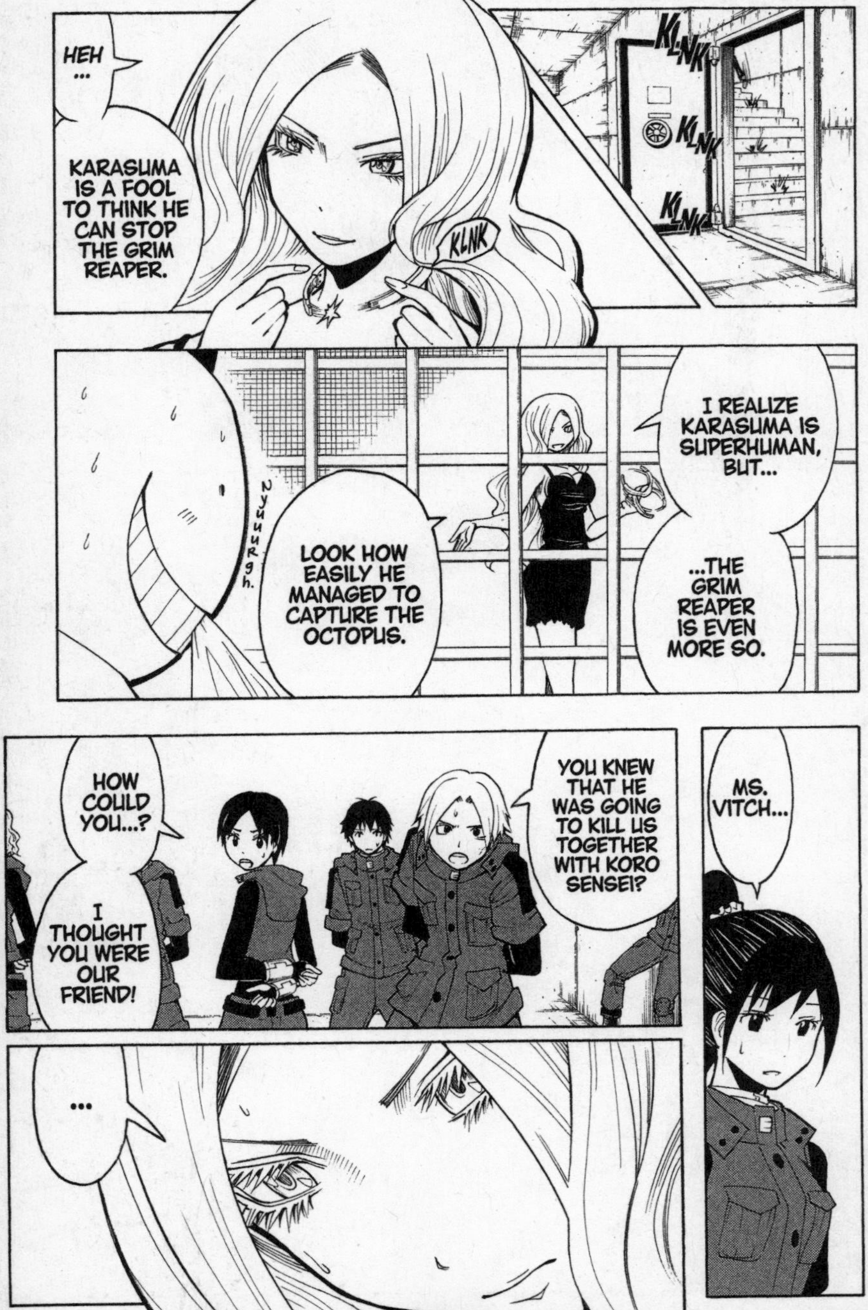
KLNK
KLNK
KLNK
HEH ...
KARASUMA IS A FOOL TO THINK HE CAN STOP THE GRIM REAPER.
KLNK
I REALIZE KARASUMA IS SUPERHUMAN, BUT...
...THE GRIM REAPER IS EVEN MORE SO.
LOOK HOW EASILY HE MANAGED TO CAPTURE THE OCTOPUS.
Nyuuurgh.
MS. VITCH...
YOU KNEW THAT HE WAS GOING TO KILL US TOGETHER WITH KORO SENSEI?
HOW COULD YOU...?
I THOUGHT YOU WERE OUR FRIEND!
...

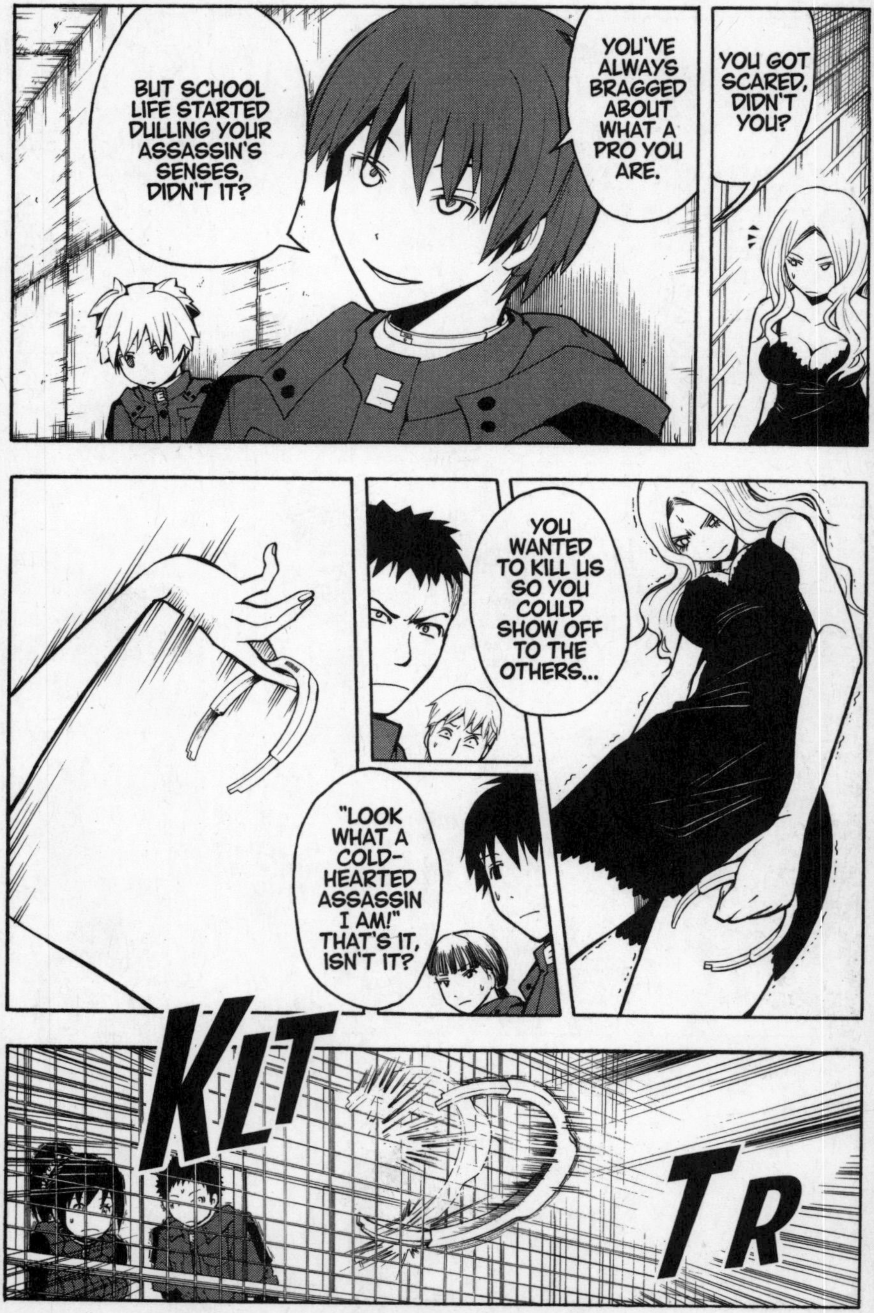
YOU GOT SCARED, DIDN'T YOU?
YOU'VE ALWAYS BRAGGED ABOUT WHAT A PRO YOU ARE.
BUT SCHOOL LIFE STARTED DULLING YOUR ASSASSIN'S SENSES, DIDN'T IT?
YOU WANTED TO KILL US SO YOU COULD SHOW OFF TO THE OTHERS...
"LOOK WHAT A COLD-HEARTED ASSASSIN I AM!" THAT'S IT, ISN'T IT?
KLIT
TR

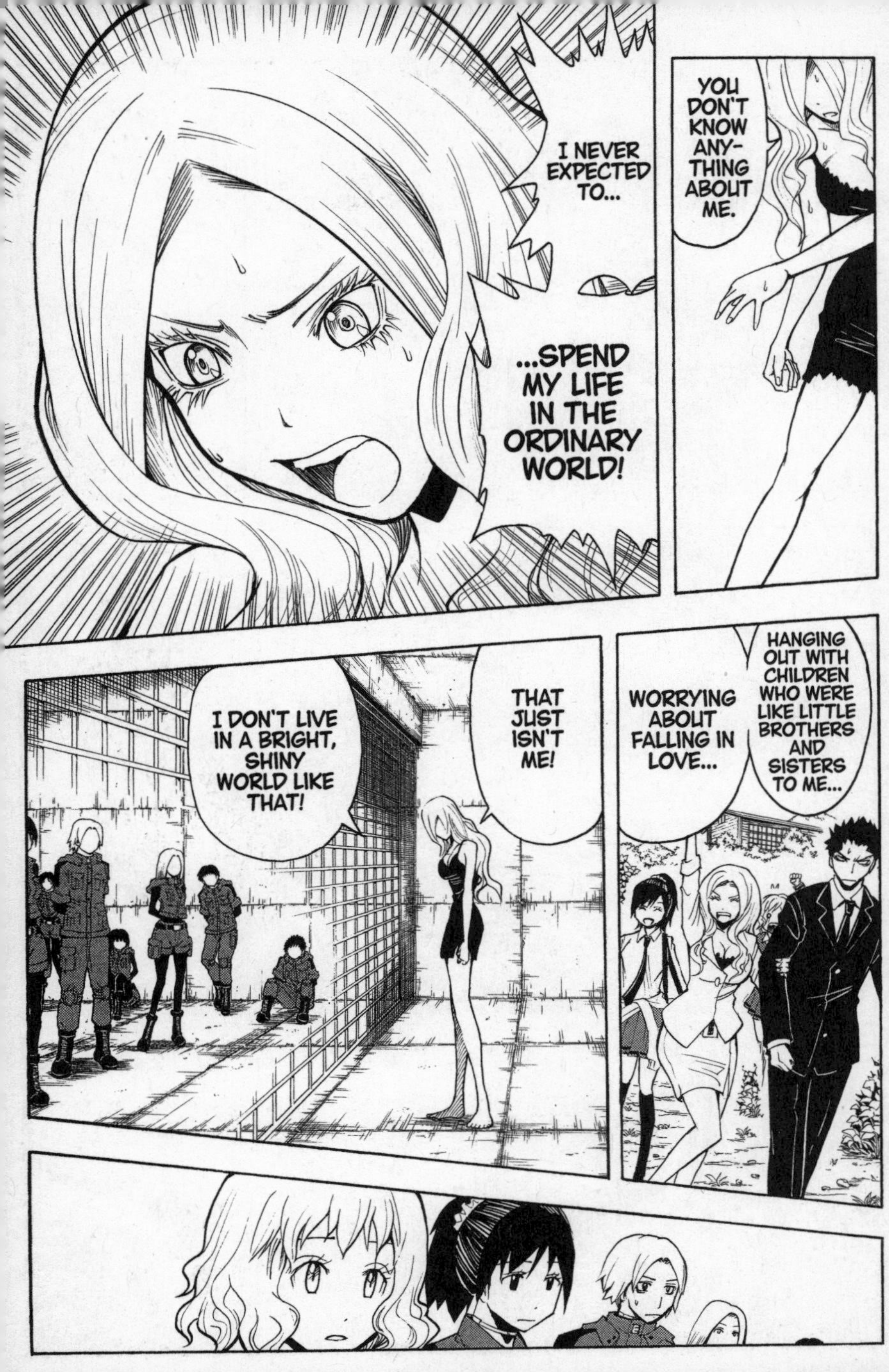
YOU DON'T KNOW ANY-THING ABOUT ME.
I NEVER EXPECTED TO...
...SPEND MY LIFE IN THE ORDINARY WORLD!
HANGING OUT WITH CHILDREN WHO WERE LIKE LITTLE BROTHERS AND SISTERS TO ME...
WORRYING ABOUT FALLING IN LOVE...
THAT JUST ISN'T ME!
I DON'T LIVE IN A BRIGHT, SHINY WORLD LIKE THAT!

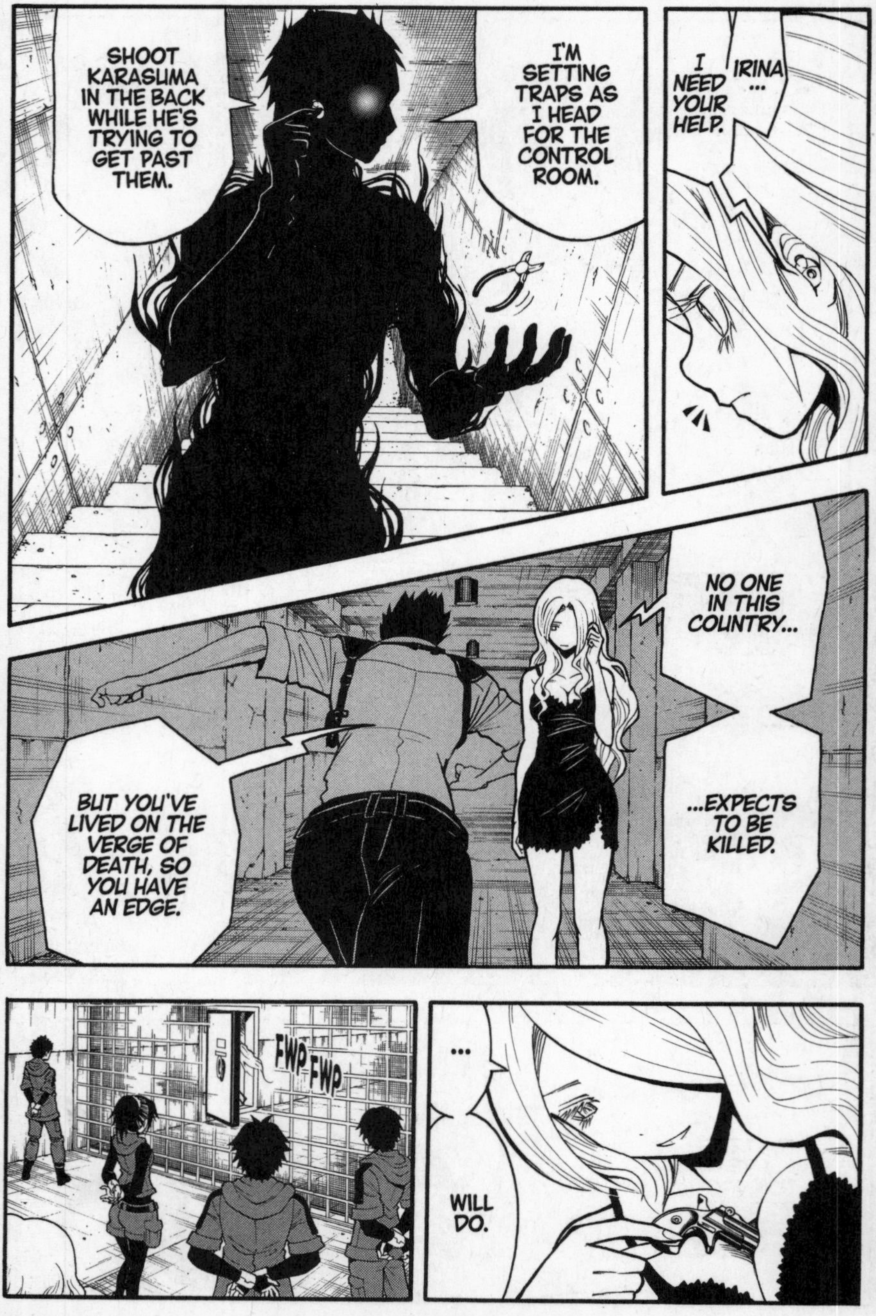
IRINA...
I NEED YOUR HELP.
I'M SETTING TRAPS AS I HEAD FOR THE CONTROL ROOM.
SHOOT KARASUMA IN THE BACK WHILE HE'S TRYING TO GET PAST THEM.
NO ONE IN THIS COUNTRY...
...EXPECTS TO BE KILLED.
BUT YOU'VE LIVED ON THE VERGE OF DEATH, SO YOU HAVE AN EDGE.
...
WILL DO.
FWP FWP

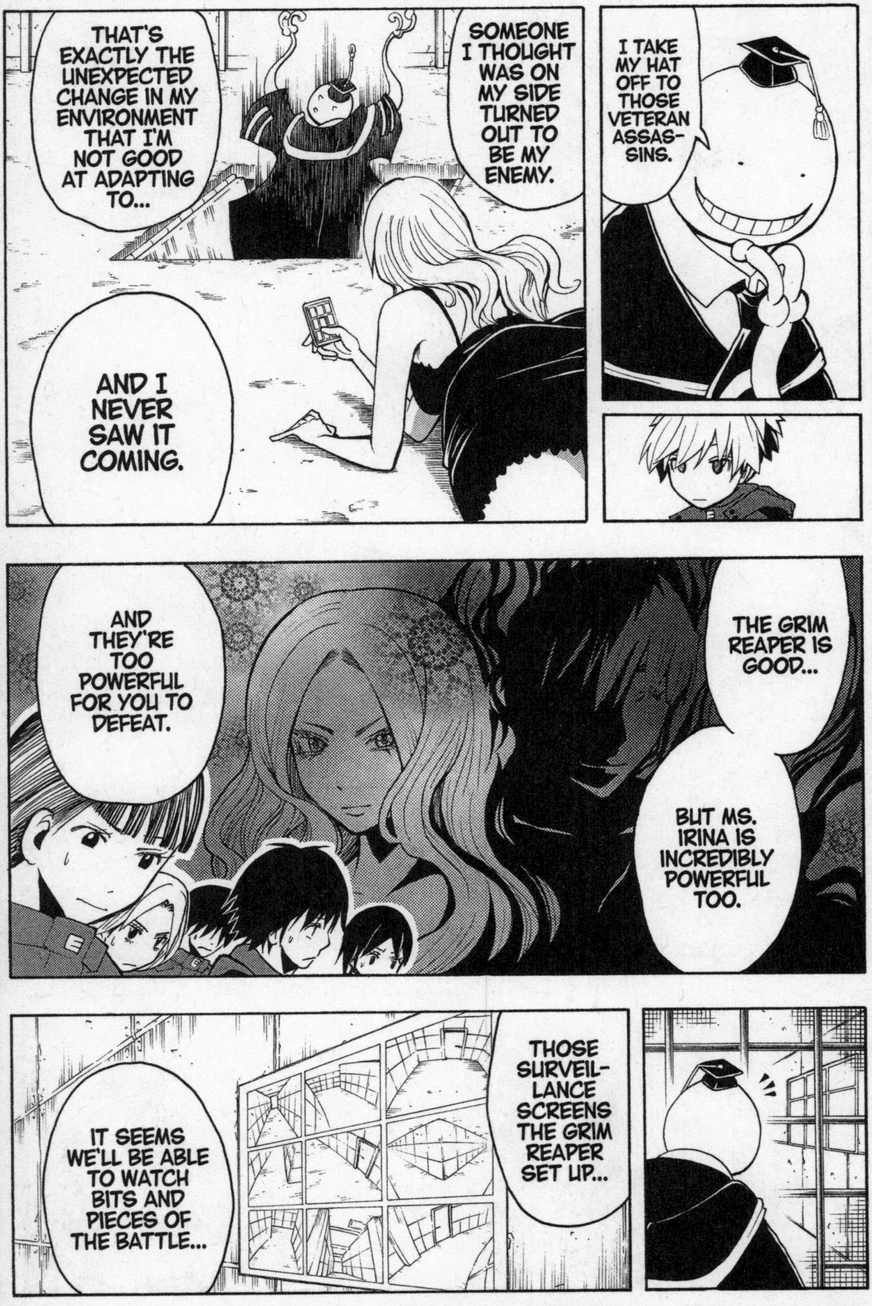
I TAKE MY HAT OFF TO THOSE VETERAN ASSAS-SINS.
SOMEONE I THOUGHT WAS ON MY SIDE TURNED OUT TO BE MY ENEMY.
THAT'S EXACTLY THE UNEXPECTED CHANGE IN MY ENVIRONMENT THAT I'M NOT GOOD AT ADAPTING TO...
AND I NEVER SAW IT COMING.
THE GRIM REAPER IS GOOD...
BUT MS. IRINA IS INCREDIBLY POWERFUL TOO.
AND THEY'RE TOO POWERFUL FOR YOU TO DEFEAT.
THOSE SURVEIL-LANCE SCREENS THE GRIM REAPER SET UP...
IT SEEMS WE'LL BE ABLE TO WATCH BITS AND PIECES OF THE BATTLE...

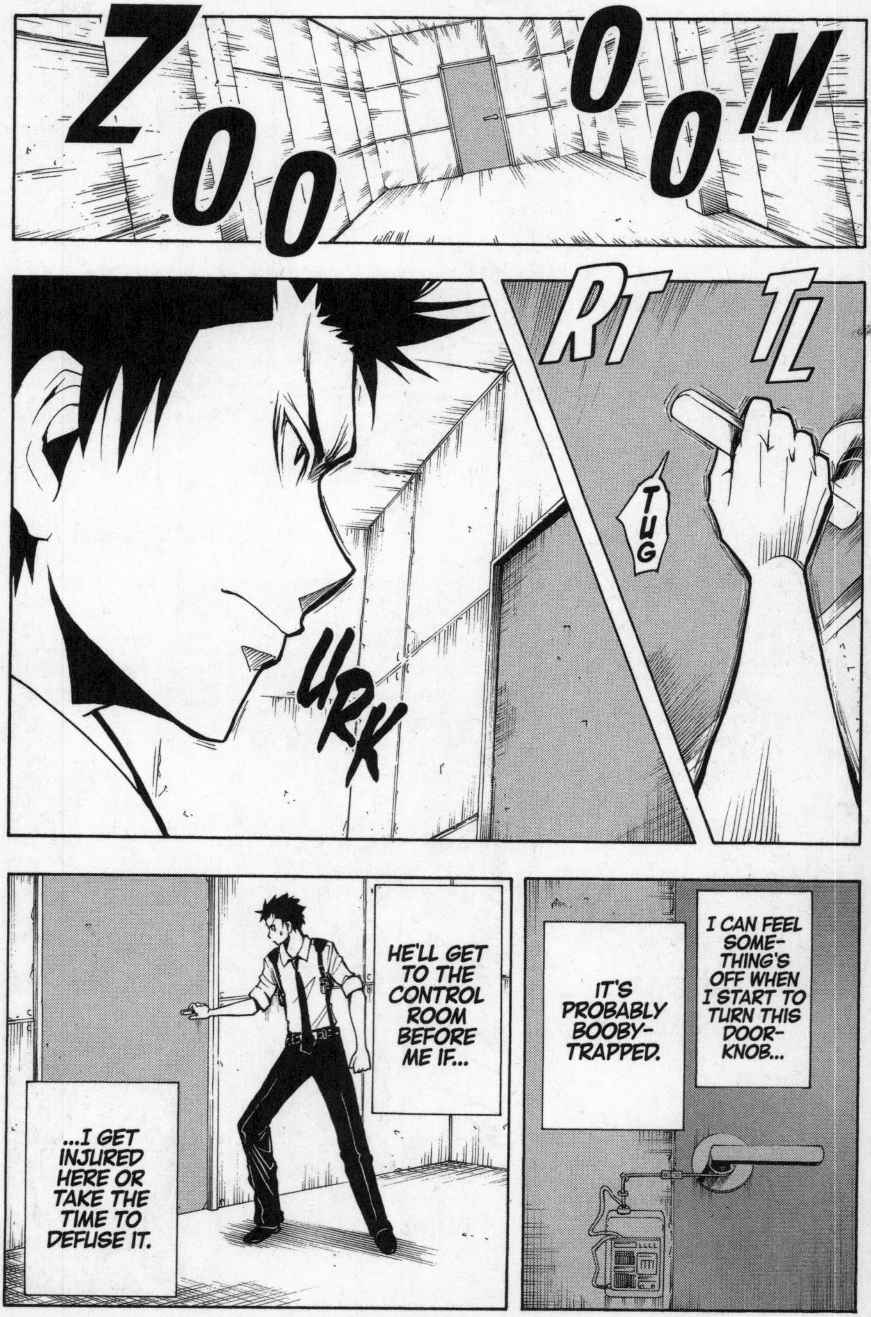
ZOOOOM
RTTL
TUG
URK
I CAN FEEL SOME-THING'S OFF WHEN I START TO TURN THIS DOOR-KNOB...
IT'S PROBABLY BOOBY-TRAPPED.
HE'LL GET TO THE CONTROL ROOM BEFORE ME IF...
...I GET INJURED HERE OR TAKE THE TIME TO DEFUSE IT.

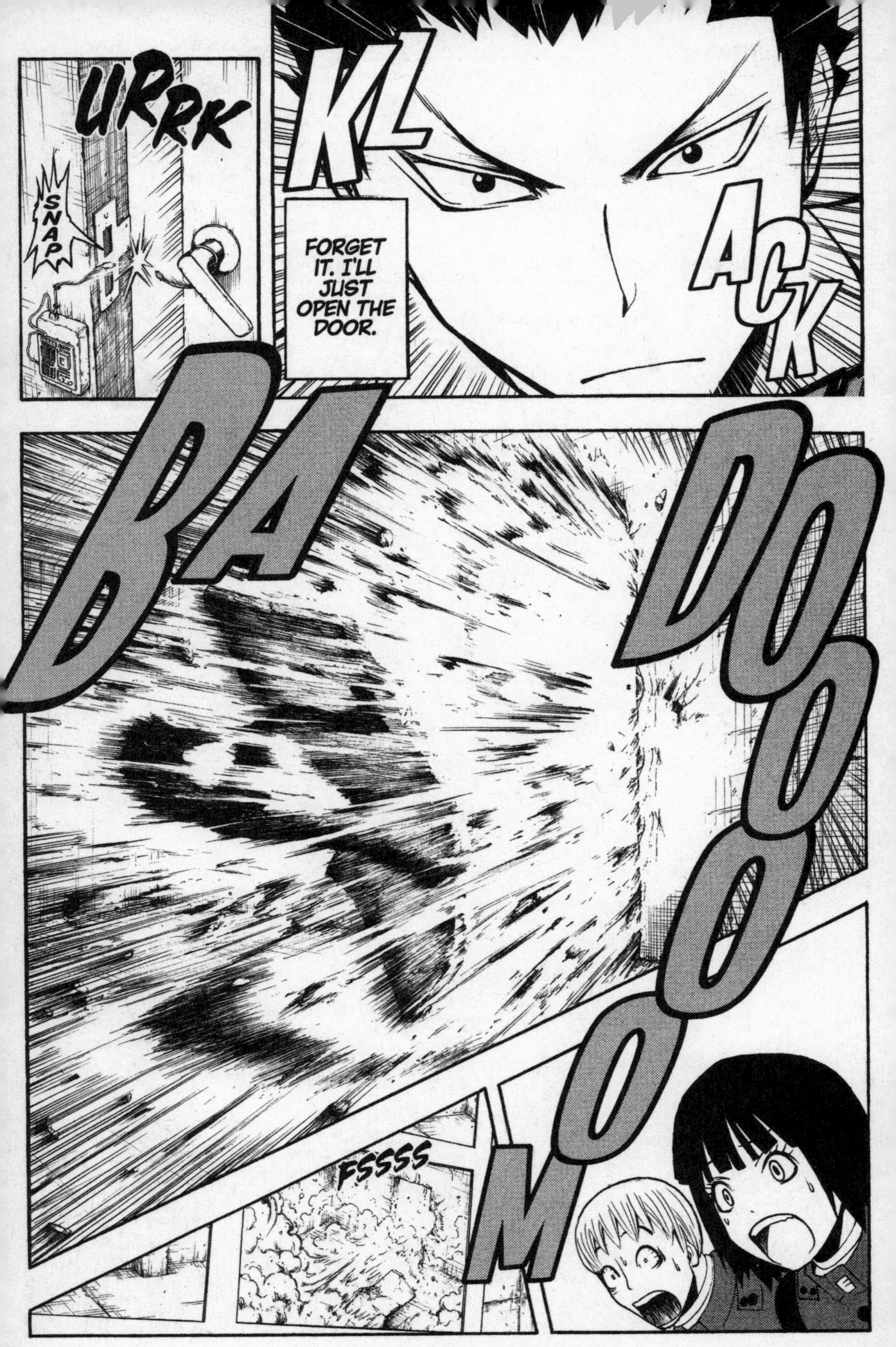
KLACK
FORGET IT. I'LL JUST OPEN THE DOOR.
URRK
SNAP
BADOOOOOM
FSSSS

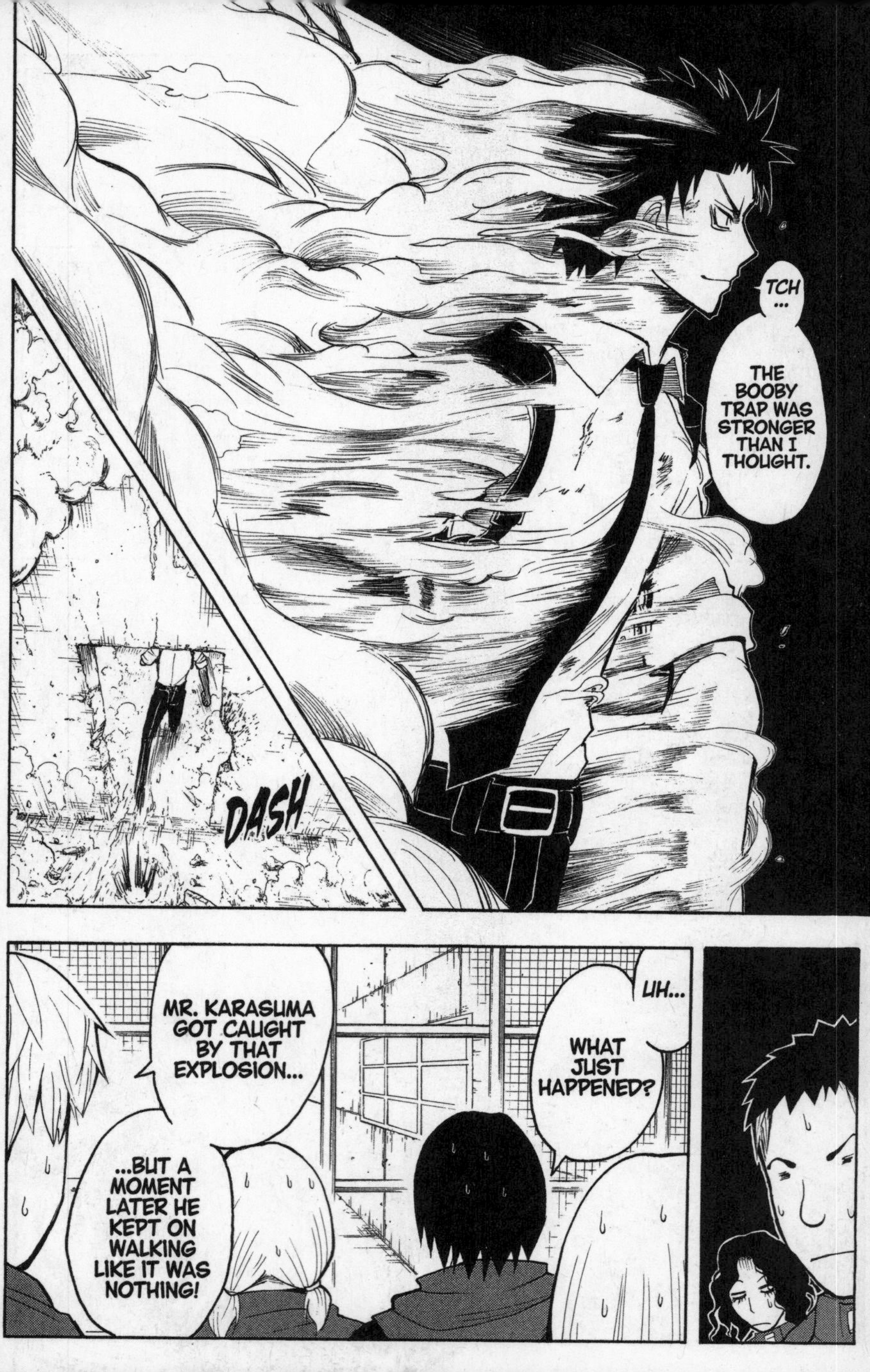
TCH...
THE BOOBY TRAP WAS STRONGER THAN I THOUGHT.
DASH
UH...
WHAT JUST HAPPENED?
MR. KARASUMA GOT CAUGHT BY THAT EXPLOSION...
...BUT A MOMENT LATER HE KEPT ON WALKING LIKE IT WAS NOTHING!

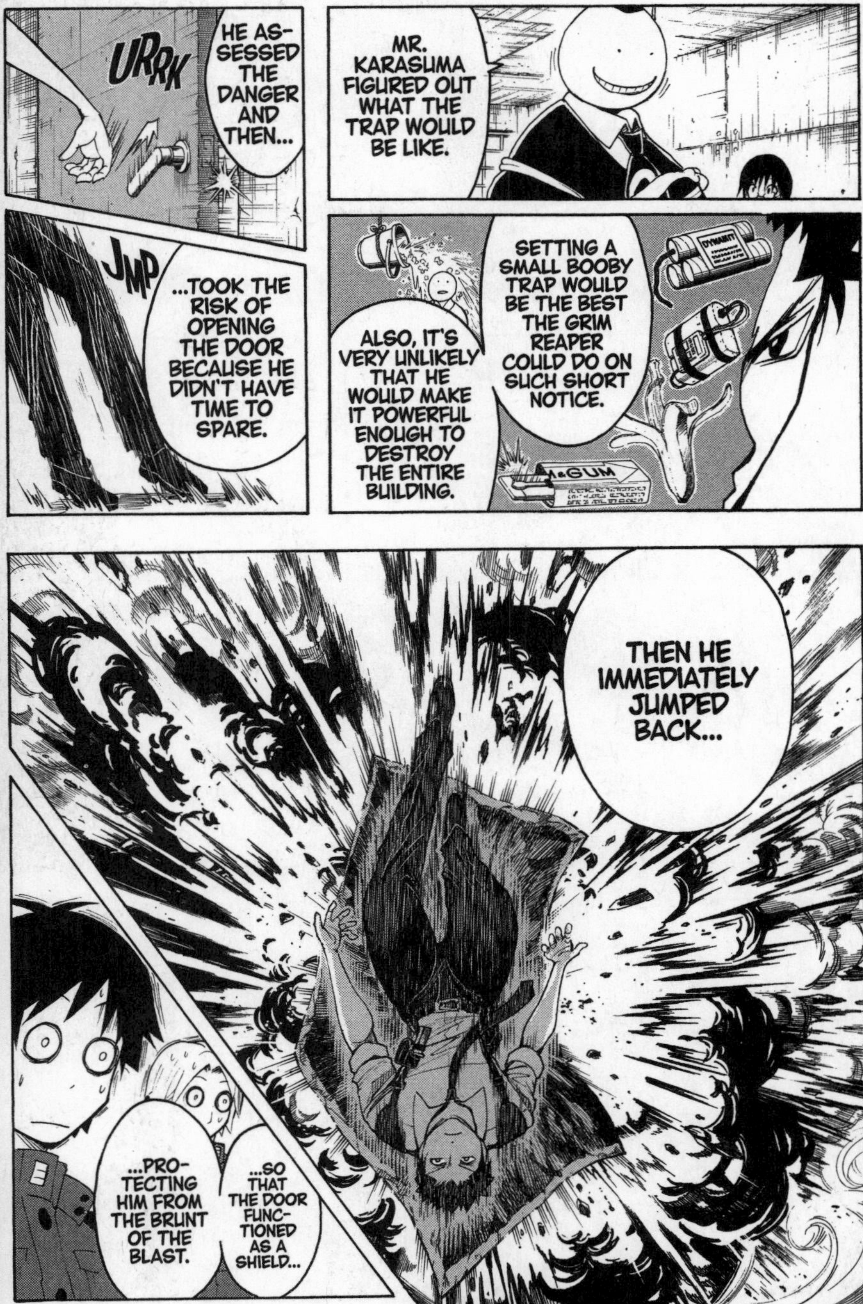
MR. KARASUMA FIGURED OUT WHAT THE TRAP WOULD BE LIKE.
URRK
HE AS-SESSED THE DANGER AND THEN...
SETTING A SMALL BOOBY TRAP WOULD BE THE BEST THE GRIM REAPER COULD DO ON SUCH SHORT NOTICE.
DYNAMIT
M&GUM
ALSO, IT'S VERY UNLIKELY THAT HE WOULD MAKE IT POWERFUL ENOUGH TO DESTROY THE ENTIRE BUILDING.
JMP
...TOOK THE RISK OF OPENING THE DOOR BECAUSE HE DIDN'T HAVE TIME TO SPARE.
THEN HE IMMEDIATELY JUMPED BACK...
...SO THAT THE DOOR FUNC-TIONED AS A SHIELD...
...PRO-TECTING HIM FROM THE BRUNT OF THE BLAST.

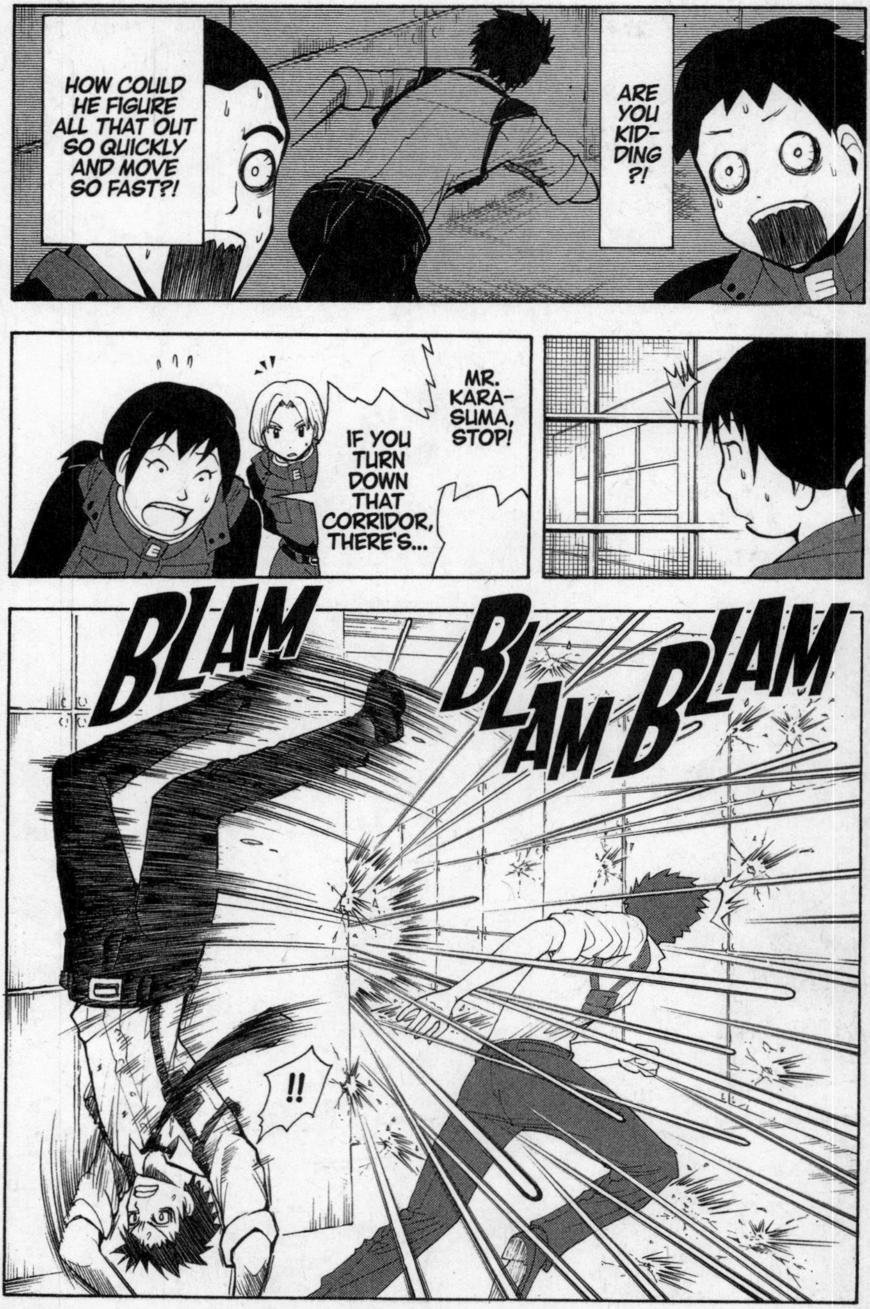
ARE YOU KID-DING?!
HOW COULD HE FIGURE ALL THAT OUT SO QUICKLY AND MOVE SO FAST?!
MR. KARA-SUMA, STOP!
IF YOU TURN DOWN THAT CORRIDOR, THERE'S...
BLAM BLAM
BLAM
!!

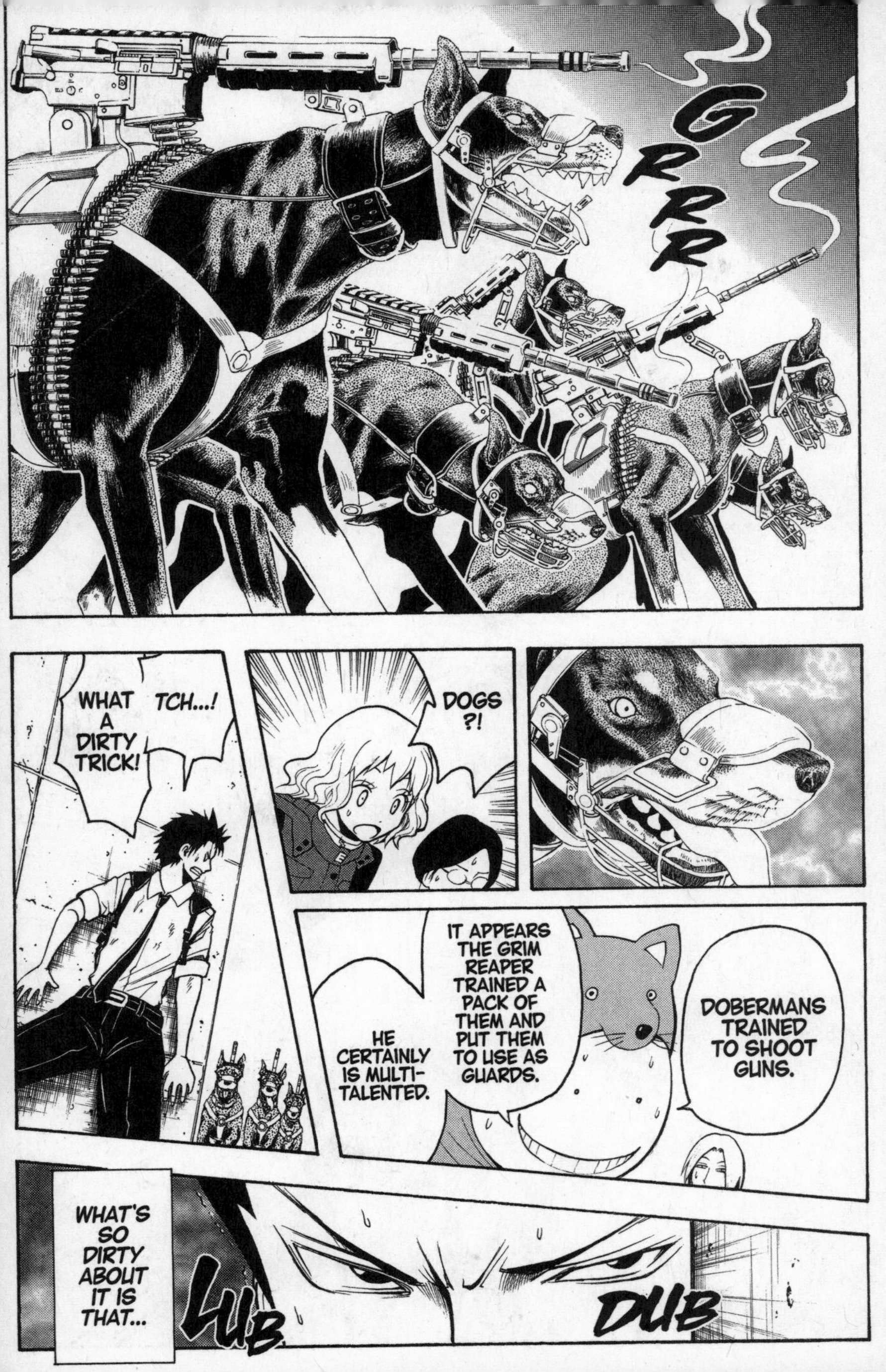
GRRR
DOGS ?!
DOBERMANS TRAINED TO SHOOT GUNS.
IT APPEARS THE GRIM REAPER TRAINED A PACK OF THEM AND PUT THEM TO USE AS GUARDS.
HE CERTAINLY IS MULTI-TALENTED.
TCH...!
WHAT A DIRTY TRICK!
DUB
WHAT'S SO DIRTY ABOUT IT IS THAT...
LUB

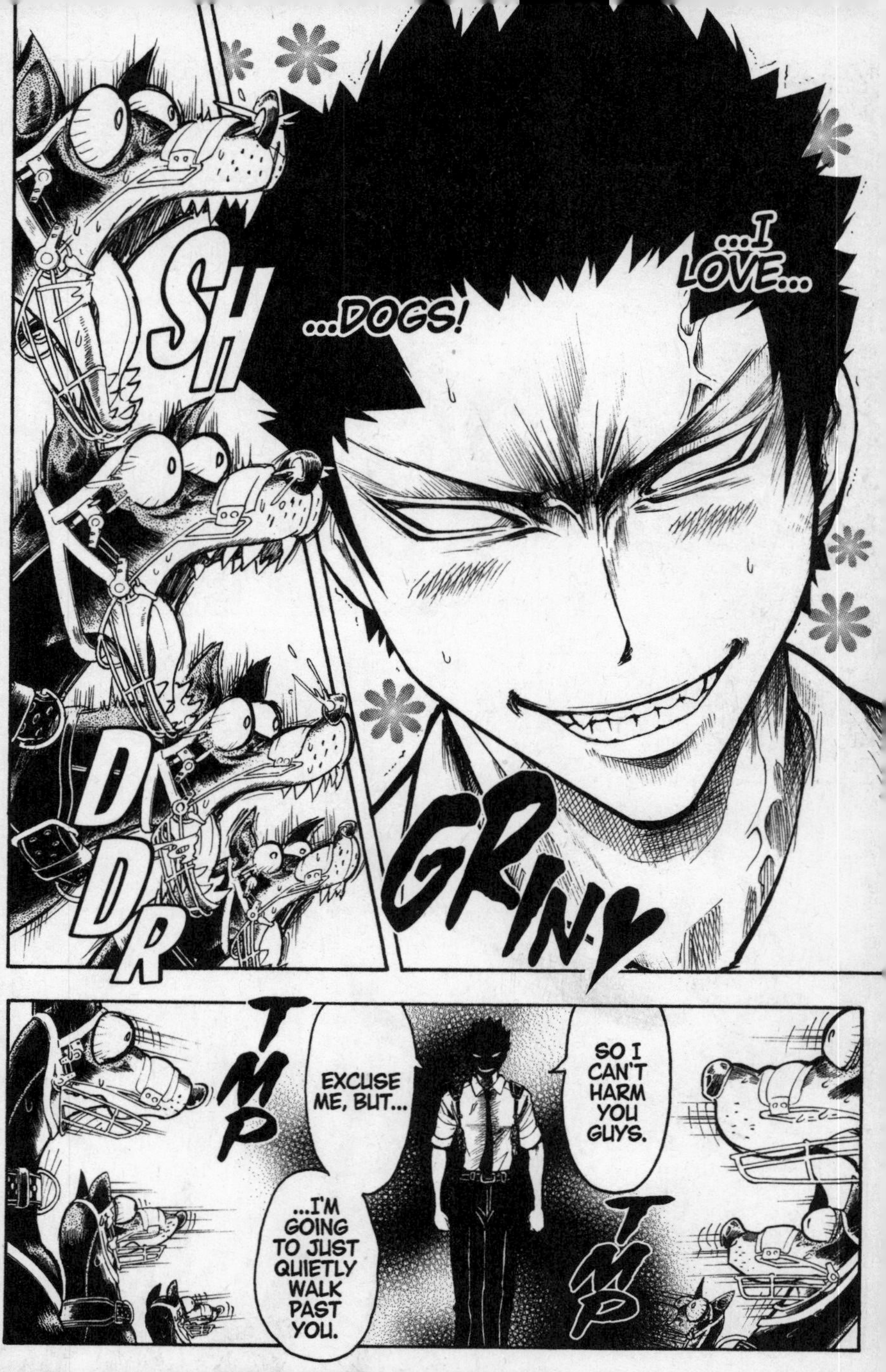
...I LOVE...
...DOGS!
SH
GRINY
DDR
TMP
SO I CAN'T HARM YOU GUYS.
EXCUSE ME, BUT...
...I'M GOING TO JUST QUIETLY WALK PAST YOU.
TMP

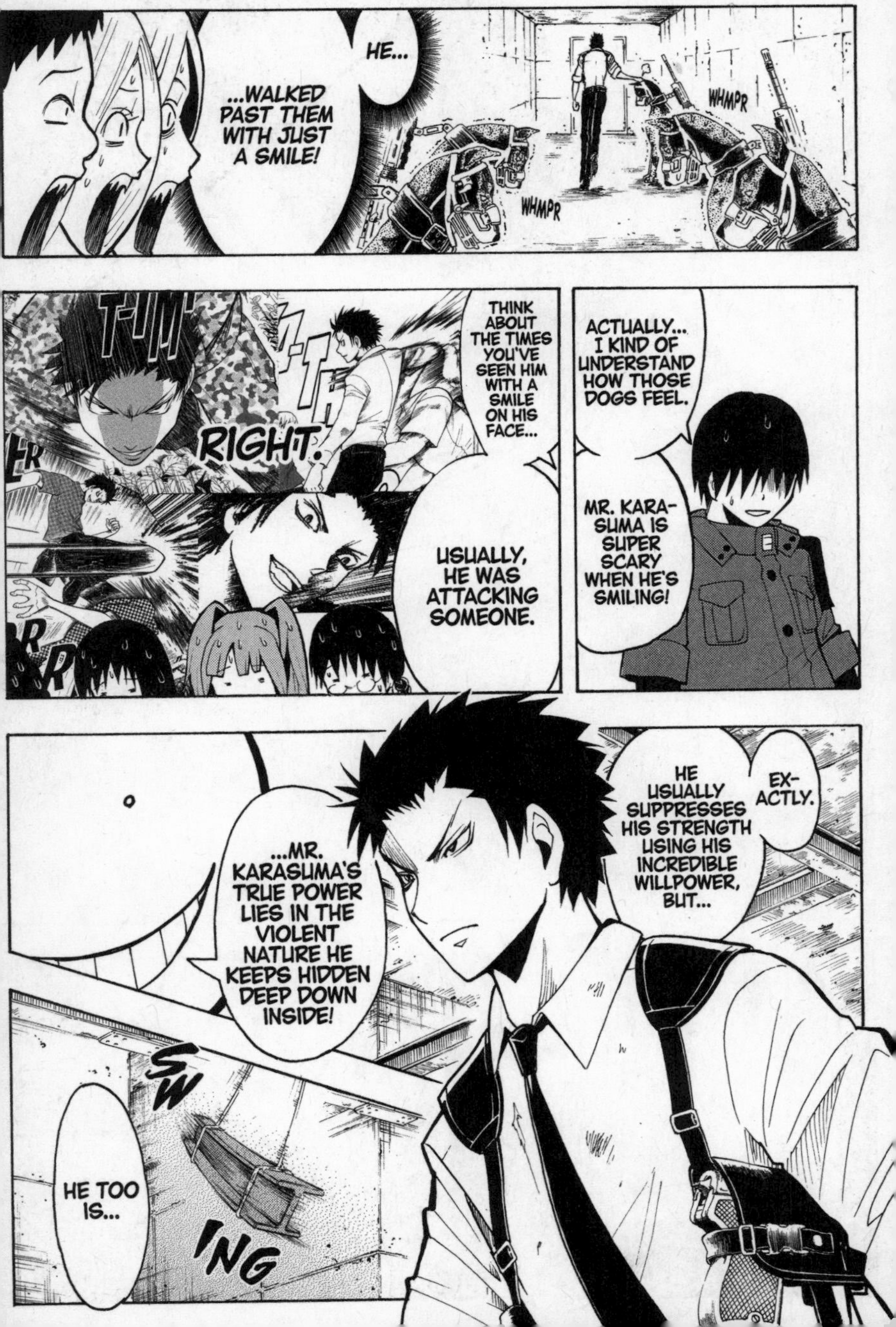
WHMPR
HE...
...WALKED PAST THEM WITH JUST A SMILE!
WHMPR
ACTUALLY... I KIND OF UNDERSTAND HOW THOSE DOGS FEEL.
MR. KARASUMA IS SUPER SCARY WHEN HE'S SMILING!
THINK ABOUT THE TIMES YOU'VE SEEN HIM WITH A SMILE ON HIS FACE...
RIGHT.
USUALLY, HE WAS ATTACKING SOMEONE.
EX-ACTLY.
HE USUALLY SUPPRESSES HIS STRENGTH USING HIS INCREDIBLE WILLPOWER, BUT...
...MR. KARASUMA'S TRUE POWER LIES IN THE VIOLENT NATURE HE KEEPS HIDDEN DEEP DOWN INSIDE!
SWING
HE TOO IS...

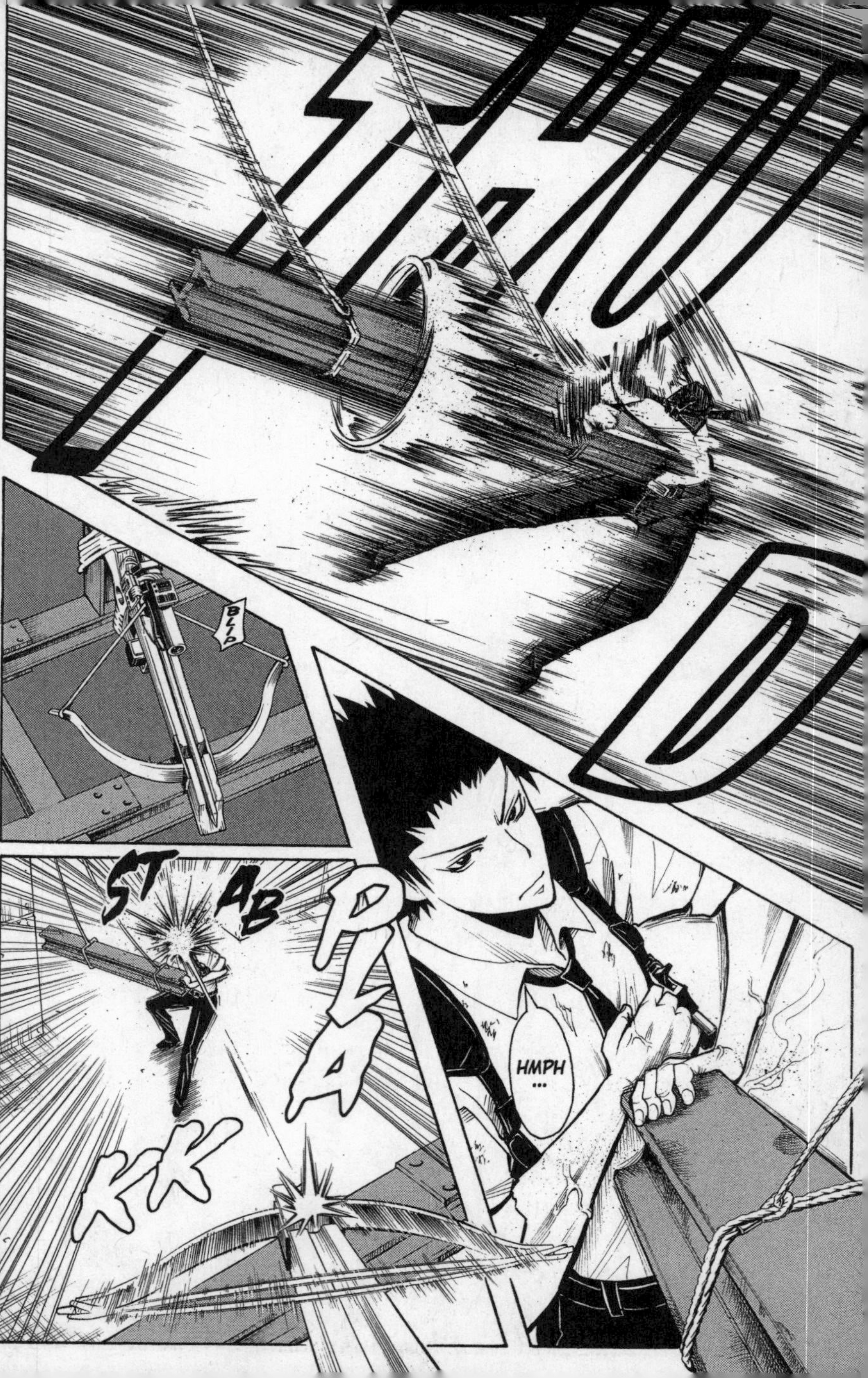
HMPH ...
BLIP
STAB
PLAKK

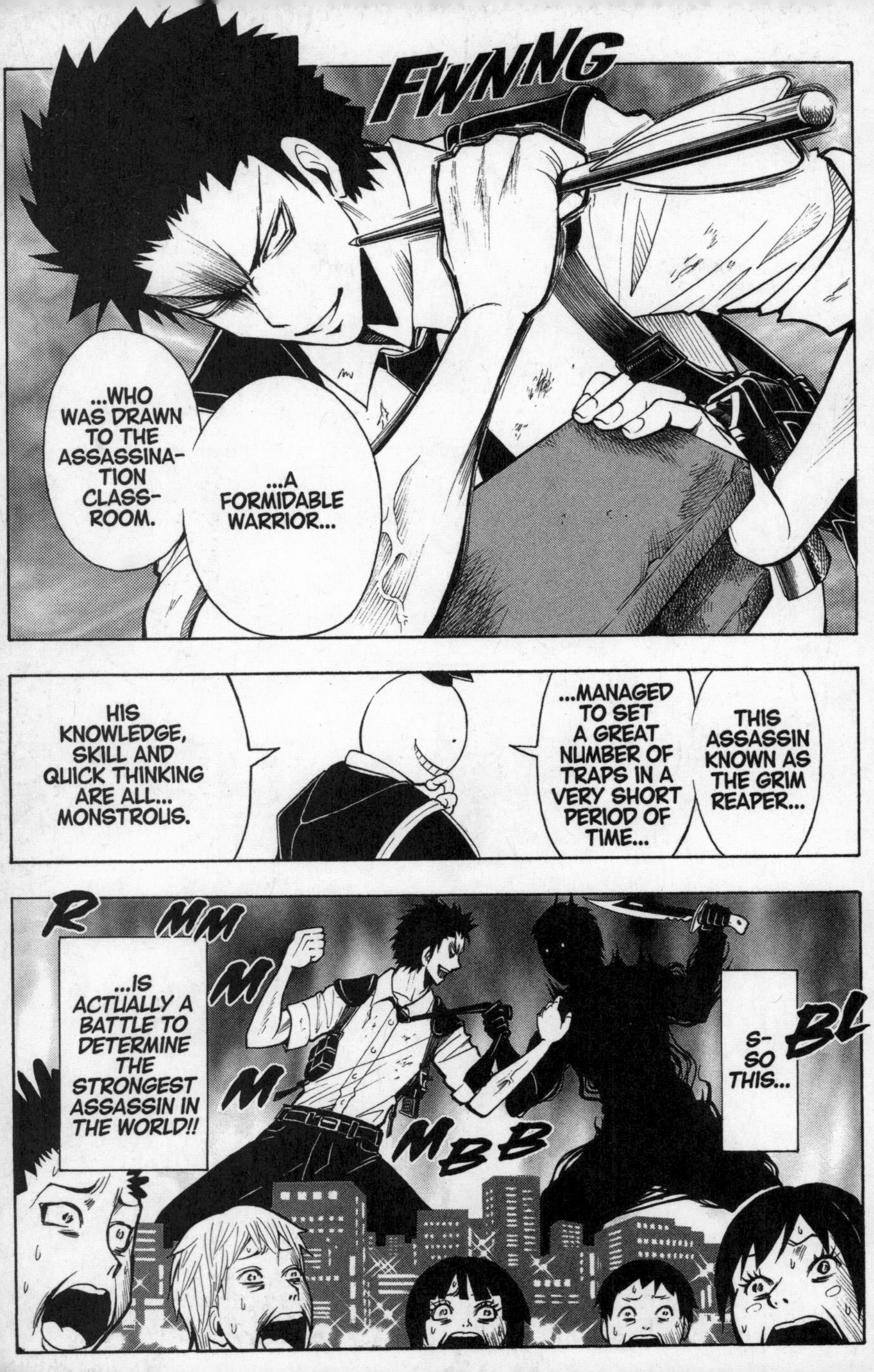
FWNNG
...A FORMIDABLE WARRIOR...
...WHO WAS DRAWN TO THE ASSASSINATION CLASSROOM.
THIS ASSASSIN KNOWN AS THE GRIM REAPER...
...MANAGED TO SET A GREAT NUMBER OF TRAPS IN A VERY SHORT PERIOD OF TIME...
HIS KNOWLEDGE, SKILL AND QUICK THINKING ARE ALL... MONSTROUS.
BL
S-SO THIS...
RMMMM-MBB
...IS ACTUALLY A BATTLE TO DETERMINE THE STRONGEST ASSASSIN IN THE WORLD!!

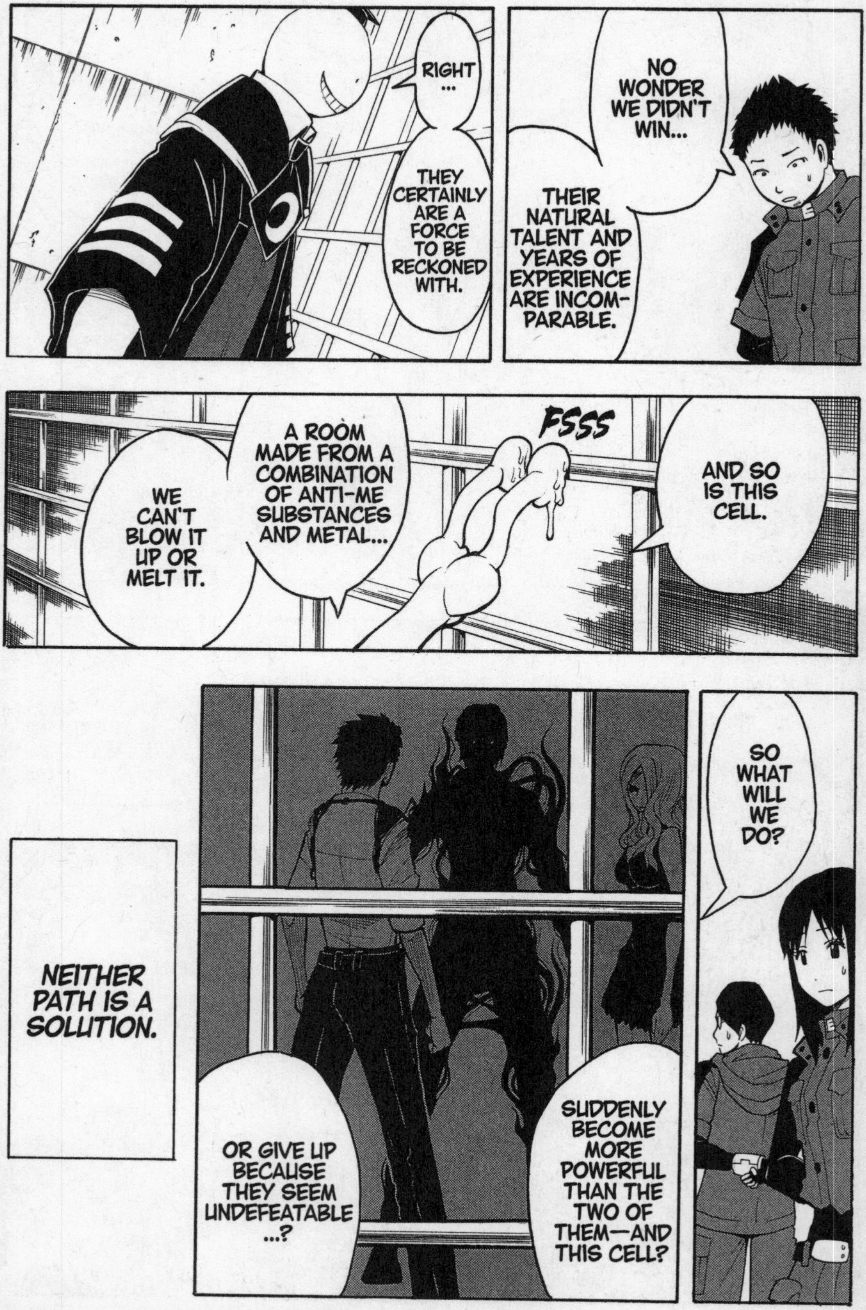
NO WONDER WE DIDN'T WIN...
THEIR NATURAL TALENT AND YEARS OF EXPERIENCE ARE INCOMPARABLE.
RIGHT...
THEY CERTAINLY ARE A FORCE TO BE RECKONED WITH.
AND SO IS THIS CELL.
FSSS
A ROOM MADE FROM A COMBINATION OF ANTI-ME SUBSTANCES AND METAL...
WE CAN'T BLOW IT UP OR MELT IT.
SO WHAT WILL WE DO?
SUDDENLY BECOME MORE POWERFUL THAN THE TWO OF THEM—AND THIS CELL?
OR GIVE UP BECAUSE THEY SEEM UNDEFEATABLE...?
NEITHER PATH IS A SOLUTION.

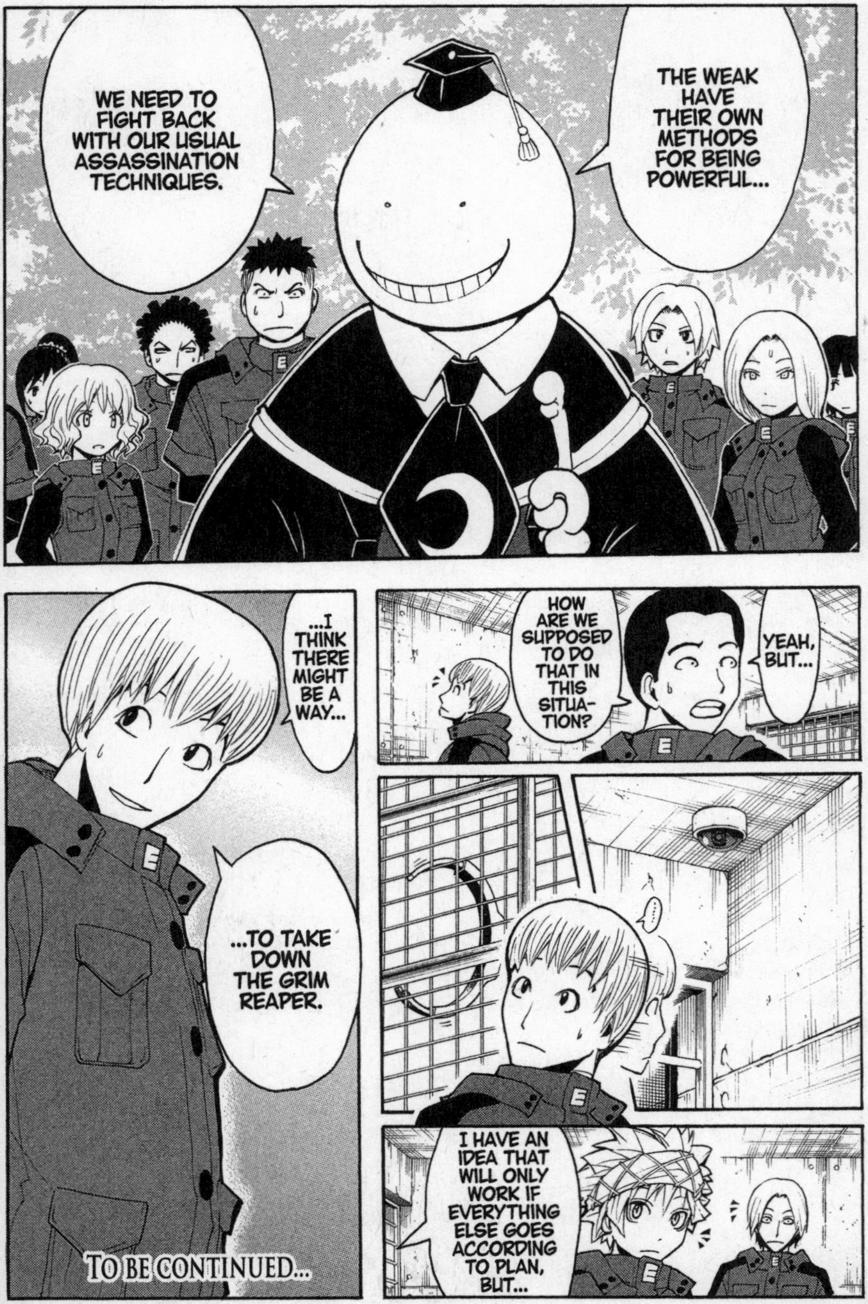
THE WEAK HAVE THEIR OWN METHODS FOR BEING POWERFUL...
WE NEED TO FIGHT BACK WITH OUR USUAL ASSASSINATION TECHNIQUES.
YEAH, BUT...
HOW ARE WE SUPPOSED TO DO THAT IN THIS SITUA-TION?
I HAVE AN IDEA THAT WILL ONLY WORK IF EVERYTHING ELSE GOES ACCORDING TO PLAN, BUT...
...I THINK THERE MIGHT BE A WAY...
...TO TAKE DOWN THE GRIM REAPER.
TO BE CONTINUED...

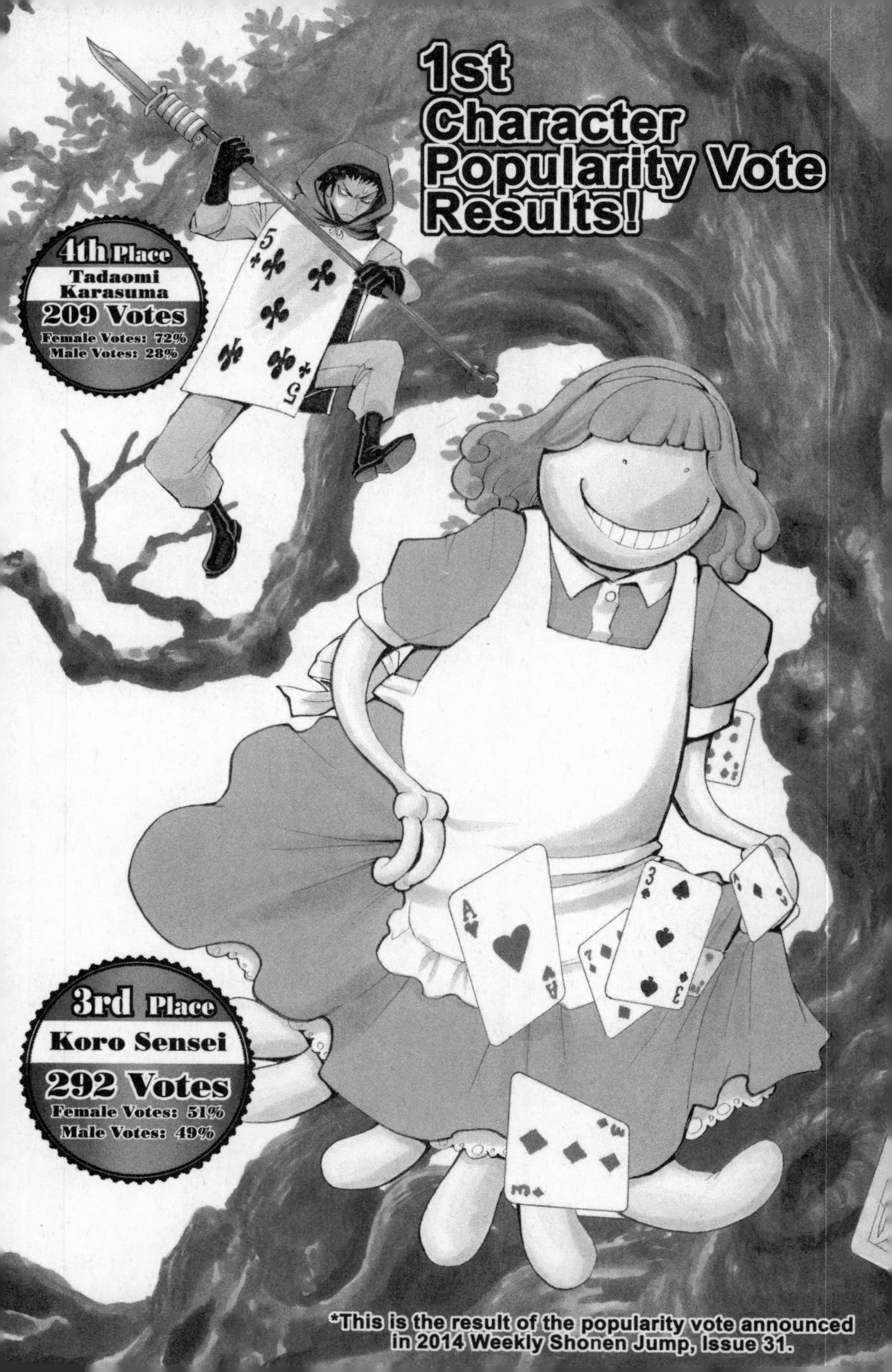
1st Character Popularity Vote Results!
4th Place
Tadaomi Karasuma
209 Votes
Female Votes: 72%
Male Votes: 28%
3rd Place
Koro Sensei
292 Votes
Female Votes: 51%
Male Votes: 49%
*This is the result of the popularity vote announced in 2014 Weekly Shonen Jump, Issue 31.

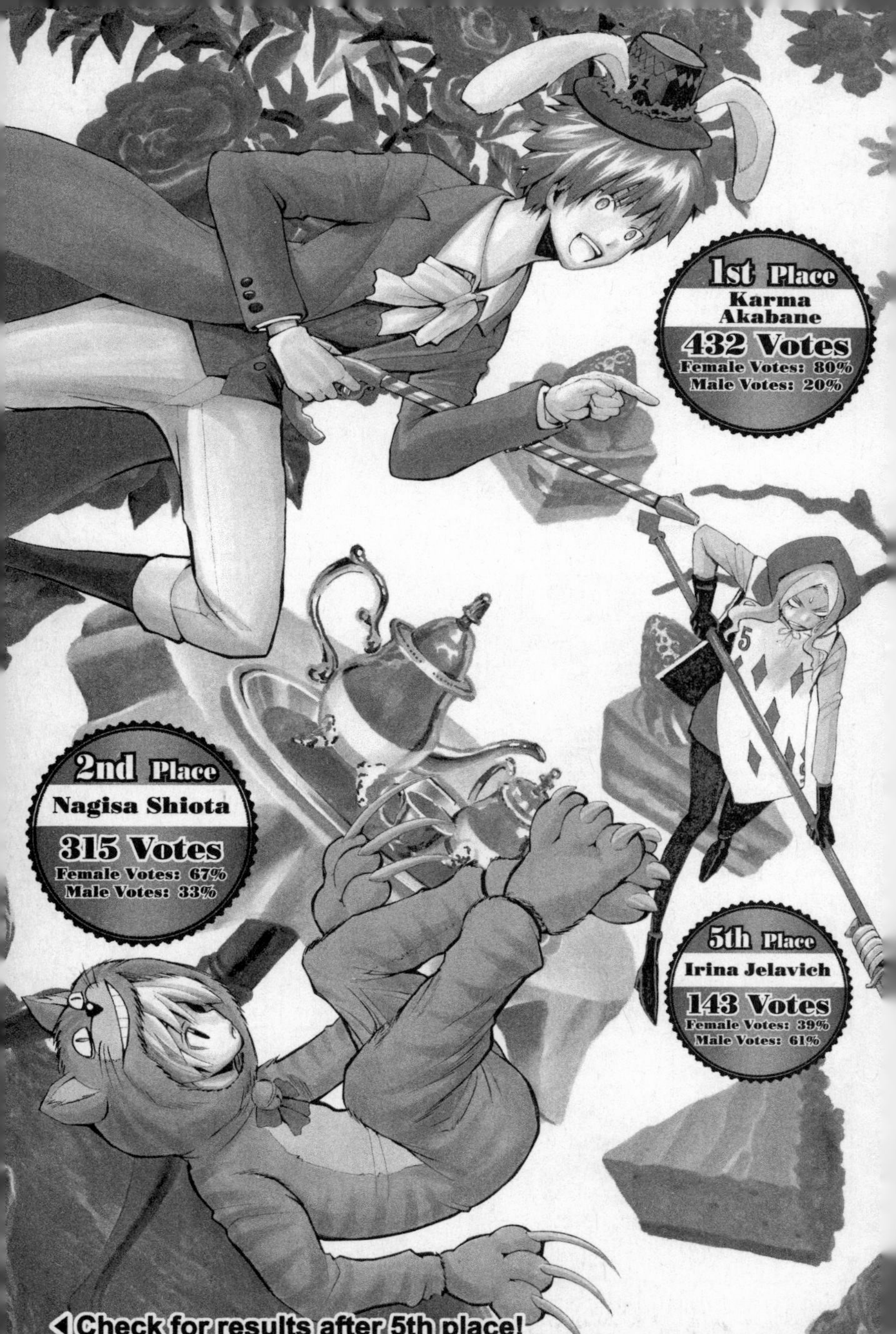
1st Place
Karma Akabane
432 Votes
Female Votes: 80%
Male Votes: 20%
5th Place
Irina Jelavich
143 Votes
Female Votes: 39%
Male Votes: 61%
2nd Place
Nagisa Shiota
315 Votes
Female Votes: 67%
Male Votes: 33%

◀Check for results after 5th place!

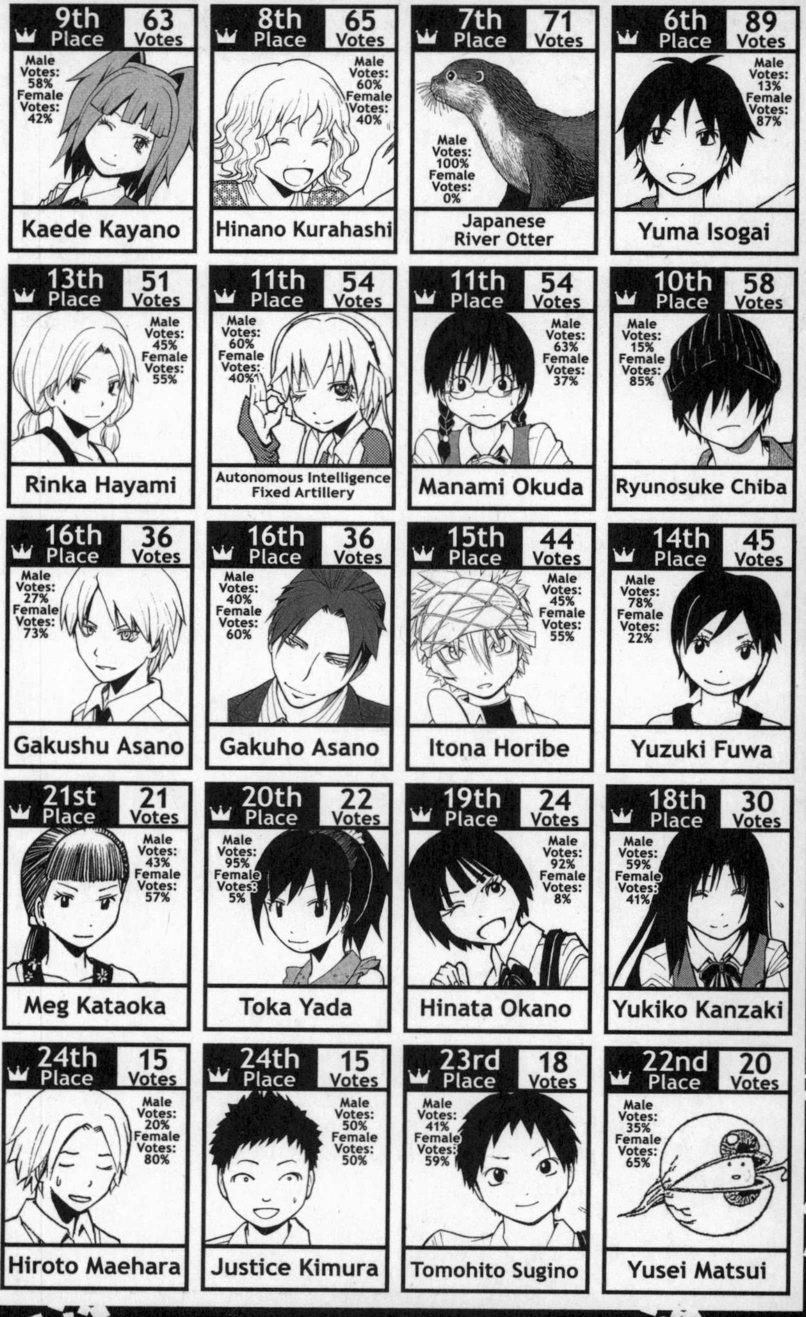
6th Place
89 Votes
Male Votes: 13%
Female Votes: 87%
Yuma Isogai
7th Place
71 Votes
Male Votes: 100%
Female Votes: 0%
Japanese River Otter
8th Place
65 Votes
Male Votes: 60%
Female Votes: 40%
Hinano Kurahashi
9th Place
63 Votes
Male Votes: 58%
Female Votes: 42%
Kaede Kayano
10th Place
58 Votes
Male Votes: 15%
Female Votes: 85%
Ryunosuke Chiba
11th Place
54 Votes
Male Votes: 63%
Female Votes: 37%
Manami Okuda
11th Place
54 Votes
Male Votes: 60%
Female Votes: 40%
Autonomous Intelligence Fixed Artillery
13th Place
51 Votes
Male Votes: 45%
Female Votes: 55%
Rinka Hayami
14th Place
45 Votes
Male Votes: 78%
Female Votes: 22%
Yuzuki Fuwa
15th Place
44 Votes
Male Votes: 45%
Female Votes: 55%
Itona Horibe
16th Place
36 Votes
Male Votes: 40%
Female Votes: 60%
Gakuho Asano
16th Place
36 Votes
Male Votes: 27%
Female Votes: 73%
Gakushu Asano
18th Place
30 Votes
Male Votes: 59%
Female Votes: 41%
Yukiko Kanzaki
19th Place
24 Votes
Male Votes: 92%
Female Votes: 8%
Hinata Okano
20th Place
22 Votes
Male Votes: 95%
Female Votes: 5%
Toka Yada
21st Place
21 Votes
Male Votes: 43%
Female Votes: 57%
Meg Kataoka
22nd Place
20 Votes
Male Votes: 35%
Female Votes: 65%
Yusei Matsui
23rd Place
18 Votes
Male Votes: 41%
Female Votes: 59%
Tomohito Sugino
24th Place
15 Votes
Male Votes: 50%
Female Votes: 50%
Justice Kimura
24th Place
15 Votes
Male Votes: 20%
Female Votes: 80%
Hiroto Maehara

29th Place | 11 Votes

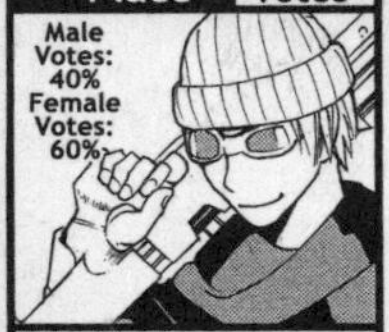

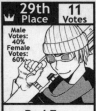

Male Votes: 40%
Female Votes: 60%

Red Eye

29th Place | 13 Votes

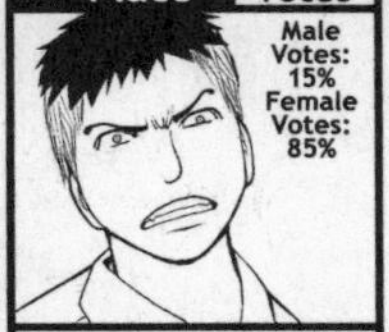

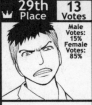

Male Votes: 15%
Female Votes: 85%

Ryoma Terasaka

24th Place | 15 Votes

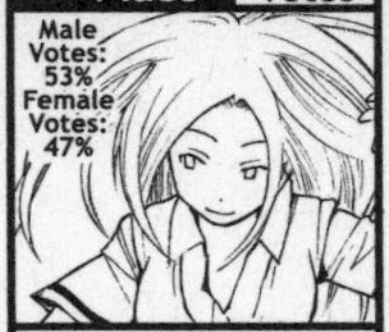

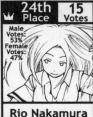

Male Votes: 53%
Female Votes: 47%

Rio Nakamura

24th Place | 15 Votes

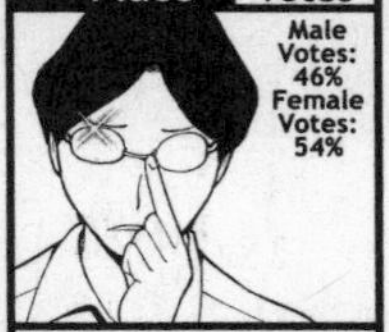

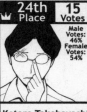

Male Votes: 46%
Female Votes: 54%

Kotaro Takebayashi

Character ranking from 30th place (with few votes)

58th place Kokona Tagawa
Kevin
Ryuki
Yuya Higuchi *(NEURO: Supernatural Detective)*
Setsuna Honjo *(NEURO: Supernatural Detective)*
Suzume Sonokawa
Hirokazu Tsuruta
Miss Yukimura, the former teacher
The 70% disintegrated moon
The downright adorable tentacle (Class 2)
The VIP bodyguard Ms. Vitch eliminated (Class 10)
Question 11 of the first trimester midterm (Class 14)
The background character in Class 16, page 17, who looks a bit like Usui from *NEURO*
The guy who knows all the best places to see on the school trip: Ryuki
Ritsu's Master (Class 22)
The convenience store worker who's trying to stop the fight for the restroom between Seo and Tsuchiya (Class 24)
The Kung-Fu Master in Class 41, page 8.
The girl who gave a love letter to Meg Kataoka (Class 44)
Fish-Fish (Class 45)
Fish King (Class 45)
The character that looks like Funassyi (Class 64)
The Giant Anti-Koro Sensei Explosive Pudding (Class 80)
The female news reporter who also appeared in *NEURO* (Class 85)
The weasel that attacked Itona's radio control car (Class 88)
The goldfish Isogai cooked and Maehara ate (Class 90)
The women on the cover of the porn magazine Koro Sensei reads
Atsuko Maeda (Class 18)
David Ito in Volume 2, page 193
Editor Murakoshi
Y-san from Chiba Prefecture (An infamous *Nisekoi: False Love* fan popularity contest voter)
Others - 1 Vote

30th place Sumire Hara - 10 Votes

31st place Kirara Hazama - 9 Votes
32nd place Taiga Okajima - 8 Votes

33rd place Sosuke Sugaya
Shiro - 7 Votes

35th place Grip
Cross-Dressed Nagisa - 6 Votes

37th place Sakura
Kunudon - 5 Votes

39th place Akira Takaoka - 4 Votes

40th place Takuya Muramatsu
Fake Ritsu
Lovro Brovski
Gastro
The Grim Reaper
Irumanju
Virus Anpanman
Neuro Nogami *(NEURO: Supernatural Detective)*
Eishi Sasazuka *(NEURO: Supernatural Detective)* - 3 Votes

49th place Taisei Yoshida
Natsuhiko Koyama
Sang-hyeok
Prime Minister Takanojo Migitsuma *(NEURO: Supernatural Detective)*
The high school girl who keeps getting tortured in the *Jump* detective manga (Class 63)
Maeda, who's scheduled to go abroad (Class 78)
Kikuchi, the donut lover (Class 78)
Tsunemi, the fiery sister (Class 78)
Yako Katsuragi *(NEURO: Supernatural Detective)* - 2 Votes

58th place Koki Mimura
Teppei Araki
Ren Sakakibara
Nobuta Tanaka
Kaho Tsuchiya - 1 Vote

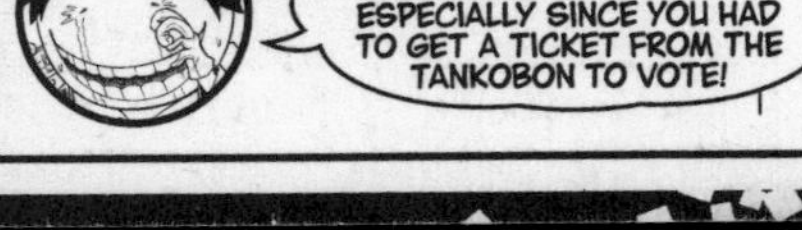
I CANNOT THANK THE FANS ENOUGH FOR TAKING PART, ESPECIALLY SINCE YOU HAD TO GET A TICKET FROM THE TANKOBON TO VOTE!

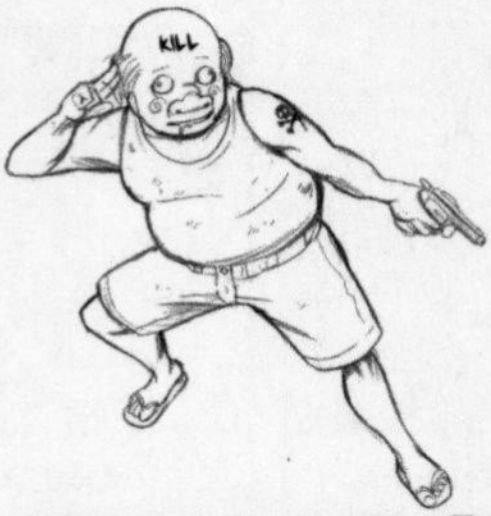
KILL

Abebe British Bulldog Futoshi

- Birthday: February 29 (48 years old)
- Height: 5' 10"
- Weight: 225 lbs.
- Career History: President of a certain African country →British Foot Guard →Police officer in Japan →Security guard in Japan→Part-time worker in Japan →Empty trashcan collector in Japan
- Hobby/Skill: Kabaddi, Cricket, Gateball
- Motto: The more character background, the better
- Weakness: Dog hater, cat hater, bad gambler, kind to women, awful cook
- Karasuma's Evaluation: "He's all over the place."

Wall

Poke

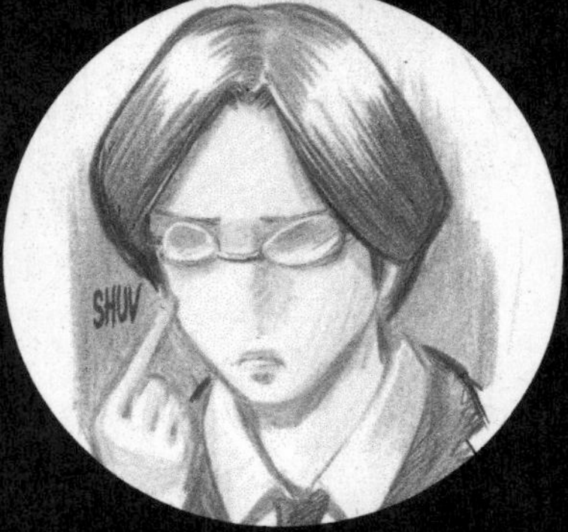
SHUV

I've introduced patterns to the cover to add more variety. How do you like it?

I was thinking about changing things up after vol. 10, so the designer presented me with a variety of patterns, all of which are wonderful.

I'm going to use them on the even-numbered volumes. I have so many patterns to choose from that I can't wait to choose the one for the next volume!

I hope you're looking forward to them too!

—Yusei Matsui

Yusei Matsui was born on the last day of January in Saitama Prefecture, Japan. He has been drawing manga since elementary school. Some of his favorite manga series are *Bobobo-bo Bo-bobo*, *JoJo's Bizarre Adventure* and *Ultimate Muscle*. Matsui learned his trade working as an assistant to manga artist Yoshio Sawai, creator of *Bobobo-bo Bo-bobo*. In 2005, Matsui debuted his original manga *Neuro: Supernatural Detective* in *Weekly Shonen Jump*. In 2007, *Neuro* was adapted into an anime. In 2012, *Assassination Classroom* began serialization in *Weekly Shonen Jump*.

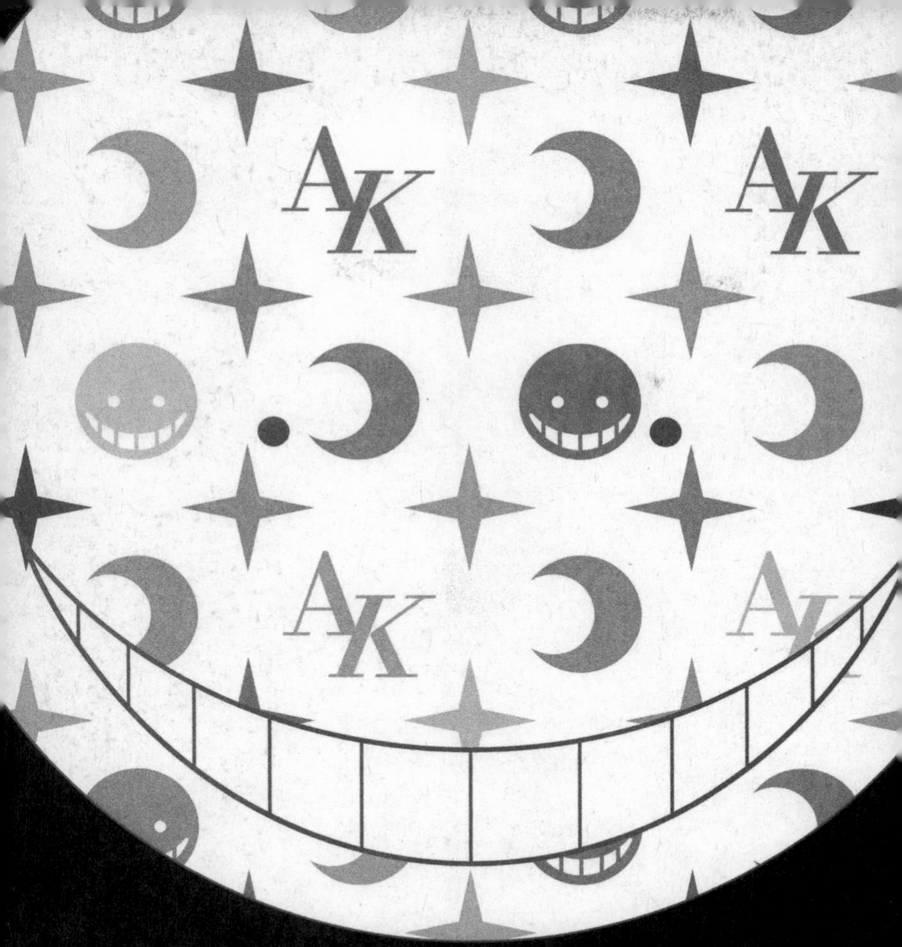

A new pattern design from Koro Sensei. This "Korogram" pattern will make your $10 graphic novel look like it cost a hundred bucks. Buy one for your girlfriend to give her a moment of fleeting happiness.

ASSASSINATION CLASSROOM

YUSEI MATSUI

12

TIME FOR THE GRIM REAPER

A MOMENT OF TENTACLE ZEN

Tentacles on,
tentacles off!

-The Tentacler

A S S A S S I N A T I O N
CLASSROOM

Volume 12
SHONEN JUMP ADVANCED Manga Edition

Story and Art by YUSEI MATSUI

Translation/Tetsuichiro Miyaki
English Adaptation/Bryant Turnage
Touch-up Art & Lettering/Stephen Dutro
Cover & Interior Design/Sam Elzway
Editor/Annette Roman

ANSATSU KYOSHITSU © 2012 by Yusei Matsui
All rights reserved.
First published in Japan in 2012 by SHUEISHA Inc., Tokyo.
English translation rights arranged by SHUEISHA Inc.

Printed in the U.S.A.

Published by VIZ Media, LLC
P.O. Box 77010
San Francisco, CA 94107

10 9 8 7 6 5 4 3 2 1
First printing, October 2016

www.viz.com

The Grim Reaper sets up a lethal trap that buries Mr. Karasuma and Ms. Vitch alive. Will Mr. Karasuma's repressed feelings surface before he and Ms. Vitch do? And how will Mr. Karasuma face Death? Then, despite his vow to destroy the planet in March, Koro Sensei offers career counseling to his students. Nagisa's professional goal raises some serious issues. And finally, it's time for the next school festival showdown. Class E and Class A compete for the most customers. If they build it, will they come... to the top of 3-E's remote mountaintop?

Available December 2016!

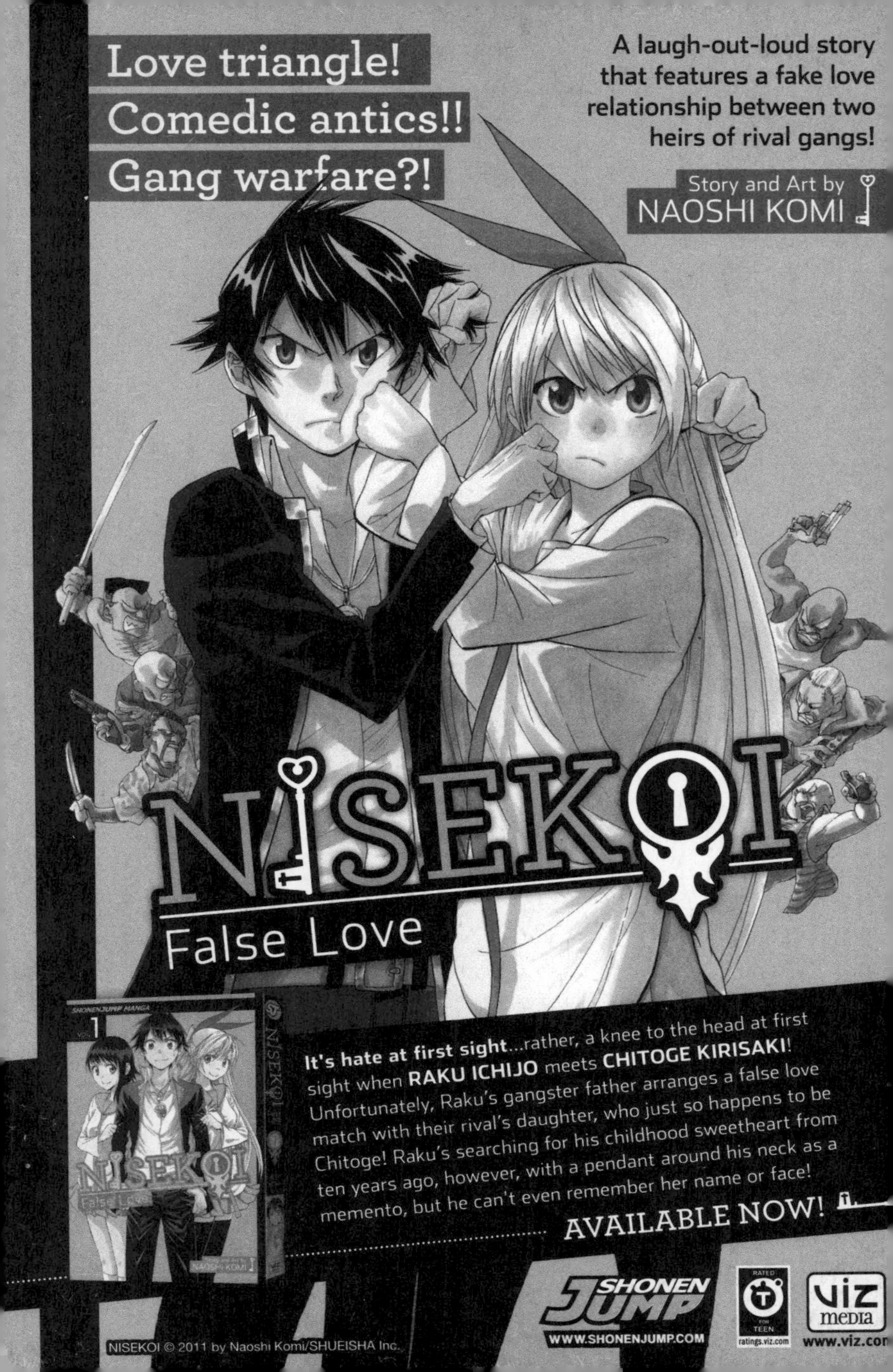
Love triangle!
Comedic antics!!
Gang warfare?!
A laugh-out-loud story that features a fake love relationship between two heirs of rival gangs!
Story and Art by NAOSHI KOMI
NISEKOI
False Love
SHONENJUMP MANGA
vol. 1
It's hate at first sight...rather, a knee to the head at first sight when RAKU ICHIJO meets CHITOGE KIRISAKI! Unfortunately, Raku's gangster father arranges a false love match with their rival's daughter, who just so happens to be Chitoge! Raku's searching for his childhood sweetheart from ten years ago, however, with a pendant around his neck as a memento, but he can't even remember her name or face!
AVAILABLE NOW!
SHONEN JUMP
WWW.SHONENJUMP.COM
RATED T FOR TEEN
ratings.viz.com
viz media
www.viz.com
NISEKOI © 2011 by Naoshi Komi/SHUEISHA Inc.